WORKSHOPS IN COMPUTING
Series edited by C. J. van Rijsbergen

W0107062

Also in this series

continued on back page...

J.P. Bowen and J.E. Nicholls (Eds.)

Z User Workshop, London 1992

Proceedings of the Seventh Annual
Z User Meeting, London
14–15 December 1992

Springer-Verlag Berlin Heidelberg GmbH

J.P. Bowen, MA

J.E. Nicholls, MA

Oxford University Computing Laboratory
Programming Research Group
11 Keble Road
Oxford, OX1 3QD, UK

ISBN 978-3-540-19818-5

British Library Cataloguing in Publication Data
Z User Workshop, London 1992 : Proceedings of the Seventh Annual Z User
Meeting, London, 14–15 December 1992. – (Workshops in Computing)
    I.   Bowen, Jonathan Peter
    II. Nicholls, J.E.   III.   Series
    005.133
ISBN 978-3-540-19818-5

Library of Congress Cataloging-in-Publication Data
Z User Workshop (7th : 1992 : London, England)
    Z User Workshop, London 1992 : proceedings of the Seventh annual
Z User Meeting, London, 14–15 December 1992 / J.P. Bowen and
J.E. Nicholls (eds.)
      p. cm. – (Workshops in computing)
    Includes bibliographical references and index.
    ISBN 978-3-540-19818-5   ISBN 978-1-4471-3556-2 (eBook)
    DOI 10.1007/978-1-4471-3556-2
    1. Z (Computer program language)–Congresses.   I.   Bowen, J. P.
(Jonathan Peter), 1956–   .   II.   Nicholls, John E.   III. Title.
IV.   Series.
QA76.73.Z2Z2 1992   93-3819
005.1'2–dc20   CIP

Apart from any fair dealing for the purposes of research or private study, or
criticism or review, as permitted under the Copyright, Designs and Patents Act
1988, this publication may only be reproduced, stored or transmitted, in any form,
or by any means, with the prior permission in writing of the publishers, or in the
case of reprographic reproduction in accordance with the terms of licences issued
by the Copyright Licensing Agency. Enquiries concerning reproduction outside
those terms should be sent to the publishers.

© Springer-Verlag Berlin Heidelberg 1993
Originally published by Springer-Verlag Berlin Heidelberg New York in 1993

The use of registered names, trademarks etc. in this publication does not imply,
even in the absence of a specific statement, that such names are exempt from the
relevant laws and regulations and therefore free for general use.

The publisher makes no representation, express or implied, with regard to the
accuracy of the information contained in this book and cannot accept any legal
responsibility or liability for any errors or omissions that may be made.

Typesetting: Camera ready by contributors

34/3830-543210 Printed on acid-free paper

Introduction and Opening Remarks

J.E. Nicholls
(Chairman, Z User Group)
Oxford University Computing Laboratory
Programming Research Group

When we started planning for this, the Seventh Z User Meeting, one of our first decisions was to decide on a theme for the meeting. The papers collected in these proceedings reflect our decision to base the meeting on *Industrial Applications*. The presentations demonstrated a growing maturity and breadth of application of work with Z; in addition, about half the audience consisted of people from industry or with strong industrial affiliations. Thus, although it is recognised that work remains to be done on the underlying mathematical theory of Z, a major focus of attention is now moving to the establishment of techniques and tools that will encourage the wider application of Z and other formal notations and methods.

The meeting was held at our regular time just before Christmas, and at first it seemed there might have to be two meetings at about the same time – our regular annual user meeting, and a further meeting to mark the end of the ZIP project, a collaborative project which has worked on Z standards, tools and methods. We discussed various arrangements, including a 'ZIP day' attached to the user meeting, but finally settled on the idea that ZIP presentations should be interspersed with submitted and invited papers. This offered several advantages: for users, an opportunity to see the work of a sustained effort on Z development, for the ZIP project, an opportunity to present to, and obtain feedback from, an audience of informed users.

The industrial theme of the meeting is represented by the papers of our invited speakers, and we heard from the UK speakers of several different views of how formal methods are being introduced. The other invited speaker gave news from a survey of the use of formal methods in several countries, including the USA and his home country, Canada, and provided a reminder of the work that remains to be done to make these methods an accepted part of software development.

The ZIP presentations illustrated the progress of the project in its three main areas of work. One of the work packages of the ZIP project has involved the development of a proposed standard for Z and those attending the meeting were given a copy of the first publicly available version of the draft *Z Base Standard*. British Aerospace, project managers of the ZIP project, generously supported the printing costs for these copies. In addition to those presented here, other papers have been generated from the ZIP project and will be published later. We are grateful to the DTI for its role in providing support and funding for the ZIP project, and also for acting as hosts for this meeting. Simon Attwood has been the DTI representative for the ZIP project and helped in the local arrangements for the meeting.

In addition to the papers by invited speakers, several submitted papers discussed the industrial use of Z, and two in particular gave extremely interesting talks on *safety-critical* applications, surely one of the key areas of use for formal notations such as Z.

Finally I should like to mention that during the past year public recognition of the importance of formal methods in industry was given by the granting of the Queen's Award for Technical Achievement for work with Z to two of the organisations that have played prominent parts in the development and application of Z: the CICS group from IBM United Kingdom Laboratories, Hursley, and the Programming Research Group, Oxford University.

As usual, the work of organising the meeting was shared by many people. Members of the Programme Committee helped in planning the meeting, refereeing papers and chairing the sessions. Committee members and officers of the Z User Group responsible for the seventh meeting were:

> Rosalind Barden, Logica Cambridge Ltd
> Jonathan Bowen, Oxford University PRG (*Secretary*)
> Elspeth Cusack, British Telecom
> David Duce, Rutherford Appleton Laboratories
> Anthony Hall, Praxis plc
> Howard Haughton, Lloyd's Register
> Brian Hepworth, British Aerospace
> Michael Hinchey, Cambridge University (*Treasurer*)
> Darrell Ince, The Open University
> Peter Lupton, IBM Hursley
> John McDermid, University of York
> Silvio Meira, University of Pernambuco, Brazil
> John Nicholls, Oxford University PRG (*Chair*)
> Gordon Rose, University of Queensland
> Chris Sennett, DRA Malvern
> Sam Valentine, Brighton University
> Jim Woodcock, Oxford University PRG
> John Wordsworth, IBM Hursley

The committee is grateful to Mrs Joan Arnold who once again carried out the essential and arduous secretarial duties involved in organising the meeting.

Finally I should like to express my regrets that, at very short notice, I was unable to attend the meeting itself. I should like to thank those who covered my duties – John Wordsworth for introducing and chairing the opening session of the meeting, Stephen Brien for delivering the paper on the *Z Base Standard*, and Jonathan Bowen for jointly editing these proceedings.

Contents

Object-Oriented Systems

Information Systems

Methods, Quality and Animation

Appendices

An International Survey of Industrial Applications of Formal Methods

Dan Craigen
ORA Canada
dan@ora.on.ca

Susan Gerhart
National Science Foundation
sgerhart@nsf.gov

Ted Ralston
Ralston Research Associates
ralston@cli.com

Abstract

At the 7th Z User Meeting, the first author gave an invited presentation on an international survey of industrial applications of formal methods. The survey was performed by the three authors in 1992. In this short paper, we briefly overview the survey and provide pointers to more extensive reports.

1 Introduction

During 1992, the three authors systematically surveyed and analyzed 12 cases of industrial use of formal methods. The purpose of the survey was threefold [5]:

1. To provide an authoritative record on the practical experience to date.

2. To better inform industry and government bodies developing standards and regulations.

3. To provide pointers to future research and technology transfer needs.

   Our final report [5] discusses the surveyed cases in detail and provides an analysis of the effect of formal methods on each case. In addition, the report describes the methodology used; the limitations of the methodology; provides a cluster-by-cluster analysis; provides recommendations for formal methods R&D; and presents a general set of findings, observations and conclusions. Note that the report includes details of the cases; consequently, readers of the report will be able to draw their own conclusions and interpretations.

   Two companion papers highlight different aspects of the survey. The first paper [10] provides key observations, in software engineering terms, about formal methods practice, but without emphasising the particular formal methods techniques used. A second paper [6] emphasises the formal methods techniques used.

   The reader is urged to read the final report and the two companion papers, as the current paper is meant primarily to be a pointer to our other, more substantial, efforts.

2 Case Studies

In brief, the twelve cases were:[1]

1. Darlington Trip Computer Software (DNGS) [1]: Decision making logic for the shutdown systems of the Darlington Nuclear Generating Station was implemented in software (primarily Pascal and FORTRAN) and proven to be in conformance with requirements. SCR specifications were used.

2. Multinet Gateway System (MGS) [8]: The MGS is a secure Internet device for the transmission of datagrams. Formal methods were used to explicate the security model. The Gypsy Verification Environment was the primary formal methods tool.

3. SACEM [11]: SACEM is computer-controlled automated train protection system that allowed for the reduction in train separation times (from 2min 30sec to 2min) on one of the Paris RER lines, while maintaining safety margins. Hoare assertions and B abstract machines were used.

4. Traffic Alert and Collision Avoidance System (TCAS) [15]: TCAS is an on-board device that is to reduce the risk of mid-air and near mid-air collisions. Formal methods, using a modified version of Statecharts and focusing on a readable formal notation, was used to clarify the requirements of a complex digital avionics system.

5. Customer Information Control System (CICS) [12]: CICS is a large transaction processing system and Z was used to re-engineer a number of modules and to specify new features. Formal methods were being used to improve quality and reduce development costs.

6. Cleanroom [16]: The Cleanroom methodology was applied, by IBM, to a COBOL restructuring facility and, by Goddard, to a satellite attitude control system. Cleanroom combines formal methods techniques and statistical testing based on usage patterns.

7. Software Infrastructure (Tektronix) [9]: Tektronix used Z to develop a software infrastructure for a family of oscilloscope products with the intention of shortening time-to-market through a reusable software platform.

8. Transputer (inmos) [2]: Used formal methods (Z, Occam and HOL) to analyze components of three generations of their transputer. For example, Z was used to specify the IEEE floating point unit.

9. SSADM Toolset [4]: Praxis developed a toolset supporting the SSADM structured analysis method (SSADM is an acronym for Structured Systems Analysis and Design Method). Z was used to describe the toolset infrastructure and some of the tools.

10. Large Correct Systems (LaCoS) [14]: An Esprit project which is experimentally applying Raise to a number of industrial applications.

---

[1] We provide a single reference for each of the cases.

11. Token Based Access Control System (TBACS) [13]: The Formal Development Methodology was used to gain experience with formal methods through the specification and proof of security properties for a smartcard.

12. Analytical Information Base (HP) [3]: HP used their VDM-based specification language (HP-SL) to develop an application running on an HP patient monitoring system—a real-time database.

3 Clusters

To aid in our analysis, we divided the 12 cases into three clusters: Regulatory, Commercial and Exploratory. The Regulatory cluster (consisting of DNGS, MGS, SACEM and TCAS) included the cases which required a certification for the product and/or its development process. The Commercial cluster (consisting of CICS, Cleanroom, Tektronix, inmos and SSADM) consisted of the cases where an organisations was producing a product in which quality or productivity were of concern. The Exploratory cluster (consisting of LaCoS, TBACS and HP) included cases where organisations were exploring the efficacy of formal methods on a specific product or in its development process.

By clustering the cases in the above manner, we were able to elicit some common themes within the clusters and draw distinctions between the clusters. So, for example, in the Regulatory cluster we found that first-order logic was the most common logical framework; that specification style was often based on a state-machine paradigm; that demonstrating conformance of code to specification was of importance; that the tools being used were inadequate; and that there was a need to integrate formal methods with other validation techniques. An example distinction between clusters was the difference of importance of demonstrating conformance of code to specifications. While important in the Regulatory cluster, it had only limited application in the Commercial cluster.

4 Conclusions

In this concluding section, we highlight some of our conclusions arising from the survey.

The authors concluded that formal methods are currently being used on important, sometimes critical, systems. From the cases studies, we found that formal methods are being used:[2]

- to attain high degrees of confidence in systems;

- to support domain analysis;

- to facilitate communication between interested parties;

- to re-engineer legacy code; and

- to provide evidence of best practice.

---

[2]No single case incorporated all of these uses.

There is no doubt that the technology is evolving and is expanding the range of applications.

There are, however, various difficulties. For example, many of the available tools are ineffectual, exceedingly difficult to master, and are isolated from other software engineering tools. On the other hand, we concluded that tools were not always a prerequisite to the successful use of formal methods. We found that some of the formal methods notations have been impediments to the uptake of formal methods. Many software engineers and domain experts are not willing to come to grips with quantified formulae or first-order logic. Finally, there are rather severe difficulties of technology transfer. It is not easy for organisations to assimilate sophisticated technologies such as formal methods; careful consideration of transfer paths are required.

We note that two particular areas where useful R&D could be performed are (i) the inclusion of formal methods with other assurance techniques (such as testing) and (ii) the integration of formal methods with new or existing design methods.

Numerous other observations and conclusions are discussed in the final report and the companion papers.

5   Acknowledgements

The study was sponsored by the U.S. National Institute for Standards and Technology, the U.S. Naval Research Laboratory, and the Atomic Energy Control Board of Canada. The U.S. National Science Foundation also provided independent research time for the second author. Previous studies of trends in commercial and regulatory applications of formal methods were performed in conjunction with the organisation of the FM89 [7] conference and the MCC Formal Methods Transition Study.

The authors wish to thank the interviewees for their time, professional information, and openness. The advisory committee was also exceptionally helpful: Adele Goldberg, John Marciniak, Morven Gentleman, Lorraine Duvall, and John Gannon.

References

[1] G. Archinoff, *et al.* Verification of the Shutdown System Software at the Darlington Nuclear Generating Station. In Proceedings of the International Conference on Control and Instrumentation in Nuclear Installations, Glasgow, Scotland, May 1990.

[2] G. Barrett. Formal Methods Applied to a Floating Point Number System. IEEE Transactions on Software Engineering, 15:611–621, 1989.

[3] Stephen Bear. An Overview of HP-SL. In Proceedings of VDM'91: Formal Development Methods, Volume 551, pp 571–587, Lecture Notes in Computer Science, Springer-Verlag, December 1991.

[4] David Brownbridge. Using Z to Develop a CASE Toolset. In J.E. Nicholls (Ed.), Z User Workshop, Oxford 1989, pp 142–149, Workshops in Computing, Springer-Verlag, 1990.

[5] Dan Craigen, Susan Gerhart, Ted Ralston. An International Survey of Industrial Applications of Formal Methods. Reports to be published by NIST, NRL, and AECB, 1993.

[6] Dan Craigen, Susan Gerhart, Ted Ralston. Formal Methods Reality Check: Industrial Usage. In Proceedings of FME'93 (Formal Methods Europe), Odense, Denmark, (April 1993).

[7] Dan Craigen, Karen Summerskill (Eds.): Formal Methods for Trustworthy Computer Systems (FM89). Springer-Verlag, 1990.

[8] George Dinolt, et al. Multinet Gateway – Towards A1 Certification. In Proceedings of the IEEE Symposium on Security and Privacy, 1984.

[9] David Garlan and Norman Delisle. Formal Specifications as Reusable Frameworks. VDM'90: VDM and Z!, Springer-Verlag, 1990.

[10] Susan Gerhart, Dan Craigen, Ted Ralston. Observations on Industrial Practice Using Formal Methods. In Proceedings of the 15th International Conference on Software Engineering, Baltimore, Maryland, (May 1993).

[11] G. Guiho, C. Hennebert. SACEM Software Validation. In Proceedings of the 12th International Conference on Software Engineering, 1990.

[12] Iain Houston and Steve King. CICS Project Report: Experiences and Results from the use of Z. In Proceedings of VDM'91: Formal Development Methods, Volume 551, pp 588–596, Lecture Notes in Computer Science, Springer-Verlag, December 1991.

[13] D. Richard Kuhn and James F. Dray. Formal Specification and Verification of Control Software for Cryptographic Equipment. In Proceedings of the 6th Computer Security Applications Conference, Phoenix, Arizona, December 1990.

[14] Experiences from Applications of RAISE. LaCoS project reports LA-COS/CRI/CONS/13/V1 and LACOS/CRI/CONS/20/V1, of June 1991 and March 1992 respectively.

[15] Nancy Leveson, et al. Experiences using Statecharts for a System Requirements Specification. Submitted for publication.

[16] Richard Linger and Harlan Mills. A Case Study in Cleanroom Software Engineering: the IBM COBOL Structuring Facility. COMPSAC, IEEE Computer Society, 1988.

Language Issues and Reuse

Putting Numbers into the Mathematical Toolkit

Samuel H Valentine,
University of Brighton

Summary

The support for numbers in the current mathematical tool-kit of Z extends only to integers, and even for them most actual definitions are omitted. This paper supplies all necessary definitions and extends support to real numbers and to intervals which may be used to approximate them.

The work was undertaken as part of the RECOUP project, under SERC grant number GR/F 99656/4/1/2152.

Introduction

The Z language is extensible. Many of the sets, relations and functions which one uses in practice are defined in the Mathematical Tool-kit, written in Z itself. J. M. Spivey's book "The Z Notation — A Reference Manual" (second edition, 1992) gives a version of the Tool-kit which includes those sets which are currently regarded as standard in Z. Any specifier is at liberty to add new sets, relations and functions which may be used for a document, or for all of a specification containing many documents, or for all of the work of a particular author or at a particular installation, for example.

The mathematical tool-kit as given in Spivey 92 contains a type $\mathbb{Z}$ which is stated to represent the integers, but not formally defined. The relations $<$, $\leq$, $\geq$ and $>$ and functions $+$, $-$, $*$, div and mod are given signatures but the predicate part of the definitions contains only the words " ... definitions omitted ...". The provision of formal definitions is essential for complete rigorous proof, and in any case is desirable for didactic purposes.

Models of real-world systems often involve non-integral numbers, precise or approximate. The more theoretical models may involve coefficients which may be non-integral or even irrational, such as e and π. Computer programming languages usually support a type called REAL, which is typically implemented as a binary floating-point representation. The RECOUP project, for which this work has been undertaken, is concerned with the recovery of programs written in Fortran, where REAL numbers of this form are used with great frequency.

A specification language needs to be able to express precise statements about any models of systems, and about the computer programs which are intended to reflect or to control them. We therefore need the means to discuss any rational or irrational numbers. It is also useful to have the concept of the "interval", that is, bounds within which a real number is known to lie, which we use to describe an approximation to a real number with a known tolerance.

Because of the strong type system in Z, it is desirable that all sorts of number should be of the same Z type. So a new numeric type has been defined, whose most general useful form is given by the set "interval". Subsets of this are the bounded intervals, "boundedInterval", the real numbers, $\mathbb{R}$, the rational numbers, $\mathbb{Q}$, and the integers, $\mathbb{Z}$. Thus the existing type $\mathbb{Z}$ has been redefined to become a subset of the new type. We have the subsetting:

$$\mathbb{N}_1 \subset \mathbb{N} \subset \mathbb{Z} \subset \mathbb{Q} \subset \mathbb{R} \subset \text{boundedInterval} \subset \text{interval}$$

The comparison operations, $\_<\_, \_\leq\_, \_\geq\_, \_>\_$ are total orders over the real numbers, and, as we shall describe, partial orders over the intervals. In order to facilitate the discussion we introduce formal definitions of partial and total orders.

The widening of the numeric type has caused generalisation of all functions and relations which use numbers, and has instigated the introduction of some new ones. Since all that is being changed is the widening of domains of relations and functions, existing well-defined specifications will retain the same meaning under the enhanced tool-kit unless they make explicit reference to the domains or ranges of the altered functions or relations.

It follows also that these generalisations cannot make proof, in any particular case, harder than it was before. This is because any properties which were true under the old definition using only integers will remain theorems applicable to at least that domain, and once we have proved that the new definitions endow the integer parts of their domains with all the properties which we had assumed for them, which is a task which need be done once only, we can inherit all proofs. If we wish to work entirely with integers, we can carry on exactly as before.

Summary of Objects Reviewed

po	Partial orders	Added
ipo	Irreflexive partial orders	Added
rpo	Reflexive partial orders	Added
to	Total orders	Added
rto	Reflexive total orders	Added
ito	Irreflexive total orders	Added
interval	Intervals of rational numbers	Added
boundedInterval	Bounded intervals	Added
$\mathbb{R}$	Real numbers	Added
$\mathbb{Q}$	Rational real numbers	Added
$\mathbb{Z}$	Real integers	Redefined
$\mathbb{N}$	Non-negative real integers	Redefined
$\mathbb{N}_1$	Positive real integers	Redefined
0, 1	Integers zero and one	Defined
plusInfinity	Positive infinity	Added
minusInfinity	Negative infinity	Added
<	Less than	Defined
>	Greater than	Defined
$\leq$	Less than or equal to	Defined
$\geq$	Greater than or equal to	Defined
within	Closer approximation	Added
intervalMonotonic	Monotonic functions on intervals	
		Added
withinPair	Within for two arguments	Added
intervalPairMonotonic	Monotonic for two arguments	Added
+	Plus	Defined
–	Minus, Negate	Defined
*	Multiply	Defined
/	Divide	Added
2, 3, 4, 5, 6, 7, 8, 9, 10		
	Integers 2 to 10	Defined
mod	Modulo	Defined
div	Divide	Defined
min	Minimum of a set of intervals	
		Generalised
max	Maximum of a set of intervals	
		Generalised
glb	Greatest lower bound	Added
lub	Least upper bound	Added
makeInterval	Interval containing others	Added
consistent	Overlapping intervals	Added
joinInterval	Interval contained in others	Added

"Shorties", and the Style of Writing Z

There is an issue which has received some discussion in the Z literature, namely, whether a very compressed form of expression is desirable. As an example, we may take the definition of transitivity which we are about to use. We shall define a relation

$$R: X \leftrightarrow X$$

as "transitive" if we have that

$$R \; \natural \; R \subseteq R$$

This definition may not immediately evoke the notion of transitivity in the reader's mind, since it differs in form from that usually given in textbooks. It can however be expanded using the definition of relational composition, to give the equivalent predicate

$$\{ x, y, z: X \mid x \underline{R} y \wedge y \underline{R} z \bullet x \mapsto z \} \subseteq R$$

which in turn implies

$$\forall x, y, z: X \mid x \underline{R} y \wedge y \underline{R} z \bullet x \underline{R} z$$

which now begins to look more like the familiar form.

In general, "shorties", as they are often colloquially known, arise where there is a brief predicate on sets, which is equivalent to a less brief predicate on the elements of those sets.

The purpose of specification is the sharing of information, and any form of expression which is incomprehensible is therefore useless in specification work. There is no point in using shorties if they cannot be understood. On the other hand, it is generally quite straightforward to expand a shortie using its definition, so at worst we are talking about a slight delay in comprehension. It is recommended that any form of shortie should be explained in the accompanying natural language description when it is first used. The advantages of shorties are that
a) being short, they are less liable to typographical error;
b) they generally avoid the use of one or more bound variables required in the equivalent more explicit quantification;
c) once a particular shortie becomes familiar, it comes to seem simpler than the fuller form;
d) shorties can be used inside other expressions where the fuller form would look impossibly long and complex.

In the end, the recommendation is that shorties should be used as if they were definitions of auxiliary functions. That is, one could define "transitive" as a generic set or as a prefix relation. Instead, one introduces the shortie

$$R \; \natural \; R \subseteq R$$

and explains what it means, and then one can use that as an equivalent to an auxiliary definition.

Partial and Total Orders

Name

po	—	Partial orders
ipo	—	Irreflexive partial orders
rpo	—	Reflexive partial orders
to	—	Total orders
rto	—	Reflexive total orders
ito	—	Irreflexive total orders

Definition

partialOrder X ==
$\{$ R: X $\leftrightarrow$ X $|$

$\quad$ R $;$ R $\subseteq$ R $\wedge$ R $\cap$ R˘ $\subseteq$ id X $\}$

po X == $\quad$ partialOrder X

irreflexivePartialOrder X == $\quad$ $\{$ R: po X $|$ R $\cap$ id X $= \emptyset$ $\}$

ipo X == $\quad$ irreflexivePartialOrder X

reflexivePartialOrder X == $\quad$ $\{$ R: po X $|$ id X $\subseteq$ R $\}$

rpo X == $\quad$ reflexivePartialOrder X

totalOrder X == $\quad$ $\{$ R: po X $|$ R $\cup$ R˘ $\cup$ id X $=$ X × X $\}$

to X == $\quad$ totalOrder X

irreflexiveTotalOrder X == $\quad$ to X $\cap$ ipo X

ito X == $\quad$ irreflexiveTotalOrder X

reflexiveTotalOrder X == $\quad$ to X $\cap$ rpo X

rto X == $\quad$ reflexiveTotalOrder X

Description

A relation R: X $\leftrightarrow$ X is "transitive" if R $;$ R $\subseteq$ R, and is "antisymmetric" if R $\cap$ R˘ $\subseteq$ id X. A relation which is both transitive and antisymmetric is a "partial order" over X.

A relation is "irreflexive" if R $\cap$ id X $= \emptyset$, and is "reflexive" if id X $\subseteq$ R. A partial order which is irreflexive is an "irreflexive partial order" over X. To every such relation there is a corresponding "reflexive partial order" obtained by including the identity relation. In general, a partial order need be neither reflexive nor irreflexive.

If a partial order is such that every possible unequal pair is a member either of the order or of its inverse, it is a "total order". As with partial orders, we have the possibility to restrict to the reflexive or to the irreflexive form.

Examples

_⊆_ [X] ∈ rpo X
_⊂_ [X] ∈ ipo X

Laws

∀ V: ℙ X; R: partialOrder X •   id V ∈ partialOrder X
                                      R ∪ id V ∈ partialOrder X
                                      R \ id V ∈ partialOrder X
                                      R ∩ (V × V) ∈ partialOrder X
∀ R, S: partialOrder X • R ∩ S ∈ partialOrder X

Theorem

$$\{ R: X \leftrightarrow X \mid R \text{ ; } R \subseteq R \land R \cap id\ X = \varnothing \} =$$
$$\text{irreflexivePartialOrder } X$$

that is, if a relation is transitive and irreflexive, it is antisymmetric, and
therefore a partial order.

Proof

$R \text{ ; } R \subseteq R \land R \cap id\ X = \varnothing$

⊢

$(R \text{ ; } R) \cap id\ X = \varnothing$

⊢

$R^\sim \text{ ; } (R \text{ ; } R) \cap id\ X = R^\sim \text{ ; } \varnothing$

⊢

$(R^\sim \text{ ; } R \text{ ; } R) \cap (R^\sim \text{ ; } id\ X) = \varnothing$

⊢

$(id\ (ran\ R) \text{ ; } R) \cap R^\sim = \varnothing$

⊢

$(ran\ R \lhd R) \cap R^\sim = \varnothing$

⊢

$R \cap R^\sim = \varnothing$

⊢

$R \cap R^\sim \subseteq id\ X$

⊢

$R \in partialOrder\ X$

References

Hayes (1987) gives "partial_order X" for rpo X and "total_order X" for
rto X on page 14, and "(strict) total order on X" for ito X on pages 45-
46.

Charles Baudelaire (1821 - 1867) writes
  "Là, tout n'est qu'ordre et beauté, Luxe, calme et volupté"

Numbers

We derive numbers in a fully formal way, and generalise to allow intervals and reals. The development proceeds as follows:

1. We define the set of positive natural numbers, "positive", as a free type. We define arithmetic functions such as "padd" for addition of these elements, and so on.

2. We define the positive fractions, "fraction" as the set of pairs of positives in lowest terms. We define arithmetic functions such as "fadd" for addition of these elements, and so on.

3. We define the rational numbers, "rational" as the set of signed fractions or zero. We define arithmetic functions such as "qadd" for addition of these elements, and so on.

4. We define the intervals, "interval" as similar to the set of Dedekind cuts on the rationals, that is, an interval is defined as being two disjoint open convex sets of rationals, a lower set not bounded below and an upper set not bounded above. We define arithmetic functions such as "+" for addition of these elements, and so on.

5. We introduce successive subsets of "interval" namely "boundedInterval", those intervals which have finite bounds, and $\mathbb{R}$, the real numbers. We define $\mathbb{Q}$, the rational real numbers, which is isomorphic to the original set "rational" but of the same type as "interval". Similarly we introduce $\mathbb{Z}$, the real integers. Thus the existing type $\mathbb{Z}$ has been redefined to become a subset of the new type. We have the subsetting
  $\mathbb{N}_1 \subset \mathbb{N} \subset \mathbb{Z} \subset \mathbb{Q} \subset \mathbb{R} \subset$ boundedInterval $\subset$ interval
where all of these sets are considered to be of the same type.

Theory of Positive Natural Numbers

We start with the definition, as a free type, of the positive integers.
  positive::= unit | succ ◄ positive ►
where "succ" is the function which gives us the successor of each positive integer and "unit" is the first of them. This gives us the following properties (see Spivey "The Z Notation", section 3.10):

The effective declarations
>   unit: positive
>   succ: positive $\rightarrowtail$ positive

and the axioms
>   unit $\notin$ ran succ
> $\forall$ S: $\mathbb{P}$ positive | unit $\in$ S $\wedge$ succ $(\!S\!) \subseteq$ S • S = positive

where this latter axiom is the principle of induction.

An immediate consequence of the axiom of induction is that
>   positive = { unit } $\cup$ ran succ

We define addition:

---

padd: positive × positive → positive

> $\forall$ a: positive •   a padd unit =   succ a
> $\forall$ a, b: positive •   a padd (succ b) =   succ (a padd b)

---

and we can prove lots of theorems, using induction:
> $\forall$ b: positive • unit padd b = succ b
> $\forall$ a, b: positive • succ a padd b = succ (a padd b)
> $\forall$ a, b: positive • a padd b = b padd a
> $\forall$ a, b, c: positive • (a padd b) padd c = a padd (b padd c)
> $\forall$ a, b, c: positive | a padd c = b padd c • a = b
> $\forall$ a, b, c: positive | c padd a = c padd b • a = b
> $\forall$ a, b: positive • a padd b $\neq$ b
> $\forall$ a, b: positive • a padd b $\neq$ a

We define "greater than" and "greater than or equal to".

---

pgt, pge: positive $\leftrightarrow$ positive

> $\forall$ a, b: positive •   a pgt b $\Leftrightarrow$ ($\exists$ c: positive • a = b padd c)
>   a pge b $\Leftrightarrow$ a = b $\vee$ a pgt b

---

and we can show that
>   pgt $\in$ irreflexivePartialOrder positive
>   pge $\in$ reflexivePartialOrder positive
> $\forall$ a: positive • a pge unit
> $\forall$ a, b: positive • a pgt b $\Leftrightarrow$ succ a pgt succ b
> $\forall$ a, b: positive • a pge b $\Leftrightarrow$ succ a pge succ b
> $\forall$ a, b: positive • a pge b $\vee$ b pge a

pge ∈ reflexiveTotalOrder positive
pgt ∈ irreflexiveTotalOrder positive

We define multiplication

---

pmult: positive × positive → positive

∀ a: positive •   a pmult unit =   a
∀ a, b: positive •   a pmult (succ b) =   a padd (a pmult b)

---

and we give the following laws:
    ∀ b: positive • unit pmult b = b
    ∀ a, b: positive • (succ a) pmult b = b padd (a pmult b)
    ∀ a, b: positive • a pmult b = b pmult a
    ∀ a, b, c: positive • a pmult (b pmult c) = (a pmult b) pmult c
    ∀ a, b, c: positive • a pmult c = b pmult c ⇒ a = b
    ∀ a, b, c: positive •
        a pmult (b padd c) = (a pmult b) padd (a pmult c)

Theory of Rational Numbers

The rational numbers are derived from the positive integers by allowing free use of subtraction and division. We start with division, and define a fraction as a pair of positive integers in lowest terms, that is

fraction ==
    { a, b: positive |
        (∀ c, p, q: positive |
            c pmult p = a ∧ c pmult q = b •
                c = unit) }

We need a function to reduce a pair of integers to lowest terms, namely

---

reduce: positive × positive → fraction

∀ x, y: positive; r: fraction •
    reduce (x, y) = r ⇔ x pmult second r = y pmult first r

---

which we can prove to be a function using the laws quoted above, and we define addition and multiplication on fractions:

fadd, _fmult_:
    (positive × positive) × (positive × positive) → fraction

∀ a, b, c, d: positive •
    (a, b) fadd (c, d) =
           reduce ((a pmult d) padd (b pmult c), b pmult d)
    (a, b) fmult (c, d) = reduce (a pmult c, b pmult d)

We define the rational numbers in terms of positive fractions
        rational ::= zero | plus ◄ fraction ► | minus ◄ fraction ►
where "plus" and "minus" are functions which convert fractions into
rationals, and "zero" is a separate special rational. We define the
arithmetic functions. First addition:

---

qadd: rational × rational → rational

∀ a, b: fraction; s, t: { plus, minus } | s ≠ t •
    s a qadd t a = zero
    s a qadd s b = s (a fadd b)
    s (a fadd b) qadd t b = s a
∀ x, y: rational •
    y qadd x = x qadd y
    x qadd zero = x

and multiplication:

---

qmult: rational × rational → rational

∀ a, b: fraction; s, t: { plus, minus } | s ≠ t •
    s a qmult s b = plus (a fmult b)
    s a qmult t b = minus (a fmult b)
∀ x: rational •
    x qmult zero = zero qmult x = zero

then subtraction and division as their inverses:

```
  _qsub_: rational × rational → rational
  _qdivide_: rational × (rational \ { zero }) → rational
─────────────────────────────────────────────────────────────
  ∀ x, y: rational •                    (x qadd y) qsub y = x
  ∀ x, y: rational | y ≠ zero •         (x qmult y) qdivide y = x
```

and we can establish order

```
  qgt, qlt: irreflexiveTotalOrder rational
  qge, qle: reflexiveTotalOrder rational
─────────────────────────────────────────────────────────────
  ∀ x, y: rational • x qgt y ⟺ x qsub y ∈ ran plus
  qge = qgt ∪ id rational
  qlt = qgt˘
  qle = qge˘
```

The unit number, as a rational is
$$qunit == plus\ (unit,\ unit)$$

The set of rational positive integers is the set
$$qpositive == \{\ p: positive • plus\ (p, unit)\ \}$$
and the whole set of rational integers is the set
$$qinteger == \{\ zero\ \} ∪$$
$$\{\ p: positive;\ s: \{\ plus,\ minus\ \} • s\ (p, unit)\ \}$$

A principle of induction, rephrased for the rationals, is
$$∀\ S: \mathbf{P}\ qpositive\ |$$
$$qunit ∈ S ∧ ∀\ q: S • q\ qadd\ qunit ∈ S •$$
$$S = qpositive$$

Theory of Rational Intervals and Reals

We define a rational interval as a pair of disjoint open convex sets of rationals, the one not bounded below, the other not bounded above.

```
interval == { lower, upper: P rational |    lower ∩ upper = Ø ∧
                                            qgt ( lower ) = lower ∧
                                            qlt ( upper ) = upper }
```

In this definition we have defined two sets, the lower set and the upper set, with the following properties:

1. The lower set and the upper set are disjoint.
2. The rather terse predicate

qgt (lower) = lower

can be split into two conjuncts:

qgt (lower) ⊆ lower ∧ lower ⊆ qgt (lower)

and this in turn can be made more explicit as

(∀ r: lower; t: rational | r qgt t • t ∈ lower) ∧

∀ r: lower • ∃ u: lower • u qgt r

Thus any rational which is less than any member of the lower set is also a member of the lower set, so the lower set is convex and unbounded below. And given any member of the lower set, there is a rational greater than it, also in the lower set. That is, the lower set is open above, and has no greatest member.
3. Similarly, the upper set is convex, unbounded above, and open below.

The definition is framed in this way to allow us to extend our concept of number beyond the rationals. The lower set corresponds to the set of rationals which we wish to regard as being less than the number we are defining, and the upper set to the set of rationals which we wish to regard as greater than the number we are defining. This works for any boundary value whether or not it corresponds to any rational number. It also works for numbers specified imprecisely, where there is a boundary region containing many rationals.

To help us talk about intervals we define the following functions

qbelow, qabove, qbetween: interval → ℙ rational

∀ i: interval •   i = (qbelow i, qabove i)
                     qbetween i = rational \ qbelow i \ qabove i

We can easily show that

∀ i: interval •   ∀ x: qbelow i; z: qabove i • x qlt z
                     ∀ x: qbelow i; y: qbetween i • x qlt y
                     ∀ y: qbetween i; z: qabove i • y qlt z

An important particular case of intervals is the set ℚ, the rational reals:

ℚ == { r: rational • (qgt ({ r }), qlt ({ r })) }

It is plain that if we have some r: rational and some x: ℚ with

x = (qgt ({ r }), qlt ({ r }))

then

qbetween x = { r }

The definition establishes a bijection between the rationals and ℚ. Our subsequent definitions treat the rational reals isomorphically to the rationals, and in Z specifications we will normally use only the former.

We define the set of integer reals, $\mathbb{Z}$, which is a subset of ℚ
$$\mathbb{Z} == \{ \text{ n: qinteger } \bullet \text{ (qgt } (\{ n \}), \text{ qlt } (\{ n \})) \}$$

We define two particular integer reals
$$0 == (\text{ran minus, ran plus})$$
$$1 == (\text{qgt } (\{ \text{ qunit } \}), \text{ qlt } (\{ \text{ qunit } \}))$$
and further subsets of $\mathbb{Z}$
$$\mathbb{N}_1 == \{ \text{ n: qpositive } \bullet \text{ (qgt } (\{ n \}), \text{ qlt } (\{ n \})) \}$$
$$\mathbb{N} == \mathbb{N}_1 \cup \{ 0 \}$$

We can create the two simple infinite values:

---

plusInfinity, minusInfinity: interval

---

plusInfinity = (rational, ∅)
minusInfinity = (∅, rational)

The bounded intervals are those where the upper and lower sets are both non-empty, so the interval may not extend to infinity in either direction.
$$\text{boundedInterval} == \{ \text{ i: interval } | \text{ qbelow i } \neq \varnothing \neq \text{ qabove i } \}$$

The set of real numbers, $\mathbb{R}$, is the set of those bounded intervals, i, where (qbetween i) either has a single member or is empty. The case where (qbetween i) has a single member corresponds to the rational reals, as we have just seen.
$$\mathbb{R} == \mathbb{Q} \cup \{ \text{ i: boundedInterval } | \text{ qbetween i } = \varnothing \}$$

The set $\mathbb{R} \setminus \mathbb{Q}$ is called the set of irrational real numbers.

We exclude the simple infinite values from $\mathbb{R}$ in accordance with the usual practice. We shall refer to the set
$$\mathbb{R} \cup \{ \text{ plusInfinity, minusInfinity } \}$$
as "the extended real numbers".

It is easy to show that
$$\forall \ x, y: \mathbb{R} \ | \ \text{qabove } x = \text{qabove } y \bullet x = y$$
and
$$\forall \ x, y: \mathbb{R} \ | \ \text{qbelow } x = \text{qbelow } y \bullet x = y$$

Example of an Irrational Real

The rational number whose value is two can be defined formally as
   qtwo == qunit qadd qunit

The positive square root of two will be represented, as a real number, as

   root2 == (ran minus ∪ { r: rational | r qmult r qlt qtwo },
            { r: ran plus | r qmult r qgt qtwo })

The lower set is all the negative rationals, together with those positive rationals whose square is less than two. The upper set is the set of all positive rationals whose square is greater than two. Since there is no rational whose square is equal to two, we can easily show that
(qbetween root2 = ∅), and that we have defined an irrational real number.

End of Example

In general an interval, i, has more than one element in (qbetween i). In this case we say that the interval is non-trivial. Non-trivial intervals describe numbers which are incompletely specified or worked out. In particular they model numbers held with limited precision in computers or other digital devices, or written on paper with a limited number of decimal places, for example. Thus when we say that
   $\pi = 3.1416$
we can take this as meaning something like
   $3.14155 \leq \pi \leq 3.14165$
The theory being developed here allows one to treat such an approximation as a single element, and to define the correct results for arithmetic operations carried out on it

We use the word "precision" when discussing how much information is represented, as in the example above. The word "accuracy" we prefer to use only to describe how closely the value in a mathematical model represents the value in the external system being modelled. The value of π, for example, is known with perfect accuracy, although difficult to state numerically with perfect precision. We shall not address the issue of accuracy here.

Comparison Relations on Intervals

We extend the usual numeric relations _<_, _>_, _≤_, _≥_ to apply to intervals. We also introduce a new relation "within" for use with non-trivial intervals.

First let us note that equality in Z is not part of the Mathematical Tool-kit; it is a fundamental concept in the notation which we cannot redefine. If we have some

i. j: interval

then the predicate

i = j

is true if i and j are identical intervals, and is false otherwise. It could be that i and j overlap, and therefore represent different approximations to the same underlying real number. In that case we say that the intervals are "consistent". Equality is stronger than that — and indeed is too strong for many practical purposes.

We can, however, define the other comparison relations _<_, _>_, _≤_, _≥_ to be whatever seems most useful. We define _<_ so that if we have

i < j

we can be sure that the real number approximated by i is less than the real number approximated by j, that is, the intervals do not overlap and all the rationals in (qbetween i) are less than all the rationals in (qbetween j). So we define

---

_<_, _>_: irreflexivePartialOrder interval

∀ i, j: interval •
    i < j ⇔ qbelow j ∩ qabove i ≠ ∅
    i > j ⇔ j < i

The predicate (i < j) is true if there is definitely a rational above i and below j. If i and j are distinct non-trivial intervals, neither (i < j) nor (j < i) is counted as true if the intervals overlap, so _<_ is a partial order, but not a total order, for intervals in general.

If we restrict both operands to be real numbers, _<_ and _>_ become total orders.

_<_ ∩ ℝ × ℝ ∈ irreflexiveTotalOrder ℝ
_>_ ∩ ℝ × ℝ ∈ irreflexiveTotalOrder ℝ

We define

i ≤ j

to be true if we can guarantee that the real number approximated by i is less than or equal to the real number approximated by j. So we say

---

$\leq$_, _$\geq$_: partialOrder interval

$\forall$ i, j: interval •
    i $\leq$ j $\Leftrightarrow$ i < j $\vee$ (qbelow j, qabove i) $\in$ $\mathbb{R}$
    i $\geq$ j $\Leftrightarrow$ j $\leq$ i

The predicate (i $\leq$ j) is defined to be true if (i < j) is true, or if the intervals touch end to end without non-trivial overlap. Thus _$\leq$_ is a partial order, which is neither reflexive nor irreflexive for intervals in general.

If we restrict both operands to be real numbers, _$\leq$_ and _$\geq$_ become total orders, and reflexive.

    $\leq$ $\cap$ $\mathbb{R}$ × $\mathbb{R}$ $\in$ reflexiveTotalOrder $\mathbb{R}$
    $\geq$ $\cap$ $\mathbb{R}$ × $\mathbb{R}$ $\in$ reflexiveTotalOrder $\mathbb{R}$

If one interval is wholly contained within another, it gives a better approximation to the underlying value. Formally we define the relation "within":

---

within: reflexivePartialOrder interval

$\forall$ i, j: interval • i within j $\Leftrightarrow$
        qbelow j $\subseteq$ qbelow i $\wedge$ qabove j $\subseteq$ qabove i

---

We can show that
      $\forall$ i, j: interval | i within j • qbetween i $\subseteq$ qbetween j
and
      $\forall$ i, j: interval | $\emptyset$ $\neq$ qbetween i $\subseteq$ qbetween j • i within j
but note that in the second case we can draw no similar conclusion if (qbetween i) is empty.

Defining an Interval from its Between Set

In general an interval is defined by its "between" set provide that the between set is non-empty. In order to be valid, the between set must be convex, that is, it must contain every rational between any pair of its members, and it must be such as to leave the "above" and "below" sets both open. When we come to define arithmetic functions on intervals, it is often straightforward to describe a new between set in terms of the between sets of the operands, provided the operands are non-trivial intervals. Where the intervals concerned have irrational end-points, however, and the result has a rational end-point corresponding to it (which can easily occur), the most direct expression may exclude that end-point from the candidate "between" set.

The function "outside" directly constructs the "below" and "above" sets from the proposed "between" set, omitting any rational end-point. It defines a valid interval for all non-empty values of its argument, whether or not the argument set is closed or is convex.

---

outside: P_1 rational $\rightarrow$ interval

---

outside =
    λ S: P_1 rational •
        ({ q: rational | ($\exists$ r: rational • $\forall$ s: S • q $\underline{qlt}$ r $\underline{qlt}$ s) },
        { q: rational | ($\exists$ r: rational • $\forall$ s: S • q $\underline{qgt}$ r $\underline{qgt}$ s) })

We can show that
    $\forall$ i: interval | qbetween i $\neq \emptyset$ • outside (qbetween i) = i
and
    $\forall$ S: P_1 rational • S $\subseteq$ qbetween (outside S)
and also
    $\forall$ S, T: P_1 rational | S $\subseteq$ T • outside S within outside T

In order to define functions on intervals which also apply to irrational numbers, we can use the fact that there are non-trivial intervals which approximate them as closely as we please. We therefore need some criterion of well-behavedness, to constrain the function to conform to our intuition of the treatment of an interval as an approximation to an underlying value. We define the set of functions we want as being "interval monotonic"

intervalMonotonic ==
    { f: interval $\nrightarrow$ interval |
          ($\forall$ i: interval; j: dom f |
              i within j •
                  i $\in$ dom f $\wedge$ f i within f j) }

Suppose we apply a function to some interval argument, and the result is some interval. If the function is interval monotonic, whenever we apply it to some contained interval, the result will be an interval contained within the original result.

We are motivated in particular by the special case
∀ f: intervalMonotonic •
        ∀ x: ℝ; j: dom f | x within j • x ∈ dom f ∧ f x within f j

We define versions of "within" and of "intervalMonotonic" where we want to consider functions of two arguments:

---

withinPair: reflexivePartialOrder (interval × interval)

∀ p, q: interval × interval •
    p withinPair q ⇔
            first p within first q ∧ second p within second q

---

intervalPairMonotonic ==
        { f: interval × interval ↦ interval |
                    (∀ p: interval × interval; q: dom f | p withinPair q •
                            p ∈ dom f ∧ f p within f q) }

Defining Arithmetic Functions –
Addition and Subtraction

We start with subtraction, from which we derive negation and addition.

_−_, _+_: interval × interval → interval
−: interval → interval

_−_ ∈ intervalPairMonotonic
∀ i, j: interval | qbetween i ≠ ∅ ≠ qbetween j •
    i − j = outside { q: qbetween i; r: qbetween j • q qsub r }
∀ i: interval • − i = 0 − i
∀ i, j: interval • i + j = i − (− j)

We can easily show that the part of the subtraction function given explicitly is itself already intervalPairMonotonic. The case not covered explicitly is where one or both arguments is an irrational number. The requirement that subtraction is to be intervalPairMonotonic makes sure that it is defined in that case, and that its value is the limit of the subtraction of the intervals which approximate the irrational value or values concerned. The derivation from subtraction of negation and of addition is straightforward.

Note

For
> { q: qbetween i; r: qbetween j • q qsub r }

we could have written
> _qsub_ (qbetween i × qbetween j)

which would be legal, briefer, but perhaps not very clear. A nicer way would be
> (qbetween i) qsub (qbetween j)

which is not legal Z syntax, and which it is not currently possible to define as an extension, but which would evoke precisely the meaning wanted.

End of Note

Laws

$\forall$ i, j, k: interval •
> i + j = j + i
>
> (i + j) + k = i + (j + k)

$\forall$ i, j: interval; k: boundedInterval •
> i + k = j + k $\Leftrightarrow$ i = j

$\forall$ i: interval •
> 0 within i − i

This means that where we have two, perhaps different, underlying values, for which we have the same range of possibilities, and we subtract the one from the other, the result is an interval containing the value 0, since the underlying values might have been equal, but including in general other values too.

$\forall$ i, j, k: interval •
> i + k > j + k $\Rightarrow$ i > j

If we restrict to real numbers, we get stronger laws:

$\forall$ i, j: interval; x: $\mathbb{R}$ •
> x − x = 0
>
> i + x > j + x $\Leftrightarrow$ i > j

and we have the well-known properties:

$\forall$ x, y: $\mathbb{R}$ • $\quad$ − x $\in$ $\mathbb{R}$ $\wedge$ $\quad$ x + y $\in$ $\mathbb{R}$ $\wedge$ $\quad$ x − y $\in$ $\mathbb{R}$

$\forall$ x, y: $\mathbb{Q}$ • $\quad$ − x $\in$ $\mathbb{Q}$ $\wedge$ $\quad$ x + y $\in$ $\mathbb{Q}$ $\wedge$ $\quad$ x − y $\in$ $\mathbb{Q}$

$\forall$ x, y: $\mathbb{Z}$ • $\quad$ − x $\in$ $\mathbb{Z}$ $\wedge$ $\quad$ x + y $\in$ $\mathbb{Z}$ $\wedge$ $\quad$ x − y $\in$ $\mathbb{Z}$

Induction

We can state a principle of induction for integer real numbers, namely:

$$\forall \ S: \mathbb{P} \ N_1 \ |$$
$$1 \in S \wedge (\forall \ n: S \bullet n + 1 \in S) \bullet$$
$$S = N_1$$

Multiplication and Division

Multiplication and division are defined in a way similar to that used for subtraction

---

_*_: interval × interval → interval
_/_: interval × { i: interval | ¬ 0 within i } → interval

_*_ ∈ intervalPairMonotonic
_/_ ∈ intervalPairMonotonic
∀ i, j: interval | qbetween i ≠ Ø ≠ qbetween j •
    i * j = outside { q: qbetween i; r: qbetween j • q qmult r }
∀ i, j: interval | qbetween i ≠ Ø ≠ qbetween j ∧ ¬ 0 within j •
    i / j = outside { q: qbetween i; r: qbetween j • q qdivide r }

Laws

∀ i, j, k: interval •
    i * j = j * i
    (i * j) * k = i * (j * k)
    ¬ 0 within j * k ⇒ (i / j) / k = i / (j * k)
∀ i, j: interval; k: boundedInterval •
    ¬ 0 within k ⇒ (i * k = j * k ⇔ i = j)

    ¬ 0 within i ⇒ 0 within i / i
    k > 0 ∧ i * k > j * k ⇒ i > j
    (i + j) * k within i * k + j * k
    i * j > 0 ⇒ (i + j) * k = i * k + j * k

If we restrict to real numbers, we get stronger laws:

∀ i, j: interval; x: ℝ •
    x ≠ 0 ⇒ x / x = 1
    x > 0 ⇒ (i * x > j * x ⇔ i > j)
    (i + j) * x = i * x + j * x

and we have the well-known properties:
$\forall$ x, y: $\mathbb{R}$ • $\quad$ x $*$ y $\in$ $\mathbb{R}$ $\wedge$ $\quad$ y $\neq$ 0 $\Rightarrow$ x / y $\in$ $\mathbb{R}$
$\forall$ x, y: $\mathbb{Q}$ • $\quad$ x $*$ y $\in$ $\mathbb{Q}$ $\wedge$ $\quad$ y $\neq$ 0 $\Rightarrow$ x / y $\in$ $\mathbb{Q}$
$\forall$ x, y: $\mathbb{Z}$ • $\quad$ x $*$ y $\in$ $\mathbb{Z}$

References for Discussion of Laws

R. E. Moore - Methods and Applications of Interval Analysis,
$\hfill$ SIAM 1979
U W Kulisch & W L Miranker -
$\quad$ Computer Arithmetic in Theory and Practice,
$\hfill$ Academic Press 1981

Representation of Particular Rational Reals

We make the well-known definitions
$\qquad$ 2 == 1 + 1
$\qquad$ 3 == 2 + 1
$\qquad$ 4 == 3 + 1
$\qquad$ 5 == 4 + 1
$\qquad$ 6 == 5 + 1
$\qquad$ 7 == 6 + 1
$\qquad$ 8 == 7 + 1
$\qquad$ 9 == 8 + 1
$\qquad$ 10 == 9 + 1

We then affirm the standard convention, which cannot be stated formally within the mechanism on the Z Tool-kit but is assumed to be a part of the concrete syntax of Z, that any identifier wholly composed of the digits
$\qquad$ 0, 1, 2, 3, 4, 5, 6, 7, 8, 9
which we write as
$\qquad$ sd
where s is a digit string and d is a digit, has the value given recursively by the rule
$\qquad$ sd = (10 $*$ s) + d

It is then posssible to write simple expressions to represent any member of $\mathbb{Q}$, for example
$\qquad$ – 3
or
$\qquad$ 355 / 113

Precedence of Arithmetic Functions

We follow Spivey 92 (section 3.1.2) in giving some infix arithmetic functions higher syntactic priority than others. For the functions under discussion here, Spivey gives

       Priority 3:   + −

       Priority 4:   * div mod

and we will amend that so that division, _/_, is also included at priority 4, giving us

       Priority 3:   + −

       Priority 4:   * / div mod

This means that when we write, for example,

       33 + 1 / 3

we mean

       33 + (1 / 3)

rather than

       (33 + 1) / 3

Mod and Div

Name

       mod   —   Modulo

       div   —   Divide

Definition

mod: interval × interval ↦ interval
div: interval × interval ↦ Z

---

div =
   { a, b: interval; n: Z | ¬ 0 within b ∧ n ≤ a / b < n + 1 •
                                    (a, b) ↦ n }
mod =
   { a, b: interval; n: Z |
       (¬ 0 within b ∧ n ≤ a / b < n + 1) ∨ b = 0 •
                               (a, b) ↦ a − (b * n) }

Laws

$\mathbb{R} \times (\mathbb{R} \setminus \{ 0 \}) \subseteq$ dom _div_
$\mathbb{R} \times \mathbb{R} \subseteq$ dom _mod_

$\forall$ a, b: interval | (a, b) $\in$ dom _div_ •
       b > 0 $\Rightarrow$ 0 $\leq$ a mod b < b
       b < 0 $\Rightarrow$ b < a mod b $\leq$ 0
       a − (a div b) $*$ b = a mod b
$\forall$ a, b: interval; c: $\mathbb{R}$ | (a, b) $\in$ dom _div_ $\wedge$ c $\neq$ 0 •
       (a $*$ c) div (b $*$ c) = a div b
$\forall$ a, b: interval; c: $\mathbb{R}$ | (a, b) $\in$ dom _mod_ •
       (a $*$ c) mod (b $*$ c) = c $*$ (a mod b)
$\forall$ a: interval; b: $\mathbb{R}$; c: $\mathbb{Z}$ | (a, b) $\in$ dom _div_ •
       (a + b $*$ c) mod b = a mod b
       (a + b $*$ c) div b = a div b + c

Rounding Down and Up

Note that for any x: interval, provided it has an unambiguous integral part, we can round down and express its integer part by writing
     x div 1
We can round up by writing
     − (x div −1)

similarly we can express the fractional part by writing
     x mod 1
and so on.

Minimum and Maximum

Name

min	—	Minimum of a set of intervals
max	—	Maximum of a set of intervals

Definition

min: $\mathbf{P}_1$ interval $\nrightarrow$ interval
max: $\mathbf{P}_1$ interval $\nrightarrow$ interval

---

min =
    { S: $\mathbf{P}_1$ interval; m: interval |
            m $\in$ S $\wedge$ ($\forall$ i: S \ { m } $\bullet$ m $\leq$ i) $\bullet$

                                            S $\mapsto$ m }
max =
    { S: $\mathbf{P}_1$ interval; m: interval |
            m $\in$ S $\wedge$ ($\forall$ i: S \ { m } $\bullet$ m $\geq$ i) $\bullet$

                                            S $\mapsto$ m }

Description

The minimum of a set S of intervals is that element which is smaller than any other, if any. The maximum of S is that element which is larger than any other, if any.

Laws

$\mathbf{F}_1$ $\mathbb{R}$ $\subseteq$ dom min
$\mathbf{F}_1$ $\mathbb{R}$ $\subseteq$ dom max
$\mathbf{P}$ $\mathbb{N}$ $\cap$ dom min = $\mathbf{P}_1$ $\mathbb{N}$
$\mathbf{P}$ $\mathbb{N}$ $\cap$ dom max = $\mathbf{F}_1$ $\mathbb{N}$

$\forall$ S, T: dom min | S $\cup$ T $\in$ dom min $\bullet$
                        min (S $\cup$ T) = min { min S, min T }
$\forall$ S, T: dom max | S $\cup$ T $\in$ dom max $\bullet$
                        max (S $\cup$ T) = max { max S, max T }

$\forall$ S, T: $\mathbb{R}$ | S $\in$ dom min $\wedge$ S $\cap$ T $\in$ dom min $\bullet$
                        min (S $\cap$ T) $\geq$ min S
$\forall$ S, T: $\mathbb{R}$ | S $\in$ dom max $\wedge$ S $\cap$ T $\in$ dom max $\bullet$
                        max (S $\cap$ T) $\leq$ max S

$\forall$ a, b: $\mathbb{Z}$ | a $\leq$ b $\bullet$ min (a .. b) = a $\wedge$ max (a .. b) = b
$\forall$ a, b, c, d: $\mathbb{Z}$ $\bullet$ (a .. b) $\cap$ (c .. d) = max { a, c } .. min { b, d }

Greatest Lower Bound and Least Upper Bound

Name

glb	—	Greatest lower bound of a set of intervals
lub	—	Least upper bound of a set of intervals

Definition

glb, lub: P_1 interval → interval

$\forall$ S: P_1 interval •
    glb S = (qgt (∩ (qbelow (S))), ∪ (qabove (S)))
    lub S = (∪ (qbelow (S)), qlt (∩ (qabove (S))))

Description

In describing these functions, we give the name "the extended real numbers" to the set
    $\mathbb{R}$ ∪ { minusInfinity, plusInfinity }

Then we can describe glb and lub as follows.

The greatest lower bound of a set of extended real numbers is the greatest possible extended real number which is less than or equal to all the numbers in the set. The greatest lower bound of a set of intervals is the narrowest interval within which must lie the greatest lower bound of the extended real numbers approximated by those intervals.

The least upper bound of a set of extended real numbers is the smallest possible exended real number which is greater than or equal to all the numbers in the set. The least upper bound of a set of intervals is the narrowest interval within which must lie the least upper bound of the extended real numbers approximated by those intervals.

Discussion of Definition

The "qbelow" and "qabove" sets of the intervals in the set are used to define the qbelow and qabove sets of the result using generalised union and intersection. Where generalised intersection is used on an infinite set of open sets, the result may be closed, so it is necessary to omit any possible rational end-point by writing

$$\text{(qgt } (\cap (\text{qbelow } (S))))$$

instead of just

$$(\cap (\text{qbelow } (S)))$$

in the definition of glb, and similarly in the case of lub.

Laws

glb $(P_1 R) = R \cup \{ \text{minusInfinity} \}$
glb $(F_1 R) = R$
lub $(P_1 R) = R \cup \{ \text{plusInfinity} \}$
lub $(F_1 R) = R$

$\forall S: \text{dom min} \bullet \text{glb } S = \text{min } S$
$\forall S: \text{dom max} \bullet \text{lub } S = \text{max } S$

Operations to Manipulate Intervals

Name

makeInterval	—	Interval containing a set of intervals
consistent	—	Overlapping intervals
joinInterval	—	Interval within a set of intervals

Definition

makeInterval: P_1 interval → interval
consistent_: P (P interval)
joinInterval: P interval ↦ interval

$\forall S: P_1$ interval •
   makeInterval S =
        (qgt $(\cap$ (qbelow $(S)))$, qlt $(\cap$ (qabove $(S)))$
$\forall S: P$ interval •
   consistent S ⇔ $\forall$ i, j: S • qbelow i $\cap$ qabove j = $\emptyset$
joinInterval =
   λ S: P interval | consistent S •
       $\cup$ (qbelow (S), $\cup$ (qabove (S))

Description

"makeInterval" defines the smallest interval which has all elements of a given set of intervals within it. This can be used to create an interval explicitly from its end-points. "consistent" is a prefix relation defining a set of intervals which overlap, and which could be approximations to the same underlying value. "joinInterval" defines the widest possible interval which is within all elements of a given set of consistent intervals.

Examples of Use

We can directly express any interval with rational end-points by writing expressions like

makeInterval { − 17, 17 + 1 ∕ 2 }

for example. Note that { 3, 5 }, { 5, 3 } and

{ 5, 4, 3, 7 / 2, 4 + 1 / 2 }

are all the same interval.

"joinInterval" can be used to define the overlap region of any set of consistent intervals, but most usefully it represents the limit of a perhaps infinite sequence of approximations to a value, so that

joinInterval

{ p, q: $\mathbb{Q}$ |

$p * p < 2 \wedge q > 0 \wedge q * q > 2$ •

makeInterval { p, q } }

represents the square root of 2.

Conclusions and Suggestions for Further Work

This paper does not advocate any particular approach to numerical specification or programming. Its aim is only to provide the basis for a language suitable for precise discussion of exact and inexact numbers, whether they are to be processed in floating-point, using true rational representations, using interval arithmetic, or whatever.

We have shown how to define in Z integers, reals and intervals. It should be apparent that we can go further in various ways. In fact we can transcribe into Z the whole content of textbooks on calculus, on numerical analysis, on interval analysis, and related topics. More specifically, we can
a) define complex numbers, vectors, tensors etc. and operations on them;

b) state in Z and study the assumptions which it is reasonable to make about floating-point arithmetic, and the characteristics of actual implementations;
c) rework the definitions of numbers and operations on them in Z-- (Valentine 91), in order to show the extent to which they are operationally effective.

References and Bibliography

Aberth O. Computable Analysis. McGraw Hill 1980

Hardy G H. A Course in Pure Mathematics.
        Cambridge University Press (first edition 1908 ...)

Hayes I (ed). Specification Case Studies, Prentice Hall 1987

Kulisch U W, & Miranker W L.
        Computer Arithmetic in Theory and Practice.
        Academic Press 1981

Moore R E. Methods and Applications of Interval Analysis. SIAM 1979

Spivey J M. The Z Notation — A Reference Manual (second edition).
        Prentice Hall 1992

Suppes P. Axiomatic Set Theory. Van Nostrand 1960, Dover 1972

Valentine S H. Z--, an Executable Subset of Z.
        In: Nicholls J E (ed) Proceedings of Sixth Z User Meeting,
                Dec 1991. Springer 1992

Valentine S H. Enhancements to the Z Mathematical Toolkit.
        University of Brighton, Computer Dept Technical Report, 1993

Towards Libraries for Z

Ian Hayes
Luke Wildman
Department of Computer Science, University of Queensland
Brisbane, Australia

Abstract

We consider adding parametrised libraries to Z as a strict extension to
the current notation. We examine a simple modularisation facility with
only generic sets as parameters, similar to current Z generic schemas.

In examining parameters other than generic sets we consider both an
explicit parameter section at the beginning of the library and a more general alternative allowing any variable in the library to be instantiated as a
parameter. It turns out, however, that the same effect as the latter form
of parametrisation can be achieved with just the simple modularisation,
that is, with only generic set parameters.

Finally, we consider interactions between the modularisation facility
and current Z notation. In particular, we consider the problem of allowing
flexibility in using free types and schema types as parameters.

1 Introduction

The objective of this paper is to examine the possibilities and problems involved
with adding parametrised libraries to Z [13]. Our aim is to preserve as much as
possible the basic Z language, so that modularisation becomes a straightforward
language extension.

We would like the modularisation facility to be usable with all forms of
Z specifications, not just those making use of the conventions for specifying
sequential programs (that is, specifications written in terms of a state and a
number of state-to-state operations using conventions such as primed and unprimed variables, delta schemas, etc.). Hence our approach differs from that
of Object-Z [5], OOZE [1], Z++ [9], and MooZ [10] (see [14] for a comparison
of these). These introduce modularisation features centred around modelling
abstract data types with state and operations. For this paper, we see a modularisation facility as a way of grouping together, and perhaps parametrising, a
number of definitions, in the same way that a schema groups together components. A library can thus be viewed as a super-schema. The two approaches
have different aims and should not really be seen as in competition. Our work
is closer to that of Duke [2, 3].

Currently, Z has little in the way of facilities for modularisation.

- One can refer to definitions in a library.

- One can define a schema to collect together a number of components,
  along with a predicate linking these components. These components can
  only be variables, not nested definitions.

In both cases the definitions may be generic and the formal parameters are unstructured sets. The actual parameters may be structured sets. However, no knowledge of this structure is available within the library.

In Section 2 we present a simple modularisation facility, which can be viewed as an extension of generic schemas. Only (unstructured) sets are allowed as parameters to these libraries. These simple facilities are quite useful in practice and allow, for example, a well-structured presentation of the CAVIAR specification [7]. A full treatment of the CAVIAR specification using libraries similar to those in this paper is given in [8]. In Section 3 we consider parameters other than unstructured sets, and dependencies between parameters. These lead to some interactions with other Z notation. These problems are discussed in Section 4.

2 Simple modularisation

2.1 No parameters

The simplest form of modularisation is just to allow the collecting together of a set of definitions into a single library. Mathematical libraries, such as sequences, bags, etc., are commonly used with Z specifications, so it is essential that a modularisation facility at least support this requirement. This is not difficult.

As a Z specification is viewed as a document it is appropriate to view a library as a chapter or section of a specification document. In fact, the term chapter has been used for such libraries in Z for many years [12].

One problem with using such libraries is that, especially in the case of libraries developed independently, the same name may be used in more than one library. If one would like to use these libraries together within a specification, then there needs to be some way of disambiguating references to a common name. A simple way of doing this is to qualify references to common names with the library's name to make the reference unambiguous (assuming of course that the libraries themselves have been given different names).

This ability to create separate name spaces and disambiguate references to names is the first advantage of having a modularisation facility. With the possibility of multiple instantiations of the same library, disambiguation of names becomes essential.

2.2 Z-style generic parameters

The next level of facility we consider is allowing generic libraries. The parameters allowed are unstructured sets, similar to those currently allowed in Z for generic definitions. This allows us to group together a collection of related definitions *generic as a whole* in the parameter sets. When such a library is used, its generic sets need to be instantiated. An instantiation of the library provides all the definitions within the library instantiated with the actual parameter sets.

2.2.1   Z generic definitions

As with Z generic definitions, different instantiations need to be distinguished.
With current Z generics, the context of an instantiation often uniquely determines the parameter set, but in general the parameter set may need to be
specified explicitly. For example, given a generic function *length* defined by

$$
\begin{array}{|l}
\hline\!\![X]\!\!=\!\!=\!\!=\!\!=\!\!=\!\!=\!\!=\!\!=\!\!=\!\!=\!\!=\!\!=\!\!=\\
\quad length : \operatorname{seq} X \to \mathbb{N} \\
\hline
\quad length(s) = \#s \\
\hline
\end{array}
$$

then for s : seq $\mathbb{N}$ in the context '$length(s)$', *length* is taken to mean $length[\mathbb{N}]$
as its type is uniquely determined by the type of s. However, in the context
'$length(\langle\rangle)$' the type of the empty sequence, $\langle\rangle$, cannot be uniquely determined,
and hence the type of *length* cannot be uniquely determined. In this case we
can write $length[\mathbb{N}](\langle\rangle)$ to fully determine the type of *length*.

For the current generic definitions in Z, there is a requirement that the
object being defined is uniquely determined by the definition for any given
actual parameter set(s). This requirement was introduced because every use of
a generic definition is considered to be a separate instantiation of that definition
(see [13] for more details). As the objects being defined may be used within
expressions, two instances of a definition with the same parameter set(s) are
required to have the same value in order to maintain referential transparency. In
the use of such a generic definition, as the actual parameters uniquely determine
its value, no further disambiguation is required.

2.2.2   Generic libraries

While the approach of requiring each generic definition to be uniquely defined
for every actual generic parameter is appropriate for single generic definitions,
for the case of a generic library containing a number of *variable declarations* as
well as definitions, the same approach is not suitable.

First and foremost one would like to be able to include variables within a
generic library whose values are not uniquely determined by the generic set
parameters. Different instantiations of the same library, even with the same
generic parameters, could then use different values for their respective variables.
A not uncommon mistake in Z specifications is to write generic definitions of
variables that are not uniquely determined by the generic sets. We would like
to provide a facility for doing this correctly.

Secondly, if one separates the instantiation of a library from the use of that
instantiation's definitions, then there is only one instantiation and the reason
for the uniqueness condition for Z generics disappears.

For multiple instantiations of the same library one needs to be able to
distinguish variables in one instantiation from variables in another. This can be
achieved straightforwardly by providing a mechanism for naming instantiations.
We shall do this by prefixing the instantiation with a name followed by '::'. This
not only allows us to distinguish different instantiations of a definition without
having to supply the generic sets, but also allows us to distinguish different
instantiations with the same generic sets.

2.2.3   Example: grammar library

As an example let us consider a library useful for dealing with context-free grammars. The library is generic over the symbol set and has four variables defining the grammar: the terminal symbols, the nonterminal symbols, the set of productions and the starter symbol. Within the library from which this example was taken, a number of useful derived variables determined from the grammar are specified. Here we limit ourselves to the single derived variable *derives*.

The library appears as Section 2.2.4 below. The title of the section consists of '*Library:*' followed by the name of the library, followed by an optional list of generic set formal parameters in square brackets.

Within a library, a formal parameter set acts like a basic type in a normal Z specification. The scope of variables and schemas defined within a library is limited to the library. However, a specification (or another library) may gain access to the definitions within a library by instantiating the library.

When a library is instantiated, actual parameter sets are specified. For example, the *GrammarOps* library of Section 2.2.4 can be instantiated with the actual set of symbols AS by the declaration,

> $GrammarOps[AS]$.

All the definitions of the library *GrammarOps* are available within the specification that included the instantiation. However, every occurrence of a formal parameter within the library definition is replaced by the corresponding actual parameter set within the instantiation.

When a library is instantiated, its name may also be qualified to distinguish definitions with the same name in different libraries. The qualification consists of a name followed by '::'. For example, we may instantiate *GrammarOps* with qualifier A as follows.

> $A{::}GrammarOps[AS]$

The qualifier is applied to all names defined in the library. We discuss the special case of qualification of schemas in Section 3.2.

2.2.4   Library: GrammarOps[S]

This library is parametrised by the set of symbols to be used with the grammar, S. The types of the four variables that define the grammar are all defined in terms of this generic symbol set, S.

$$
\begin{array}{|l}
productions : S \leftrightarrow \operatorname{seq} S \\
terminals, nonterminals : \mathbf{P}\, S \\
starter : S \\
\hline
starter \in nonterminals \\
terminals \cap nonterminals = \{\} \\
\operatorname{dom} productions \subseteq nonterminals \\
(\forall\, s : \operatorname{ran} productions \bullet \operatorname{ran} s \subseteq terminals \cup nonterminals)
\end{array}
$$

In order for the grammar to be valid these variables satisfy a set of constraints: the starter symbol must be a nonterminal, the terminal and nonterminal symbols should be disjoint, only nonterminals may appear on the left side of a production, and only terminals and nonterminals may appear on the right side of a production.

The *derives* relation is derived from the grammar as follows: if a nonterminal N can produce the string of symbols (terminals and nonterminals) β, then a string of symbols containing N can derive the same string with N replaced by β.

$$derives : \text{seq } S \leftrightarrow \text{seq } S$$

$$\forall \alpha, \beta, \gamma : \text{seq } S; N : nonterminals \bullet$$
$$(\alpha \frown \langle N \rangle \frown \gamma, \alpha \frown \beta \frown \gamma) \in derives \Leftrightarrow (N, \beta) \in productions$$

3 Parameters other than generic sets

The parametrisation mechanism discussed above only allows unstructured sets as parameters. The next logical step is to allow parameters other than generic sets. We can allow values including (structured) sets as parameters and allow dependencies between parameters to be specified. We considered two approaches to providing more general parameters:

- having an explicit parameters section at the head of a library to specify the types of and constraints on the parameters, and

- allowing any of the variables declared in the library to be a parameter.

The first approach allows the simple syntax of positional parameters, but fixes once and for all the parameters to the library. If partial instantiation of parameters is required — because not all the parameters are known at the point of initial instantiation — a special mechanism needs to be introduced.

In the second approach any variable in the library may be regarded as a parameter and instantiated to a value. This requires the use of a keyword parameter mechanism on instantiation, but in allowing any of the variables in a library to be considered as parameters it treats partial instantiation as the norm.

The second approach is appealing as it would appear to allow libraries to be used in contexts not previously considered by the author of the library, using a different set of parameters to those used originally, without the necessity to revise the definition of the library. This leads to the library being more general than a statically parametrised library and able to be *re-used* in more contexts.

From the preceding discussion it is clear that we prefer the second, more flexible, approach outlined above. The real surprise is that one can achieve the same overall effect as the second approach with the simple generic libraries of Section 2! One instantiates a library with appropriate sets for the generic set parameters. Any of the variables of the library can then be effectively instantiated to a value by simply adding a normal Z predicate equating the variable to the value. In fact, this approach is more general: the predicate need not be an equality, but may just further constrain the value of the variable. So, we get not only partial instantiation in the sense of only *equating* some of the variables to be particular values, but also in the sense of only *constraining* some of the variables. The generality and simplicity of this approach are appealing.

For this approach the grammar library is as in Section 2.2.4, that is, with only generic set parameters. The library can be instantiated with its generic set:

$A::GrammarOps[AS]$,

and then any parameters are effectly instantiated by adding normal Z predicates after the library instantiation. For example, the variables describing a grammar may be instantiated as follows.

$A::productions = Aprod$
$A::terminals = Aterm$
$A::nonterminals = Anonterm$
$A::starter = Astart$

A 'with' construct This last predicate giving the values for the grammar variables requires multiple uses of the qualifier '$A::$'. This repetition can be avoided by the introduction of a **with** construct similar to that available in many programming languages. The above predicate can then be written

with A •
> $productions = Aprod$
> $terminals = Aterm$
> $nonterminals = Anonterm$
> $starter = Astart$

Renaming on instantiation Another useful facility is the ability to change the name of variables or definitions within a module on instantiation of the module. This can be provided by extending the renaming capability for Z schemas to apply to libraries as well. This is straightforward.

3.1 An example: A resource-user system

As a second example we consider a resource-user system parametrised over three generic sets: T, R, U. This example is a simplified version of the resource-user system in the CAVIAR specification [7]. Informally, T is to be thought of as a set of *time slots*, R is a set of *resources* and U is a set of *users*. We describe a general resource-user system as a function from T to the set of relations between R and U. Thus we have a rather general framework: for each time slot $t \in T$, some users are occupying or using some resources. The specification of the resource-user system follows as Section 3.1.1.

3.1.1 Library: ResourceUser[T,R,U]

The state of a resource-user system is modelled by a function ru which for every time t gives the relationship between resources and users at that time.

```
┌─ State ──────────────────────────────────────
│  ru : T → (R ↔ U)
└──────────────────────────────────────────────
```

This state allows both multiple users of a resource, and a user to have multiple resources.

The *initial state* of this system is defined by making $ru(t)$ the empty relation for each t.

$$Init \; \widehat{=} \; [State \mid \mathrm{ran}(ru) = \{\{\}\}]$$

A resource $r?$ may be booked by user $u?$ for all the times in the set $t?$ provided the user has not already booked that resource for any of those times.

```
┌─ Book ─────────────────────────────────────────────
│ ΔState
│ t? : P T
│ r? : R
│ u? : U
├────────────────────────────────────────────────────
│ ∀ t : t? •
│       (r? ↦ u?) ∉ ru(t) ∧
│       ru'(t) = ru(t) ∪ {r? ↦ u?}
│ t? ◁ ru' = t? ◁ ru
└────────────────────────────────────────────────────
```

The resource-user relation is updated to record the booking for only those times in $t?$.

A user $u?$ may cancel a booking for a resource $r?$ for a set of times $t?$, provided the user has the resource booked for all those times.

```
┌─ Cancel ───────────────────────────────────────────
│ ΔState
│ t? : P T
│ r? : R
│ u? : U
├────────────────────────────────────────────────────
│ ∀ t : t? •
│       (r? ↦ u?) ∈ ru(t) ∧
│       ru'(t) = ru(t) \ {r? ↦ u?}
│ t? ◁ ru' = t? ◁ ru
└────────────────────────────────────────────────────
```

The resource-user relation is updated to remove the bookings for only those times in $t?$.

3.2   Decoration of components of schemas

The resource-user library can be instantiated for different types of resources and users and even different types of times. In the CAVIAR specification there are multiple instantiations of this library in different guises. For illustration we consider two instantiations:

- reservations of hotel rooms, *HotelRm*, for visitors, V, on dates, *Date*, and

- reservations for transport, *Trans*, for visitors, V, at times, *Time*.

The instantiations follow.

$HR :: ResourceUser[Date, HotelRm, V]$
$TR :: ResourceUser[Time, Trans, V]$

(Please ignore the fact that multiple bookings of a room for the same date are allowed; this is avoided in the full CAVIAR specification, but ignored here for simplicity.) The above instantiations give us two state schemas, $HR::State$ and $TR::State$. For the full CAVIAR system we need to combine both these states (and more) together into a system state schema. We can write,

$$
\boxed{\begin{array}{l}
\underline{\ CAVIAR\_State} \\
HR::State \\
TR::State
\end{array}}
$$

However, we need to be careful how we interpret a reference like $HR::State$:

- We can interpret it to mean that just the name of the schema is qualified. In which case it is equivalent to

$$
\boxed{\begin{array}{l}
\underline{\ HR::State} \\
ru : Date \rightarrow (HotelRm \leftrightarrow V)
\end{array}}
$$

- Alternatively, the qualification '$HR::$' can be used as a decoration on the schema components as well. In which case it is equivalent to

$$
\boxed{\begin{array}{l}
\underline{\ HR::State} \\
HR::ru : Date \rightarrow (HotelRm \leftrightarrow V)
\end{array}}
$$

If we take the former meaning then the definition of $CAVIAR\_State$ is invalid as it attempts to merge two incompatible ru components. For the second interpretation, the names $HR::ru$ and $TR::ru$ are distinct and the definition of $CAVIAR\_State$ is valid. Further, as the schema component names are distinct, operations defined by combining hotel reservation and transport reservation operations are well defined. For example, an operation to book a hotel room and leave the transport reservations unchanged can be defined by

$$Book\_HR \mathrel{\widehat{=}} HR::Book \wedge TR::\Xi State.$$

If we reconsider the first alternative (qualification but no decoration), then we need to distinguish the hotel and transport reservations. This could be done by declaring two variables of the appropriate type of state:

$$
\boxed{\begin{array}{l}
\underline{\ CAVIAR\_State} \\
hr : HR::State \\
tr : TR::State
\end{array}}
$$

The problem now becomes defining operations on this state, such as an operation to book a hotel room. In order to do this we need to define an operation which performs a booking operation on the hr component of the above state:

$$
\begin{array}{l}
\rule{10cm}{0.4pt}\\
\textit{Book\_HR} \rule{8cm}{0pt}\\
\Delta CAVIAR\_State\\
t? : \mathbf{P}\ Date\\
r? : HotelRm\\
u? : V\\
\rule{10cm}{0.4pt}\\
tr' = tr\\
\exists\,\Delta HR::State\ \bullet\\
\quad \theta HR::State = hr\ \wedge\\
\quad HR::Book\ \wedge\\
\quad hr' = \theta HR::State'\\
\rule{10cm}{0.4pt}
\end{array}
$$

This definition is more complicated than the version given above which assumes decoration of schemas.

While automatically decorating the components of a schema with a library qualifier works well for the example given above (and also for the full CAVIAR specification - see [8]), it is not necessarily the preferred approach in general. It requires that component names are always decorated even when there are no clashes and decoration is not necessary, and it also precludes the merging of components of schemas from two separate libraries if this were desired.

One approach to having a relatively simple specification of such operations without automatically decorating the components of a schema with the library qualifier, is to allow explicit decoration of schemas. The CAVIAR state could then be written

$$
\begin{array}{l}
\rule{8cm}{0pt}\\
\textit{CAVIAR\_State} \rule{5cm}{0pt}\\
hr\text{-}HR::State\\
tr\text{-}TR::State\\
\rule{8cm}{0.4pt}
\end{array}
$$

where 'hr-' is a decoration, but 'HR' is only a name qualifier. This expands to

$$
\begin{array}{l}
\rule{8cm}{0pt}\\
\textit{CAVIAR\_State} \rule{5cm}{0pt}\\
hr\text{-}ru : Date \rightarrow (HotelRm \leftrightarrow V)\\
tr\text{-}ru : Time \rightarrow (Trans \leftrightarrow V)\\
\rule{8cm}{0.4pt}
\end{array}
$$

The booking operation can then be written as follows.

$$Book\_HR \;\hat{=}\; hr\text{-}HR::Book \wedge tr\text{-}TR::\Xi State.$$

This approach has the appeal that it separates the concerns of qualification and decoration. These two notational devices become primitives that may be used either independently or combined together to create the effect desired by the specifier. Although this approach is slightly more cumbersome than automatic decoration of schema components, it is no where near as complicated as having no decoration at all. (Such named decoration would be useful in Z regardless of libraries.)

4   Structured set parameters

One area of interest is if a library requires some knowledge of the internal structure of a generic set parameter. For example, the library may assume that the generic set is a Cartesian product of two sets X and Y. This case can be handled simply by making both X and Y generic set parameters, rather than their Cartesian product. The Cartesian product can then be defined in terms of X and Y within the library. Of more interest are the cases when the generic set is expected to be a free type (Section 4.1) or a schema type (Section 4.2).

4.1 Free type

A free type may be used as part of a library. For example, the free type may be of the form,

$$T ::= x \langle\!\langle X \rangle\!\rangle \mid y \langle\!\langle Y \rangle\!\rangle,$$

where the sets X and Y may or may not be generic set parameters to the library.

In some cases, however, one would like the free type T to be treated like a parameter and to be equated with a subset of some existing free type which has constructors of the same type as x and y, but may also have other constructors. For example, consider the set $T2$

$$T2 ::= x2 \langle\!\langle X \rangle\!\rangle \mid y2 \langle\!\langle Y \rangle\!\rangle \mid z2 \langle\!\langle Z \rangle\!\rangle,$$

which is similar to T. It can be thought of as a superset of T.

To see how we can achieve this it is instructive to expand the free type definition of T above. T is introduced as a basic type:

$$[T],$$

with two total one-to-one constructor functions x and y. The ranges of these constructor functions are disjoint (1a) and together they construct the whole of T (2a).

$$
\begin{array}{|l}
x : X \rightarrowtail T \\
y : Y \rightarrowtail T \\
\hline
\text{disjoint} \langle \operatorname{ran} x, \operatorname{ran} y \rangle \hfill (1a) \\
\bigcup \{ \operatorname{ran} x, \operatorname{ran} y \} = T. \hfill (2a)
\end{array}
$$

In this form it is clear that if we equate T with $T2$, x with $x2$ and y with $y2$, that constraint (2a) is not satisfied. However, if we remove constraint (2a), we can make T a generic parameter which we can instantiate with $T2$, and then equate x with $x2$ and y with $y2$ to achieve the desired effect. So, by using the expanded form of the definition of T without constraint (2a), we can achieve our objective.

For free types within a library that we wish to allow to be substituted by 'super' types, we could allow the following syntactic sugar as a predicate within a library:

$$T \supseteq x \langle\!\langle X \rangle\!\rangle \mid y \langle\!\langle Y \rangle\!\rangle.$$

T would be a generic parameter, and x and y can be equated with the actual constructor functions.

Recursive free types The principle used above may be applied to free types whose definitions involve recursion, however, the expansion of the free type definition in this case involves a more general version of condition (2a). We consider a simplified example of abstract syntax for boolean expressions and assertions taken from a specification of a simple programming language.

$$BE ::= const\langle\!\langle Boolean\rangle\!\rangle \mid var\langle\!\langle Id\rangle\!\rangle \mid and\langle\!\langle BE \times BE\rangle\!\rangle$$

The expansion of this definition introduces the basic type BE,

$$[BE]$$

and defines the constructor functions *const*, *var* and *and*:

$$
\begin{array}{|l}
const : Boolean \rightarrowtail BE \\
var : Id \rightarrowtail BE \\
and : BE \times BE \rightarrowtail BE \\
\hline
\text{disjoint } \langle \text{ran } const, \text{ran } var, \text{ran } and\rangle \\
\forall\, W : \mathbb{P}\, BE \bullet \\
\quad const(\!|Boolean|\!) \cup var(\!|Id|\!) \cup and(\!|W \times W|\!) \subseteq W \\
\quad \Rightarrow BE \subseteq W.
\end{array}
$$

$\qquad\qquad\qquad\qquad\qquad\qquad\qquad\qquad\qquad\qquad$ (1b)
$\qquad\qquad\qquad\qquad\qquad\qquad\qquad\qquad\qquad\qquad$ (2b)

A 'superset' of boolean expressions are assertions with the following abstract syntax:

$$
\begin{aligned}
Assertion ::=\ &Aconst\langle\!\langle Boolean\rangle\!\rangle \mid Avar\langle\!\langle Id\rangle\!\rangle \\
&\mid\ Aand\langle\!\langle Assertion \times Assertion\rangle\!\rangle \\
&\mid\ forall\langle\!\langle Id \times Assertion\rangle\!\rangle.
\end{aligned}
$$

To pass *Assertion* for *BE* we need to drop condition (2b) and equate the corresponding constructor functions.

Note that the constructors *Aconst*, *Avar* and *Aand* do not generate all possible assertions. However, *BE* has been instantiated to the set of all assertions, so *Aand* is of type

$$Aand : Assertion \times Assertion \rightarrowtail Assertion.$$

The arguments to this constructor may be any assertions, including assertions not generated solely with the three constructor functions, ie, they involve the *forall* constructor. Care should be taken within the library as to whether such constructed objects are desirable or not.

4.2   Schema type

As with free types it is useful if a library may expect the structure of a set passed to it to be a schema with certain components. For example, a library may expect a parameter to be of the form

$$
\begin{array}{|l}
\underline{\ S\ }\qquad\qquad\qquad\qquad\qquad\qquad\qquad\qquad \\
c : C \\
d : D \\
\hline
P(c, d) \\
\hline
\end{array}
$$

where P is some predicate possibly involving c and d, and the sets C and D may or not be generic set parameters. It is useful to allow sets that are *similar* to S to be passed as parameters as well. For example, consider the schema $S2$ similar to S.

```
┌─ S2 ─────────────────────────────
│  c2 : C
│  d2 : D
│  e2 : E
├──────────────────────────────────
│  P(c2, d2) ∧ Q(c2, d2, e2)
└──────────────────────────────────
```

As with free types, it is useful to break the schema S down into an *almost* equivalent form. S is considered to be a basic type with two total selector functions c and d and an onto constructor function mkS.

$[S]$

The components $c(s)$ and $d(s)$ of any element of $s \in S$ satisfy the predicate P (3), and for any pair, $cx : C$ and $dx : D$ that satisfy P, a corresponding element of S exists (4) and this element is unique (5). The constructor function mkS can build any element of S (it is onto) given a pair cx and dx satisfying P (6), and the c and d components of such a constructed element are cx and dx respectively (7). (There is quite a deal of redundancy in the conditions (4)–(7), but this is useful to keep the concepts involved separate.)

$$
\begin{array}{l}
c : S \rightarrow C \\
d : S \rightarrow D \\
mkS : C \times D \twoheadrightarrow S \\
\hline
(\forall s : S \bullet P(c(s), d(s))) \hfill (3) \\
(\forall cx : C;\ dx : D \mid P(cx, dx) \bullet \\
\quad (\exists s : S \bullet cx = c(s) \wedge dx = d(s))) \hfill (4) \\
(\forall s1, s2 : S \bullet \\
\quad c(s1) = c(s2) \wedge d(s1) = d(s2) \Rightarrow s1 = s2) \hfill (5) \\
\operatorname{dom} mkS = \{cx : C;\ dx : D \mid P(cx, dx)\} \hfill (6) \\
(\forall cx : C;\ dx : D \mid P(cx, dx) \bullet \\
\quad c(mkS(cx, dx)) = cx \wedge d(mkS(cx, dx)) = dx) \hfill (7)
\end{array}
$$

If we are to allow schemas with additional fields, such as $S2$ to be substituted in place of S, then we can no longer insist on the uniqueness condition (5) — because two elements of $S2$ with the same $c2$ and $d2$ fields may have different $e2$ fields — nor can we make use of the constructor function mkS (plus (6) and (7)) — because we need to know the value of component $e2$ to construct a value of $S2$. Provided $S2$ satisfies conditions (3) and (4), we can instantiate S to $S2$ and the selector function c to $(\lambda\, S2 \bullet c2)$ and d to $(\lambda\, S2 \bullet d2)$.

If $S2$ puts a tighter constraint on fields $c2$ and $d2$ (via predicate Q) than S does, then we cannot insist that that there exist a value of s corresponding to every pair $cx : C$ and $dx : D$ such that $P(cx, dx)$ holds, thus eliminating condition (4) as well. In this case the declarations within the library become

$$
\begin{array}{|l}
c : S \to C \\
d : S \to D \\
\hline
\forall\, s : S \bullet P(c(s), d(s))
\end{array}
$$

and we can substitute $S2$ for S as above. As these declarations are quite straightforward, we will not bother introducing any syntactic sugar for this case.

Although the above allows compatible schemas to be treated as parameters, it only allows the schemas to be treated as sets. It does not allow for schema operators. It is not clear how one would go about allowing schema operators in such a context. Duke discusses extensions to the schema operators in a similar context in [3, 4].

5 Conclusions

By far the most significant conclusion of this work is that parametrised libraries may be added to Z by simply adding libraries with generic set parameters. The effect of parameters other than generic sets may be achieved by equating variables declared within an instantiation of a library with the desired value. In fact, the mechanism is more general than explicit parametrisation, as we may just place constraints on the value of the variable, rather than giving an explicit value. In addition, any of the variables declared within a module can be thought of as a parameter. This provides a more flexible modularisation and parametrisation mechanism than statically predetermined parameters. We envisage that this could lead to easier reuse of libraries.

It was a revelation to us that such a simple mechanism could provide such a flexible modularisation facility.

The approach that we have taken with schemas has been to only qualify the name of the schema with the library's qualifier and not decorate the schema's components with the qualifier. The problem of combining schemas to represent an operation on states made up from multiple instantiations of a library is solved by allowing schemas to be decorated with a name as described in Section 3.2. This approach has been taken because it separates the concerns of qualification of names and decoration of schemas. Providing these two facilities separately allows the specifier the flexibility of combining them or using them independently as needed.

If a library needs some knowledge of the internal structure of a generic parameter set, this can be provided. The more interesting cases are free types (Section 4.1) and schema types (Section 4.2). Access to the structure of these types can be provided via constructor functions and selector functions, respectively. In general, one would like to be able to supply compatible sets as parameters by relaxing some of the conditions of the normal definitions. This can already be done by simply writing out the required conditions explicitly, but may be aided by new notation to help express the desired constraints more succinctly. This is an area for further investigation.

The libraries presented here can be thought of as super schemas. Or, put the other way around, a schema can be thought of as a mini library. In fact, there are no difficulties in allowing a schema to be instantiated just like a library.

We would recommend allowing such instantiations. The main differences between schemas and libraries are that schemas can be used as types and can be combined using schema operators. Neither of these two facilities is applicable to libraries.

One point that has not been discussed so far is the inclusion of the same library in unqualified form more than once in the same specification. For example, a mathematical library (like bags) could be included in two separate libraries. If both of these libraries are included (unqualified) then the mathematical library definitions have been included more than once in the same specification. As both these inclusions derive from the same source it seems reasonable to merge their definitions, rather than treat this as an error. The same approach would not be recommended for two definitions with the same name that derive from different sources. For further discussion on this point see [6].

6 Acknowledgements

This work has benefited from discussions with Bill Flinn, Ib Holm Sørensen and Mike Spivey, on the modularisation of the CAVIAR specification, and from the work of David Duke [2, 3]. Luke Wildman is supported by an Australian Postgraduate Research Award. We would also like to acknowledge our collaboration with Jim Welsh and David Carrington on an Australian Research Council supported grant entitled *Modularity in the Derivation of Verified Software* (A48931426).

References

[1] Alencar A, Goguen J. OOZE: An object-oriented Z environment. In America P (ed), Proc. ECOOP'91 European Conference on Object-Oriented Programming, vol 512 of Lecture Notes in Computer Science, pp 180–199. Springer-Verlag, 1991.

[2] Duke D. Structuring Z specifications. In Proc. 14th Australian Computer Science Conference, 1991.

[3] Duke D. Enhancing the structure of Z specifications. In Nicholls J (ed), Z User Workshop, York 1991, Workshops in Computing, pp 329–351. Springer-Verlag, 1992.

[4] Duke D. Object-Oriented Formal Specification. PhD thesis, Department of Computer Science, University of Queensland, 1992.

[5] Duke R, King P, Rose G, Smith G. The Object-Z specification language version 1. Technical Report SVRC 91-1, Department of Computer Science, University of Queensland, QLD 4072, Australia, 1991.

[6] Fitzgerald J. Modularity in model-oriented formal specifications and its interaction with formal reasoning. PhD thesis, Department of Computer Science, University of Manchester, 1991.

[7] Flinn B, Sørensen I. CAVIAR: A case study in specification. In Hayes I (ed), Specification Case Studies, International Series in Computer Science, pp 141–188. Prentice Hall International, Hemel Hempstead, Hertfordshire, UK, 1987.

[8] Flinn B, Sørensen I. CAVIAR: A case study in specification. In Hayes I (ed), Specification Case Studies, International Series in Computer Science, pp 79–110. Prentice Hall International, Hemel Hempstead, Hertfordshire, UK, second edition, 1993. To appear.

[9] Lano K. Z^{++}: An object-orientated extension to Z. In Nicholls [11], pp 151–172.

[10] Meira S, Cavalcanti A. Modular object-oriented Z specifications. In Nicholls [11], pp 173–192.

[11] Nicholls J (ed). Z User Workshop, Oxford 1990, Workshops in Computing. Springer-Verlag, 1991.

[12] Sørensen I. A specification language. In Staunstrup J (ed), Program Specification: Proceedings of a Workshop, vol 134 of Lecture Notes in Computer Science, pp 381–401. Springer-Verlag, 1981.

[13] Spivey J. The Z Notation: A Reference Manual. International Series in Computer Science. Prentice Hall, Hemel Hempstead, Hertfordshire, UK, 2nd edition, 1992.

[14] Stepney S. Comparative study of object orientation in Z. Technical Report ZIP/Logica/90/046, Issue 3.0, Logica Cambridge Ltd, Betjeman House, 104 Hills Road, Cambridge CB2 1LQ, UK, 1990.

Plain guide to the Z Base Standard

J. E. Nicholls
Oxford University Computing Laboratory
Programming Research Group
11 Keble Road Oxford OX1 3QD

Abstract: This paper provides a brief introduction to the *Z Base Standard* published in November 1992 and made available for the first time at the Seventh Z User Meeting. Topics include:

Why? (reasons for developing a Z standard)
How? (technique of description)
What? (outline of contents & structure)
Help! (guidelines for reading the standard)
What next? (status and direction)

Acknowledgement: Preparation of this paper has been undertaken as part of the ZIP project. ZIP — A unification initiative for Z Standards, Methods and Tools has been partially funded by the Department of Trade and Industry and the Science and Engineering Council under their joint Information Engineering Advanced Technology Programme.

Introduction

As a delegate to the Seventh Z User Meeting you will have received a copy of Version 1.0 of the *Z Base Standard* [1], developed as part of the ZIP project. When you first open the document you may find it somewhat daunting, but you should bear in mind that in preparing this version our first objective has been to make its technical contents as precise, accurate and complete as possible. Later, we plan to improve its readability and make it more accessible to its intended users — in following sections of the paper, I propose some objectives for this aspect of the work.

The aim of this paper is to introduce the standard to non-specialist readers, to summarise the reasons for developing a Z standard, to introduce the techniques of description used, and to indicate the current status of standards activities.

Reasons for developing a Z standard

Why a Z standard?

- stability
- control over development
- quality of description
- standards are mandatory in some situations

If you look at mathematics text books, even on established subjects such as set theory, algebra or mathematical logic, you will see a variety of notations, concepts and methods of presentation—inventing new notations is an integral part of doing mathematics. It follows that many mathematicians are not naturally predisposed to the establishment of notational standards, which might be seen to inhibit their natural way of working. On the other hand engineers (and many physical scientists) generally understand the importance of standards, which are essential if large, complex systems are going to work.

Z is "a way of writing mathematics" but it is also a tool for software engineers. A standard for Z is needed to make it possible to use Z over *space* (by groups of people) and over *time* (since a project started one year may not finish until several years later).

A decision about the timing for standards development is important. Too soon, and the notation may not yet have been fully evaluated. Too late, and there may already be several dialects. The *Proposal for a New Work Item* submitted to ISO [2] provides a statement of the current use of Z and a rationale for developing a standard at this time. I suspect I do not need to labour the point to this audience, since it was at one of the early Z User Meetings in Oxford that the needs for a Z standard were first publicly expressed.

Summary: some advantages of standardisation

Stability.
Z specifications are widely distributed
they are shared by many people
Z specifications persist over time

Standards development: a means of recognising user needs.
reconciliation of different ideas about the language
confirmation of completeness and sufficiency of design
agreement on the form and content of standards documents

Quality.
> established techniques of validation
> statements of conformity
> establish links with (and use of) other standards

Accessibility.
> standards are: published, available, maintained

Techniques for defining Z

Required properties of a language description

- precision
- completeness, consistency, soundness
- intelligibility

As we advocate the use of formal descriptions of systems, we also wish to provide a formal description of the notation itself.

Syntax. Syntax deals with all matters relating to the representation of Z and the structure of well-formed specifications.

In the Z definition, the usual distinction is made between concrete and abstract syntax. The *concrete syntaxes* deal with how Z is written and appears in print or on a screen. In addition, a form of representation in computer codes is given, using the framework of SGML [3]. This standard form of representation, increasingly used for system documentation, allows the editing, storing and retrieval of Z documents in a machine independent way. It provides a way for Z documents to be structured and the parts linked together as in hypertext.

The *abstract syntax* defines the underlying structure of Z and establishes the named entities to be used in defining the semantics.

Semantics. Semantics provides a theory that allows *meaning* to be given to well-formed Z documents. Since the definition applies to the entire language and not just to a specific text, we base the description on the *syntax* of the language. We have made the abstract syntax the centre for the description, since this is more amenable to mathematical reasoning and proof than the concrete syntax.

In the approach taken in the Base Standard, we do not define the meaning of the underlying set theory and logic—these are regarded as given. However, we do need to provide mathematical definitions of Z concepts that do not appear in conventional mathematics. These include two that have been introduced to help in writing system descriptions:

the Z *type system*
the Z *schema*

We require not just to explain these (this can be done informally) but to give a formal definition so that users can confidently calculate, reason and prove results about Z specifications.

Several approaches (operational, axiomatic, denotational, algebraic) are used for providing formal descriptions of programming language semantics. In the *Z Base Standard* a denotational method is used — the approach is to provide a function that associates with each syntactic element of the language an abstract value which may be a number, a truth value or a function. These functions are applied recursively to the whole language.

We believe the techniques used in the *Z Base Standard* are the best to satisfy the first two of the "Required properties" listed above — work remains to be done to satisfy the third.

The Z Base Standard

Several descriptions of Z have been published, although in one way or another they have lacked completeness and/or formality. Version 1.0 of the *Z Base Standard* brings together for the first time formal definitions of all elements commonly understood to be part of Z, together with additional elements considered necessary to make it a viable standard for its intended use. The structure of the document is as follows:

Introductory sections. These sections contain statements of scope, design principles and the aims of standardisation, together with a brief history of development. The statements of scope and design principles of Z are important in guiding future development; I believe one of the special merits of Z is its breadth of scope and open-ended design.
An important part of the introductory section, still under discussion, is the statement of rules of conformance.

Method of description. These sections explain the method of description and define the metalanguage and the definitional framework used in the rest of the document. In formal methods of language definition, 'meaning' is defined mathematically in terms of set theory and logic. The *semantic universe* is a collection of all possible meanings (i.e. sets) and is defined first as part of the framework.

Language description. This is the central part of the document and contains definitions of elements of the language, corresponding to the structure of the abstract syntax.

Annexes. These comprise the following sections:

> abstract syntax
> representation syntax
> mathematical toolkit
> interchange format
> character set
> a deductive system

The annexes containing the syntaxes and character set collect together information listed in the Language Description. The other annexes contain additional information and in the case of the *Interchange Format* and the description of *A deductive system*, are published for the first time in this version.

References. A collection of historical and technical references.

Syntactic Categories defined in sections of the Language Description

Expression (with 17 subsections)

Predicate (13 subsections)

Declaration (4 subsections)

Schema Text (2 subsections)

Schema (15 subsections)

Paragraph (6 subsections)

Specification (1 subsection)

Descriptions are written so that all information about a language element is grouped together. At the end of each section, tables of *free variables* and *alphabets* are given. Within each of the main sections, the format of each language description follows a consistent pattern, each entry is subdivided into the following subsections:

    abstract syntax
    representation & transformation
    type
    meaning or value

Each entry contains a formal description in metalanguage, together with explanatory English commentary. At the end of the document (in Annexes) the complete syntaxes are repeated, so that they can reviewed as a whole.

A guide for readers

Language standards are not generally regarded as providing as easy read. This preliminary version of the *Z Base Standard* is no exception, but we intend to try and make this not only the most complete and accurate description of Z, but also, of its kind, the most readable. We put forward the following general principle:

Principle of accessibility

Those who can use Z should be able to read and understand the Z Base Standard

---

The document which defines the Z notation is itself a formal specification. It is written in mathematics rather than Z, and readers will need to know something of the general principles of language definition. We can therefore divide the background needed for understanding the standard into *general concepts* (typically found in computer science courses and text books), and *Z-related concepts* included specifically for use in the definition.

General concepts

        set theory and logic
        principles of formal definition
        techniques of syntax definition
            concrete and abstract syntax
        principles of denotational semantics
            the (denotational) sense of 'meaning'
            semantic universe

The mathematical basis for the definition is ZF set theory and first order logic.

Functional and relational operators are introduced in the definition (some of them being similar to those in Z). All notation that is likely to be unfamiliar is defined in the text.

Readers should be familiar with the principle of separating representational aspects of language and the concept of abstract syntax. Denotational methods of language description are described in several recent text books — see for example the book by Meyer [4].

Z-related concepts

Many of the concepts introduced in the standard are needed to provide a formal basis for the treatment of Z types and schemas. The introductory sections of the standard include, or will include, explanations of the following:

> **Z types.** Summary of reasons for introducing types in a specification language. Mathematical basis of the Z type system.

> **Carrier set.** Every type has an associated set of values, its carrier set.

> **Z schemas.** Properties of Z schemas (Note: schemas are not macros). Scope properties; free variables and declarations. Schemas as types; schema operations. Effects on semantics and proof methods.

> **Signature.** A mapping from names to types. Used in the definition of the type of a schema.

> **Binding.** A mapping from names to values. Used in defining the value of an element of a schema.

> **Environment.** A function from names to (possibly generic) elements. Used to record the information contained in a specification.

Standards activities

The numbering of the current *Z Base Standard* as Version 1.0 disguises the activities that have preceded its publication. There have been six full versions of the Base Standard before this one (details are listed in copyright notices at the beginning of the document), and many other draft document and working papers have been produced. Previous versions have included experiments with different layouts and structures of the document. As work on the foundational aspects of Z (including the semantics and the proposals for a deductive system) has progressed, alternative approaches have been tried. Throughout, members of the Standards Review Committee (listed in the document) have played a vital role in reviewing and advising on the best structures for the form of the document.

BSI and ISO. In the past year we applied to BSI for the establishment of a Standards Panel for Z and this has been approved; the Panel is: *IST/5/-/52: Z Notation.* Shortly after the decision to form this Panel, ISO committee SC22 approved the formation of a New Work Item, and as part of the normal procedure for new items, the decision is currently under ballot.

Status of standards activities

The current document is: Version 1.0 of the *Z Base Standard* [1]

This includes: the first formal description of all parts of Z
                    integrated descriptions of syntaxes and semantics
                    a *deductive system* for reasoning and proof

Earlier versions have been reviewed by the
    Standards Review Committee
    there is a plan for a full validation

Implementation of parts of the standard has been carried out
    as part of the work of the Tools group of the ZIP project
    and by other implementors

A BSI Standards Panel is in place
    a proposal for an ISO *New Work Item* is currently under ballot

Version 1.0 is a proposed *Working Draft* for the Standards Panel

Comments are invited

Standards work within the current ZIP project will come to an end at the end of 1992, with publication of Version 1.0. We have applied for funding to continue the work in the Programming Research Group, where the bulk of the work on the current standard has been done. Standards work will necessarily take on a new flavour as it passes to national and international representation. We have anticipated this by inviting international representatives on the Standards Review Committee and we hope these experts will continue to advise on the directions that should be taken for the standard.

Directions

Z has been shown to be a simple, compact and robust notation with considerable expressive powers. It has been successful in a wide variety of environments. I believe its success has come about because of its closeness to conventional mathematics and its capability for being used in many different ways. In the Case

Studies that have formed an important part of the history of Z development, there are reports of many kinds of use, from a minimal use to model a local aspect of a system, to the most whole-hearted formalist definition of complete systems, including the use of formal reasoning and proof.

In spite of the acknowledged success of Z and other notations in key case studies, the general use of formal methods in industry remains very low. I believe that future work on the development of Z should include studies of what is needed of the notation (and its supporting environment) to improve the general use of formal methods.

Improving the use of formal methods

- better understanding of the development process for use with formal methods

- improved integration with other notations and methods, including:
    structured methods
    object-oriented approaches

- research on techniques of refinement and code generation

- better ways of presenting and teaching the use of formal methods

---

An understanding of the form and meaning of Z is important for its proper use, and I believe the *Z Base Standard*, instead of being a dusty document on library shelves, should provide a source of general understanding of the language and its mathematical foundations.

Acknowledgements

Acknowledgements for the development of Z are given in the document and will be supplemented by a *History of Z* to be prepared. The current version of the *Z Base Standard* has been as a result of extensive work by the Standards Review Committee especially those listed at the front.

Finally I should like to acknowledge the work of Stephen Brien, whose name properly leads the attributions in [1]. He is not only the major editor, but also the major author of the *Z Base Standard*.

References

1. *Z Base Standard* (editors: Stephen Brien, John Nicholls), Version 1.0 dated 30th November 1992. Document ZIP/PRG/92/121 (obtainable from Programming Research Group, 11 Keble Road, Oxford OX1 3QD).

   The current version of the draft *Z Base Standard*, developed as part of the ZIP project and currently under review by the Z Standards Review Committee. It is proposed to submit this as a Working Draft to the BSI Z Standards Panel.

2. *Proposal for a New Work Item: Z Specification Language*, Document ISO/IEC JTC 1 N2159 dated 1992-10-09.

3. **ISO 8879-1986 (E)** *Information Processing—Text and Office Systems—Standard Generalised Markup Language (SGML)*, Geneva: ISO, 1986.

4. Meyer, B., *Introduction to the theory of programming languages*, Prentice-Hall, 1990.

Reuse and Adaptation of Z Specifications

K. Lano

Applied Information Engineering,
Lloyd's Register
29 Wellesley Rd.
Croydon
CR0 2AJ

H. Haughton

Applied Information Engineering,
Lloyd's Register
29 Wellesley Rd.
Croydon
CR0 2AJ

Abstract

This paper discusses the reuse and adaptation of specifications in Z and object oriented Z, and provides techniques based on a calculus of refinements and on measures of specification design quality, which attempt to address these issues. This calculus will form the basis of a proposal to extend the logic W for standard Z [40] to a reasoning formalism suitable for proving relationships between specifications at a global level. Comparisons with the facilities offered by object oriented specification languages, and with the B abstract machine notation are given. Examples from industrial case studies of the applications of these techniques are also provided.

1 Introduction

Reusability of components of the software process has been seen as a central means to resolve the 'software crisis': the accelerating cost of new development and the backlog of maintenance and adaptation requests for existing applications [7, 26]. Development of systems from an entirely 'clean slate' is becoming seen as something to be avoided if possible, and even in the world of safety-critical systems there are economic and technical pressures to move away from bespoke, one-of-a-kind systems towards reuse of existing components: both to reduce costs, and to gain in reliability due to the proven track-record of used components [25]. In the commercial DP world, the immense investment in existing systems (IBM estimate that there are 80 billion lines of COBOL in applications across the world, of which 55 billion are in old unstructured systems) means that re-writing applications from scratch is infeasible, and reverse-engineering and translation techniques are being developed to convert these applications into new improved forms [35].

There are many forms and levels of reuse: at the most basic (and successful) there are subroutine libraries, such as those for mathematical functions for C and FORTRAN. At a higher level, one can attempt to reuse designs or specifications, and to reuse the knowledge which has underlain design or implementation decisions. None of these higher-level forms of reuse has succeeded to any great extent in practice, because of the technical and organisational issues which mitigate against reuse: in order to reuse a component safely, there must be some way in which the reuser can certify that it meets their requirements - that is, there must be some formal specification of its semantics. There must also be a means by which the reuser can adapt the components to meet their own needs, whilst still being guaranteed their basic properties. Organisational barriers include commercial secrecy, competition, the 'not invented here' syndrome, and portability barriers between differing hardware and systems software.

Proposals for getting around these commercial barriers, for example, by paying a fee for every *use* of a software product, rather than for every purchase, aim to encourage a culture in which it becomes profitable for much effort to be spent on producing high quality reusable components - because these will have extended lifetimes and repeated applications - rather than on unmaintainable 'throwaway' products (which nonetheless often have lifetimes much longer than expected because of the cost of redevelopment or because they are a unique embodiment of knowledge).

Component libraries have been developed for object-oriented languages such as Smalltalk, C++ and Eiffel [8], but with the possible exception of Eiffel, none of these include any specification aspects: a reuser must delve into the code details if they really want to know what their components do. Some authors propose an approach whereby a few software factories employing formal methods experts and tools to generate high-quality reusable components are used to meet primary software needs [31]. One could also envisage certification institutions for components produced by 'outsiders' which are candidates for inclusion in a library. Other 'software factory' proposals include an approach [3] in which new stages are added to the development process for the consolidation and packaging of components for reuse in other projects.

Z specifications potentially provide an excellent medium for reuse and adaptation since they combine a precise description of functionality together with a design of a system. Formal specifications, unlike other means of describing reusable components, are *objective*; they cannot be given two different interpretations by the developer and the user of the component. A Z specification of a system or system component can also be highly abstract, describing only the functionality and purpose of the component, rather than the details of its implementation.

Using tools such as the B system [1], and the results of ongoing work on converting (a subset of) Z to B abstract machine notation, it should even be possible to generate C or Ada code from such specifications, although tailoring of this code to particular environments may be needed.

If Z is to become a widely used specification language, it is inevitable that there will be a need to reuse existing specifications and developments. Methods and techniques for reuse of specifications should therefore be available. In the remainder of the paper, we will address the issue of how Z specifications can be structured and designed to facilitate reuse and adaptation, assuming that adaptations to specifications can be carried down into new code using suitable tools and techniques [16, 18].

2 Software Evolution

Nothing is more pervasive in the world of software than the need for change and adaptation of systems: either because the original requirements specification did not capture the real requirements, or because the environment in which the application must operate changes, in technical or social ways, or the end users discover new requirements as a result of using the system in practice. Traditionally all such changes are carried out on the code, with design documentation not being updated in line with the code: the structured notation diagrams become 'dead documents', which no-one ever reads again (if they do they may be misled since the documents may be out of date, and because they are relatively free of semantics and formal links to the code) [34].

Z specifications, if organised into a design which mirrors the entities of the real world domain, can serve to alleviate these problems in the following ways:

1. providing a common language between the system specifier and the user [9]: any design changes or conceptual difficulties can be discussed using the interfaces of specification modules, without translation barriers;

2. maintaining formal links between the code and the specification: it should be possible to formulate mathematical conditions which guarantee the correctness of the change (for instance, that a modification to an implementation of an operation for efficiency reasons still satisfies its specification);

3. redesigns of a system can be expressed at the specification level, where there is less implementation detail, and mapped back to code, so guaranteeing correctness.

It is important to realise that the enabling technology for such a process, in the form of the B Toolkit and other formal methods tools, is already present in prototype form, and methods for successful use of this technology are now needed.

3 Specification Construction for Reuse

3.1 Modularity

Meyer [26] identifies several forms of modularity which a language can possess, and several criteria on the concept of a module which enables reuse of such modules. We will not reiterate these arguments here, however it is clear that an adequate notion of modularity requires a corresponding syntactic language construct: it is not sufficient to simply say that a module 'extends from page 2 to page 9' of a specification! For both Z and the B abstract machine notation (AMN), distinctions must be made between language features used to *construct* specifications and constructs which correspond to conceptual design modules. In Z, schemas are used pervasively to provide a means of building a specification, allowing reuse of declarations, of predicates, and of operations. These can also correspond to conceptual units (and indeed should where reasonable) of system state and system services. It is not however possible to control the scope of such items as axiomatic definitions or type definitions, a problem which was repeatedly encountered in the specification of a large software engineering repository [29], involving some 200 functions and type definitions, which needed to be (semantically) grouped into conceptually meaningful subsets relating to the object language components.

In B, the **INCLUDES** and **USES** facilities for incremental specification construction are distinguished from the **IMPORTS** facility for reuse of existing specifications. Modules in B are not simply abstract machines (similar to Ada packages) but can also be collections of 'sibling' machines representing linked entities in an entity-relationship-attribute model of a system or domain. The corresponding units of modularity for reuse in Z are entire subspecifications, consisting of a state, an invariant on this state, possible auxilliary type and function definitions, and a series of operations on the state. No explicit execution order is imposed on these operations, so allowing alternative implementations and adaptation to meet new functional requirements. Such units can also correspond to coherent conceptual units in the application domain (such as an *Account* with characteristic operations, or a subsystem of a process control application dealing with a particular device). We will use a subset of the Object-Z [11] notation to denote such a unit. This notation can be automatically generated from the Z^{++} notation [15]. We will use the Z^{++} semantics of classes, and will also use Z^{++} syntax for concepts which cannot be naturally expressed in Object-Z.

A class in Object-Z is denoted by a schema box containing definitions of inherited classes, local types and functions (axiomatic definitions), a state schema (un-named) and definitions of an initialisation method *Init* and of general methods of the class, expressed as schemas. Methods from classes which are used as types in the specification, such as *Clock* below, are applied by prefixing the name of the instance to which they are applied to the name of the method, with parameters supplied via substitution where needed. A general class definition has the following form:

$$
\begin{array}{|l}
\hline
\_\,ClassName[generic\ \ parameters]\,\underline{\hspace{4cm}} \\
\quad inherited\ \ classes \\
\quad type\ \ definitions \\
\quad constant\ \ definitions \\
\quad state\ \ schema \\
\quad initial\ \ state\ \ schema \\
\quad operation\ \ schemas \\
\hline
\quad history\ \ invariant \\
\hline
\end{array}
$$

An example, from an industrial case study [38, 19] is as follows:

$$
\begin{array}{|l}
\hline
\_\,Tool\,\underline{\hspace{5cm}} \\
\quad State ::= down \mid up \mid none \\
\quad \cdot\mid\ \ descent\_time : \mathbb{N} \\
\quad \text{The time it takes the tool to descend.} \\
\hline
\end{array}
$$

$$
\begin{array}{|l}
\hline
state : State; \\
ptimer : Clock; \\
holding : 0 \mathinner{\ldotp\ldotp} 1 \\
\hline
\end{array}
$$

___INIT_____
state' = up ∧
holding' = 0 ∧
ptimer.Init
_____

___In_Motion_____
Ξ(state, ptimer, holding)
_____
state = none ∧
ptimer.Counting
_____

___Start_Descent_____
Δ(state, ptimer, holding)
_____
state = up ∧
state' = none ∧
holding' = holding ∧
ptimer.Start_Count[descent_time/n?]
_____

___Finish_Descent_____
Δ(state, ptimer, holding)
_____
state = none ∧
state' = down ∧
ptimer.Finish_Count ∧
holding' = holding
_____

___Pick_Up_____
Δ(state, ptimer, holding)
_____
state = down ∧
holding = 0 ∧
holding' = 1 ∧
state' = state ∧
ptimer' = ptimer
_____

In the above class, the Δ notation defines the list of variables which are liable to be modified by an operation. The Ξ notation indicates that all variables are not modified by an operation.

In Z^{++} notation *Clock* is the class

```
CLASS Clock
OWNS
  stop_time  :  N;
  elapsed   :  N
INVARIANT
```

$$elapsed \leq stop\_time$$

RETURNS
$Counting : \rightarrow;$
$Finished\_Count : \rightarrow$

OPERATIONS
$Init : \rightarrow;$
$Start\_Count : \mathbb{N} \rightarrow;$
$Finish\_Count : \rightarrow;$
* $Tick : \rightarrow$

ACTIONS
$Init ==> stop\_time' = 0 \land elapsed' = 0;$
$Start\_Count\ n? ==> stop\_time' = n? \land elapsed' = 0;$
* $elapsed < stop\_time$ &
$Tick ==> elapsed' = elapsed + 1;$
$Counting ==> elapsed < stop\_time;$
$elapsed = stop\_time - 1$ &
$Finish\_Count ==>$
$$elapsed' = stop\_time;$$
$Finished\_Count ==> elapsed = stop\_time$

HISTORY
$Init \land \Box(Start\_Count \Rightarrow$
$$(\ (Tick \lor Counting)\ \underline{until}\ Finish\_Count)\ )$$

END CLASS

We use Z^{++} notation here to express concepts which are not included in Object-Z: the idea of a spontaneous internal action ($Tick$) which cannot be called by clients or descendants of the class, but which can occur at any time when its precondition allows; and the idea of preconditioning operations explicitly by the notation

$$Pre_{C,m}\ \&$$
$$m\ x\ y\ ==>\ Def_{C,m}$$

The BNF syntax of Z^{++} is provided in Appendix A.

The *Tool* specification describes a controlled tool which has an initialisation operation (producing an initial state), a predicate which is true when the tool is in motion (*In_Motion*), an operation to initiate descent (*Start_Descent*), an operation which can only succeed if the tool is ready to complete its descent (as determined by the internal timer) *Finish_Descent*, and an operation to actually perform a grasping operation once it has descended (*Pick_Up*).

The *Clock* in the above specification is a class which encapsulates the concept of a timer. Note that other means of control of the *Tool* instances could have been alternatively specified: by means of a sensor, or by means of external control. Such a change (in the controlled system, or in the interface of the *Tool* to the rest of the system), would require a form of reuse and adaptation of the above specification.

A temporal constraint could be added, to provide additional information on the concept that the specification represents:

$$Init \land \Box(Start\_Descent\ \underline{before}\ Finish\_Descent \land$$
$$Finish\_Descent\ \underline{before}\ Pick\_Up)$$

The semantics of temporal constructs are given in terms of finite or infinite sequences of states of the class which satisfy the class invariant, and which are obtained by application of a method to a preceding state to obtain its successor. A *history* of a class C is a finite or infinite sequence $s : C^*$ of tuples (v, x, m, v', y) where $v, v' : V$, $Inv_C(v)$, $Inv_C(v')$, $x : X$, $y : Y$, $Pre_{C,m}(v, x)$ and $Def_{C,m}(v, x, v', y)$, $m \in \underline{methods}(C)$, and X is the input type of m, Y the output type, and V the cross product of the types of the attributes of C. Inv_C is the invariant predicate of C. We also require that post and pre states match, that is, for $i + 1 \in \mathrm{dom}(s)$, $s(i).4 = s(i+1).1$. If θ is a temporal logic predicate in the language of C, and s is a history of C, $s \models \theta$ is defined by the following clauses, together with the above restriction.

$$
\begin{aligned}
s(i) &\models \Box\theta & &\equiv (\forall j \geq i)(j \in \mathrm{dom}(s) \Rightarrow s(j) \models \theta) \\
s(i) &\models \odot\theta & &\equiv (i+1 \in \mathrm{dom}(s) \wedge s(i+1) \models \theta) \vee (i+1 > \#s) \\
s(i) &\models \bigcirc\theta & &\equiv i+1 \in \mathrm{dom}(s) \wedge s(i+1) \models \theta \\
s(i) &\models \Diamond\theta & &\equiv (\exists j \geq i)(j \in \mathrm{dom}(s) \wedge s(j) \models \theta) \\
s(i) &\models (\theta \; \underline{before} \; \psi) & &\equiv i \in \mathrm{dom}(s) \; \wedge \\
& & & \quad \forall j > i \mid j \in \mathrm{dom}(s) \bullet s(j) \models \psi \Rightarrow \\
& & & \qquad (\exists k \geq i \mid k \leq j \bullet \\
& & & \qquad\quad s(k) \models \theta) \\
s(i) &\models (\theta \; \underline{until} \; \psi) & &\equiv i \in \mathrm{dom}(s) \; \wedge \\
& & & \quad \forall j \geq i \mid j \in \mathrm{dom}(s) \bullet \neg (s(j) \models \theta) \Rightarrow \\
& & & \qquad (\exists k \geq i \mid k \leq j \bullet \\
& & & \qquad\quad s(k) \models \psi) \\
s(i) &\models m & &\equiv m = s(i).3
\end{aligned}
$$

where in the last definition, m is a method of the class. $\underline{methods}(C)$ for a class C is the set of methods of C.

Note that, for simplicity in defining refinement, the only symbols allowed in a temporal constraint are method names and logical connectives.

In a specification unit the state schema does not need to be named, and the enclosing box acts to gather the related state, type, and operation components into a syntactic and semantic whole: it defines a type which can be used just as the corresponding state schema in Z, with the critical difference that direct access to the attributes of the state is forbidden outside the class and its descendants: instances $a : C$ of a class C can only be modified by applications of operations M defined in the class. A method has a definition which is dependent both upon the actual text of its schema and the class in which it is defined: $\Delta(v)$ for a variable list v denotes the 'frame' of the operation in the context of the class, the subset of variables that the operation may change. In the above specification we have chosen to use the standard explicit form of specifying state changes, so that the frame of each operation is the set of attributes of the class.

Generic parameters are distinguished from locally defined given types by listing them after the name of the class:

```
┌─ List[X] ─────────────────────────────
│
│   ...
│
└───────────────────────────────────────
```

Temporal logic constraints can be adjoined to specify an intended execution order:

Seq_Tool ————————————————————————————
$Tool$
$\Box(Start\_Descent \Rightarrow \Diamond Pick\_Up)$

The default temporal constraint is that some operation of the system can occur at any time:

$$\Box(M_1 \vee \ldots \vee M_n)$$

where the M_i are all the operations of the specification. As temporal constraints can be strengthened in refinements, these will allow fewer possible execution sequences, and the refined class will be more deterministic.

For simplicity we will only consider. specifications without algebraic constraints in the following. Algebraic constraints are principally useful as a summarisation of the properties of the methods of a class and their relationships with each other: and hence, as a summary description of the meaning of the class for a specification library browser, etc. Both these and temporal constraints are important in providing an overview of the meaning of a specification, which can be expanded if necessary by reference to the internal (state-based) specification of the operations.

3.2   The Philosophy of Refinement

The concept of refinement is central to reuse and adaptation: after any change to a system we will usually require that it performs at least the services that it did before, and that it can be used as it previously was. In this sense, refinement should coincide with the object-oriented concept of type compatibility: for specifications (classes) C and D, if $C \sqsubseteq D$ (C is refined by D), we should have that instances of D can be viewed as instances of C (ie, any implementation of D can serve as an implementation of C). What is needed for reuse and adaptation is a means by which we can prove refinements of composed systems from refinements of subsystems, and for proving that certain useful transformation operations on specifications are actually refinements (or equivalences).

It is also useful for refinement to correspond to *theory extension*: any property provable about C should be provable also about a refinement D, in a certain sense. This is particularly important with regard to security and temporal constraints: such integrity constraints must be preserved from specifications through to final implementations. The refinement concept of RSL, for instance, implies theory extension [41]. Refinement also should be consistent with a move away from abstraction and towards implementation. In practice it is not possible to completely satisfy all these requirements. Temporal constraints are a significant difficulty: if we wish a strengthening of temporal logic constraints on the admissible sequences of operation invocations of a class to be a refinement (so that required properties concerning liveness, safety, etc are preserved), we cannot also have type compatibility: a client of the refined class may not be able to execute certain sequences of operations upon it that it could on its predecessor. The way around this is to incorporate in the invariant some indication of which required behaviours are desired for the class and its refinements by clients. The concept of refinement which we propose for classes corresponds closely to that adopted for classical Z and for B abstract machines. It has strong semantic properties, and provides a category structure for the set of all classes and types. This category has products, co-products and initial and terminal objects.

Given two classes C, D, refinement is defined in terms of a pair ϕ, R, where ϕ is a mapping from the method names of C to those of D, and R is a predicate defining a relation between the other features of C and D (ie, those type, constant and variable identifiers declared in C and D).

Let $\pi(C)$ for a class C denote the declaration of the class, that is, the schema text $c \mid Inv_C(c)$ of the state schema of C, together with the other declarations of the class, excepting the definitions of the methods, and including those declarations of types made visible to it via module importation [15]. For a method m, $Def_{C,m}$ denotes the predicate of the schema of m as defined in the context of the class C, $Pre_{C,m}$ denotes the explicit precondition of the method.

Inv_C denotes the state invariant. $\pi(D)'$ denotes the state schema of D in which attributes are replaced by their dashed versions, c' denotes the declaration of C in which attributes are postdecorated by a $'$. d, d' are the attribute declaration of D and the postdecorated attribute declaration of D. We assume that the names of the features of C are disjoint from the names of the features of D.

We use sequents of the form $Premise \vdash Conclusions$, where $Premise$ is a list of declarations and predicates, and $Conclusions$ is a list of predicates. The intuitive meaning is that if all the premises hold, at least one conclusion holds.

Then we require:

1. $c;\ d \vdash R \wedge Inv_D \Rightarrow Inv_C$

2. $d \vdash Inv_D \Rightarrow \exists c \mid Inv_C \bullet R$

3. $\pi(C);\ d \vdash R \wedge Pre_{C,m} \Rightarrow Pre_{D,\phi(m)}$

4. $\pi(C);\ \pi(D);\ d' \vdash R \wedge Pre_{C,m}\ \wedge$
   $Def_{D,\phi(m)} \Rightarrow \exists c' \mid Inv'_C \bullet R' \wedge Def_{C,m}$

5. $\vdash_{TL} \underline{history(D)} \Rightarrow \phi(\underline{history(C)})$

$\vdash_{TL}$ denotes inference in first order predicate calculus enhanced with a linear temporal logic [2].

Three and four hold for each method m of C: it is required that each method m of C has some corresponding interpretation method $\phi(m)$ in D, and that this method is more refined than m in the standard sense [13].

The notation $C \sqsubseteq_{\phi,R} D$ denotes the existence of such a refinement, this can be simplified to $C \sqsubseteq_\phi D$, $C \sqsubseteq_R D$ or $C \sqsubseteq D$ in the case that the specific interpretation function or the predicate R are not of interest.

The notation $A \equiv B$ denotes that $A \sqsubseteq B$ and $B \sqsubseteq A$: such specifications can effectively be considered equivalent (semantically). We have not adopted the more general concept of refinement given in [10], in which input and output parameter types of methods can be refined, since we require that interfaces to methods be preserved in order for refinement to imply type-compatibility. In B interfaces of operations must remain constant during refinement, so enabling abstract specifications to be used in place of their (assumed) implementations in C code.

Refinement is reflexive: $A \sqsubseteq_{id,true} A$, and transitive: $A \sqsubseteq_{\phi,R} B$ and $B \sqsubseteq_{\psi,S} C$ implies $A \sqsubseteq_{\phi;\psi,\exists\pi(B)\bullet R \wedge S} C$ where all classes here are consistent.

Internal consistency of a specification requires that its state and type declarations are consistent (they have a model), and that the definitions of the operations preserve the invariant of the state:

1. $\vdash \exists c \mid Inv_C$;

2. $c \vdash Pre_{C,m} \wedge Inv_C \Rightarrow \exists c' \mid Inv'_C \bullet Def_{C,m}$;

3. $c;\ c' \vdash Pre_{C,m} \wedge Inv_C \wedge Def_{C,m} \Rightarrow Inv'_C$.

The second condition states that the explicit precondition which a user declares for an operation must imply the actual precondition. The third asserts that each operation preserves the state invariant.

Classes in which one or more operations violate these criteria are probably incomplete (for instance, if the specifier has omitted to provide an explicit action by which an operation preserves an invariant), or are erroneous and poor starting points for an implementation. They may even be 'miraculous' in the sense of [28]: never fully implementable. The class *false* with *false* invariant (and at least one operation) is the most refined class, and is completely unimplementable: it has no models. In contrast, the (pseudo) initial object in the category of classes and refinements is the class $\underline{\varnothing}$ with no attributes or operations, and with the empty schema type $\{\varnothing\}$ as its state space [42, page 18], it is refined by any class, and can be considered to have any model of set theory as a model.

The B method requires that each machine (specification module) be proved internally consistent: this is necessary for a system aimed at developing implementable code from specifications, and should be a component of any system of this kind based on Z. Certainly any library component should come with rigorous proofs of internal consistency and proofs that it meets (refines) its specification (interface).

3.3 An Algebra of Classes

In order to facilitate manipulation of specification structures, the following operations on classes are provided. All (with the exception of hiding) are syntactically definable, as well as satisfying laws in the semantics of refinement.

$$
\begin{aligned}
ClassExp ::= \ &ClassIdentifier \\
\mid\ &ClassExp \setminus (FeatureList) \\
\mid\ &ClassExp[RenameList] \\
\mid\ &GenClassExp[ParameterList] \\
\mid\ &ClassExp \mathbin{\underline{+}} ClassExp
\end{aligned}
$$

A *ClassIdentifier* is an identifier used in a definition of a class as above, and *FeatureList* is a list of method names from the given class. *RenameList* is a list of substitutions *new/old*, where *old* is an attribute, constant or method name of the class, and *new* is an appropriate substitution: an identifier in the case that *old* is a method or attribute, an identifier or value (expression) in the case that *old* is a constant. We make the restriction that the new names must all be distinct and must not already by used as features or local variables in the class. In the forth form above, the *ParameterList* must be a list of valid types, and must contain exactly as many generic parameters as are required by the generic class.

These notations have the following meaning. Hiding features of a class by the form $C \setminus (m_1, \ldots, m_n)$ has the effect that the m_i cannot be used by descendants or clients of the class. This is similar to the hiding constructs of languages such as RSL [41], and is useful for purposes of reusability and separate refinement. It allows the separation of the 'destructive' forms of inheritance which violate refinement, such as deletion of a method, and the constructive forms. Renaming, by the syntax $C[e_1/v_1, \ldots, e_n/v_n]$, allows a class to be reused for a different conceptual purpose by changing the names of (semantically identical) features. It also enables classes to be explicitly renamed to avoid name clashes between features upon extension (which would otherwise be resolved automatically). It provides an indirect way of replacing general constants of a class by specific constants / values which satisfy their axioms.

$C \pm D$ denotes the co-product of the classes C and D in terms of the category of classes and refinements: it is the 'least common refinement' of C and D, and also corresponds to certain forms of inheritance, described below.

We have the following basic laws:

$$A \setminus M \sqsubseteq A$$
$$A \pm A \equiv A$$
$$A \times A \equiv A$$
$$A \pm \emptyset \equiv A$$

In contrast to Eiffel, our inheritance construct does not allow the dropping of features from an inherited class. Such a 'non-monotonic' form of inheritance leads to considerable problems in structuring specifications [8], and is not a refinement. Concealment of methods of a class from descendants and clients must be explicitly signalled by use of the $\setminus$ operation on a class.

A specification defines a directed acyclic graph of classes in terms of the inheritance relationship $C < D$ "D inherits C". We denote by $C <_i D$ the transitive closure of the relation $\ll$ (strict inheritance). Similarly, we do not allow cycles in the client relation (D is a client of C if C is used as a type in the definition of an attribute of D): such cycles are unnecessary since we can use the free type constructions of Z to build recursive data-structures such as trees.

In the following section we will show how properties of refinement preservation can support the safe adaptation and reuse of specifications and specification components. The situation we aim for is to be able to change the implementation of a specification (either an existing specification component or a requirements definition for such a component) without changing the system that uses it.

4   Laws of Refinement Preservation

As with previous work in this area [24], we aim to break up the task of proving refinements into manageable portions, and to reduce this task to that of proving suitable side-conditions for general inferences of the form

$$\frac{Premises}{C \sqsubseteq_{\phi,R} D}$$

rather than trying to prove each refinement from first principles.

As an instance of a generally applicable law which allows a reuser to implement a class method by any refining operation, we have that if a method $M1$ is replaced by a procedural refinement $M2$, the result is a refined class:

$(M1):$

$$\pi(C);\ d \vdash\ Pre_{C,M1} \wedge R \Rightarrow Pre_{D,M2}$$
$$\frac{\pi(C);\ \pi(D);\ d' \vdash\ Pre_{C,M1} \wedge R \wedge Def_{D,M2} \Rightarrow \exists\, c' \mid Inv'_C \bullet R' \wedge Def_{C,M1}}{\vdash C \sqsubseteq_{\phi,R} D}$$

D is the class C with method $M1$ replaced by $M2$ and ϕ is the map taking $M1$ to $M2$ and leaving other methods unchanged. Variables are renamed 1-1 via R.

$(M2):$

$$\frac{\vdash A \sqsubseteq_{\phi,R} B}{\vdash A \sqsubseteq_{\phi,R} C}$$

where C is B with a new method M on the state of B, not occurring in A or B.

Clearly, replacing a literal value with a new axiomatic definition of a constant with this value, and substituting this function for the literal value in the predicate of a method or in the invariant, is also a refinement, allowing the modifiability of an application to be increased.

4.1   Laws for Inheritance

In the first instance, we would like to be able to show that common forms of extension to a specification preserve refinement (ie, preserve its properties for external users of the specification). A general form of inheritance which preserves refinement is *strict* inheritance: this is the form denoted by $C \ll D$. **Definition** *Strict inheritance* of a class C in a class D is defined as follows. Let E be the class defined as D but without C mentioned in its EXTENDS list. Then rename features of C until the set of names used for attributes, methods and types defined in C are disjoint from those defined in E, to form a class C'. The class D has attributes and methods the union of those of C' and E, algebraic constraints and history invariant the conjunction of those of C' and E, and invariant the conjunction of those of C' and E. All these conjunctions are modulo the renamings of attributes and methods.

Similarly in the case of multiple strict inheritance, whereby several classes are inherited in another class, and common features are renamed if necessary to distinguish them. No features are merged implicitly: the specifier must explicitly signal any required identities. This is in keeping with the spirit of Z. The mutual strict inheritance of C and D in $\varnothing$ is the *co-product* $C + D$.

General inheritance is defined as above but without attribute renaming taking place. It is denoted by $C < D$. We have the following rule which allows a specifier to restate the logical aspects of a class in a way which preserves their semantic meaning under the declarations of the class.

$(I1):$
$$\vdash \pi(D) \Leftrightarrow \pi(C)$$
$$\vdash C < D$$
$$\overline{\vdash C \sqsubseteq_{id,true} D}$$

d is the declaration of D, c of C. Similarly, it is possible to restate the definitions and explicit preconditions of methods in forms which are logically equivalent under the invariant of the class and the relevant declarations of attributes and parameters. The same applies to temporal constraints. It is clear that such a transformation preserves consistency of C to D, provided the new operations preserve the new invariant and have non-empty domain (this is similar to the condition B requires for its version of inheritance to preserve internal consistency of 'machines').

If we define new attributes of a class, together with new invariants which do not invalidate models of the original class (a 'conservative extension'), then we have a refinement:

$(I2):$
$$\vdash C < D$$
$$c \vdash Inv_C \Rightarrow \exists\, u \bullet Inv_D$$
$$\overline{\vdash C \sqsubseteq_{id,true} D}$$

E is the class D with C removed from its **EXTENDS** list, u is the declaration of E, c of C, and the attribute names in u and c are disjoint. Each operation of C is extended in D by new conjuncts which ensure conditions 2 and 3 of the internal consistency of D:

$$Def_{m,D} \equiv Def_{m,C} \wedge \psi_m$$

An example would be the introduction of new attributes in E which are purely auxilliary functions of the attributes of C. Again, consistency is preserved provided the new operations preserve the new invariant and are non-empty.

A series of simple transformations, such as finite differencing (replacing a computed function by a new state variable), 1-1 renaming, and replacement of an output variable of a method by a new state variable (thus allowing the strict command/query format advocated by [26] to be adopted) have been shown to be refinements [20].

Indeed, a 1-1 renaming is an isomorphism:

$$C\ R \equiv C$$

if R is a 1-1 renaming of features of C.

Products and co-products are defined abstractly as follows:

$$(CP1): \quad A \sqsubseteq_f D \wedge B \sqsubseteq_g D \;\Rightarrow\; (A \pm B) \sqsubseteq_{f \pm g} D$$
$$(CP2): \quad A \sqsubseteq_{\rho_1} A \pm B \;\wedge\; B \sqsubseteq_{\rho_2} A \pm B$$

where $f \pm g$ can be defined from f and g, and ρ_1, ρ_2 are the canonical embeddings;

$$(P1): \quad D \sqsubseteq_f A \wedge D \sqsubseteq_g B \;\Rightarrow\; D \sqsubseteq_{f \underline{\times} g} (A \underline{\times} B)$$
$$(P2): \quad (A \underline{\times} B) \sqsubseteq_{\pi_1} A \;\wedge\; (A \underline{\times} B) \sqsubseteq_{\pi_2} B$$

The laws $(CP1)$ and $(CP2)$ lead to the useful law that strict inheritance preserves refinement:

$$(I3): $$
$$\vdash A \sqsubseteq_f A'$$
$$\vdash C = A \pm B$$
$$\underline{\vdash C' = A' \pm B}$$
$$\vdash C \sqsubseteq_{f \pm id} C'$$

Thus, in any specification S in which class C is used by other classes only by means of strict inheritance, refinement of C to C' will lead to a refined specification S'. If A and B are consistent, then $A \pm B$ is consistent.

However there are other, more complex ways in which one class (specification) can be used in another:

1. as a parameter instantiation in a generic class;

2. as a type in an attribute declaration (as a *supplier*);

3. as a parameter type in a method.

We will consider these below.

4.2   Laws for Generic Parameters and Supplier Classes

Ideally, we would like generic classes to preserve refinements of their parameters (so that they are *functors* of the category of classes, in the sense of category theory). This is almost trivial in the case that the generic class uses no methods of the parameter classes, but in the general case it is closely related to the need to prove that *promotion* of operations preserves refinement [24]: there is a similar distinction between global and local states, and a requirement that the global specification should not unduly constrain the effect of the local update.

4.2.1 Preservation of Procedural Refinement

We have to consider the ways in which a method from a parameter or supplier class can be used within the methods of its client, and the ways in which a supplier class can be used as a type within its client. Many common constructs on relations preserve relational refinement $\sqsubseteq$ of their components, for instance, the following three rules hold:

$$(R1): \quad \frac{f, f' : A \nrightarrow B \quad g, g' : B \nrightarrow C \quad f \sqsubseteq f' \quad g \sqsubseteq g'}{f\,\mathring{\,}\,g \sqsubseteq f'\,\mathring{\,}\,g'}$$

$$(R2): \quad \frac{R, R' : A \leftrightarrow B \quad S, S' : A \leftrightarrow B}{R \sqsubseteq R' \quad S \sqsubseteq S' \quad \operatorname{dom} R' \cap \operatorname{dom} S' = \varnothing}{R \cup S \sqsubseteq R' \cup S'}$$

$$(R3): \quad \frac{R, R' : A \leftrightarrow B \quad S, S' : C \leftrightarrow D \quad R \sqsubseteq R' \quad S \sqsubseteq S'}{R \times S \sqsubseteq R' \times S'}$$

As a consequence the disjoint union constructor preserves refinement of its components: this is a common means of building schemas in Z and object-oriented extensions to Z. The facility for hiding methods of a class can be used to hide the internal methods

```
┌─ Op_Ok ─────────────────────────────
│ Δ(v)
│ x : X
│ y : Y
├─────────────────────────────────────
│ Pre_Ok ∧
│ Def_Ok
└─────────────────────────────────────
```

and its *Error_Op* counterpart from descendants and clients, since these should only legitimately use the *Op* method, where $Op \stackrel{\wedge}{=} Op\_Ok \vee Error\_Op$. This distinction could not be directly stated in a Z specification.

4.2.2 Preservation of Data Refinement

In order to lift a data-refinement $r : S \leftrightarrow T$ to a data-refinement $con[r]$ between types $con[S]$ and $con[T]$ built from S and T, we need laws to determine when these refinements can be lifted, and the properties which are preserved.

In general we want these lifting operations to preserve relational composition: $con[f\,\mathring{\,}\,g] = con[f]\,\mathring{\,}\,con[g]$ and identity: $con[id_A] = id_{con[A]}$ in addition to totality and functionhood.

We have the following:

(*Power set 2*) :

$R : W \leftrightarrow V$

$\mathbf{P_2}[R] : \mathbf{P}\ W \leftrightarrow \mathbf{P}\ V$
$\qquad a \longmapsto b \quad where\ b \subseteq R\ (\!|\ a\ |\!)$

This constructor preserves totality of R, but not functionhood. It does not preserve identity, but does preserve composition.

(*Cartesian product*) :

$r : W \leftrightarrow V$

$(\times X)[r] : W \times X \leftrightarrow$
$\qquad\qquad V \times X$
$\qquad (w, x) \longmapsto (v, x)$
$\qquad where\ (w, v) \in r$

(*Function lift*) :

$r : W \leftrightarrow V$

$(X \twoheadrightarrow)[r] : (X \twoheadrightarrow W) \leftrightarrow$
$\qquad\qquad\quad (X \twoheadrightarrow V)$
$\qquad t \longmapsto s$
$\qquad where\ \operatorname{dom} t = \operatorname{dom} s\ \wedge$
$\qquad \forall x : \operatorname{dom} t \bullet$
$\qquad\qquad (t(x), s(x)) \in r$

Both of these preserve totality and functionhood, identity and composition.

(*Sequence*) :

$r : S \leftrightarrow T$

$seq[r] : \operatorname{seq} S \leftrightarrow \operatorname{seq} T$

where $(s, t) \in seq[r] \equiv (\#s = \#t \wedge \forall i : 1 .. \#s \bullet (s(i), t(i)) \in r)$. This is a special case of relation lifting.

The above lead to the rules [G1], [G2] and [G3] for generic classes given in [20].

A consequence of these laws is that the addition of new methods to a supplier class always preserves the semantics of its clients. In addition, if the supplier class is replaced by a class with identical features but with a logically weaker history predicate, then the resulting client classes are refinements of the original clients. It is also possible to strengthen the history predicate of a supplier class, provided that this strengthening does not invalidate sequences of method applications upon it which can be required by its client. In this case, history predicate strengthening is a preserved refinement. These rules are quite similar to those for the valid use of *imported* machines in B [22].

5 The Process of Reuse and Adaptation

5.1 Feasibility of Reuse

Basili and Caldieri [3] consider that reuse will only be feasible if the cost of reusing a component in a new project is considerably less than the cost of developing it from scratch. Moreover, it is not simply components (specifications) which are reused in isolation, but the experience and the context in which they have been constructed. In our terms, this means the specifications which have been used to build these components, such as their ancestors or suppliers. Such a context provides additional meaning and understanding about the role and purpose of the component which may be essential in determining its reusability and in determining sensible and feasible adaptations.

The general process of reuse will involve (i): a recognition of certain (quite abstract) requirements Req, (ii): an analysis of what components $Comp$ are available which meet (or nearly meet) parts of this requirement, in the context of a suitable library Lib, and (iii): an estimation of the cost saving produced. Such a process fits quite well into the spiral model [7, 4]. In formal terms, selection of the specification $Comp$ – assumed to have an implementation Imp – means that we replace the long and expensive task of formal data-refinement of Req to a implementable system by (i): adaptation of $Comp$ to a specification $Comp'$; (ii): verification that $Comp'$ meets Req, and (iii): adaptation of the development of Imp to a development of Imp' which implements $Comp'$. This reuse will only be feasible if the adaptation and recognition steps are relatively inexpensive compared to the cost of new development. Measures of specification similarity should be available, so that some guidance is possible in the component selection process.

In the formal framework above, assessment of component similarity can be based upon several aspects of a specification: its context, ie, the specifications used to construct or derive it; the informal descriptions of the meanings of its features; the temporal constraint, which gives an overview of its intended behaviour, and any algebraic constraints on the methods, which would enable the 'abstract data type' which the specification implements to be recognised. Adaptation of developments is facilitated by laws concerning refinement preservation: if a new component is a refinement of an old one, and the way it is used by the enclosing system is refinement preserving, then all we need to do is textually replace the old features of the used component by the new ones.

The B Method approach to reuse follows the above process. An abstract machine $A.mch$ (corresponding to a Z^{++} object class in which other classes cannot be used as types) will have an implementation $A.imp$, in a fully completed development, and new requirements, formalised in an abstract specification $B.mch$, can reuse the development A by importing the abstract specification $A.mch$ into the implementation $B.imp$ of $B.mch$. Code of a development is reused (operations of an imported machine can be used to perform parts of the functionality of the operations of the importing machine), but only indirectly via the (hopefully more concise and comprehensible) abstract specification of the development. Significantly, we know that refinement of the imported machine $A.mch$ is preserved by the importing, so that 'improvements' to A will lead to improvements to B.

We propose to adopt this approach within a method based upon an object-oriented Z, by identifying a subset of Z constructs which preserve refinement of their components, and which are close to imperative code constructs. This subset will be used in the classes which implement new requirements in terms of existing abstract classes. B generalised substitution notation would be an obvious candidate for a notation for the methods of such classes, given semantic mappings between Z and B [17].

5.2   Dealing with Change Requests

The majority of maintenance requests are of an adaptive or enhancement nature [23]. An adaptation request includes porting of an application to another environment, changing the internal details of a class which interfaces directly with the environment (and which therefore, is in conceptual terms at the lowest level of the specification), or changing the internal organisation of classes. An enhancement request involves adding new functionality, including new descendants of existing classes. In the case of adaptive requests, we should aim to minimise the extent of the specification which is affected by the change: the classes which are directly involved in the change should be isolated and where possible, the classes which use them should be preserved in definition. It may be necessary to improve the way in which these classes use the modified classes in order to enable refinement preservation (this is a *preventative* maintenance activity). Basic enhancement is clearly a refinement activity: we require new functions in addition to existing functionality, which we do not want to be affected. Adding functions to classes at a certain level of the specification hierarchy should only require additional functions at higher levels of the hierarchy which allow user access to these functions. Proofs of internal consistency will need to be performed, but these can be limited to the new features of the classes.

In general, while it is clear that not all maintenance activities will be refinements, there are many cases in which it is economically essential for existing functionality to be preserved: this is functionality which may be depended upon by many existing clients of the organisation responsible for the application, and cannot safely be deleted (or worse, changed in its semantics). Often, organisations phase out functionality gradually, announcing future deletions a release or version in advance so that users can cope with changes which are not refinements.

Perhaps the main difficulty for maintainers will remain the process of translating a change request (expressed in domain terms) into one expressed in terms of the specification. It is here that a formalism which allows a clear expression of designs and real-world concepts can be of great assistance in reducing the effort of this translation.

5.3   Examples

5.3.1   Adaptive Change: Modification of System Environment

Using the previously given specification, we show how a request to adapt this to use a sensor in place of an internal timer could be handled. This request is a simplified example of the type of adaptive request which occurs in practice: an application with a specific interface to systems software or hardware must be modified to deal with a slightly different operational environment. In this respect, we have the outline requirements for the same high-level operations to be available (*INIT*, *In_Motion*, *Start_Descent*, *Finish_Descent*, *Pick_Up*), but we require the environment in which the specification operates to change. In this case we have to use a system *Sensor*, with operations *Init*, *Activate*, *Make_Contact*, and returnable function *In_Contact*. The similarity we may then build up, as a result of our understanding of the system, is that the supplier class *Clock* of our existing component *Tool* corresponds to the supplier class *Sensor* of our required component *Handler*, and that the operation *Clock.Init* corresponds to *Handler.Init*, that *Start_Count* corresponds to *Activate*, and that *Finish_Count* corresponds to *Make_Contact* (with *Counting* corresponding to ¬ (*In_Contact*)). Conjuncts of the temporal constraints of the two supplier classes are also a key factor in recognising these similarities:

HISTORY
$$Init \ \wedge \ \Box(Start\_Count \ \Rightarrow$$
$$(\ (Tick \ \vee \ Counting) \ \underline{until} \ Finish\_Count) \ )$$

for the *Clock*, and

HISTORY
$$Init \ \wedge \ \Box(Activate \ \Rightarrow$$
$$(Check\_Contact \ \underline{until} \ Make\_Contact) \ )$$

for the *Sensor*.

We must check that the way in which we wish to use the *Sensor* is consistent with its internal behaviour. Re-implementation is in this case trivial, involving simply a change in the number of arguments to the *Start_Count* function.

The new system specification is then:

```
┌─ Handler ──────────────────────────────────────────────
│ State ::= down | up | none
│ ┌──────────────────────────────────────────────────────
│ │ state : State;
│ │ psensor : Sensor;
│ │ holding : 0 .. 1
│ ├─ INIT ───────────────────────────────────────────────
│ │ state' = up  ∧
│ │ holding' = 0  ∧
│ │ psensor.Init
│ ├─ In_Motion ──────────────────────────────────────────
│ │ Ξ(state, psensor, holding)
│ │ ──────────────────────────────────────────────────────
│ │ state = none  ∧
│ │ ¬ (psensor.In_Contact)
```

Start_Descent
$\Delta(state, psensor, holding)$

$state = up \;\wedge$
$state' = none \;\wedge$
$holding' = holding \;\wedge$
$psensor.Activate$

Finish_Descent
$\Delta(state, psensor, holding)$

$state = none \;\wedge$
$psensor.Make\_Contact \;\wedge$
$state' = down \;\wedge$
$holding' = holding$

Pick_Up
$\Delta(state, psensor, holding)$

$state = down \;\wedge$
$holding = 0 \;\wedge$
$holding' = 1 \;\wedge$
$state' = state \;\wedge$
$psensor' = psensor$

As with the timed system, the *Sensor* instance *psensor* is entirely internal to an instance of *Handler*; is value is not returned by the *Handler*, and no other class instance can share it or refer to it. Any information required by an external system about the state of this sensor has to be routed through the *Handler*. This corresponds to the real-world situation, where these components may be very closely associated (physically and conceptually).

An example of a pure enhancement change would be the addition of an operation to query the current value of the attribute *elapsed* of the *Clock*. This would require the addition of operations to *Clock* and to *Tool*. Such a change is a refinement, provided that it does not require a weakening of the class or history invariant of either class.

5.3.2 Adaptive Change: Transformation to Query / Update form

Given a specification of the form

```
CLASS Stack0
OWNS
  contents : seq(N)
OPERATIONS
  Init : →;
  Push : N →;
  Pop : → N
ACTIONS
```

$$Init \;\;==> \;\;\; contents' \;=\; \langle \; \rangle;$$
$$Push \;\; xx? \;\;==>$$
$$contents' \;=\; \langle \; xx? \; \rangle \;^\frown\; contents;$$
$$Pop \;\; vv! \;\;==>$$
$$contents' \;=\; tail(contents) \;\land$$
$$vv! \;=\; contents(1)$$
END CLASS

in which an operation (*Pop*) has a side-effect in addition to producing a result, we can adapt this by means of a standard transformation which factors out the side-effects from such operations:

CLASS *Stack*1
OWNS
  contents : seq($\mathbf{N}$)
OPERATIONS
  *Init*1 : →;
  *Push*1 : $\mathbf{N}$ →;
  *Pop*1 : →;
  Top : → $\mathbf{N}$
ACTIONS
  $Init1 \;\;==> \;\;\; contents' \;=\; \langle \; \rangle;$
  $Push1 \;\; xx? \;\;==>$
    $contents' \;=\; \langle \; xx? \; \rangle \;^\frown\; contents;$
  $Pop1 \;\;==>$
    $contents' \;=\; tail(contents);$
  $Top \;\; vv! \;\;==>$
    $vv! \;=\; contents(1)$
END CLASS

It is direct to prove that the class

CLASS *Stack*2
  EXTENDS *Stack*1
OPERATIONS
  *Pop*2 : → $\mathbf{N}$
ACTIONS
  $Pop2 \;\; vv! \;\;==>$
    $Top \;\; {}_9^o \;\; Pop1$
END CLASS

refines *Stack*0 via the identity predicate and the mapping

$$\{ \; Init \mapsto Init1,$$
$$Push \mapsto Push1,$$
$$Pop \mapsto Pop2 \; \}$$

of methods. Thus all services which could be required of the original class can be carried out in an equivalent manner by the new low-level class *Stack*1, via *Stack*2.

6 Measures of Reusability

Several difficulties have been found in maintaining and understanding object-oriented programs [39, 30]. The definition of an operation may be excessively factored into conjuncts by means of inheritance, so that it is hard to determine its full meaning. This can be addressed by automatic tools which will expand out a full version of a class in which all inheritance is removed. In addition dynamic binding and the use of polymorphism leads to confusion over which definition of a method is being applied. We have avoided the use of reference semantics because of the similar problems which are caused by aliasing (concerning sharing of an object by several other objects).

Whilst inheritance can be used to express similarity relationships, it is important not to confuse the use of inheritance to support subtyping and to describe similarities. For instance, we may, in a specification dealing with graphical figures, define a *Polygon* class which has a method *Add_Vertex* for adding a vertex to a polygon. Some libraries for object-oriented languages then define a class *Rectangle* (for instance) as a descendant of this class, with the *Add_Vertex* method hidden (since you cannot add vertices to a rectangle). This leads to considerable confusion when the hierarchy is extended to include many inheritors of *Polygon*, some of which are mutable shapes and some immutable. A better approach would be to define a *GeneralPolygon* class, without the *Add_Vertex* operation, and to define *Mutable_Polygon* and *Immutable_Polygon* as descendants of this, with *Rectangle* as a descendant of the latter. The degree of similarity between two classes would be expressed by the degree of refinement of their greatest common ancestor $C \pm_{Spec} D$ in the given specification.

In general, common factors of two classes in a hierarchy should exist in that hierarchy, if this commonality is conceptually significant (and may form the basis of further extensions). The issue is related to the use of *derived types* in Pascal and Ada [5]: two semantically identical (in terms of their machine representation) types can be used to represent distinct concepts, and in this case $\pm$ and explicit inheritance may be a better measure of similarity between components than $\times$ and refinement. It is for this reason that we do not propose that the category of classes be factored by its equivalence classes under $\equiv$. Conceptually distinct classes may be semantically identical when only their internal implementation is considered, yet quite different in terms of the hierarchy of specifications which have been used to construct them, and this hierarchy provides future resources and a meaningful context for their adaptation and extension.

Experience from Smalltalk has shown that libraries of reusable components are themselves highly prone to suggestions for changes and restructuring, and should not be envisaged as a fixed structure for all time. Naturally, changes to a library should usually be refinements, to enable compatibility with existing users.

Some authors [35] recommend that no class should possess more than 100 attributes or more than 10 methods, that methods should contain no more than 20 atomic statements, and messages should pass no more than five parameters. Advice can then be given to a user to reduce the fragmentation of a method, or conversely, to split up the definition of an overly complex method into two or more classes.

In the case of specifications, we should also measure (and aim to increase) the proportion of class usage relationships which preserve refinement. This is a high-level semantic counterpart of the 'minimise module coupling' quality measure for systems [12]. Is-a relationships are often asserted on the basis of the static aspects of an object class alone, without concern for dynamic behaviour. We could name such a general relationship by the term 'specialisation', and require that this be implied by subtyping, but not conversely. As an example where this issue arises, the specification of geometric shapes defined in [37] can be analysed.

The entities defined in this specification are: *Quadrilateral*, *Parallelogram*, *Rhombus*, *Rectangle* and *Square*. Intuitively, one might expect that the inheritance hierarchy is such that *Parallelogram* inherits from *Quadrilateral*, *Rhombus* and *Rectangle* inherit from *Parallelogram*, and *Square* inherits from both *Rhombus* and *Rectangle*. Indeed, if one considers only the state components of the corresponding classes, then the inheritance hierarchy of this form is also a subtyping hierarchy. That is, the state of *Rhombus* is more restrictive than the states of its ancestors, and so forth. Therefore, the specialisation relation between these concepts follows the above pattern.

But in the object-oriented paradigm, concepts are represented both by a certain state, and by characteristic operations over this state. The combination of these aspects is significant for determining refinement (ie, subtyping). In this case for example, we might consider operations of *Shearing* a quadrilateral through a specified angle, and an operation to determine the *Angle* of any shape which is at least a *Parallelogram*.

Unfortunately, the *Shear* operation does not preserve the property of being a *Rhombus* or of being a *Rectangle*, so for no proper descendant of *Parallelogram* is it an appropriate method. This means in addition that there is not a simple refinement relation between *Parallelogram* or *Rhombus*, or between *Parallelogram* and *Square*. In practical use, one could not safely use an instance of the *Square* class as an instance of *Parallelogram*, since applying a non-trivial *Shear* operation to this instance would result in a violation of the invariant of *Square*. Instead, the OOZE specification of the problem in [37] considers the following hierarchy: *Quadrilateral*, inherited by *Parallelogram* and *ShearableQuadrilateral* (ie, the *Quadrilateral* class with the method *Shear* added), and with *Rectangle* and *Rhombus* inheriting from *Parallelogram*, *Square* inheriting from *Rectangle* and *Rhombus*, and *ShearableParallelogram* inheriting from *ShearableQuadrilateral* and *Parallelogram*. Viewed in this way, every inheritance relationship is also a refinement relationship, and hence, type-compatibility is correctly expressed in the class hierarchy.

7 Reuse in B

The B abstract machine notation provides a language for specification which ranges from abstract set theoretical statements to procedural code (in Dijkstra's guarded command language).

In B, components and (formalised) requirements will be abstract specifications, and reuse typically takes place using the IMPORTS machine inclusion clause [1]. This enables the abstract specification of a system to be used to provide services needed by a new set of requirements. The machine which links the existing specification to the new requirements will itself act as an implementation of the new requirements. Thus reuse can take place without the code details of the existing system needing to be analysed: their semantics is guaranteed by the formal development of the code by refinement from the abstract specifiations.

8 Conclusion

We have discussed the issues involved in supporting practical reuse and adaptation using Z and object-oriented Z specifications, and have outlined a rigorous theory of refinement and refinement preservation to enable proof techniques to be applied to validate system changes. Three aspects of a specification which are useful for the support of reusability have been identified: (i), a syntactic construct for the units of modularity (specifications with state and operations) used in a system; (ii), a description of the way the operations of a specification interact, and (iii), a representation of the intended order of execution of the operations. All these aspects assist in component recognition and adaptation.

A particular approach to the reuse of existing specifications has been identifed, which adapts the B Method approach by using implementation-oriented classes in place of the IMPLEMENTATION machines of B, and abstract specification classes in place of the abstract machines of B.

Tools supporting elements of this process, such as reverse-engineering for the extraction of specifications of reusable components from existing code, proof-obligation generation and interfaces with structured notations have been developed [14, 15, 21], and could form the basis of a formally based reuse and maintenance system.

Acknowledgement

The research conducted in this paper was partially funded by the DTI under IEATP project IED4/1/2182 "B User Trials". The authors wish to thank the Committee of Lloyd's Register for permission to publish this paper. The views expressed in the paper are the opinions of the authors and are not necessarily the views of Lloyd's Register.

References

[1] J.-R. Abrial, **Assigning Programs to Meaning**, Prentice Hall, 1993.

[2] H. Barringer, R. Kuiper, *Hierarchical Development of Concurrent Systems in a Temporal Logic Framework*, Springer Verlag Lecture Notes in Computer Science Vol 197, **Seminar in Concurrency**, 1984.

[3] V. R. Basili, G. Caldiera, *Identifying and Qualifying Reusable Software Components*, **Computer**, Feb. 1991, 61 - 71.

[4] B. W. Boehm, *A Spiral Model of Software Development and Enhancements*, **IEEE Computer**, Vol 21, No 5, May 1988.

[5] G. Booch, **Software Engineering with Ada**, 2nd Edition, Benjamin Cummings, 1987.

[6] A. De Bunje, R. J. Bril, *The Specification of Synchronised Actions*, In: **IEEE CompEuro 92 Proceedings**, P. Dewilde, J. Vandewalle (Eds.), IEEE Press, 1992, pp. 520 - 525.

[7] E. Burd, *The Spiral Model and Object Orientation: A Path towards Successful Reuse*, KBSL Conference on Requirements and Design Methods for Object-Oriented Environments, 1992.

[8] E. Casais, *An Incremental Class Reorganisation Approach*, **ECOOP '92 Proceedings**, Springer-Verlag LNCS, Vol. 615, 114 - 132.

[9] D. Clarke, *Object Insider Column*, **Object Magazine**, May/June 1992.

[10] E. Cusack, *Object-Oriented Modelling in Z*, **ECOOP '91 Proceedings**, Springer-Verlag Lecture Notes in Computer Science, 1991.

[11] D. Duke, R. Duke, P. King, G. A. Rose, G. Smith, *Object-Z: An Object-Oriented Extension to Z*, in **Formal Description Techniques, II (FORTE'89)**, Vancouver, Canada, December 1989, North-Holland, 1990, 281-296. A technical report: 91-1, Software Verification Research Centre, The University of Queensland.

[12] M. Eva, **SSADM Version 4: A User's Guide**, McGraw Hill International Series in Software Engineering, 1992.

[13] M. Josephs, *The Data-Refinement Calculator for Specifications*, **Information Processing Letters** Vol 27, No 1, pp 29-33, 1988.

[14] K. Lano, H. Haughton, *Extracting Design and Functionality from Code*, **CASE '92 Proceedings**, IEEE Press, 1992.

[15] K. Lano, H. Haughton, *The Z^{++} Manual*, Lloyd's Register, 1992.

[16] K. Lano, *Restructuring and Adapting B Specifications*, Lloyd's Register, BUT/LLOYDS/KL/5/V1, July 1992.

[17] K. Lano, *Theoretical Results for Refinement and Proof*, Lloyd's Register, BUT/LLOYDS/KL/15/V1, January 1993.

[18] K. Lano, H. Haughton, *A Specification-Based Approach to Maintenance*, **Journal of Software Maintenance**, December 1991.

[19] K. Lano, H. Haughton, *Object-Oriented Z Specifications for Safety-Critical Software*, KBSL Conference on Requirements and Design Methods for Object-Oriented Environments, 1992.

[20] K. Lano, H. Haughton, *Reasoning and Refinement in Object-Oriented Specification Languages*, **ECOOP '92 Proceedings**, Springer-Verlag LNCS Vol. 615.

[21] K. Lano, H. Haughton, *Integrating Formal and Structured Methods in Reverse-Engineering*, **Proceedings of Working Conference on Reverse Engineering**, IEEE Press, 1993.

[22] K. Lano, H. Haughton, *B Method Manual Vol. 4: Specification Design and Reuse*, Lloyd's Register, 1992.

[23] B. Lientz, E. Swanson, G. Tompkins, *Characteristics of Application Software Maintenance*, **Communications of the ACM**, Vol. 21, No. 6, (June 1978), 466 - 471.

[24] P. Lupton, *Promoting Forward Simulation*, **Z User Meeting 1990**, Nicholls J., (Ed.), Springer-Verlag Workshops in Computer Science, 1991.

[25] R. Malcolm, *Safety Critical Systems: Technological and Market developments*, Lloyd's Register, March 1991.

[26] B. Meyer, **Object-Oriented Software Construction**, Prentice Hall 1988.

[27] B. Meyer, *Tools for the New Culture: Lessons from the Design of the Eiffel Libraries*, **Communications of the ACM**, September 1990, Vol 33, No. 9.

[28] C. Morgan, K. Robinson, P. Gardiner, *On The Refinement Calculus*, PRG Monograph PRG-70, 1988, Oxford University Programming Research Group.

[29] G. Ostrolenk, *A Specification of the UNIFORM Schema*, Lloyd's Register, 1992.

[30] C. Ponder, B. Bush, *Polymorphism Considered Harmful*, **ACM Sigplan Notices**, Volume 27, No. 6, June 1992.

[31] D. R. Pyle, *Specifying Object Semantics*, KBSL Conference on Requirements and Design Methods for Object-oriented Environments, Leeds 1992.

[32] D. R. Pyle, M. Josephs, *Enriching a Structured Method with Z*, Oxford University Programming Research Group, 1991.

[33] D. R. Pyle, M. Josephs, *Entity-Relationship Models Expressed in Z: A Synthesis of Structured and Formal Methods*, Oxford University Programming Research Group, 1991.

[34] C. A. Richter, *An Assessment of Structured Analysis and Structured Design*, **Software Engineering Notes**, Vol 11, No 4, August 1986, 75 - 83.

[35] H. Sneed, *Migration of Procedurally oriented COBOL programs in an Object-oriented architecture*, **IEEE Conference on Software Maintenance**, IEEE Press, 1992.

[36] M. Spivey, **The Z Notation: A Reference Manual**, Prentice Hall, 1989.

[37] S. Stepney, R. Barden, D. Cooper, **Object Orientation in Z**, Springer-Verlag Workshops in Computer Science, 1992.

[38] B. Vergauwen, J. Levi, *Formal Verifications: An Industrial Case Study*, **IEEE CompEuro 92 Proceedings**, P. Dewilde, J. Vandewalle (Eds.), IEEE Press, 1992, pp. 208 - 213.

[39] N. Wilde, R. Huitt, *Maintenance Support for Object-Oriented Programs*, **Proceedings of Conference on Software Maintenance 1991**, Sorrento, Italy, IEEE Computer Society Press, 1991.

[40] J.C.P. Woodcock, S. M. Brien, W: *A Logic for Z*, Programming Research Group, 1991.

[41] The RAISE Language Group, **The RAISE Specification Language**, Prentice Hall 1991.

[42] S. Brien, J. Nicholls (Eds.), *Z Base Standard*, Version 0.5, March 1992, Oxford University Programming Research Group.

A Syntax

The BNF description of a Z^{++} class declaration is:

```
Object_Class ::= CLASS Identifier TypeParameters
                 [EXTENDS Imported]
                 { [TYPES Types]
                 [FUNCTIONS Axdefs] }*
                 [OWNS Locals]
                 [RETURNS Optypes]
                 [OPERATIONS Optypes]
                 [INVARIANT Predicate]
                 [ACTIONS Acts]
                 [CONSTRAINTS Constraints]
                 [HISTORY History]
                 END CLASS
```

```
TypeParameters ::= [ "[" Parlist "]" ]
```

$$
\begin{array}{ll}
Parlist & ::= Identifier\ [,\ Parlist] \\
& |\ \ Identifier \ll Identifier\ [,\ Parlist] \\
Imported & ::= Idlist \\
Types & ::= Type\_Declarations \\
Locals & ::= Identifier : Type\ ;\ \ Locals \\
& |\ \ Identifier : Type \\
Optypes & ::= [*]\ Identifier : Idlist\ \longrightarrow\ Idlist\ ;\ \ Optypes \\
& |\ \ [*]\ Identifier : Idlist\ \longrightarrow\ Idlist \\
Acts & ::= [*]\ [Expression\ \&]\ Identifier\ Idlist\ ==>\ \ Code\ ;\ \ Acts \\
& |\ \ [*]\ [Expression\ \&]\ Identifier\ Idlist\ ==>\ \ Code \\
Constraints & ::= Equation \\
& |\ \ Equation\ ;\ \ Constraints \\
History & ::= Fmla_{LTL}
\end{array}
$$

The *TypeParameters* are a list (possibly empty) of *generic* type parameters used in the class definition. A parameter X can be required to be a descendent of a class A via the notation $A \ll X$ here. The **EXTENDS** list is the set of previously defined classes that we are inheriting in this class. The *Types* are type declarations of type identifiers used in declarations of the local variables of the object. The *Locals* variable declarations are attribute declarations, in the style of variable declarations in Z. The **OPERATIONS** list declares the types of the operations, as functions from a sequence of input domains to an output domain. The **RETURNS** list of operations defines the output type of those attributes and functions of the objects internal state that are externally visible; these are operations with no side-effect on the state. The **INVARIANT** gives a predicate that specifies the properties of the internal state, in terms of the local variables of the object. This predicate is guaranteed to be true of the state of an object class instance between executions of the operations of the object instance. The default invariant (ie, if this clause is omitted) is *true*.

The **ACTIONS** list gives the definitions of the various operations that can be performed on instances of the object; for instance we would write: $READ\ x$ $==>$ $q' = tail\ q\ \wedge\ x = head\ q$ in a specification of queues with contents q. The default action for a method, if no action for it is listed, is the completely non-deterministic operation on the state of the class and its parameters.

The input parameters are listed before the output parameters in the action definitions. *Code* includes Z predicates. Operations can be given explicit preconditions by the notation

$$
\begin{array}{l}
Pre_{C,m}\ \& \\
\quad\ \ m\ x\ y\ \ \ ==>\ \ \ Def_{C,m}
\end{array}
$$

The default precondition is *true*.

Operations prefixed by a * are *spontaneous internal actions*: they correspond to *daemons* in object-oriented terminology.

The **HISTORY** predicate specifies the admissible execution sequences of objects of the class, using linear temporal logic formulae with operators □ (henceforth), ○ (next), and ◇ (eventually). Further temporal logic operators, such as ; 'chop', * 'iterate', and <u>until</u> 'until', can also be defined. For simplicity in our definition of refinement, it is assumed that only method names from the class and logical connectives can occur in the history of a class, in addition to the predicates *true* and *false*. The default history constraint is *true*, or []*true* equivalently. The history predicate of class C is denoted by *history*(C).

Safety-Critical Systems and Timing

Requirements for Defence Standard 00-55

Invited talk: author's abstract

Andrew Bradley
Head of Systems Computing
British Aerospace Defence
Military Aircraft Division

Interim Defence Standard 00-55 'The Procurement of Safety Critical Software in Defence Equipment' mandates the use of formal methods in a large, influential UK industrial sector and is therefore of particular significance for the Z community.

In the first of three parts, the presentation outlined the history of Def Stan 00-55 and its relationship to other software safety standards (RTCA DO 178A/B, MIL STD 882B, Def Stan 00-56, ...). Its technical content was described in some detail, structured around a phased lifecycle and intermediate design products:

- Software Requirements Specification — Informal / Structured

  - Software Specification — Formal + Informal Commentary

    - Software Design — Formal + Informal Commentary

      - Code — Formal, High Order Language

Verification activities required by the standard include in-phase syntax checking, type checking, proof of internal consistency, flow analysis and testing, as well as phase to phase verification by formal proof. Validation activities include animation of the specification using a formally derived executable prototype, comparative testing of code against the executable prototype, comparative testing of code against the executable prototype and the more traditional validation of code against the software requirements specification.

The second section of the presentation summarised BAe Military Division's experience of developing and applying such software engineering techniques on projects including Jaguar Fly-by-wire and the Experimental Aircraft Programme (EAP). The experience accumulated over 2 decades now includes routine use of analyzable high order language subsets such as SPADE PASCAL and SPARK ADA, accompanied by design annotation and flow analysis, as well as extensive experience of specification animation and the use of executable prototypes. Formal specification, refinement and proof techniques have been applied on Research and Development programmes and on some focused project applications, and tool support is assessed to be improving rapidly.

In the final section of the presentation more speculative views on the future outlook for formal methods and their use in industry were put forward. The relationship between graphical specification notations (Yourdon, CORE, . . .) and mathematically formal notations has developed over the last 10 years from being initially one of 'alternatives', through 'complementarity' to one where, in future, the formal notation is seen as 'underpinning' a graphical/textual notation suitable for large systems. Proof of emergent properties, particularly safety, is envisaged as being concentrated at the specification stage of development, complemented by automatic code generation. Similarly, testing is expected to be concentrated around the specification phase, with testing at the build and integration stages being confirmatory rather than exploratory.

In the longer term it is viewed as preferable for cross-sector or European standards to emerge and replace Def Stan 00-55 and much of BAe's research into formal methods involves collaboration with European partners covering non-defence industries. BAe have also established the Dependable Computing Systems Centre at York / Newcastle Universities to perform generic research for safe and reliable systems. The issue of technology transfer onto large scale projects, as always, is key to the successful exploitation of formal methods research.

Formal Specification and Development of Control System Input/Output

Jonathan Jacky

Department of Radiation Oncology RC-08

University of Washington,

Seattle WA 98195, USA

Abstract

This paper presents a formal specification in the Z notation for computations that calculate control system state variables from input/output
device register contents (and vice-versa). The specification is motivated
by a particular medical device but is quite generic and should be widely
applicable. The specification is parameterised so that an implementation
can be adapted to different control systems by providing tables of configuration data, rather than changing executable code. Specified behaviours
include detection of errors (where clients invoke operations with invalid
parameters) and faults (where input/output devices report invalid data).
The specification is not merely descriptive, but is also used in the formal
development (or "refinement") of a detailed design. From an initial specification which naturally expresses the requirements, but is abstract and
non-constructive, we derive a functionally equivalent specification (also
in Z), which suggests a straightforward and efficient implementation in an
imperative programming language. Formal justification is provided for
each step in the derivation. Theorems are stated that formalise claims
such as "All inputs are handled properly." Proving the theorems checks
for errors in the derivation, and provides confidence that the formal specification expresses the intended requirements.

1   Introduction

The Clinical Neutron Therapy System at the University of Washington is a
cyclotron and treatment facility that provides particle beams for cancer treatments with fast neutrons, production of medical isotopes, and physics experiments. The facility was installed in 1984, and includes a computer control
system provided by the cyclotron vendor [6]. Devices under computer control include a 900 amp electromagnet and a 30 ton rotating gantry, as well as
four terminals at three operator consoles. The control system handles over one
thousand input and output signals, and includes six programmable processors
as well as some nonprogrammable (hard-wired) controls. The University is
now developing a new, successor control system [4]. This development project
is motivated by requirements to make the system easier and quicker to use,
easier to maintain, and able to accommodate future hardware and software
modifications.

We are attempting to achieve high reliability and safety by applying rigorous software development and quality assurance practices. Safety-critical control systems are often advocated as ideal applications for formal software development methods [1]. However, few published case studies apply formal methods to a problem of central importance in these applications: low level input/output.

2 Requirements

A vital activity in most control systems is the processing of unscaled, unencoded contents of the input/output device registers that are attached to the transducers that sense and control some physical process. Register contents must be translated to the values of the state variables that occur in the control laws that the system is supposed to obey. For example, analog quantities must be scaled and offset to match analog-to-digital converters (ADC's) and DAC's and often must be adjusted according to calibration curves. Groups of digital signals must be encoded as discrete variables. Translations must be computed in both directions: register contents are encoded into variables on input, and state variables are decoded back to register contents on output. Obviously, the correctness of the entire system depends critically upon such translations.

It is also necessary to detect errors (where clients invoke operations with invalid parameters) and faults (where operations fail despite valid invocation by the client). In most computing applications, it is expected that programs should detect and report errors, but it is left to the users to deal with faults. Control systems differ from other computing applications in part because they are expected to handle some faults.

Our system is large, but most of its size derives from repetition of similar elements. We hope to produce a manageable system by basing the implementation on tables that describe the system configuration. For example, one table, the "wiring list," tells which signals are connected to particular input/output device register addresses; another table, the "crate diagram," tells which kind of device is present at each address. It should be possible to accommodate most configuration changes simply by editing tables, rather than changing executable code. Changing the routing between signals and devices, or adding additional signals and devices similar to those already present, should only require changing tables. Accommodating new kinds of signals and devices should only require adding the minimal amount of code needed to deal with their specific characteristics.

The requirements are not difficult to understand, but a large control system provides many opportunities for confusion and error. We decided it would be useful to conduct a formal development. The purpose of the effort reported here was to determine what the tables should contain and how the implementation should interpret their contents. The objective was to produce a specification that was sufficiently detailed so that its implementation in an imperative programming language would be a straightforward exercise, and it would be clear how to construct and fill in the tables to describe any particular control system configuration. We intended that the development should be sufficiently rigorous that we could use proofs to support claims we would like to make, for example, "All possible inputs will be handled properly," or "Every output will be valid."

We used the Z notation [7] for this work because it seemed a good match to our chosen table-driven strategy: global functions and relations in Z correspond to our configuration tables. Some of our preliminary experiments with Z appear in [2], and a more detailed report of the present work appears in [3]. The Z text in this paper was found free of syntax and type errors by a type-checker [8].

3   The system configuration and the system state

At the lowest level, input/output is accomplished by data converter hardware. Data converters accommodate *signals* connected to the controlled process. Signals may be digital or analog, and carry information which is input or output with respect to the computer.

Data converters contain *registers*. Every register is identified by a unique *address*, and holds *contents* that encode the value of one signal in a form intelligible to the computer. In any particular configuration, a fixed set of addresses is populated with registers.

We distinguish register contents from control program *state variables*. While registers hold contents, *variables* have *values*.

Expressed formally, we have:

$$[ADDR, CONTENTS, VAR, VALUE]$$

$$
\begin{array}{|l}
ioreg : \mathbb{P}\ ADDR \\
iovar : \mathbb{P}\ VAR \\
map : VAR \leftrightarrow ADDR \\
\hline
map\langle\!\langle iovar \rangle\!\rangle \subseteq ioreg
\end{array}
$$

$$
\begin{array}{|l}
\underline{\ Sys\ } \\
register : ADDR \nrightarrow CONTENTS \\
variable : VAR \nrightarrow VALUE \\
\hline
\text{dom } register = ioreg \\
\text{dom } variable \cap \text{dom } map \subseteq iovar
\end{array}
$$

The sets *ioreg* and *iovar*, and the relation *map* model some of the tables that describe the configuration. The set *ioreg* lists the populated register addresses, *iovar* lists the variables that can be named as parameters in input or output operations, and *map* relates those variables to the registers from which they are derived. We do not model any operations that change the configuration tables.

The schema *Sys* models the registers along with their contents, and the variables with their values. There is a fixed set of registers in the configuration; only their contents may change. The set of variables may change as the program executes, as different subroutines are invoked or dynamic data structures evolve.

Our choice of the words "register" and "address" does not mean this model is limited to memory-mapped devices. A register could be any distinguishable item of data, including a named element accessed through a "smart" controller, and an address might be a name derived from an English word, instead of a number. Moreover, values need not be scalar; variables might have complex internal structure.

4   Translating between register contents and state variable values

The higher-order function *encode* determines the translation between variable values and register contents. When applied to the *register*, *encode* returns a function from variables to values; changing the contents of the registers causes a different function to be returned. The operation schema *Translate* uses *encode* to calculate variable values from register contents (or vice versa).

$$
\mid \quad encode : (ADDR \nrightarrow CONTENTS) \nrightarrow VAR \nrightarrow VALUE
$$

```
┌─ Translate ─────────────────────────────────────
│ ΔSys
│ vars? : P VAR
├──────────────────────────────────────────────────
│ variable' = variable ⊕ (vars? ◁ (encode register'))
```

This schema can be specialised in each direction.

$Encode \mathrel{\widehat{=}} [\, Translate \mid register' = register \,]$

$Decode \mathrel{\widehat{=}} [\, Translate \mid variable' = variable \,]$

These operations are called *Encode* and *Decode*, not *Input* and *Output*, because they are only intended to model the translation between register contents and state variable values; they do not necessarily include the transfer of data between the registers and the transducers connected to the controlled process. In some systems, those transfers are separate operations.

We have not yet shown how the function *encode* is constructed. That is the subject of the following sections.

5   Some useful preliminaries

In this section we define several items that are used to construct the function *encode*. The construction itself will be performed in the next section.

5.1   Only consider items that are related

The signature of *encode* suggests that all registers must be examined to determine the value of any variable. In fact, usually only one, or a few, registers are related to any variable. To use this observation, we must introduce more information that describes how the system is wired together.

Variables are ultimately derived from *signals* obtained from transducers that are connected to the controlled process. Each signal is connected to a particular register. The signal routing is recorded in voluminous wiring lists that are part of the documentation for any configuration. The relation *map* introduced in section 3 is composed from this information.

[*SIGNAL*]

$$
\begin{array}{l}
signal : VAR \leftrightarrow SIGNAL \\
routing : SIGNAL \twoheadrightarrow ADDR \\
\hline
map = signal \,\mathbf{;}\, routing
\end{array}
$$

This representation makes it easy to change *routing* as needed, for example to bypass a faulty data converter channel.

5.2   Collect similar elements into groups

Most of our system's size derives from repetition of similar elements; we can achieve efficiencies by grouping similar elements together and treating them all in the same way. This section introduces relations and functions that classify signals and variables into groups.

Each variable belongs to a *class*, and every instance of each class is derived from items called *members*. Each signal is associated with a particular member. In our system there are hundreds of variables and signals, but only a few dozen classes and members. For example, most of the signals in our system are contributed by about forty high-current power supplies for magnets that confine, focus and steer the particle beam. "Power supply contactor" is a class; the contactor for Quadrupole Magnet 2B is one of many variables which are an instances of that class. Also, "contactor on-bit" and "contactor off-bit" are members of the contactor class; the contactor on- and off-bits for Quadrupole 2B are two of the many signals that correspond to those members. Some formally worked-out examples appear below in section 6.1.

Signals are assigned to variables such that all variables of the same class are associated with signals that have the same membership. Moreover, to enable the members within each class to be distinguished from each other, each signal associated with a class must have a different membership.

[*CLASS, MEMBER*]

$$
\begin{array}{l}
class : VAR \twoheadrightarrow CLASS \\
member : SIGNAL \twoheadrightarrow MEMBER \\
classdef : CLASS \leftrightarrow MEMBER \\
\hline
\forall v : \mathrm{dom}\ class \bullet \\
\quad classdef \langle\!|\{class\ v\}|\!\rangle = member \langle\!|signal \langle\!|\{v\}|\!\rangle|\!\rangle \\
\forall c : \mathrm{dom}\ classdef \bullet \\
\quad member \rhd classdef \langle\!|\{c\}|\!\rangle \in SIGNAL \twoheadrightarrow MEMBER
\end{array}
$$

Our choice of names is influenced by the "object-oriented programming" school; in fact we anticipate specifying another view of the system where the variables are instances ("objects") of abstract data types ("classes") defined by Z schemas.

It turns out to be useful to define the function *amember*, that associates each address with the membership of its attached signal, and *rmember*, that expresses registers in terms of membership rather than addresses:

$$
\begin{aligned}
&amember : ADDR \twoheadrightarrow MEMBER \\
&rmember : (ADDR \twoheadrightarrow CONTENTS) \twoheadrightarrow (MEMBER \twoheadrightarrow CONTENTS)
\end{aligned}
$$

$$
\begin{aligned}
&routing \,\S\, amember = member \\
&\forall\, reg : \text{dom}\, rmember \bullet \\
&\qquad rmember\, reg = \{\, a : \text{dom}\, reg \bullet amember\, a \mapsto reg\, a \,\}
\end{aligned}
$$

Each element in the range of *rmember* is still a function because all signals associated with a class have a different membership.

5.3 Limit the values that elements may assume

Each kind of signal and variable is only supposed to take on certain values. For analog quantities, these usually form a continuous range that represents physically reasonable values. For digital elements, these form a meaningful set of discrete indications.

$$
\begin{aligned}
&mrange : MEMBER \leftrightarrow CONTENTS \\
&crange : CLASS \leftrightarrow VALUE
\end{aligned}
$$

Register contents and variable values that do not lie within the ranges specified by these two relations are considered faulty.

The relation *mrange* constrains the contents of each register, considered by itself. Registers are sometimes collected together in groups, where the entire group encodes some variable. The schema *Combination* associates each class with all of its members and all combinations of their permitted values.

$$
\begin{array}{|l}
\hline
\text{\textit{Combination}} \\
\hline
cclass : CLASS \\
contents : MEMBER \twoheadrightarrow CONTENTS \\
\hline
\text{dom}\, contents = classdef(\!|\{cclass\}|\!) \\
contents \subseteq mrange \\
\hline
\end{array}
$$

This schema will be used later to define *encode* and specify faults.

5.4 Replace functions with sequences

It is sometimes more efficient to replace functions with sequences. For many input/output devices it is usual to transfer the contents of a long sequence of consecutive addresses in a single operation (for example, in *direct memory access* (DMA) transfers). In such cases, we do not need to associate addresses with items, because the source of each item is indicated by its position in the sequence. Also, in most programming languages, parameters to operations (procedure calls, function applications etc.) are distinguished by their position in a sequence.

Therefore, for each class, we choose a particular sequence of the associated members. This determines a sequence of addresses associated with each variable.

$$member\_seq : CLASS \nrightarrow \text{iseq } MEMBER$$
$$addr\_seq : VAR \nrightarrow \text{iseq } ADDR$$

$\forall t : \text{dom } classdef \bullet$
  $\text{ran} (member\_seq\, t) = classdef (\!|\{t\}|\!)$
$\forall v : \text{dom } class \bullet$
  $(addr\_seq\, v) \,\sfrac\, amember = (class \,\sfrac\, member\_seq)\, v$

6 Constructing *encode*

We now have enough pieces in place to construct the function *encode*. The construction is performed in several steps.

6.1 Define the translation tables

We begin by defining the higher-order function *translate*, which provides a way for system designers to describe the translation function for each class. When *translate* is applied to some class c, it returns a function that associates values with certain patterns of members and contents.

$$translate : CLASS \nrightarrow (MEMBER \nrightarrow CONTENTS) \nrightarrow VALUE$$

$\forall c : \text{dom } translate \bullet$
  $\text{dom} (translate\, c) \subseteq \{\, Combination \mid cclass = c \bullet contents \,\} \wedge$
  $\text{ran} (translate\, c) \subseteq crange (\!|\{c\}|\!)$

Using this predicate as a template, for any *translate c* we can use the schema *Combination* to construct the domain of the function, and then use our knowledge of the application to assign each corresponding *VALUE*. For analog quantities it is usually effective to represent this assignment by a formula; for digital elements, a table is often preferred.

Filling in *translate c* for each class is a central task in creating the detailed specification for a particular control system. For example, the class *contactor* indicates whether a power supply is on or off. This is not derived from a single binary signal; it is good practice to use a separate binary signal to provide a positive indication of each condition. Since is derived from two binary signals, it has four values. Two should not normally occur. The relevant fragments of the tables are:

102

$$
\begin{array}{|l}
contactor : CLASS \\
o\!f\!f\_bit, on\_bit : MEMBER \\
clear, set : CONTENTS \\
o\!f\!f, on, both\_clear, both\_set : VALUE \\
\hline
translate\ contactor\ \{o\!f\!f\_bit \mapsto set, on\_bit \mapsto clear\} = o\!f\!f \\
translate\ contactor\ \{o\!f\!f\_bit \mapsto clear, on\_bit \mapsto set\} = on \\
translate\ contactor\ \{o\!f\!f\_bit \mapsto clear, on\_bit \mapsto clear\} = both\_clear \\
translate\ contactor\ \{o\!f\!f\_bit \mapsto set, on\_bit \mapsto set\} = both\_set
\end{array}
$$

The predicate does not require all possible patterns allowed by *Combination* to appear in the domain of each *translate c*. It is usual for some patterns to be omitted because they indicate faulty signal values or combinations. The last two entries in the preceding fragment might be omitted for this reason.

Here is a second example, where the translation function is defined by a formula. The *current* class represents an analog quantity, the current output from a power supply in units of amperes. The sole member in this class is *adc*, whose contents is the pattern of binary digits that appears in the register of an analog-to-digital converter (ADC). The translation function applies an offset and scaling factor, something like

$$
\begin{array}{|l}
current : CLASS \\
adc : MEMBER \\
\hline
\forall bits : mrange(\!\{adc\}\!) \bullet \\
\quad translate\ current\ \{adc \mapsto bits\} = m * bits + k
\end{array}
$$

where m and k are parameters that describe the translation between the ADC contents interpreted as unscaled integers and the value of current in amperes. (This fragment is a bit informal because we have not explained how *CONTENTS* and *VALUE* can be interpreted as numbers).

Some of our classes incorporate features of both of these examples. To measure vacuum pressure, at each measurement site we must use two sensors that are effective in different pressure ranges. The members for our "vacuum gauge" class include digital signals that indicate which sensor is in use, as well as analog signals from both sensors. The translation function decodes the sensor selection signals and applies a different nonlinear calibration curve, depending on which sensor is active.

The translation functions determine which situations are considered erroneous or exceptional. By first limiting the permitted ranges in *mrange* and *crange*, and then choosing which patterns of those defined by *Combination* belong to the domain of each *translate c* when we configure a system, we can determine which patterns of register contents represent valid encodings of any given set of variables. This is so important that we define a schema to describe it:

$$
\begin{array}{|l}
\underline{\ RegValid\ } \\
vars? : \mathbb{P}\ VAR \\
reg : ADDR \nrightarrow CONTENTS \\
\hline
dom\ reg = map(\!|vars?|\!) \\
\forall v : vars? \bullet \forall rs : \mathbb{P}\ reg \mid dom\ rs = map(\!|\{v\}|\!) \bullet \\
\quad rmember\ rs \in dom\ (translate\ (class\ v))
\end{array}
$$

This schema is used in subsequent developments to describe correctness (section 7) and specify faults (section 8).

6.2 Define *encode*

Next, we propose a definition for *encode*. If we already know the class c that a variable belongs to, and which registers *reg* determine the variable's value, *encode* can be derived from *translate* by using *rmember* to adjust the type of *reg*:

$$encode \; reg \; v = translate \; c \; (rmember \; reg)$$

In fact v is related to c and *reg* through *class* and *map*, respectively, so:

$$encode \; register \; v = translate \; (class \; v) \; (rmember \; (map \{\!| \{v\} |\!\} \lhd register))$$

6.3 Make *encode* more efficient

In this development step, we increase efficiency by replacing functions with sequences. This is an example of *data refinement* [5, 7]. From the function *translate* we derive *translate_seq*:

> *translate_seq* : $CLASS \nrightarrow$ iseq $CONTENTS \nrightarrow VALUE$
>
> $\forall \, c : \text{dom} \, translate \bullet translate\_seq \; c =$
> $\quad \{ \, ccontents : \text{dom} \, (translate \; c) \bullet$
> $\qquad member\_seq \; c \, \mathring{,} \; ccontents \mapsto translate \; c \; ccontents \, \}$

Then *encode* can be expressed:

$$encode \; register \; v = translate\_seq \; (class \; v) \; (addr\_seq \; v \, \mathring{,} \; register)$$

This suggests an efficient implementation in an imperative programming language (as described in section 10).

6.4 Make definitions constructive

In this final development step we derive constructive specifications from non-constructive ones. The expression $code\_seq \; (class \; v) \; (addr\_seq \; v \, \mathring{,} \; register)$ derived in the previous step almost resembles an executable statement in a functional programming language. However, this expression could not be evaluated because we have not yet shown how to construct the function $addr\_seq$. It is defined non-constructively (in section 5.4), as are several other items. A non-constructive definition is one where the item being defined does not appear by itself on one side of an equal sign.

Non-constructive definitions are often natural and concise, but they create an obligation to show that the items so defined can be implemented efficiently. In the full report [3] we discharged those obligations by calculating constructive definitions from non-constructive ones, using laws from [7] and some additional lemmas we proved ourselves.

7 Checking the development by calculation and proof

We are fallible, so our formal specification may fail to express the intended requirements, and any of the steps we used to construct the function *encode* might be wrong. An important advantage of formal specifications is that they can be analyzed, and developments based upon them can be checked by calculation and proof. We find that the theorem we pose to check some informal requirements also serves to check our construction.

We would like to claim,

"All possible inputs will be handled properly"

but this statement is much too vague to relate to our formal specification. Trying again, we say,

"If the configuration tables are accurate, then valid input signals will be translated to the proper state variable values, and invalid input signals will be detected."

Here the features of the formal specification begin to emerge, but we need still more detail. Trying once again, we begin,

"If a group of signals are entered into the routing table, and the addresses to which the signals are connected are populated, and the signals are found in the tables to be members of recognised classes, and the value of each signal falls within the permitted range for its class membership, and ..."

This is beginning to assume the prolix but shallow quality of most theorems in software verification. Rather than press on in this vein, we resort to formal notation. We are trying to state a hypotheses about signals:

$$
\begin{array}{|l}
\hline
\text{\_\_} \textit{SigValid} \text{_____} \\
\textit{sigs} : \mathbf{P} \; \textit{SIGNAL} \\
\textit{scontents} : \textit{SIGNAL} \nrightarrow \textit{CONTENTS} \\
\hline
\textit{sigs} = \mathrm{dom} \; \textit{scontents} \\
\textit{routing} (\textit{sigs}) \subseteq \textit{ioreg} \\
\textit{member} (\textit{sigs}) \subseteq \mathrm{ran} \; \textit{classdef} \\
\exists \; \textit{RegValid} \; \bullet \\
\quad \textit{sigs} = \textit{signal} (\textit{vars?}) \; \wedge \\
\quad \textit{scontents} = \{ \, a : \mathrm{dom} \; \textit{reg} \; \bullet \; \textit{routing}^{\sim} a \mapsto \textit{reg} \; a \, \} \\
\hline
\end{array}
$$

Here, we use the *RegValid* schema defined in section 6.1. We wish to relate the signals *sigs* in these hypotheses to the *vars?* parameter in the *Encode* operation schema, so we also need:

$$
\begin{array}{|l}
\hline
\text{\_\_} \textit{SigMatchVar} \text{_____} \\
\textit{sigs} : \mathbf{P} \; \textit{SIGNAL} \\
\textit{vars?} : \mathbf{P} \; \textit{VAR} \\
\hline
\textit{sigs} = \textit{signal} (\textit{vars?}) \\
\hline
\end{array}
$$

Now we can state the entire theorem, which formalises the requirement, "All valid signals will be handled properly".

$$SigValid \land SigMatchVar \land Encode \vdash$$
$$\forall v : vars? \bullet \exists c : CLASS \bullet c = class\ v \land$$
$$variable'\ v = translate\ c\ \{s : sigs \bullet member\ s \mapsto scontents\ s\}$$

The conclusion says that the variables should have the values required for the signals' contents by the tables and formulas for the signals' class membership.

Our proof of this theorem appears in the full report [3]. The proof provides confidence that the formal specification expresses the informally stated requirement. It also serves as a good check on the development steps, since the hypothesis $SigValid$ and the conclusion are expressed in terms of signals, classes, members, and the function *translate*, while the schema that describes the operation, $Encode$, is expressed in terms of registers, variables, and the function *encode*. The schema $SigMatchVar$ ties the two representations together.

Our development, and the theorem we stated to check it, are closely related to *refinement* as described by Spivey [7] and Potter, et al. [5]. To justify a refinement, one should prove a *correctness theorem* that has the form:

$$\text{pre } AOp \land Retr \land COp \land Retr' \vdash AOp$$

Where AOp is the operation schema for the abstract state, $Retr$ is the schema describing the retrieve relation, and Cop is the operation schema for the concrete operation.

This is almost the same as our own theorem; our hypotheses $SigValid$ corresponds to pre AOp, our $SigMatchVar$ to $Retr$, our $Encode$ to COp, and our conclusion to AOp. The similarity is clear, except our development proceeded from the "concrete" to the "abstract" representation! We should not feel obligated to follow the recommended sequence too dogmatically, but instead should consider refinement a useful collection of methods for checking development steps, regardless of the order in which they are discovered.

8 Detecting errors and faults

An important specification task is to enumerate the errors and faults that might occur in each operation and determine how to handle them. An advantage of a formal specification is that it is not necessary to rely solely on inspiration to discover potential errors and faults; some of them can be calculated. In Z, they can often be determined by calculating preconditions. States which do not satisfy the precondition of an operation are usually those that designers consider erroneous or faulty.

For example, the precondition of the operation $Encode$ is:

$$
\begin{array}{|l}
\hline
\text{\textit{PreEncode}} \\\hline
Sys \\
vars? : \mathbf{P}\ VAR \\\hline
vars? \subseteq iovar \\
\exists reg : \mathbf{P}\ register \bullet RegValid \\
\hline
\end{array}
$$

The essential requirement expressed here is that the expression *vars?* $\lhd$ *encode register* from *Encode* must be defined. Therefore, *vars?* must lie within the domain of *encode register*; failure to satisfy this predicate is an error. Also, *register* must lie within the domain of *encode*; failure to satisfy this predicate is a fault.

Now we can follow usual Z style for extending partial operations. When an error or fault is detected, it should be reported, but the system state must not otherwise change, for example:

```
┌─ BadReg ─────────────────────────────────────────
│ ΞSys
│ vars? : P VAR
│ status : STATUS
├───────────────────────────────────────────────────
│ status = badreg
│ ¬ (∃ reg : P register • RegValid)
└───────────────────────────────────────────────────
```

A similar schema *BadVar* describes the case where the input variables are not valid. Then the *Encode* operation can be extended:

$$T\_Encode \,\hat{=}\, (Encode \wedge Success) \vee BadVar \vee BadReg$$

These three outcomes exhaust all possibilities.

9 Inverse operations

Non-constructive notations make it easy to define inverse operations. One example is the definition of the *Decode* operation that translates state variable values to register contents (section 4). It contains the predicate

$$variable = variable \oplus (vars? \lhd (encode\ register'))$$

This is nonconstructive because *register'* is the item being defined. We can define a constructive version of *Decode* by analogy with *Encode*:

$$|\quad decode : (VAR \nrightarrow VALUE) \nrightarrow ADDR \nrightarrow CONTENTS$$

```
┌─ Decode ─────────────────────────────────────────
│ ΔSys
│ vars? : P VAR
├───────────────────────────────────────────────────
│ variable' = variable
│ register' = register ⊕ (map⦇vars?⦈ ⊲ (decode variable))
└───────────────────────────────────────────────────
```

It seems clear that *decode* should be the inverse of *encode*. If we already knew which variable v was associated with a particular register address, we could derive *decode* from the inverse of *translate*:

$$decode\ variable\ a = (translate\ (class\ v))^{\sim}\ (variable\ v)\ (amember\ a)$$

In fact v is related to a through the function *map*, so we can just use the preceding definition, where it is understood that $v \in map^{\sim}(\{a\})$ (any element will do).

The function *decode* is expressed here in terms of previously-defined items. Thefore, we do not need to define any additional configuration tables. Where evaluating *translate c* is implemented by table lookup, the implementation of $(translate\,(class\,v))^{\sim}$ can use the same table, with the direction of lookup reversed.

The development in this section could be checked by proving the conjecture

$$Encode \;\mathbf{;}\; Decode \vdash register' = register$$

10   Towards an implementation

In this section we show how the final development of our specification suggests an efficient and straightforward implementation in an imperative programming language.

Given sets, global functions and relations can be implemented as tables that are loaded when the control system is initialised; the predicates for these items suggest acceptance tests that could be performed when the tables are produced, or run-time checks to be performed each time the tables are loaded. Application of a higher-order function to its first argument can be implemented as code that dispatches to a handler for that particular case. Ordinary function application can be implemented as table lookup or formula evaluation, whichever is more efficient.

The specification appears sufficiently detailed to serve as a basis for formal verification of the implementation, if we wish to attempt it.

11   Discussion

Critics charge that many formal developments are described in retrospect, merely casting into formal notations work that has already been developed intuitively. Our own experience refutes that cynical assessment.

Our results may seem obvious; in fact, we made several false starts that led to cumbersome specifications and unfinished developments. The formal notation, by providing compact descriptions that can be manipulated and checked algebraically, was quite helpful for identifying problems, exploring alternatives, and expressing a detailed solution. The development was easy to calculate, but might have been difficult to intuit or improvise. Had we plunged on into implementation without the formal development, we might have begun building a less satisfactory alternative.

The existing implementation provides some indication of the difficulties we have avoided (we are developing a replacement for the control system that was provided by the cyclotron vendor when the facility was installed [6]). The code seems unnecessarily large and is quite difficult to follow. There was some attempt to make the system table-driven, but reconfiguring it to accommodate different converter hardware, or even to move a signal from a failed converter, cannot be accomplished by changing table entries; it is necessary to modify executable code. There is little error checking; it is not clear what errors are checked. A manual startup sequence is necessary because the system can set outputs before valid register contents are established.

The formally-developed replacement described in this paper has not yet been implemented, but we are confident that it will not be difficult, and will provide much improvement over the present system.

12 Acknowledgments

The author thanks three anonymous reviewers for suggestions that improved the clarity and accuracy of this version of the paper.

References

[1] Craigen D. FM89: Assessment of formal methods for trustworthy computer systems. In 12th International Conference on Software Engineering Proceedings, pp 233 – 235. IEEE Computer Society, 1990.

[2] Jacky J. Formal specifications for a clinical cyclotron control system. In Moriconi M (ed), Proceedings of the ACM SIGSOFT International Workshop on Formal Methods in Software Development, pp 45 – 54, Napa, California, USA, 1990. (also in *ACM Software Engineering Notes*, 15(4), Sept. 1990).

[3] Jacky J. Formal specification and development of control system input/output (revised). Technical Report 92-11-02, Radiation Oncology Department, University of Washington, Seattle, WA, 1992.

[4] Jacky J, Risler R, Kalet I, Wootton P. Clinical neutron therapy system, control system specification, part i: System overview and hardware organization. Technical Report 90-12-01, Radiation Oncology Department, University of Washington, Seattle, WA, 1990.

[5] Potter B, Sinclair J, Till D. An Introduction to Formal Specification and Z. Prentice Hall International (UK) Ltd, Hemel Hempstead, Hertfordshire, 1991.

[6] Risler R, Eenmaa J, Jacky JP, Kalet IJ, Wootton P, Lindbaeck S. Installation of the cyclotron based clinical neutron therapy system in Seattle. In Proceedings of the Tenth International Conference on Cyclotrons and their Applications, pp 428 – 430, East Lansing, Michigan, 1984. IEEE.

[7] Spivey JM. The Z Notation: A Reference Manual. Prentice-Hall, New York, 1989.

[8] Spivey JM. The FUZZ Manual. J. M. Spivey Computing Science Consultancy, Oxford, 1991. Second Printing.

Preliminary Experience Using Z to Specify a Safety-Critical System†

John C. Knight   Darrell M. Kienzle
Department of Computer Science, University of Virginia
Charlottesville, VA, USA

Abstract

We present our experiences in developing and using the specification for a safety-critical system. This system is an experimental medical device that is designed to perform robotic human neurosurgery. Our goal is to use this system as a case study to examine the role of software in such systems and the role of specification in achieving safe operation. Our experience with this case study has taught us that although formal specifications are of great value, their use alone is not sufficient to achieve high levels of safety. Required in addition are a clear definition of software safety and a rigorous process for developing the necessary specifications. We present, in addition, some observations on the use of Z in safety-critical applications.

1 Introduction

In this paper, we summarize our experiences to date in developing and using the specification for a safety-critical system. This system is an experimental medical device designed to perform robotic human neurosurgery known as the *Magnetic Stereotaxis System*.

Some computer applications, such as flight-control systems, require very high *reliability*, while others, such as transaction-processing, systems require very high *availability* [1]. However, there are many computer applications in which *safety* and not reliability or availability is the overriding concern. Reduced, altered, or in some cases even no functionality is acceptable in such systems as long as no harm is done. This is the situation with the application we describe here. Our concern is with the role of software in such systems and the role of specification in achieving safe operation.

Despite their recent exploitation on a number of realistic projects, the use of formal specifications is still in its infancy. Similarly, the notations used for formal specifications are undergoing continual improvement. Since we are involved in the software development for a safety-critical application, we decided to undertake a case study in order to add to the body of experience in this area. The goal of this ongoing project is a thorough evaluation and documented demonstration of the use of formal specification in the safety-critical domain.

† Sponsored in part by NASA under grant number NAG-1-1123.

The safety-critical application that is the focus of our case study is summarized in section 2. The experiences we report are in three major areas. The first area, described in section 3, is that of definitions. Before we were able to develop the necessary specification, we had to develop suitable definitions for the major goals that the specification had to meet. A side effect of this effort was the creation of a required structure for specifications of systems that require very high levels of safety.

The second area in which we report our experiences is the process of developing a specification. Once we had the necessary definitional framework, we set out to construct the specification but found we had no particular path to follow. Our experience in developing a process for specifying safety requirements is discussed in section 4.

The third area of experience that we report is the use of Z itself [2]. We found it to be mostly excellent for our needs but we came across a number of pragmatic difficulties. We describe our experiences in this area in section 5. Finally, we present our conclusions in section 6.

2 A Safety-Critical Application

The Magnetic Stereotaxis System (MSS) is an investigational device for performing human neurosurgery being developed in a joint effort between the University of Virginia and the Department of Neurosurgery at the University of Washington [3]. It operates by manipulating a small permanent magnet (known as a "seed") within the brain using an externally applied magnetic field. By varying the magnitude and gradient of the external field, the seed can be moved along a non-linear path and positioned at a site requiring therapy, e.g., a tumor. The device can be used for hyperthermia by radio-frequency heating of the seed from an external source or for chemotherapy by using the seed to deliver drugs to a site within the brain. The MSS concept promises to be far less traumatic to the patient than present invasive approaches to such treatments.

The externally applied magnetic field of the MSS has to have a gradient of at least five Tesla per meter in order to move the seed through brain tissue. This field is produced by a set of six superconducting electromagnets that are mounted in a cryostatic enclosure that surrounds the patient's head during surgery. The seed location within the brain is monitored in real time by an X-ray imaging system that provides two perpendicular images which include views of the skull, a set of fiducial markers, and the seed. Data from these images is combined with a set of stored, pre-operative Magnetic Resonance Images (MRI's) and displayed for the neurosurgeon.

The MSS's computer system controls the X-ray, RF-heating, and electromagnetic subsystems; presents MR images and X-ray data to the neurosurgeon; and accepts the neurosurgeon's input and translates it into commands to the various subsystems.

Clearly, the MSS is a safety-critical system. The greatest concern is, of course, with patient injury; undesired seed movement, for example, could cause serious brain damage. Many different equipment failures can occur and the computer system will be expected to deal with them. For example, the X-ray imaging system could fail by leaving the X-ray source on thereby delivering an excessive X-ray dose, or it could fail by producing a defective image leading to erroneous estimation of the seed's location.

Of course, computer system failures can lead to patient injury or damage to other parts of the equipment also.

Although the MSS is a medical device, it is best thought of as a complex control system required to operate safely. There is no requirement for high reliability or high availability. As such it is not unlike safety-critical systems in many domains.

3 The Role Of Formal Specification In Software Safety

At the outset, we found it necessary to develop a framework of rigorous definitions because without them we had no precise goal for the specification we were developing. More specifically, the informal goal was to use the specification as part of a development effort that would yield software that was safe. However, there was no definition that could be applied to our application that permitted us to state what it meant for the software to be safe in a rigorous sense.

We find it surprising that some standards mandate various techniques but either give no reason why they should be used or justify them with statements that are variations of "Technique X is good and leads to better software." For safety-critical applications, it is not sufficient to seek software that is "safer" or "more reliable" in an imprecise sense because that which is achieved might still be inadequate. With no precise definition of software safety, for example, it is not possible to state that a given software entity is safe. It is pointless to develop a standard that prescribes the use of various techniques for achieving something that is itself not defined. The framework of definitions that we have developed includes a precise definition of safe software, and this definition permits a clear statement of what it means for software to be safe for a specific system. Without such a definition, there is no hope of being able to build safe software because we would never know what we were trying to achieve.

A detailed explanation of our framework of definitions together with its rationale is presented elsewhere [4]. We present here only a brief informal summary.

For systems where safety (rather than reliability or availability) is the overriding concern, we define the software specification to consist of three parts: The intrinsic-functionality specifications. The failure-interface specifications. The recovery-functionality specifications.

Informally, the intrinsic-functionality specifications state what the software is required to do during normal operation. Taken together, the intrinsic functionalities of all the elements making up a system implement the desired system functionality.

The failure-interface specifications state essentially what the software must do with a high degree of assurance. The software may fail in any manner whatsoever internally but, in the event that it is unable to provide its intrinsic functionality, the interface that it provides to other components in the system has to be its failure interface. The failure interface might be inert and safe thereby having what is generally called a fail-safe characteristic. It might also define limited functionality, essentially that functionality that must be present to ensure continued safe system operation or a controlled shutdown.

It is extremely important to note that system-level safety analysis is impossible unless certain assumptions are made about what happens when components fail. Essentially, for the system-safety analysis to be valid, each component *including the software* must present a predefined interface when it fails. If they do not, nothing precise can be said about the subsequent behavior of the system and consequently nothing can be said about the safety of the system. The notion of fail-stop computers [5], a concept fundamental to the analysis of distributed computing systems, is another example of this approach.

The recovery functionality of the software is the required functionality that must be provided in the event that another component in the system fails. It is precisely the recovery functionality of a system's software that is being used when the software checks the operation of another component or responds to a failure indication of another component.

The software in a safety-critical system is expected to comply with all three of the sets of specifications just defined. However, in a system that is required to be safe, hazards will be avoided if the system-safety analysis is correct and each component meets the second and third of the sets of specifications. This leads to the notion of the *software-safety specifications* which we define to be the combination of the failure-interface specifications and the recovery-functionality specifications.

Finally, we define software to be safe in a formal (but not necessarily intuitive) sense if it complies with its safety specifications, i.e., its failure-interface specifications and its recovery-functionality specifications. Achieving safe software, again in a formal sense, requires that the safety specifications as we have defined the term be complete and accurate, and that the subsequent implementation implements the safety specifications correctly. This is, therefore, the goal of the MSS software development, and the exact role of the specification is now clear.

4 Specification Development

Many standards exist or are being prepared that are concerned with the development of software for safety-critical systems. Typically, such standards prescribe the use of specific techniques, including in some cases formal specifications, but they do not indicate exactly how the techniques should be applied. Although the use of a formal specification in the development of a safety-critical system is very desirable, the mere use of a formal specification is not sufficient. There is no assurance, for example, that the specifications will reflect the requirements accurately nor that those using the specifications will use them correctly. We claim that a specification has to be developed and used according to a rigorous, repeatable process if the full potential of formal specification is to be achieved.

The source of the software safety specification for most safety-critical systems including the MSS is the system fault-tree analysis and the resulting *system fault trees* [6, 7]. Each system fault tree is an and/or tree that documents a hazard that can arise from the system and the events that can cause it[†]. In the MSS, for example, patient injury is a hazard, and one way that this can occur is for the X-ray source in the imaging system to remain on when it should not. This can occur if the X-ray source itself fails or the controlling software fails in such a way that it activates the X-ray source but fails to deactivate it. A system fault tree details all the different combinations of events that can lead to a hazard. Such trees are used by systems engineers to demonstrate that complete systems are safe by associating probabilities with events within the tree and showing that hazards are caused with a sufficiently small probability. The fault trees for a given system are usually built by a systems engineer working in concert with engineers in all the other disciplines involved. Typically, such fault trees usually contain software functions in a completely integrated manner. The issue of failure probabilities for software is often resolved by assuming such probabilities are either zero or one.

The software-safety specifications, according to our definition summarized above, are implicit in the system fault trees. First, consider the recovery functionality specifications. There are entries in the tree in which a hazard is avoided because software takes some action when a device fails. In the MSS, for example, the DC power to the X-ray system should be turned off if an X-ray source remains on unexpectedly. Similarly, the failure interface specifications for the software are implied by the system fault tree. If the software fails but presents a well-defined interface after doing so, hazards can be avoided. For example, if the software failure interface specifies that following detection of any internal software failure, the interface that the software presents is to shut down sources of energy, such as the MSS's electromagnets or X-ray sources, then software failure cannot lead to patient injury. We note that this is an extended form of the concept of Safe Programming introduced by Anderson and Witty [9].

The issue we faced was to process the system fault tree systematically so that a complete and correct set of software safety specifications were produced. Working with systems engineers we set out to modify the system fault tree for the MSS by including software functions at appropriate points. This turned out to be a chaotic and totally unsatisfactory approach. After developing several versions of the system fault trees each being substantially different in form but not function from the others we sought a better way.

Our better way is still under development but consists of three major steps. In the first, system fault trees are developed in which safety-related software is not considered and in which software failures are ignored. The hardware engineers append failure probabilities to these preliminary fault trees and use them to determine which hazards can occur with unacceptable probability. In the next step, software functions are added where possible to reduce the probability of hazards occurring to acceptable levels. The output of this step is the recovery-functionality specifications. In the final step, the consequences of failure of each software function are examined and constraints placed on each software function such that a software function cannot itself cause a hazard as a result of failure. It is this third step that yields the software failure-interface specifications.

---

† We note that system fault trees are not related to software fault trees [8].

5 Using Z

The software safety specifications for the Magnetic Stereotaxis System is approximately 40 pages long at this point and still considered a working draft. It is important to keep in mind that this document consists of only the failure interface specification and the recovery functionality specification. Those aspects of the intrinsic functionality which have no safety ramifications have not been formally specified. In this section, we present some of our observations about Z that have arisen as a result of building this specification.

6.2 Clarity of Specifications

Although we hope to be able to develop the final safety specifications from the associated system fault trees in a completely rigorous manner, the accuracy of both the specifications and the fault trees is a matter of judgement. It is essential that the specifications be available as a mechanism for communication between all of the engineering disciplines involved in developing the application. In our case, for example, various experts in electrical engineering, cryogenics, and magnetism need to be able to understand the specifications completely.

Whereas the formal semantic basis for Z ensures precision, it does not ensure clarity. For example, rather than stating explicitly that a display must be updated, a specification might state only that the value of some variable be changed and rely on the fact that buried in the specification is a statement that the display must always display the contents of that variable. We often found ourselves using "tricks" of this type in exactly the way we have learned *not* to do in programming.

Such specifications are correct, of course, but they tend to mask the primary purpose of the specification: clear communications. In specifying safety requirements, this is especially important. We learned this particular lesson the hard way. After translating our safety requirements into an incredibly clever and terse specification, we were stunned to realize that the specification buried the safety requirements deeply within the functionality specification. This was exactly the opposite effect of that desired.

Our conclusion from this experience is that techniques for writing clear specifications need to be developed and stressed. Although these stylistic issues may be well-known to experts in Z, they are not obvious to the novice. Documented stylistic guidelines would be very valuable.

7.3 Lifecycle Considerations

We found the common emphasis on getting the specification correct before the system is designed and built to be too restrictive. Although the rational software design process would enforce perfecting the specification before the implementation is begun, this is rarely possible. Most significant software systems require that prototyping and other risk-reduction methods be incorporated into a more realistic life-cycle, such as the spiral model [10]. Textbooks that demonstrate Z as a key element in the waterfall model are likely to be viewed as unrealistic and inconsistent with the remainder of software engineering theory. In building the MSS software, we took an iterative enhancement approach [11]. In fact, the formal safety specification was not even begun until prototype software had been completed by the system's inventors [3]. This was desirable since, in novel systems such as the MSS, the role of software can best be determined via experimentation with a prototype. This permitted us to have a very precise knowledge of the software's interaction with the safety aspects of the system because we were able to determine the functionality requirements on the software entirely. A side effect of this process was the realization that the original system hardware had to be amended to facilitate software safety. For example, separate X-ray sensors that are readable by the software will be added to permit independent checking of the state of the X-ray sources.

8.4 Limited Z Resources

An important hurdle to the widespread acceptance of Z is the relative lack of Z knowledge outside of the United Kingdom. We did not have the benefit of a resident Z expert, and acquired all of our exposure to Z from the collection of available texts, which are uniformly introductory in nature [12, 13, 14, 15]. For example, the texts to which we had access failed to mention the schema type and the selection operator, both of which we found very valuable. In addition, the texts we used gave the impression that Z is a notation best suited to specifying database systems. A more diverse collection of case studies and a few advanced texts would be very helpful.

Exacerbating the problems of limited Z knowledge is the lack of Z tools. Although the ability to create Latex specification files is quite widespread, the lack of other tools is disturbing. Some useful tools would be similar to those available for many programming languages, such as graphical syntax-directed editors, library managers, browsing and inspection utilities, and cross-reference databases.

9.5 Specification of Interfaces

Z is remarkably powerful at specifying relations between abstract entities but less able to specify how these entities relate to the physical world. Conventional Z specifications stress the relations of before and after states of certain operations but tend to gloss over the details of when these operations are invoked and precisely how they interact with external interfaces. This is a serious problem when working with safety-critical systems where interface and timing errors could cause tremendous harm. Dealing with the problem by using English text as part of the specification defeats the purpose of using a formal specification if the English contains critical information not present in the formal notation. One approach would be to use a "semi-formal" notation such as the input and output forms used in the A-7 technique [16], that utilize agreed-upon external semantics mapping formal entities to their real-world counterparts. Another would be to establish conventions in Z for items such as hardware ports, display screens, and memory-mapped input and output. These would appear as standard Z constructs but would contain other well-understood semantics that would define their relation with the real world precisely. Finally, Z is in need of conventions for building specifications for real-time systems. The existing conventions for specifying states and changes of state are quite appropriate for specifying discrete operations on databases and state-based systems, but they are not presently suitable for specifying real-time control systems. An appropriate convention for incorporating timing requirements should be formulated before a host of such "conventions" are propagated.

10.6 Specification Reuse

We observe that some classes of systems exhibit considerable similarity across entire domains. Real-time, reactive control systems, for example, tend to share a common framework, characterized by modes, events, conditions, actions, and durations, but are distinguished by the peripheral devices and the primary control logic. Developing the software safety specifications for the MSS made it painfully clear that the reuse of Z specifications would be very beneficial [17]. This reuse might take many forms including reusable parts for the specification of particular device controllers, a general framework (or skeleton) for real-time control systems, specifications of user-interface components, and other general abstract entities such as coordinate systems. Many of the entities that we have specified, for example, might be of use to others and vice versa. If significant volumes of reusable parts were available, rather than reinventing the entire framework of a specification for a new system, effort could be concentrated on those elements of the system that distinguish it from others.

Before any general reuse and sharing of parts can exist, a convention for specifying reusable parts must be adopted. Existing techniques include object-oriented extensions to Z [18], domain-specific frameworks [19], and object-oriented approaches to writing standard Z [20]. Other possibilities include new classes of schemata, macro-inclusion facilities, and Z pre-processors that resolve naming conflicts. Whatever the exact details, any such convention must be the subject of widespread agreement in order to be of real use.

Finally, the standard mathematical toolkit in Z is very useful, but we found ourselves wishing that other basic types were defined in the language. It was our experience that the basic types of integer and positive integer were simply too restrictive, and that other basic types, such as a character set (ASCII) and limited precision floating-point (IEEE 754), would make specifications simpler and clearer.

12 Conclusions

From our experience with this case study, our primary conclusion is that Z as a notation for formal specifications is an excellent start. However, a notation by itself is not sufficient to ensure that the maximum benefit from formal specification technology will be achieved. The most important addition to the notation is a rigorous process for its use. We note that this conclusion is *not* a criticism of Z but a reflection of the immature state of the software engineering field in the area of formal methods.

Our other conclusions are mainly in the area of minor improvements that we would like to see made to Z and to the way that it is used. Guidance for the novice user on style and technique together with more extensive and more widely available tools and conventions will do a great deal to enhance the utility and success of formal specification in Z.

References

1. Siewiorek DP, Swarz RS. The theory and practice of reliable system design. Digital Press, Bedford, Massachusetts 1982
2. Spivey M. The Z notation: a reference manual. Prentice Hall International 1989
3. Wika KG, Lawson MA, Gillies GT, Ritter RC. A user interface and control algorithm for the video tumor fighter. Technical Report UVA/640419/NEEP91/112, Department of Nuclear Engineering and Engineering Physics, University of Virginia, 1991
4. Knight JC, Kienzle DM. Safety-critical computer applications: the role of software engineering. Technical Report TR-92-23, Department of Computer Science, University of Virginia, 1992
5. Schlichting RD, Schneider FB. Fail-stop processors: an approach to designing fault-tolerant computing systems. ACM Trans on Comp Sys 1983; 1(3)
6. Green A. Safety systems reliability. John Wiley & Sons, New York 1983
7. Thomson J. Engineering safety assessment. John Wiley & Sons, New York 1987
8. Leveson N, Harvey P. Analyzing software safety. IEEE Trans on Soft Eng 1983; SE-9(5)
9. Anderson T, Witty R. Safe programming. Bit 1978; 18
10. Boehm BW. A spiral model of software development and enhancement. IEEE Computer 1988; 21(5)
11. Basili VR, Turner AJ. Iterative enhancement: a practical technique for software development. IEEE Trans on Soft Eng 1975; SE-1(4)
12. Diller A. Z: an introduction to formal methods. John Wiley & Sons, New York 1990
13. Ince DC. An introduction to discrete mathematics and formal system specification. Oxford University Press, New York 1988
14. Potter B, Sinclair J, Till D. An introduction to formal specification and Z. Prentice Hall, New York 1991
15. Woodcock JCP, Loomes M. Software engineering mathematics. Addison-Wesley, Reading, Massachusetts 1988
16. Heninger KL. Specifying software requirements for complex systems: new techniques and their application. IEEE Trans on Soft Eng 1980; SE-6(1)
17. Tracz W (editor). Software reuse: emerging technology. IEEE Computer Society Press, 1988
18. Duke D, Duke R. Towards a semantics for Object-Z. VDM '90: VDM and Z - formal methods in software development. Proceedings, 3rd VDM-Europe symposium 1990, Kiel, FRG, Springer-Verlag 1990
19. Delisle N, Garlan D. Formal specifications as reusable frameworks. VDM '90: VDM and Z - formal methods in software development. Proceedings,

3rd VDM-Europe symposium 1990, Kiel, FRG, Springer-Verlag 1990

20. Hall A. Using Z as a specification calculus for object-oriented systems. VDM '90: VDM and Z - formal methods in software development. Proceedings, 3rd VDM-Europe symposium 1990, Kiel, FRG, Springer-Verlag 1990

Using Diagrams to give a Formal Specification of Timing Constraints in Z

A. C. Coombes, J. A. McDermid
Dependable Computing Systems Centre,
Department of Computer Scicnce,
University of York,
Heslington, York, YO1 5DD

Abstract

The need to represent timing requirements for computer systems in a formal way is being addressed by a growing number of specification techniques. However, a common weakness in these techniques is **understandability**, as a specification is often used to communicate between interested parties who may not possess the skills necessary to interpret a formal specification. Some atemporal specification languages deal with this problem by means of graphical notations with associated formal semantics (e.g. statecharts), although to the knowledge of the author, no such technique exists for dealing with temporal constraints in such a way. This paper presents causal timing diagrams, one possible approach for describing timing requirements graphically with an underlying formal semantics.

1. Introduction

Where computer systems are to be used within high-integrity or safety-critical applications, it is essential that the risk of any kind of failure is minimised. The use of formal methods as a means to reduce the chance of a *design failure* is growing in popularity (indeed the interim defence standard 00-55 [12] mandates the use of formal methods for software specification).

Although the use of formal methods does confer many advantages to the developer of a software system, there is one major disadvantage; namely that of understandability[1]. In order to assist with this problem, various techniques have been suggested whereby a graphical specification can be transformed into a formal one, or where a formal specification can be derived from a diagram [4, 13, 6].

However, to the author's knowledge, none of the 'formal graphical' methods adequately deal with the issue of time. The major reason for this seems to be that many of the mainstream formal methods (on which the graphical techniques are

---

[1] Particularly where 'non-technical' staff (i.e. those who don't have the skills necessary to read specifications written in a particular formal language) need to understand the specification.

mostly based) do not, in their 'basic' versions, possess any notion of time, although it has been recognised that in some systems, the specification of timeliness properties is needed (particularly in safety-critical systems, which are often time critical) [10], therefore provision for representing time has been made in extensions to some of the well-known formal languages [5, 6, 7, 1].

This paper describes one possible approach to representing timing constraints graphically, but in a way that also permits them to be transformed into Z. The causal timing diagrams described in this study are based upon timing diagrams, a technique used by electronic engineers to describe the temporal properties of digital devices. It is the thesis of this paper that these diagrams can be adapted for use in software engineering environments. Section 2 gives an informal overview of the timing diagrams that we propose, and indicates how they differ from those used by electronic engineers. Section 3 describes the formal representation of the causal timing diagrams, briefly summarises a technique for representing time in Z, and indicates how a mapping from the diagrams to the Z specification language might be achieved. Finally, Section 4 gives a summary, and outlines possible future directions for research.

2. Overview of Timing Diagrams

Our aim here is to give an informal overview of the expressiveness of causal timing diagrams, and to explain the reasons for some of the more significant design decisions. These design decisions are mostly manifested in the differences between the diagrams given here, and those used by electronic engineers.

Timing diagrams have been used by electronic engineers for some time as a means of describing the behaviour of digital circuits (see, for instance [16]). While the approach that is being taken here bears some similarities to that used in electronics design (indeed the approach described here was inspired by electronic timing diagrams), there are a number of significant differences between the two approaches, specifically:

- Causal timing diagrams show a much more explicit causal relationship (e.g. If this set of events occur, that event will result) which assists in the specification of the system under consideration, whereas the timing diagrams of electronics show an example of the system's behaviour over time, which is extrapolated to give a general view of timing behaviour. The electronic diagrams could be represented as a causal timing diagram, but to do this it would be necessary to insert a 'cause line' to indicate which part of the diagram is cause and which is effect.

- The 'state space' of the method described here is discrete, but consists of arbitrarily many states, unlike the electronics timing diagrams where the state space ostensibly deals with only two states, but these two states are treated in a 'continuous way', for example the voltage thresholds to change from one state to another will typically be some fractional distance between the two states.

- The temporal domain of the electronics timing diagram is considered to be 'real time', whereas the abstraction of timing grids (a form of discrete time) is used to represent time here.

- The technique described here can be represented formally, unlike the electronics model, which, apparently, possesses no formal model[2].

In order to put the concepts presented here into context, an example of a timing diagram is given. Suppose access to a single lane road is controlled by traffic lights on the east and west sides of the lane. Figure 1 shows that a vehicle arriving from the west is sufficient to cause the lights at the east to change from green (via amber) to red. Time constraints on this are represented as horizontal lines at the bottom of the diagram, for which the dashed vertical lines provide the start and end points. The measurements state that EastLight has the value Amber for a period of exactly 'ChangeTime', and that the time between the rising edge of WestSensor, and EastLight becoming Amber is less than or equal to 'StartChange'. The dotted vertical line shows the separation between cause and effect, and the annotation 'SC' indicates that the cause is a sufficient condition for the effect. The dashed horizontal lines in WestSensor indicate where the behaviour of WestSensor is no longer considered relevant. The text 'Local' in the top left of the diagram indicates the timing grid which is used to measure time.

Local

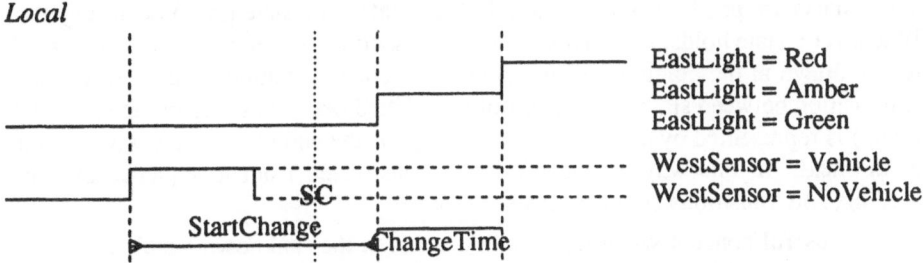

EastLight = Red
EastLight = Amber
EastLight = Green

WestSensor = Vehicle
WestSensor = NoVehicle

Figure 1: Fragment of East/West Traffic Controller Specification

In order to gain a complete picture of the use of causal timing diagrams for temporal specification, there are four main areas which must be elaborated upon, these being:

① How states are represented.

② The issues of representing causality.

③ Using time grids to represent time.

④ Describing deadlines with measurements.

---

[2] After surveying the literature, we could find no references to published models of the semantics of timing diagrams.

2.1. Representation of States

One of the basic concepts of causal timing diagrams is representing the states, and transitions between states for entities within the specification. It will be noted that transitions only ever occur between certain subsets of all of the states in a diagram. These subsets are termed **state groups**, and are perhaps most easily thought of as the states which can be reached by a state machine typically representing some physical entity in the environment of the computer system.

In the definition of causal timing diagrams given here, a state is considered to hold whenever a given predicate is true for a particular variable. A state group is defined by a countable set of mutually exclusive predicates which all refer to a given variable, and provide complete coverage of the variable (i.e. for any value of the variable, exactly one of the predicates will hold). It should be seen that constructing a state group from predicates on a variable is more flexible than considering that a state holds when a variable is equal to some value, since this permits causal timing diagrams to encompass variables of types which are infinitely large (although the example given in Figure 1 uses only equality).

The predicate corresponding to each state is assigned a position on the vertical axis. States are positioned such that all of the states in a state group occur together. Whenever a state holds, a horizontal line (representing the period that the state holds for) is drawn at the height corresponding to the state's position on the vertical axis. A transition between states (which is only permitted between states in the same state group) is represented by a vertical line which joins the end of one state with the start of the next. In this way, a 'waveform' is constructed from a sequence of states holding, and transitions between states.

A useful concept when representing states is the 'unknown state', where it is not necessary to know which state out of a given group is holding. This is represented as a dashed horizontal line in each of the states of a state group. It suggests that the state which is currently holding might be any of the states in the group. While the waveform is in this condition the state may change any number of times.

A reduced form of the unknown state is for the dashed line only to be present in *some* of the states (at least two, otherwise it isn't an unknown state). This implies that although the state is unknown, it is not permitted to be in certain states.

2.2. Causality

An important concept which is embodied by causal timing diagrams is **causality**, where some condition is said to **cause** another. This concept permits us to frame our specifications in a behavioural way.

Causality has always been considered to be a difficult and controversial subject from the philosophical viewpoint, particularly when one attempts to describe any single event as the cause of some outcome. For instance, it can be seen that the statement "the fire was caused by a match" omits many details such as the match being alight, air being present together with someone to strike the match. This problem can be eliminated by adopting the notion of a causal field, suggested by

Mackie [11], where the field is a sub-set of all the possible conditions that might occur. Thus where causal timing diagrams specify computer systems, we consider the field to be "correctly functioning systems operating in the environment for which they were intended".

Further problems arise when we consider the exact relationship between cause and effect. One property of a causal relationship which is universally agreed on is that of temporal precedence (the cause must occur before the effect). However, if the cause and effect were to be expressed as predicates, how would the relationship between them be defined? One of the most common interpretations is for the cause to logically imply the effect, which could be stated as "the cause is sufficient for the effect". Other relationships which may be used in such a temporal specification are that the cause is necessary for the effect (cause $\Leftarrow$ effect), or that the cause is sufficient and necessary for the effect (cause $\Leftrightarrow$ effect). A further relationship which might also be represented is the INUS (Insufficient and Necessary part of an Unnecessary and Sufficient) condition [8]. An example of INUS conditions are the predicates $A..H$, below:

$$(A \wedge B \wedge C) \vee (D \wedge E \wedge F) \vee (G \wedge H) \Leftrightarrow \text{Effect}$$

Here, each disjunct is sufficient, but not necessary to cause the effect, and each conjunct within a disjunct is necessary, but not sufficient for that disjunct to cause the effect. Since the timing diagram will only permit one to represent a conjunction of predicates as a cause or an effect, it will not be possible to represent an INUS condition as one diagram. Instead a number of diagrams, one for each disjunct of the INUS condition, are required, each with an identical effect part, and some means of establishing a relationship between the diagrams. This relation is provided by the causal relationship being written as $INUS_i$, where i is an identifier for a particular INUS condition.

When a group of diagrams are given as an INUS condition in the way suggested above, each diagram introduces an abstract state, S, which is given as if it is a necessary and sufficient effect of the cause part of the diagram and is therefore represented as follows:

$$\text{Cause} \Leftrightarrow S$$

The abstract states from each diagram in a complete INUS condition are disjoined to give a necessary and sufficient condition for the effect:

$$(S_1 \vee S_2 \vee \cdots \vee S_n) \Leftrightarrow \text{Effect}$$

As indicated above, to determine the predicate which represents the cause or effect in a causal timing diagram, we derive a predicate which describes the progression of states for each waveform, and conjoin them. For instance, the cause of Figure 1 could be represented from a trace of values as follows:

$$\text{EastLight}(1) = \text{Green} \wedge$$
$$\text{WestSensor}(1) = \text{NoVehicle} \wedge$$

WestSensor(2) = Vehicle

Also conjoined with this predicate must be any relationships between different waveforms (for instance, both waveforms changing state "at the same time"), and any measurements ending in this part of the causal relationship.

2.3. Time Grids

One of the major problems facing the specifier of a distributed system is in dealing with the problems of unsynchronised clocks. To provide a solution to this problem, the notion of **time grids** has been introduced [2, 9]. A time grid is defined as "the set of points on the timeline, equidistant except for small variations in the clock speed". Using this abstraction permits us to view a single continuous timeline as an arbitrary number of unrelated discrete timelines. The major property possessed by a time grid is its granularity (the distance between adjacent points). It is the granularity of a time grid which permits us to control the precision of time measurements that may be made (i.e. measurements may be made with a precision of ± the granularity divided by 2). The granularity also allows a control on the level of atomicity of behaviour to be made, since all than one actions occurring between two adjacent 'ticks' are treated as atomic with respect to that grid. Similarly, two actions occurring 'simultaneously' with respect to a grid can occur at slightly differing times.

There will be typically, more than one time grid in a system, for instance there may be one grid per processor clock (the local grid), another grid based upon the scheduling of activities, and another which describes system-wide operation.

Grids also provide an attribute which may be exploited later in the life-cycle, namely that the error in time measurement allows temporal specifications to be experimentally verified. A more extensive treatment of grids could be given, suffice to say that they are a useful abstraction and formalisation of concepts used in the building of practical real-time distributed systems.

2.4. Time Measurement

Time measurement is the thing that differentiates real-time system specification from other types of behavioural specifications. It is clear that its major pre-requisite is some form of clock, which is provided by the time grids.

It is important to consider how measurements of time must be made. The approach which has been adopted here is for a measurement to start and finish at transitions between states (normally between two known states, but in some cases, a transition between a known and an unknown state, or vice-versa is possible). The period described by the interval between the start state and end state must be compared with a duration (expressed as an integral number of ticks of the given time grid). Four types of comparison are possible, and, in causal timing diagrams represented by different types of horizontal line drawn between the start and end transitions. These are shown in Table 1, below:

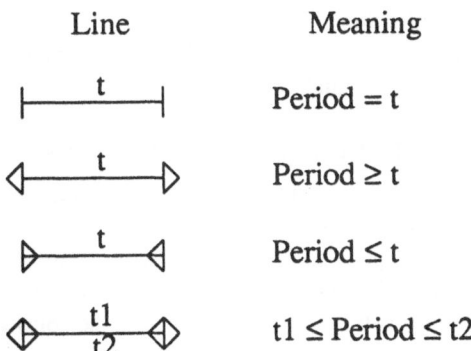

Line	Meaning
	Period = t
	Period ≥ t
	Period ≤ t
	t1 ≤ Period ≤ t2

Table 1: Measurement Types

If it is necessary to express the constraint that a given interval is greater than (or less than) some period, it can be accomplished by taking one from (or adding one to) the period. This is possible due to the discrete nature of time grids.

When a state changes from a definite state to an indefinite state, the implication is that a state change **may** take place at some time after the end of the definite state (since an indefinite state bracketed by two identical states may contain zero state changes.) The reverse holds true for a change from an indefinite state to a definite one. Thus the only type of measurements which can begin or end with a change to/from an indefinite state are the second and third in table 1. Of these the second can only begin with a change from indefinite to definite or end with a definite/indefinite change, and the third can begin with a definite/indefinite change or end with an indefinite/definite one. The reason for this restriction is primarily because the use of other measurement types in these cases would require the indefinite intervals to include at least one transition (which cannot be guaranteed by their definition).

3. Generating a Formal Specification from a Diagram

The process of generating a formal temporal specification from a causal timing diagram requires three components:

1) A formal definition of the syntax of the diagram.

2) A specification technique for expressing temporal requirements formally

3) A translation process to convert from 1) to 2). This gives us a specification for tool support, and also defines the semantics of the diagram.

These three components are described in greater detail in Section 3.1, 3.2, and 3.3 respectively.

Each of the above three components can be described in the Z specification language [15]. Z has been chosen for this purpose for a variety of reasons, namely: Z is one of the more widely used specification languages, which benefits from well defined semantics [14] and widespread tool support; it provides a means for structuring specifications, and extensions have been suggested for the representation of time (specifically the Itrace concept, which is the approach taken here). This concept underpins a novel interval logic. A non-standard logic is needed in order to cater for the real-world concerns of grids.

3.1. Formal Definition of a Causal Timing Diagram

There are two major benefits of giving a formal definition of syntax for causal timing diagrams: it allows us to give an unambiguous statement of the rules for constructing causal timing diagrams, and it gives us an entity which is subject to formal manipulation. The formal definition of the diagram also establishes a partial ordering of state transitions, which consists of the following four points:

1. A total ordering exists between transitions within the same waveform, specifically for any two transitions, the one of the left occurs 'earlier' that the one on the right.

2. A total ordering exists between all transitions and the 'initial' state (i.e. the state at the left hand edge of the diagram).

3. All transitions in the cause part of the diagram occur before all transitions in the effect part of the diagram.

4. The transition which is used to mark the start of measurement occurs earlier than the transition which marks the end of the corresponding measurement.

3.2. Representing Timing Constraints in Z

The approach adopted to describe time constraints in Z is the **Itrace** [3]. Briefly, an Itrace represents a history of a variable by a mapping from non-overlapping, closed intervals of time to a value from the type of the variable[3]. The advantages of this approach are that it is an intuitive representation of time, which works well with the time grids paradigm, it is suitable for the existing semantics of Z and the 'mapping' approach gives a convenient way of determining the state of the entire system at any given point in time (usually such points will be drawn from one of the time grids, and only applied to appropriate Itraces).

The model of time underlying the Itraces is a linear, dense time, with a start point and no end point to reflect the behaviour of most real-time systems, which can use their start point as a reference point, but have no way of determining how long they will remain in an operating state. Another useful property of the model of time is the existence of atomic intervals (i.e. intervals which cannot be subdivided), which allow time points to be represented (essential for time grids).

The Z 'toolkit' which defines Itraces also provides a number of useful operations for manipulating them, such as:

---

[3] The use of non-overlapping points in time necessarily implies that even with 'adjacent' intervals, there will be some 'gap' between the intervals. At the lowest level of abstraction, this can correspond to those times in which a state transition takes place.

when *Itrace* **is** *value*. This returns the set of intervals which indicate that a given Itrace has a particular value or values.

*n*th *Itrace* **After** *interval*. This gives the interval, which represents the 'nth' interval in the Itrace after some interval (there is also a 'Before' version of this function, which works in the opposite way).

Itrace@Interval. This returns the value of the Itrace at some point in time defined by the interval. The interval should occur during one of the intervals in the domain of the Itrace.

Interval1⊔Interval2. This returns the smallest interval which contains both interval 1 and interval 2 (called interval compose).

start *Interval*, **end** *Interval*. These two functions return the start and end points (respectively) of intervals.

Interval1 **before** *Interval2*. An asymmetric, strict partial ordering over intervals.

3.3. Converting Causal Timing Diagrams to Itraces

The process of generating temporal specifications from causal timing diagrams (or at least the formal representation of the diagrams) is a procedure which is easily comprehended. However, as one considers all of the detail necessary to generate such a specification, the process becomes inevitably more complex.

It is desirable for the translation to be given formally, since this gives an unambiguous, provable translation process. Although, for our purposes here, an informal description of the translation process is much better suited, due to its brevity.

Each part of the process results in one or more predicates, each of which is either associated with the cause or effect. Each of the predicates in the cause and effect are conjoined, which results in two predicates: one for cause, and one for effect. The relationship between cause and effect is based upon the causality type, as described in Section 2.2. As it is sometimes necessary for a diagram's cause and effect to be predicated over the same variables, it is generally most convenient for a single diagram to be represented by a Z schema. The only exception to this rule is the INUS condition, where the variables of each cause will be shared the single common effect, thus the entire INUS condition (several diagrams) is represented by a single schema.

Specifying a sequence of (known) states is achieved by use of a variable defined to be the interval when the first state holds. From Figure 1, the two initial states are defined as follows:

$$i \in \textbf{when } \tau \textsf{EastLight is \{Green\}}$$

$$j \in \textbf{when } \tau \textsf{WestSensor is \{NoVehicle\}}$$

(note that, by convention, the Itrace of a variable is named by prefixing a τ to the variable name.) Subsequent known states are given as follows:

1st τEastLight After i ∈ **when** τEastLight **is** {Amber}

2nd τEastLight After i ∈ **when** τEastLight **is** {Red}

1st τWestSensor After j ∈ **when** τWestSensor **is** {Vehicle}

When a period of non-determinism (i.e. unknown states) is shown on the diagram, it will not be referred to explicitly. However, it can be indirectly alluded to, since there will be a variable for the sequence of states before the non-determinism and one associated with the state sequence which follows it. For example, between intervals i and j, only states a and b out of a possible set {a,b,c} are permitted.

$$\forall \text{ x : INTERVAL} \,|\, \textbf{start}\, i\, \textbf{before end}\, j \wedge x\, \textbf{during}\, i \sqcup j \bullet$$

$$x \in \textbf{when}\, \tau S\, \textbf{is}\, \{a,b,c\}$$

Measurements are a further source of predicates. To make measurements, the function **period** is used (in practice, a different period function is used for every time-grid). Each measurement must show temporal precedence of the start and end of the measurement. Typically, this is conjoined with the actual measurement, however if the measurement is the third type shown in Table 1, this precedence relation implies the measurement.

Using the rules described above, the formal specification of Figure 1 can be given as:

Light ::= Red | Amber | Green | RedAmber

Sensor ::= Vehicle | NoVehicle

```
┌─ Constraint ──────────────────────────────┐
│                                            │
│  τEastLight : Itrace Light                 │
│  τWestSensor : Itrace Sensor               │
│  StartChange, ChangeTime : ℕ               │
│ ├──────────────────────────────           │
│                                            │
│  ∀ i : when τEastLight is {Green};         │
│    j : when τWestSensor is {Vehicle} •     │
│       1st dom τWestSensor Before j ∈        │
│       when τWestSensor is {NoVehicle} ⇒     │
│          (start j before end i ⇒            │
│                 period (start j ⊔ end i) ≤  │
│                 StartChange) ∧              │
│          period (1st dom τEastLight After i) = │
│          ChangeTime ∧                       │
│          1st dom τEastLight After i ∈        │
│          when τEastLight is {Amber} ∧        │
│          2nd dom τEastLight After i ∈        │
│          when τEastLight is {Red}            │
│                                            │
└────────────────────────────────────────────┘
```

4. Conclusion

The specification of timing requirements can be a complex task, especially if the requirements are to be both understandable and unambiguous to the largest possible audience. This difficulty is exacerbated by the use of formal methods (that is not to say that other difficulties are not reduced as a consequence, however.) From the work described here, it seems that temporal specifications can be made more understandable using causal timing diagrams, while permitting them to be formalised at the same time.

It is intended that the approach described in this paper will form one facet of a method for specifying safety critical systems from an 'engineering' viewpoint. Each component of this method will be given a formal semantics in the Z specification language, which will provide a common basis for validation and formal refinement of specifications. Hence, future work will focus upon the issues of providing the other aspects of the method, and integrating them. An additional goal will be to provide a full, formal description of the transformation process.

Acknowledgements

This work was funded by the SERC-funded grant GR/F 01871 and by the British Aerospace Dependable Computer Systems Centre. We are also grateful to Philip Morris for enlightening discussions on causality.

References

1. J. Bowen, "Specification of Timing Constraints", *Z Forum Electronic Newsletter* 1(6) (May 1986).

2. Alan Burns and Andrew Lister, "A Framework for Building Dependable Systems", *The Computer Journal* 34(2), pp. 173-181, BCS (April 1991).

3. A. Coombes and J. McDermid, "Specifying Temporal Requirements for Distributed Real-Time Systems in Z", YCS 176, Department of Computer Science, University of York (July 1992).

4. A. C. Coombes and J. A. McDermid, "A Tool for Defining the Architecture of Z Specifications", pp. 77-92 in *Z User Workshop, Oxford 1990*, ed. J. E. Nicholls, Springer-Verlag, Oxford, UK (December 1990).

5. J. Davies and S. Schneider, "An Introduction to Timed CSP", PRG-75, Programming Research Group, Oxford University (August 1989).

6. M Diss, P Goldsack, P Harry, S Tubb and T Rush, *A Model for the Technology Transfer of Formal Method Techniques*, Information Systems Centre, HP Labs, Bristol (1989).

7. Duke, R. and Smith, G., "Temporal logic and Z specifications", *Australian Computer Journal* 21(2), pp. 62-6, Twelfth Australian Computer Science Conference (May 1989).

8. Jaegwon Kim, "Causes and Events: Mackie on Causation", pp. 48-62 in *Causation and Conditionals*, ed. Ernest Sosa, Oxford University Press (1975).

9. H. Kopetz, G. Fohler, H. Kantz et al., *Specification and Design for Timeliness PDCS Report, Subtask B2*, York, April 7th 1990.

10. N Leveson, "The Challenge of Building Process-Control Software", *IEEE Software* 7(6), pp. 55-62 (November 1990).

11. J. L. Mackie, "Causes and Conditions", pp. 15-38 in *Causation and Conditionals*, ed. Sosa, Oxford University Press, London (1975).

12. MoD, *Interim Defence Standard 00-55: Requirements for the Procurement of Safety Critical Software*, 1991.

13. Gill Randell, "Translating Data Flow Diagrams into Z (and vice-versa)", 90019, Royal Signals and Radar Establishment, Malvern (October 1990).

14. J. Michael Spivey, *Understanding Z: A Specification Language and its Formal Semantics*, Cambridge University Press, UK (January 1988).

15. J. M. Spivey, *The Z Notation: A Reference Manual*, Prentice-Hall, Hemel Hempstead, Hertfordshire HP2 4RG, UK (1989).

16. John F. Wakerly, *Digital Design Principles and Practices*, Prentice Hall (1990).

FORMAL METHODS IN THE SPECIFICATION OF REAL-TIME, SAFETY-CRITICAL CONTROL SYSTEMS

Alastair R. Ruddle

Future Systems Group, Marconi Radar and Control Systems Ltd
New Parks, Leicester, LE3 1UF, UK

Abstract

An assessment of the relative merits of two formal methods in the specification of real-time, safety-critical control systems is presented. This case study was based on a simplified pollution monitoring and control sub-system for road tunnels, and the requirements were specified using TEMPURA and Z. It is concluded that TEMPURA currently offers greater potential for use in real-time systems development since it provides a means of describing dynamic, parallel processes and utilises a notation which is more accessible to the non-specialist than Z. However, further developments of Z to meet these shortcomings, or requirements for greater formality in real-time systems development, could alter the balance if the existing weaknesses of TEMPURA in areas such as structuring, proof and refinement are not addressed.

1   Introduction

Although formal methods have been the subject of much research effort in the academic community, potential users in the electronic systems industry have been rather more sceptical about these techniques. There is considerable confusion as to the nature, applications and possible benefits of formal methods, and consequently little confidence in the value of experimentation in this field. It is a widely held belief that formal methods can only increase the overall development costs by adding a lengthy, academic exercise to the early stages of the project. Nonetheless, increasing recognition of the problems of effective requirements capture, software maintenance, and quality issues in general are leading to greater interest within the industry.

This is particularly true for real-time control systems, where the potential for tragedy is clearly enormous with aircraft, nuclear power stations, chemical plants and many other potentially hazardous applications relying on electronic control. In order for formal methods to be adopted for these applications it is first necessary to establish:

(a)   which methods are best suited to the analysis of these types of problems;
(b)   that these techniques are accessible to engineers who typically have backgrounds in electronics and physics rather than computer science and pure mathematics.

An attempt to address these issues has been carried out as part of REDO (project P2487 of the ESPRIT programme), a CEC supported collaborative project which was primarily concerned with software maintenance issues and the development of reverse engineering techniques.

2   Preliminary Investigations

An initial study [1] was concerned with the development of a specification for a radar track former using the Z notation [2]. Although this application places constraints on the time available to perform the necessary computations, there is no requirement for the more complex interactions which occur in real-time control systems. A subsequent evaluation [3] was based on the application of three different techniques to a standard numerical procedure, Gaussian Elimination with partial pivoting, which is routinely employed in the solution of large systems of linear equations [4]. These problems occur in many fields of engineering, such as network analysis, various applications of field modelling (eg. stress, thermal and electromagnetic) and regression techniques in statistical analysis. The methods which were the subject of this work included the Z notation, an algebraic technique [5] and TEMPURA [6], an executable language based on interval temporal logic. The latter was of particular interest as it seemed more relevant to the description of dynamical, real-time systems. The resulting specifications were also encoded using the programming language C, in order to investigate the problems of generating usable code from the different forms of specification.

The results of the second study indicated that while code generated from both the Z and TEMPURA specifications offer similar levels of efficiency, the development effort associated with the Z approach is significantly higher. The code derived from the algebraic specification, however, was found to require still more effort in development than Z and resulted in a program with a very much lower level of efficiency than either Z or TEMPURA. Furthermore, TEMPURA appeared to be the most accessible of the three descriptions to engineers, since the form of the statements is very similar to a programming language.

This may also account for the easier development of code from this type of specification. Thus, the executable languages which are based on Z and the algebraic technique (ie. Z-- [7] and OBJ [8]), may make the development of code from these specifications easier. However, neither of these investigations serves to illustrate the utility of these techniques in dealing with real-time control problems.

3 Real-time Systems

In applications such as data processing timing requirements are of secondary importance to the accuracy and correct ordering of computations. Temporal constraints then only arise in the form of *non-functional requirements*, such as the acceptable response time of a system with a particular hardware configuration. Although these features are important aspects of the specification, they do not directly influence the system logic. Consequently, the need to formally demonstrate compliance with such requirements is not generally regarded as a key activity for the development of such systems. These applications are sometimes described as *soft real-time*, since failure to meet the deadlines does not result in an error or system failure.

Control systems, however, are subject to more significant restrictions on information flow. This arises from the limited availability of communications channels, sensors and actuators, and from the physical laws governing the processes involved. Thus, in these applications the relative timing of processes cannot really be regarded as non-functional. Providing a result at the right time can be more important than ensuring the correctness of the result, since more accurate values can be provided later. Inability to meet the timing constraints, however, may result in catastrophic system failures. Thus, timing constraints are not peripheral issues for these *hard real-time* systems: they are key features of the system which must be satisfied. In order to be successful in these applications formal methods must provide a more reliable and efficient way of establishing these properties than conventional empirical techniques, such as testing and walk-throughs.

A further consequence of control system time constraints is that the durations of individual processes become significant parameters. Even carefully designed systems may well be subject to unpredictable disturbances, which make the quantification of process durations somewhat difficult. Thus, it would be desirable to provide some form of self-awareness in systems which can tolerate a degree of error. If it is not possible to obtain the correct results in the given time it may be acceptable, provided that the system exhibits a reasonable level of stability, to utilize less accurate but readily available results. For example, part of a recent set of sensor readings recorded by a monitoring system could be used for control purposes if it is not possible to obtain the current values from all of the instruments within the available time. This would permit a gradual degradation of performance which would reduce the possibility of system failure as well as providing a mechanism for fault recovery.

In order to investigate the utility of formal methods in the specification of real-time control system requirements, a further comparison was carried out [9], using a more representative case study. This work was based on a simplified requirement derived from a pollution monitoring and control application. The specification languages selected for evaluation in this case were Z and TEMPURA.

4   The TEMPURA Specification

Tunnel air quality control can be considered in terms of two concurrent processes: continuous monitoring of the various pollutants, and automatic control of the ventilation system. In all practical situations this monitoring activity also represents a number of concurrent processes, as measurements will gathered from a number of separate instruments. At the highest level a TEMPURA specification for this system could be:

$$POLL\_SYSTEM \equiv INITIALIZE \; ; \; [repeat \; MONITORING \; until \; UNSAFE] \wedge$$
$$[while \; (mode=0) \; do \; AUTOCONTROL].$$

Thus, *MONITORING* and *AUTOCONTROL* are parallel processes which succeed the initialisation of various system variables (*INITIALIZE*). Termination occurs under the condition *UNSAFE*, and automatic control is suspended when the system is placed under manual control (ie. *mode=1*).

The system is required to calibrate the N instruments at regular intervals, and calculate time averaged values in between these calibrations, which are described by *CALIBRATE(i)*. Thus, the calibration interval ΔT is also the interval length of the *MONITORING* process:

$$MONITORING \equiv len(\Delta T) \wedge MON(1) \wedge MON(2) \wedge ... \wedge MON(N).$$

Since the various instruments are likely to be based on different physical principles, the time τ_i required to carry out a calibration may be unique to that type of instrument. If the reading $current_i$ obtained during calibration is outside the range $calval_i \pm \delta_i$, then the operator must be informed within a period τ_D. The pollution state is indicated by the variables $state_i$, which are assigned a value '0' initially, changing to '1' if a critical level $uprlim_i$ is exceeded and remaining at 1 until the level falls below the reset threshold $lwrlim_i$. This introduces some hysteresis into the system so that the fans are not switched on and off as the levels fluctuate around the trigger points. It is assumed here that if any instrument fails the calibration then both the $state_i$ and the record $count_i$, which gives an indication of the length of time over which $state_i=1$ holds, are maintained at their previous values. This allows some recovery from transient calibration faults with little disruption to system operation.

The condition *UNSAFE* occurs when $count_i$ exceeds the exposure limit $timlim_i$ for all of the monitored pollutants. Thus, if cal_error_i represents a message describing a calibration failure in sensor i, the procedures *MON(i)* are given by:

$MON(i) \equiv len(\tau_i) \wedge CALIBRATE(i) ; [$
          if $[(current_i > cal\_val_i - \delta_i) \wedge (current_i < cal\_val_i + \delta_i)]$
          then $[len(\Delta T - \tau_i) \wedge AVERAGE(i)]$
          else [
               $len(\tau_D) \wedge display(cal\_error_i) \wedge (state_i \leftarrow state_i) \wedge$
                   $(count_i \leftarrow count_i) ;$
               $len(\Delta T - \tau_i - \tau_D)$
          ]
     ].

The procedure *AVERAGE(i)* can be described in terms of *READ(i)*, an operation which causes a reading to be taken in a time σ_i. A total of m_i readings are taken at intervals of σ_i to compute the value $average_i$, and if this average exceeds the value $intlim_i$ a report ($report_i$) must be displayed, as well as the averaged level. Similarly, if $count_i$ exceeds $timlim_i$ the operators must be alerted to the hazard by displaying $alert_i$. This process may then be repeated up to n_i times before the next calibration is initiated, thus allowing for possible variations in the time required to compute and analyze each average. Thus:

$AVERAGE(i) \equiv (j=1) \wedge$ *while* $(j \leq n_i)$ *do* [
          $ESTABLISH\_MODE \wedge (sum_i=0) \wedge$ *for* m_i *times do* [
               $len(\sigma_i) \wedge READ(i) \wedge (sum_i \leftarrow sum_i + current_i)$
          ] ; $(average_i = sum_i \div m_i) \wedge$ [
               if $(average_i > intlim_i)$
               then [
                   $EVALUATE(i) ;$
                   $len(\tau_D) \wedge display(report_i, average_i)]$
               ]
               else [
                   if $(state_i=0)$
                   then $[skip \wedge (state_i \leftarrow state_i) \wedge (count_i \leftarrow count_i)]$
                   else $[skip \wedge (state_i \leftarrow 0) \wedge (count_i \leftarrow 0)]$
               ]
          ] ; [
               if $(count_i > timlim_i)$
                then $[len(\tau_D) \wedge display(alert_i, count_i) \wedge (j \leftarrow j+1)]$
               else $[skip \wedge (j \leftarrow j+1)]$
          ]
     ].

The procedure *ESTABLISH_MODE* allows the operators to alter the control mode by entering a suitable code, and this facility is made available every time an average is computed. If the required code is not entered within the allotted period then the control mode will remain unchanged until the option to make a change becomes available again, when the next average is computed.

The procedures *EVALUATE(i)*, which both switch the *state*$_i$ between normal and critical and increment the *count*$_i$ according to the most recent averaged values, are defined as:

EVALUATE(i) ≡   *if (average*$_i$*>uprlim*$_i$*)*
                   then [
                        if (state$_i$*=0)*
                        then [skip ∧ *(state*$_i$ ← *1)* ∧ *(count*$_i$ ← *1)]*
                        else [skip ∧ *(state*$_i$ ← *state*$_i$*)* ∧ *(count*$_i$ ← *count*$_i$*+1)]*
                   ]
                   else [
                        if (average$_i$*<lwrlim*$_i$*)*
                        then [
                             if (state$_i$*=1)*
                             then [skip ∧ *(state*$_i$ ← *0)* ∧ *(count*$_i$ ← *0)]*
                             else [skip ∧ *(state*$_i$ ← *state*$_i$*)* ∧ *(count*$_i$ ← *count*$_i$*)]*
                        ]
                        else [
                             if (state$_i$*=1)*
                             then [skip ∧ *(state*$_i$ ← *state*$_i$*)* ∧
                                  (count$_i$ ← *count*$_i$*+1)]*
                             else [skip ∧ *(state*$_i$ ← *state*$_i$*)* ∧ *(count*$_i$ ← *count*$_i$*)]*
                        ]
                   ].

In the automatic control mode the ventilation must be activated if any of the pollutants is in the critical state (ie. *state*$_i$*=1*), and must remain on until all pollutants are in the normal state (ie. *state*$_i$*=0*). The ventilation system must be switched on (*FAN_ON*) or off (*FAN_OFF*) within the period τ_C, and the flag *f* set to '1' or '0', respectively. The following procedure ensures that the fans are activated correctly under automatic control:

AUTOCONTROL ≡ *len(*τ_A*)* ; *[*
                   if [(state$_1$*=0)* ∧ *(state*$_2$*=0)* ∧ ... ∧ *(state*$_N$*=0)]*
                   then [
                        if (f=1)
                        then [len(τ_C*)* ∧ *FAN_OFF* ∧ *(f* ← *0)]*
                        else [skip ∧ *(f* ← *f)]*
                   ]
                   else [
                        if (f=0)
                        then [len(τ_C*)* ∧ *FAN_ON* ∧ *(f* ← *1)]*
                        else [skip ∧ *(f* ← *f)]*
                   ]
                   ].

It is assumed that the calibration times τ_i are small compared with the time taken to compute the averages, so that the interval τ_A for *AUTOCONTROL* may be set at an acceptable level in relation to the calibration interval and the time taken to compute the averaged readings. Provided that τ_C is also small in relation to the control interval τ_A, this should ensure that control decisions are made sufficiently often to maintain the air quality at an acceptable level.

5   The Z Specification

In order to develop a similar specification for this system in Z the concurrent processes associated with the various instruments are modelled by considering operations on the set of *Measured* pollutants, and on various derived subsets which depend on the state of individual pollutants. In addition to this, time is introduced as a variable *t*, where *Time≡N* so that it is discrete as in TEMPURA. The various arrays used to represent trigger levels and readings in the TEMPURA specification are now represented as indicated below:

$$
\begin{array}{|l}
\textit{Measured} : \ \textbf{P} \ \textit{Pollutants} \\[4pt]
\textit{lwrcal, uprcal, intlim, lwrlim, uprlim} : \ \textit{Pollutants} +\!\!\to \textbf{R} \\[4pt]
\textit{timlim} : \ \textit{Pollutants} +\!\!\to \textbf{N} \\[4pt]
\textit{current} : \ \textit{Pollutants x Time} +\!\!\to \textbf{R} \\[6pt]
\hline
\textit{Dom lwrcal} \ = \textit{Measured} \\[4pt]
\textit{Dom uprcal} \ = \textit{Measured} \\[4pt]
\textit{Dom intlim} \ = \textit{Measured} \\[4pt]
\textit{Dom lwrlim} \ = \textit{Measured} \\[4pt]
\textit{Dom uprlim} \ = \textit{Measured} \\[4pt]
\textit{Dom timlim} \ = \textit{Measured} \\[4pt]
\textit{Dom current} = \textit{Measured x Time}
\end{array}
$$

Pollutants for which the counter is being incremented are regarded as *Critical*, while those for which the counter is at zero are *Normal*. Clearly, the union of the these two sets must equal *Measured*, while the intersection must be empty. Thus, these three sets, together with the partial functions *average(p)* and *count(p)* define the abstract state of the system:

POLLUTION_STATE

Normal, Critical, Measured : $\mathbf{P}$ Pollutants

average : Pollutants $+\!\!\rightarrow$ $\mathbf{R}$

count : Pollutants $+\!\!\rightarrow$ $\mathbf{N}$

Dom average = Measured

Dom count   = Measured

Normal = {p:Pollutants | p∈Measured ∧ count(p)=0}

Critical = {p:Pollutants | p∈Measured ∧ count(p)>0}

Normal ∪ Critical = Measured

Normal ∩ Critical = φ

To accommodate the repetitions a number of **while..do** loops are introduced, as in [1], which are similar to the **DO** function of Z-- [7]. A possible Z specification could then be:

POLL_SYSTEM ≙   INITIAL_STATE ;
       while [∃p∈Measured • count(p)≤timlim(p)] **do**
          while [∃t, T_1, α:Time; i:$\mathbf{N}$ • T_1=i.α ∧ t≥T_1 ∧ t<T_1+α] **do**
             CALIBRATE_SYSTEM ;
             EVALUATE_CALS ;
             RESUME_MEASURING ;
             while [∃t, T_2, β:Time • t≥T_2 ∧ t<T_2+β] **do**
                AVERAGE_VALUES ;
                EVALUATE_AVERAGES ;
                ESTABLISH_MODE ;
                CONTROL_FANS
             end do
          end do
       end do.

Thus, following the initialisation of the system, the highest level loop of the specification is repeated until *count(p)* exceeds *timlim(p)* for all measured pollutants. The intermediate loop is enabled at intervals which correspond to the calibration period α, with the start time recorded as T_1, while the lowest level loop is executed over a period β measured from the time at which the system is returned to the monitoring mode (T_2). This loop is repeated several times, with the start time for each pass recorded as T_3.

For convenience the schemas *CALIBRATE_SYSTEM* and *RESUME_MEASURING*, which describe the instructions required to initiate calibration and return the instruments to monitoring mode, will not be defined here (as in the TEMPURA specification).

Each member p of *Measured* is represented by a unique sequence of characters (eg. CO, NO_2, SOOT) which identifies it to the operators. Similarly, each real number can also be represented by a unique sequence of characters. These features are expressed as partial and total injections:

> *name* : *Pollutants* $\rightarrowtail$ *Seq[Characters]*
>
> *value* : $\mathbf{R} \rightarrowtail$ *Seq[Characters]*
>
> ─────────────────────
>
> *Dom name* = *Measured*

It is also desirable to define a further type, *Message* $\equiv \mathbf{P}$ *Seq[Characters]*, so that messages for display to the operators may be constructed by concatenation of strings of text and the mappings *name(x)* and *value(x)*. Since the messages are required to be delivered within some predetermined time, it may be useful to consider a relation *Output: Time* $\longleftrightarrow$ *Message*, with elements *op* and projection functions *what(op)* and *when(op)*. The latter is actually an injection since only one message can be delivered at a time. Thus:

> *what* : *Output* $\rightarrow$ *Seq[Characters]*
>
> *when* : *Output* $\rightarrowtail$ *Time*
>
> ─────────────────────
>
> $\forall m{:}Measured;\ t{:}Time\ |\ (m,t)\in Output \bullet what(m,t)=m \wedge when(m,t)=t$

The state of the ventilation system and the control mode are recorded by the sequences of characters:

fan_status ::= <ON> | <OFF>,
con_mode ::= <MANUAL> | <AUTOMATIC>.

At the end of the calibration period τ it is necessary to evaluate the results to identify any failures and generate reports before monitoring continues. A new set *Failed* may be constructed which contains all members of *Measured* for which the calibration results are unsatisfactory. For each member of this set a report of the failure should issued within a time δ of completion of the calibrations at time $T_1+\tau$. Data is then collected from the remaining instruments for the calculation of new averaged values, and any significant results are reported to the operators within a time δ of the last readings used for the calculation of the averages (at time T_4). The details of these processes are described by the schemas *EVALUATE_CALS* and *AVERAGE_VALUES*.

The identification of instruments which fail calibration is described by:

EVALUATE_CALS

Ξ*POLLUTION_STATE*

Failed : $\mathbf{P}$ *Pollutants*

T_1, τ, δ : *Time*

Failed = {p:Pollutants | p$\in$Measured $\wedge$ [current(p,T_1+τ)>uprcal(p) $\vee$

$$current(p,T_1+\tau)<lwrcal(p)]\}$$

$\forall p \in$ *Failed • $\exists$op!:Output •*

   what(op!)=<CAL_ERROR_> $\frown$ name(p) $\wedge$ when(op!)<T_1+τ+δ

Calculation of the time averaged pollution levels for the remaining instruments is then defined by:

AVERAGE_VALUES

Δ*POLLUTION STATE*

Failed : $\mathbf{P}$ *Pollutants*

T_3, T_4', δ, σ : *Time*

$\forall p \in$ *Measured • count'(p)=count(p)*

$\forall p \in$ *Failed • average'(p)=average(p)*

$\exists t_1,...,t_n$:*Time • [$\forall j \in$ 1..n •*

   $t_j = T_3 + j.\sigma \wedge T_4' = t_n \wedge \forall p \in$ *Measured\Failed •*

   $$average'(p)=[\sum_{j=1}^{n} current(p,t_j)]\div n$$

   $\wedge$ *average'(p)>intlim(p) $\Rightarrow$ $\exists$op!:Output •*

      what(op!)=<NB:> $\frown$ name(p) $\frown$ <LEVEL=> $\frown$ value[average'(p)]

      $\wedge$ *when(op!)<T_4'+δ]*

Normal' = Normal

Critical' = Critical

Measured' = Measured

Evaluation of the new time averaged readings for control purposes is then described by:

EVALUATE_AVERAGES

ΔPOLLUTION_STATE

Up, Down, Failed: **P** *Pollutants*

T_4, δ : *Time*

$Up = \{p:Pollutants \mid p \in Normal\backslash(Normal \cap Failed) \wedge average(p) \geq uprlim(p)\}$

$Down = \{p:Pollutants \mid p \in Critical\backslash(Critical \cap Failed) \wedge$

$$average(p) \leq lwrlim(p)\}$$

$\forall p \in Measured \bullet average'(p) = average(p)$

$\forall p \in Critical\backslash[Down \cup (Critical \cap Failed)] \bullet count'(p) = count(p) + 1$

$\forall p \in Normal\backslash Up \bullet count'(p) = count(p)$

$\forall p \in Up \bullet count'(p) = 1$

$\forall p \in Down \bullet count'(p) = 0$

$Critical' = (Critical\backslash Down) \cup Up$

$\forall p \in Critical' \bullet$

   $count'(p) \geq timlim(p) \Rightarrow \exists op!:Output \bullet$

      $what(op!) = name(p) \frown <\_HAZARD:\_DURATION => \frown value[count(p)]$

      $\wedge when(op!) \leq T_4 + 2.\delta$

$Normal' = (Normal \cup Down)\backslash Up$

$Measured' = Measured$

The final operation (*CONTROL_FANS*) comprises three alternatives, which depend on the control mode and on the current system state. This operation is then described by:

CONTROL_FANS ≙ *FAN_ON* ∨ *FAN_OFF* ∨ *STABLE_FAN*.

The operations *FAN_ON* and *FAN_OFF*, detailing the instructions which switch the ventilation system either on or off within a specified time and reset the variable T_3, will not be defined here. However, the remaining operation *STABLE_FAN* can be defined as:

STABLE_FAN

$\Xi POLLUTION\_STATE$

fan_status, fan_status', con_mode : $\mathbb{P}$ *Seq[Characters]*

$T_3, T_3', \mu :$ *Time*

$\exists t$:*Time* •

    $(t < T_3 + \mu \wedge con\_mode = <\text{MANUAL}>) \vee$

        $t < T_3 + \mu \wedge con\_mode = <\text{AUTOMATIC}> \wedge [(Critical = \phi$

        $\wedge fan\_status = <\text{OFF}>) \vee (Critical \neq \phi \wedge fan\_status = <\text{ON}>)]$

        $\Rightarrow fan\_status' = fan\_status \wedge T_3' = t$

---

where μ is the maximum permitted time to complete one pass through the lowest level loop. The remaining operation *ESTABLISH_MODE* allows the operator to change the control mode by entering a code (*new_mode?*) within some specified interval. Failure to make an appropriate entry during this period leaves the mode unchanged.

6   Discussion

The two specifications outlined above, using TEMPURA and Z, are clearly not identical. Although it would be possible to establish a closer correspondence between them, the differences serve to illustrate the relative merits of the two techniques in the development of real-time control systems.

Systems such as the example considered here, which utilize inputs from a number of separate sources of similar status, possess an inherently parallel character which is likely to be reflected in any practical implementation. In addition to this, the complex interactions which must take place between the monitoring and control functions, as well as with human decision makers, make reliable scheduling of paramount importance. Thus, the facility to represent both time constraints and parallel processes in formal specifications are fundamental requirements for these applications.

The TEMPURA notation is based upon a subset of Interval Temporal Logic (ITL), such that every valid TEMPURA statement is also a formula of ITL. It differs from other forms of temporal logic, however, in that dynamic behaviour is described in terms of finite intervals rather than individual states or events. These intervals are constructed from non-empty sequences of states, or of sub-intervals.

Consequently, TEMPURA permits the construction of compact, hierarchical specifications which can be used to describe behaviour at different levels of abstraction. At the lowest level the individual states correspond to separate instances of time, so that time in this framework is discrete rather than continuous. This, however, is effectively the reality for most electronic control systems since they are normally based on a digital clock.

In Z the abstraction is provided by considering sets and functions, with the relationships between these structures described using schemas. The Z notation is strongly typed because of this use of set theory, with the result that all of the data types used in the specification must be explicitly defined. Despite the extra effort involved, this can lead to enhanced understanding of the system and the identification of reusable components. However, there are no inherent temporal features in Z, and composite operations can only be constructed by sequential composition. Nonetheless, the use of sets can provide a convenient way of describing some types of parallel processes.

In both of these specifications calibration of all the measuring instruments is initiated at the same time, and the intervals at which calibration must be performed are explicitly defined. Any failure to complete a calibration within the allocated time results in the relevant pollution state and duration record being frozen until the next calibration occurs. The sequential nature of the Z model also constrains the averaging and evaluation of results to occur simultaneously, and compels the control functions to be interleaved with these activities. The TEMPURA version, however, permits events to develop independently for each pollutant in between calibrations, as well as supporting a separate but concurrent control process. It would also be possible, in TEMPURA, to allow the calibration times to be uncorrelated if the system required all the instruments to operate independently. This richer behaviour can be conveniently described in TEMPURA because the notation supports both parallel and sequential composition. Attempting to model similar behaviour using the mechanisms available in notations such as Z would probably prove extremely cumbersome in any practical application.

This additional flexibility which is available in TEMPURA can allow for a more positive treatment of time constraints. For example, in the TEMPURA specification the delays between the detection and display of events are explicitly defined, while in the Z model these intervals are merely constrained not to exceed some maximum value. Although the time constraints which are applied to the system ensure that a minimum number of averaged values are collected between calibrations it is still possible, in both specifications, to increase the number of averages computed between calibrations if the level of analysis and the number of outputs required are low.

The description of system outputs is more sophisticated in the Z specification, where data for display is synthesized by the concatenation of strings of text and character sequences which represent values and names for the measured pollutants. In the TEMPURA specification these outputs are defined in terms of arrays of appropriate character strings, possibly coupled with the values associated with the relevant system variables. The potential for describing textual inputs is also greater in Z, for similar reasons.

7 Conclusions

The difficulties which are currently encountered in specifying, testing and modifying real-time systems suggest that formal methods are likely to become vital for these applications in the future. Specifications for such systems contain time constraints which are effectively functional requirements and must, therefore, be representable in any successful formal description. The ability to represent these features in a mathematical notation will automatically provide a mechanism for subsequently introducing the practical time constraints arising from the final implementation. This would then permit both logical reasoning about the consequences of the time constraints in the requirements, and formal validation of the final design against the initial specification.

The increasing use of parallel processing and distributed intelligence in order to meet the demands of complex applications makes the ability to model concurrent processes, which might not necessarily be synchronised, a vital requirement for the formal analysis of real-time systems. In addition to this, the ability to provide rapid prototyping and simulation, so that a specification may be developed interactively with the customer, suggests that an executable specification language would be a considerable advantage in industry. Currently, this facility could be provided by Z--, OBJ and TEMPURA. The transputer programming language OCCAM, which can describe parallel processes, has also been proposed for system prototyping [10], although the potential for representing time constraints is not addressed.

The availability of an executable prototype is potentially dangerous as it may be assumed, in the cost-conscious industrial environment, that such a specification will not permit undesirable consequences. Thus, the facility to formally prove the required properties of the specification takes on an even more important role in formal methods which can generate an executable specification. The procedures for proving properties are currently much better developed in Z than in TEMPURA. The latter may need to be reduced from the high level executable language down to the underlying interval temporal logic before formal manipulation can be carried out. Nonetheless, it should be possible to automate this procedure since TEMPURA compilers already perform a very similar operation in reducing the specification to the executable *normal* form. However, no attempt was made to prove the properties of either of the specifications described above. A proof system could perhaps be adapted specifically for TEMPURA from a generic model of temporal proof, a process which has already been demonstrated [11] for the CSP notation [12], on which OCCAM is based.

At present there is no established procedure for constructing a TEMPURA specification, and the process of mapping the specification to the required target language is also largely undefined. The structuring and refinement of Z specifications has been the subject of much research effort, so that this notation is at an advantage in these respects. However, the earlier work [3] indicated that code derived from the TEMPURA specification required much less development effort but provided a very similar efficiency to that derived from the equivalent Z specification.

It seems likely that the closer correspondence of TEMPURA statements to high level programming languages makes the process of transcription much easier in this case.

Despite the fact that features such as refinement, proof and structuring are less well developed in TEMPURA than in Z, the importance of temporal aspects and concurrency, coupled with a more accessible notation, currently make TEMPURA the more attractive of the two methods for engineers working on real-time control applications. Nonetheless, further developments in both the capabilities of Z (including tool support) and the demand for the use of more formal techniques in industry (eg. the proposed DEF STAN 00-55 requirement) may shift the balance away from TEMPURA. In the short term, the most effective means of exploiting these techniques is probably as a medium for describing the primitive process and controller specifications which are identified through the application of structured analysis. In the longer term, the availability of notations which can describe parallel processes, such as TEMPURA, may permit control engineers to formalise, and subsequently prove, the properties of these informal models.

Acknowledgement

The author is grateful to GEC-Marconi Limited for permission to publish this paper. The views expressed in the paper are the opinion of the author and are not necessarily the views of GEC-Marconi.

References

[1] Lano K. The Specification of a Real-Time System in Z. REDO Report 2487-TN-PRG-1015, Oxford University Computing Laboratory, Programming Research Group, 11 Keble Road, Oxford, OX1 3QD, UK, 1989

[2] Spivey M. The Z Notation: A Reference Manual. Prentice-Hall International Series in Computer Science, 1989

[3] Pearson DW. An Investigation of Formal Methods Techniques Applied to Industrial Software Development. REDO Report 2487-TN-MA-1037, Marconi Radar & Control Systems Ltd, Scudamore Road, New Parks, Leicester, LE3 1UF, UK, 1991

[4] Conte SD, de Beer C. Elementary Numerical Analysis. McGraw-Hill, 1980

[5] Woodcock J, Loomes M. Software Engineering Mathematics. Pitman, 1988

[6]   Moszkowski B. Executing Temporal Logic Programs. Cambridge University Press, 1986

[7]   Valentine S. Z--, an Executable Subset of Z. Z User Workshop, York, UK, 1991

[8]   Goguen JA, Winkler T. Introducing OBJ3. Technical Report SRI-CSL-88-9, Computer Science Laboratory, SRI International, 333 Ravenswood Ave, Menlow Park, CA 94025, USA, August 1988

[9]   Ruddle AR. An Assessment of Two Formal Methods in the Specification of a Real-Time, Safety-Critical Control System. REDO Report 2487-TN-MA-1038, Marconi Radar & Control Systems Ltd, Scudamore Road, New Parks, Leicester, LE3 1UF, UK, 1991

[10]   Fensome DA. The Transputer - A Prototyping Tool for Systems. Comp. & Cont. Eng. J., Vol.1 No.1, January 1990, pp.41-45

[11]   Manna Z, Pneuli A. How to Cook a Temporal Proof System for Your Pet Language. Proc. Symp. Principles of Programming Languages, Austin, Texas, January 1983, pp.141-154

[12]   Hoare CAR. Communicating Sequential Processes. Prentice-Hall International Series in Computer Science, 1985

Object-Oriented Systems

Introducing Hyper-Z –
a New Approach to Object Orientation
in Z*

I. Maung, J.R. Howse
Software Engineering Research Group
Departments of Computing and Mathematical Sciences
University of Brighton
Brighton BN2 4GJ
e-mail: im1@uk.ac.bton
jrh3@uk.ac.bton

Abstract

We introduce Hyper-Z, yet another object-oriented version of Z. Hyper-Z differs from standard Z, and other proposed OO extensions of Z, in that its semantics (non-well-founded sets) naturally and directly supports the specification of circularly defined objects and classes. This enables us to specify classes simply as (possibly self-recursive) schemas, and gives a very simple characterization of conformant inheritance as Z subtyping. It is also extremely close to standard Z, both in its syntax and semantics (axiomatic set theory).

Keywords   *Z, object-oriented, non-well-founded sets, subtyping, inheritance.*

1. Introduction

Hyper-Z can be viewed as an object-oriented extension of Z, in the same vein as MooZ [1], and Object-Z [2]. We adopt roughly the definition of object-orientation given in [3]p.60-62. Fundamental to Hyper-Z is the conviction that classes are just types (and that *type = module*, [3]p.61), that instances of a class are just values (we are aware that some authors use *instance* as a synonym for *object*) and that objects are just variables, whose type is just the class of the object. We adopt the view (originating

---

* This work was funded by SERC grant GR/H16629.

from [4]) of [5] that 'data abstraction (encapsulation) is an orthogonal concept to inheritance (structuring)' and we focus on structuring as in [5].

The formal specification of a class should contain at least the following:

- the name of the class and its ancestors (superclasses)
- the features (methods and attributes) of the class
- the signatures of its features (i.e. the classes of method arguments and results)

These appear even in the informal class specifications given in the Eiffel class library (see Appendix 1).

One of the main advantages of object-orientation is the facility for reuse of existing code. Extensive class libraries have been produced for the object-oriented software engineering languages, C++ and Eiffel [6]. In OOD-with-reuse, the software designer is encouraged to reuse classes in the library that are relevant (possibly in modified form) to their system. In order to do so, the designer must understand the functionality of the library classes. To ensure proper understanding, it is necessary to provide precise formal specifications of class libraries. The classes NUMERIC, INT, FLOAT, DFLOAT from the Eiffel class library [6] - are all defined circularly (see also Appendix 1). So, the formal specification of self-referential classes has significant practical importance. Such classes also have deep theoretical significance (see, for example, [7], [8], [9], [10], [11], [12], [13]).

We model values by non-well-founded sets[1], rather than well-founded sets as is conventionally done in Z semantics [14]p.14, [15]p.22-23. This allows us to model self-referential classes very naturally and directly within the framework of axiomatic set theory. The theory of non-well-founded sets has been successfully exploited for the modelling of circularly defined entities in other areas of theoretical computer science [16], [17]. A non-well-founded set is sometimes called a hyper-set, hence the name Hyper-Z.

As pointed out in [3] p. 61, in OO methodology, a class serves the dual role of type and module. The module aspects of a class in Hyper-Z are represented in the usual Z way i.e. a class is a schema. The methods and attributes of a class are encapsulated as the components of the schema

---

[1]I.e. sets in a universe, V, that is a model of ZF (without replacement and without FA) &AFA - see [16] for an explanation of this notation.

representing the class. (Note that a purely object-oriented specification will just be a collection of schemas – this guarantees encapsulation.)

Furthermore, in Hyper-Z, objects, classes and instances are all *first class values* and are not distinguished from normal Z variables, types and values respectively. Hence, all the usual schema operators apply to classes and instances and the standard type operators apply to classes. In this sense, Hyper-Z is purely object-oriented. Because of this, (behaviourally conformant) inheritance[18] is a simple generalization of schema inclusion, while the (behavioural) subtype relation between classes is just the subset relation between the non-well-founded sets denoting these classes[16].

Hyper-Z has a very simple semantics and logic (simply replace the Foundation Axiom FA by the Anti Foundation Axiom AFA in the semantics and logic (W) of Z). This is much cleaner (and much closer to the spirit of Z) than, say, the history semantics of Object-Z [2]. Hyper-Z is more expressive than Z and some of its OO extensions, because it allows classes to be circularly defined using self-reference (a natural requirement – see examples in section 2 below, and Appendix 1).

We do not treat semantic issues in detail in this paper. An understanding of axiomatic set theory and AFA is not necessary to comprehend this work. A more rigorous treatment appears in [19].

Our approach requires only minor modification of the current Z standard. In Z, schemas are all that is needed (indeed all that is available) for modularising specifications. Hyper-Z also uses only schemas, since it is unnecessary to introduce new notation for modules or classes. From the point of view of a user familiar with Z, there is very little new syntax or keywords or conventions to learn; she is merely able to write self-referential schemas which are not conventionally allowed in Z – Hyper-Z just provides her with extra expressive power.

In section 2, we show the Hyper-Z method for specifying classes by means of some simple examples. We introduce an inheritance operator in section 3, and apply it to the specification of some subclasses. The standard case study [5] for comparing OO variants of Z is specified in Hyper-Z in section 4.

2. Examples of classes defined in Hyper-Z

Hyper-Z is an extension of Z. Anything that can be written in Z can be written, *in exactly the same form*, in Hyper-Z. So in order to illustrate the original features of Hyper-Z we give examples of the definition of classes (recall that a class serves the dual role of type and module). In Hyper-Z classes are defined as (possibly) self-referential schemas. Such definitions are, strictly speaking, impossible in standard Z (see [15] p.28).

The following examples illustrate the ways in which classes are (circularly) defined as self-referential schemas in Hyper-Z[2].

Example 2.1   Natural Numbers

We now give an Eiffel class library style definition of a fictitious and very simple class, NAT:

```
Class NAT

      Ancestors of class NAT:

          No ancestors.


class  interface NAT exported  features
      succ, plus, val

feature   specification
      succ : NAT
          -- the successor of the current element
      plus (other : NAT) : NAT
          -- the sum of the current element and other
      val : BITS 32
          -- the natural's internal representation
end interface -- class NAT
```

We now formally specify the class NAT in Hyper-Z, using a natural number to model the value:

---

[2]Throughout this paper, we adopt the standard convention of using upper-case-only identifiers to denote types [20].

```
┌─NAT─────────────────────────────────────
│   val : N
│   succ : NAT
│   plus : NAT → NAT
│  ────────────────────────────────────────
│   succ.val = val + 1
│   ∀n : NAT • plus(n).val = n.val + val
└──────────────────────────────────────────
```

In OO parlance ([21], [3]), *val* is an instance variable/attribute of the class NAT, and *succ* and *plus* are its methods/features. NAT is both a subtype[3] (in the standard Z schema type sense) and a module encapsulating all the necessary information. The operations *succ* and *plus* of NAT are defined in terms of NAT in the definition of NAT – a natural object-oriented definition but impossible in standard Z, because the self-reference is not allowed in schema definitions.

We can simulate the definition of NAT in Z, by treating NAT as a basic type and imposing constraints on NAT to make it equivalent to our schema definition using an axiomatic box (see [15] p.106). A detailed discussion of this possibility appears in [19].

Example 2.2   Stack

```
┌─STACK[X]────────────────────────────────
│   contents: Seq X
│   pop : STACK[X]
│   top : X
│   push : X → STACK[X]
│  ────────────────────────────────────────
│   contents ≠ ⟨⟩ ⇒ (pop.contents = tail(contents)
│                         ∧ top = head(contents))
│   ∀x : X • push(x).contents = ⟨x⟩⌢contents
└──────────────────────────────────────────
```

---

[3]It is a subtype of T where
```
┌─T───────────────────
│   val:N
│   succ : T
│   plus : P(T×T)
└─────────────────────
```

154

The class STACK[X] is a generic class having a dummy parameter X. The methods *pop* and *push* include STACK[X] in their signatures, so, again, this is a circular definition of the class and not allowed (in schema form) in standard Z.

This example will be used later to illustrate Hyper-Z's inheritance mechanism.

Example 2.3 Point

The class POINT is defined as follows (assuming that the type REAL exists – it is a fairly easy exercise to define the reals in Z). POINT is the set of all points with x and y co-ordinates that know their distance from any other point.

```
┌─POINT──────────────────────────────────────────────
│   x,y : REAL
│   d : POINT → REAL
├─────────────────────────────────────
│   ∀p : POINT •
│       (d(p))² = (p.x - x)² + (p.y - y)² ∧ d(p) ≥ 0
└──────────────────────────────────────────────────
```

The metric *d* is defined in the standard way. This example will also be used to illustrate Hyper-Z's inheritance mechanism.

3. Inheritance in Hyper-Z

Inheritance is an essential feature of an object-oriented language (see [3] p.62, [22]). In Hyper-Z, inheritance is naturally represented as schema inclusion. This can occur with or without declaration type renaming. Since standard schema inclusion is only defined for non-recursive schemas, we extend the definition to self-recursive schemas. We will illustrate Hyper-Z's inheritance mechanism in the following examples.

Example 3.1 Person and student – adding attributes only

```
┌─PERSON──────────────────────────────────
│     Name : NAME
│     Age : AGE
│
└──────────────────────────────────────────
```

```
┌─STUDENT─────────────────────────────────
│     PERSON
│     Gpa : 1..5
│
└──────────────────────────────────────────
```

STUDENT inherits the attributes *Name* and *Age* from PERSON and adds the attribute *Gpa* (Grade point average).

Example 3.2   Movable Point - adding methods only

Given the class POINT defined above we can define the schema (class) MOVABLE_POINT by including (inheriting) the schema (class) POINT and defining the extra method move[4] .

```
┌─MOVABLE_POINT───────────────────────────
│     POINT
│     move : REAL × REAL → MOVABLE_POINT
├──────────────────────────────────────────
│     ∀a, b : REAL •
│        move(a,b).x = a + x ∧ move(a,b).y = b + y
└──────────────────────────────────────────
```

Note that the type of the argument of d (i.e. POINT) is the same as for the method, d, of POINT, since a movable point knows its distance from any point, movable or not.

---

[4]Note that we are using slightly non-standard schema semantics, to ensure that MOVABLE_POINT is actually a subset of POINT. This is explained fully in Appendix 2.

In Example 3.1 there was no need to rename any part of the inherited class; however, this is not true in general. In Example 3.3 we introduce the schema operator I (the upper-case Greek letter iota (for inherits!)).

Example 3.3 Deque - adding methods only

This is a classic inheritance example: deque inheriting from stack [23].

```
┌─DEQUE[X]──────────────────────────────────────────
│    I(STACK[X])
│    append :  X → DEQUE[X]
│    bottom : X
│    pull : DEQUE[X]
│ ──────────────────────────────────────────────────
│    contents ≠ ⟨⟩  ⇒  (pull.contents = front(contents)
│                              ∧ bottom = last(contents))
│    ∀x : X • append(x).contents = contents⌢⟨x⟩
└────────────────────────────────────────────────────
```

I(STACK[X]) is an abbreviation for STACK[X](DEQUE[X]/STACK[X]) i.e. STACK[X] schema with every occurence of STACK[X] replaced by DEQUE[X]. The formal semantics of I are clear from this definition. Hence DEQUE[X] is equivalent to:

```
┌─DEQUE[X]──────────────────────────────────────────
│    contents : Seq X
│    pop : DEQUE[X]
│    top : X
│    push : X → DEQUE[X]
│    append :  X → DEQUE[X]
│    bottom : X
│    pull : DEQUE[X]
│ ──────────────────────────────────────────────────
│    contents ≠ ⟨⟩  ⇒  (pop.contents = tail(contents)
│                          ∧ top = head(contents))
│    ∀x : X • push(x).contents = ⟨x⟩⌢contents
│    contents ≠ ⟨⟩  ⇒  (pull.contents = front(contents)
│                          ∧ bottom = last(contents))
│    ∀x : X • append(x).contents = contents⌢⟨x⟩
└────────────────────────────────────────────────────
```

If we treat inheritance as strict schema inclusion (as in Example 3.1 above), then it is clear that inheritance = subtyping in the behavioural conformance sense [24]. Furthermore, type conformance is respected since the signature of inherited methods is preserved. The I operator is analogous to the use of *like Current* in Eiffel type declarations.

We can only add methods and redefine existing ones by further constraining them (otherwise, the predicate part of the schema of the class derived by inheritance becomes false (this is the subtype proof obligation), and the derived class will be an empty class).

Example 3.4 Arbitrary (unconstrained) redefinition of a method

Arbitrary redefinition of methods results in empty classes. This is illustrated by the following example.

Redefine *bottom* to return the same value as *top*.

```
─NEWDEQUE[X]────────────────────────
    I(DEQUE[X])
  ────────────────────
    bottom = top
```

We show that NEWDEQUE[X]=∅.

∀d:NEWDEQUE[X] •
d.bottom=d.top ∧ d.contents≠⟨⟩⇒head(d.contents)=last(d.contents)=y.
Pick x≠y. Now, d.push(x).bottom=y ∧ d.push(x).top=x.
So, d.push(x).bottom ≠ d.push(x).top and hence
d.push(x)∉NEWDEQUE[X], a contradiction.
Hence, d.contents=⟨⟩. But then d.push(y)=⟨y⟩ and so if
d.push(y)∈NEWDEQUE[X], we can derive a contradiction as above.
Hence, NEWDEQUE[X]=∅.

Example 3.5 Constrained redefinition of a method

Suppose that the following class has been defined:

```
┌─ABSPOINT─────────────────────────────────────────────
│     x,y : REAL
│     d : ABSPOINT → REAL
├───────────────────────────────────────────────────────
│     ∀p : ABSPOINT •
│          d(p)=0 ⇔ x=p.x ∧ y=p.y
│          ∧ d(p)≥0
└───────────────────────────────────────────────────────
```

We can then define the class POINT as follows:

```
┌─POINT─────────────────────────────────────────────────
│     I(ABSPOINT)
├───────────────────────────────────────────────────────
│     ∀p : POINT •
│          (d(p))² = (p.x - x)² + (p.y - y)²
└───────────────────────────────────────────────────────
```

The method d has been further constrained in POINT but is still consistent with its definition in ABSPOINT.

We write

```
┌─Sub───────────────────────────────────────────────────
│     I(Super{method₁,. . . ,methodₙ})
└───────────────────────────────────────────────────────
```

to mean that we don't replace Super by Sub in the type declarations of $method_1, method_2, . . . , method_n$ and the corresponding type declarations appearing in the predicate part of Super.

This is useful for the situation where some of the methods of a superclass could violate the invariant of a subclass; see for example, RECTANGLE and PARALLELOGRAM in the case study in section 4.

4. A Case Study - Drawing Package

We now specify, in Hyper-Z, the Drawing Package case study from [5], which the authors used to compare the various OO versions of Z. The following schema is quoted from [5]:

```
┌─Edges─────────────────────────────────
│    edge: seq VECTOR
│  ─────────────────────────
│    #edge = 4
│    edge 1 + edge 2 + edge 3 + edge 4 = 0
└───────────────────────────────────────
```

```
┌─QUADRILATERAL──────────────────────────────
│    Edges
│    position : VECTOR
│    move : VECTOR → QUADRILATERAL
│    shear : SHEAR → QUADRILATERAL
│  ──────────────────────────────────────────
│    0 ∉ ran edge
│    ∀v:VECTOR• move(v).position=position + v
│                  ∧ move(v).edge=edge
│    ∀s:SHEAR• shear(s)= . . . . . definition omitted
└────────────────────────────────────────────
```

The class PARALLELOGRAM inherits QUADRILATERAL, and hence the methods, *move* and *shear*. It has an extra constraint on its edges. The method *angle*, which returns the interior angle between two sides, is new.

```
┌─PARALLELOGRAM──────────────────────────
│    I(QUADRILATERAL)
│    angle : ANGLE
│  ──────────────────────────────────────
│    edge 1+edge 3 = 0
│    angle=∠(edge 1,edge 2)
└────────────────────────────────────────
```

The class RHOMBUS inherits from PARALLELOGRAM, with a stronger constraint on its edges. Unlike all the alternative specifications given in [5], we allow *shear* to be a method of RHOMBUS. If r:RHOMBUS, *r.shear(s)* is the result of shearing *r* by shear, *s*, where *r* is considered to be a parallelogram i.e. we implicitly coerce *r* to be a parallelogram (thinking operationally). The appropriate notation was introduced in section 3.

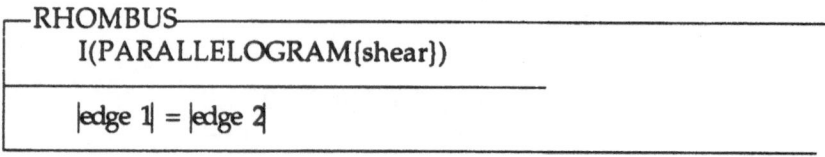

Similarly, the class RECTANGLE inherits from PARALLELOGRAM, with a stronger constraint on its edges, and the method *shear* retained as for RHOMBUS.

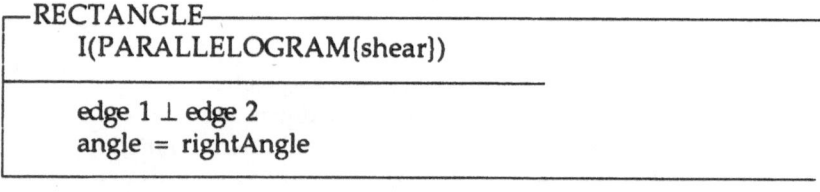

The class SQUARE multiply inherits from the classes, RHOMBUS and RECTANGLE. There are no further constraints.

```
┌─SQUARE──────────────────────────────
│     I(RECTANGLE)
│     I(RHOMBUS)
└─────────────────────────────────────
```

The state of the drawing system, *drawing*, consists of a mapping from quadrilateral identifiers, ID, to QUADRILATERAL.

```
┌─DRAWING_SYSTEM──────────────────────────────────────────
│     drawing : ID ↦ QUADRILATERAL
│     addfigure : ID × QUADRILATERAL → DRAWING_SYSTEM
│     deletefigure : ID ↦ DRAWING_SYSTEM
│     moveDS : ID × VECTOR ↦ DRAWING_SYSTEM
│     angleDS :  ID ↦ ANGLE
│     shearDS :  ID × SHEAR ↦ DRAWING_SYSTEM
├──────────────────────────────────────────────────────────
│     ∀id:ID• ∀q : QUADRILATERAL •
│     id ∉ dom drawing ⇒
│               addfigure(id,q).drawing  = drawing ∪ { id ↦q}
│     id ∈ dom drawing ⇒
│               deletefigure(id).drawing = {id} ◁ drawing
│     id ∈ dom drawing ⇒
│               (moveDS(id,v).drawing =
│                     drawing⊕{id↦drawing(id).move(v)}
│            ∧ (drawing(id) ∈PARALLELOGRAM
│                     ⇒ angleDS(id) = drawing(id).angle)
│            ∧ shearDS(id,s).drawing =
│                     drawing⊕{id↦drawing(id).shear(s)})
└──────────────────────────────────────────────────────────
```

The methods *addfigure, deletefigure* add, delete respectively a figure to/from the DRAWING_SYSTEM. The method *moveDS* moves a named figure (*drawing(id)*) within the DRAWING_SYSTEM by a given VECTOR, *v*. This works for any subclass of QUADRILATERAL (eg. RHOMBUS) automatically because eg. RHOMBUS⊆QUADRILATERAL (see Appendix 2), even though it appears only to be defined for QUADRILATERAL. *angleDS* and *shearDS* have the obvious meanings. Note that if q∈QUADRILATERAL\PARALLELOGRAM, then *q* cannot respond to an *angle* message. Strictly, we should return an error message in this case, but we do not consider error handling here, since it is ignored in [5].

5. Conclusion and future directions

We have shown that self-referential classes are important for practical object-oriented software development. The formalization of such development requires precise mathematical modelling of circularly defined classes. As far as we are aware this is the first work that directly addresses this problem. Hyper-Z solves this problem very naturally within the set-theoretic foundation of Z.

Future work will focus on giving a precise description of the semantics of Hyper-Z, its type theory and a type inference algorithm. Further detail work is required in the modification of W, the standard logic for Z, to support reasoning about Hyper-Z specifications. A complete definition of when self-referential schemas are reasonable and when they are not will be produced.

Acknowledgements

The authors wish to acknowledge the SERC whose grant GR/H16629 supported this research. We thank the anonymous referees for very helpful comments on the submitted draft, that have greatly improved both the contents and the presentation of this work. We also thank Jim Armstrong, Richard Bosworth, Franco Civello, Richard Mitchell, Dan Simpson, Rosemary Tate, and Sam Valentine, for comments on earlier drafts.

References

1. Meira S L and Cavalcanti A L C. Modular Object-Oriented Z Specifications. In: Nicholls J E (ed) Z User Workshop, Oxford 1990, Springer-Verlag, pp 173-192.
2 Duke D and Duke R. Towards a semantics for Object-Z. In: Bjorner et al (eds) VDM90, Springer-Verlag, 1990, pp 244-261 (LNCS 428).
3. Meyer B. Object Oriented Software Construction. Prentice Hall, Hemel Hempstead, 1988.
4. Wegner P. Dimensions of object-based language design. In: Meyrowitz N (ed) OOPSLA87, ACM Press, pp 168-182.
5. Stepney S, Barden R, Cooper D. A survey of object-orientation in Z. Software Engineering Journal, p.150-160, March 1992.
6 Interactive Software Engineering Eiffel: The Libraries Version 2.3. TR-EI-7/LI October 1990.
7. Canning P, Cook W, Hill W, Mitchell J, Olthoff W. F-bounded polymorphism for object-oriented programming. Proceedings of Functional Programming Languages and Computer Architecture, pp 273-280, 1989.

8. Canning P, Cook W, Hill W, Olthoff W. Interfaces for strongly-typed object-oriented programming. In: Meyrowitz N (ed) OOPSLA89, ACM Press, pp 457-467.

9. Cardelli L. Amber. In Combinators and Functional Programming Languages. Springer-Verlag, 1986, pp 21-47 (LNCS 242).

10. Cardelli L. A semantics of multiple inheritance. Information and Computation 76, pp 138-164, 1988.

11. Cook W. A denotational semantics of inheritance. PhD thesis, Brown University, 1989.

12. Cook W, Palsberg J. A denotational semantics of inheritance and its correctness. In: Meyrowitz N (ed) OOPSLA89, ACM Press, pp 433-444.

13. Cardelli L. A semantics of multiple inheritance. In: Semantics of Data Types, Springer-Verlag, pp 51-68, 1984 (LNCS 173).

14. Z Base Standard Version 0.5. ZIP/PRG/92/92, March 1992.

15. Spivey J M. Understanding Z - a specification language and its formal semantics. Cambridge Tracts in TCS 3, CUP , 1988.

16. Aczel P G H. Non-well-founded Sets. CSLI Lecture Notes 14, Stanford University, 1988.

17. Barwise J, Etchemenedy J. The Liar: An Essay on Truth and Circular Propositions. OUP, 1987.

18. Wegner P, Zdonik S B. Inheritance as an Incremental Modification Mechanism. In: ECOOP 88, pp55-77.

19. Maung I, Howse J R. Semantic Issues in the Model-based specification of Self-Referential Classes. Technical Report, Department of Computing, University of Brighton, in preparation, 1993.

20. Spivey J M. The Z Notation : A Reference Manual (2nd Edition). Prentice-Hall, Hemel Hempstead, 1992.

21. Goldberg A, Robson D. Smalltalk-80: the Language and Its Implementation. Addison-Wesley, Reading, 1983.

22. Wegner P. Concepts and paradigms of object oriented programming. OOPS Messenger, 1(1), p.7-87, 1990.

23. Snyder A. Encapsulation and Inheritance in Object-oriented Programming. In: Meyrowitz N (ed) OOPSLA86, ACM Press, pp 38-45.

24. America P. A Behavioural Approach to Subtyping in Object-Oriented Languages. In: Lenzerini et al. (ed) Inheritance Hierarchies in Knowledge Representation and Programming Languages, Wiley, Chichester, 1991.

Appendix 1 Eiffel library definition of class Numeric

10.2 Class *NUMERIC*

Ancestors of class *NUMERIC:*

No ancestors

deferred class interface *NUMERIC* **exported**
features

    infix "-", **infix** "+",
    infix "/", **infix** "*",
    prefix "-", **prefix** "+",

feature specification

    infix "-" (*other: NUMERIC*) : *NUMERIC*
    -- Difference between current element and *other*
    deferred

    infix "+" (*other: NUMERIC*) : *NUMERIC*
    -- Sum between current element and *other*
    deferred

    infix "/" (*other: NUMERIC*) : *NUMERIC*
    -- Division between current element and *other*
    deferred

    infix "*" (*other: NUMERIC*) : *NUMERIC*
    -- Product between current element and *other*
    deferred

    prefix "-" : *NUMERIC*
    -- Unary subtraction applied to current element
    deferred

    prefix "+" : *NUMERIC*
    -- Unary addition applied to current element
    deferred

end interface -- class *NUMERIC*

Reprinted from [6] with the kind permission of Professor Bertrand Meyer.

Appendix 2 - New Schema Semantics

With standard schema semantics [15] section 2.5,
MOVABLE_POINT $\not\subseteq$ POINT, because it has the extra component, *move*.

We change the denotational semantics of schemas as follows [15]p.33

$$\text{Struct} : \text{SIG} \to \mathbb{P}\,\text{STRUCT}$$

$$
\begin{aligned}
\text{Struct} = \lambda\text{SIG}\bullet \{ \text{STRUCT} \mid \\
\text{given} \subseteq \text{dom gset} \wedge \\
\text{vars} \subseteq \text{dom val} \wedge \\
(\forall v : \text{vars}\bullet \text{val } v \in \text{Carrier gset (type } v)) \}
\end{aligned}
$$

This semantics is based on the record semantics of [10].
With this definition, MOVABLE_POINT $\subseteq$ POINT, as required.

From Object-Z to C++: A Structural Mapping

G-H Bagherzadeh Rafsanjani
BT Communications Architecture Division
Bibb Way, Ipswich IP1 2EQ

S J Colwill[1]
BT Communications Architecture Division
Bibb Way, Ipswich IP1 2EQ

Abstract

We document the results of a small research project whose aim is to support the object-oriented development lifecycle with the use of a formal method. By means of case studies, we have produced a structural mapping from Object-Z to C++ which is intended to be an aid to creative programming. The mapping is justified in the context of an object model constructed for the purpose. The approach shows promise both in the context of the languages chosen and in the context of other languages and has generated considerable interest within our organisation.

1 Introduction

This paper documents the results of a small research project which has a pragmatic and empirical bias.

We have produced a mapping from an object-oriented formal specification language to an object-oriented programming language. The mapping is defined in the context of an abstract object model we produced to represent the common features of the two languages concerned in a consistent and structured manner. As a by-product, we have some observations about some aspects of the languages we have used in this context.

The aim of the project is to create a bridge between formal specification language and code, in order to help close the gap between these two. The purpose is to smooth the path from specification in a formal language to coding in one of the major programming languages. At the moment the framework is one in which a fast prototype could be created, and relates to a specific formal language and a particular programming language.

The work is aimed at object-oriented designers not necessarily committed to formal methods who are considering the use of such methods and languages in an object-oriented development.

We are committed to the use of a formal language at the specification stage for the following reasons:

- analysis of the specification is enabled–this includes type and interface consistency;

---

[1]Now with Harlequin Ltd, BarringtonHall, Barrington, Cambridge, CB2 5RG.

- properties of a system can be captured independently of the algorithms used at implementation;

- rigour is introduced at an early stage–important matters are less likely to escape to result in harm later when design re-work may become necessary;

- in addition, a formal object-oriented specification language allows the full power of the object-oriented paradigm to be deployed at an early stage.

This paper gives a structural mapping from a language known as Object-Z [4, 2] to C++ [13]. These languages were chosen for practical reasons–C++ is obviously popular and has already taken a strong hold in object-oriented development. Object-Z has been published and appears to have some of the properties necessary in a formal object-oriented specification language. It is an object-oriented extension of the well-known formal language Z [12]. The mapping itself has been found empirically by means of case studies. We take this opportunity to emphasise that we are *not* proposing any kind of translator, but rather an aid to the implementer.

We captured some of the common features of the two languages in a model produced for this purpose. In the model, we decided to avoid some aspects of these languages which we deemed to be inconsistent with good object-oriented practice. The mapping is from a subset of (a modified version of) the Object-Z to a corresponding subset of the C++ language. These subsets are determined partly by language features held in common and partly by restrictions resulting from our object model. Experimentation (case studies) and theoretical considerations (the object model) are combined to justify the mapping.

We see the uses of such a mapping as the following:

- the route from specification to code is smoothed and expedited;

- previously defined specification and code elements can be re-used;

- specification-level structuring and design decisions can be re-used in coding;

- maintainability of the product is increased as there is a clear relationship between specification (i.e. description) and code;

- design decisions are pushed back up the development trajectory thus reducing the damage and rework resulting from error;

- as a tool for aiding (not replacing) the creative programmer.

The project contained three case study investigations, one of which is the well-known shapes hierarchy as written in [4, 2]. Another case study involved the OSI Network Management Forum event reporting sieve object [8, 9]. Our implementation illustrated that the mapping could be used to prototype such services defined using a formal object-oriented language. The third case study was a partial implementation of a British Telecom office information system.

The structure of the rest of the paper is as follows. In sections 2 and 3, overviews of both Object-Z and C++ languages are presented, respectively. The mapping itself is detailed in section 4 in which we also make comments about a possible library of C++ types to support the mapping. A small example of the mapping is given. In section 5 we discuss our object model. Finally, we present our conclusions and ideas for future work in section 6.

2 Overview of Object-Z

Object-Z [4] has been proposed by researchers at the University of Queensland as an "extension" of Z ([12]) to embrace object-oriented concepts: in particular those of object, class, inheritance, and composition.

In short, this is accomplished by means of the introduction of a new schema type–the class. Each Object-Z class definition consists of what is called class constants which characterise fixed object attributes as defined by our model (see section 5), inherited classes, a state schema with predicates (invariants), an initialisation schema which defines the initial state of each object declared, and operation schemas which correspond to the methods for each object.

Inheritance in Object-Z is incremental with the subclass having access to all contents of the superclass. There is no provision for operations to be defined private to a class (used solely for internal manipulations) to be confined to objects of that class. This is reflected in our abstract model. On the other hand, we found features in Object-Z which were either not clearly defined or at variance with the stated aims of our model. For instance, Object-Z does not specifically distinguish between attributes of objects, which we regard as fixed, and their state variables. Similarly, in composition, it does not distinguish between the two forms of composition given in our model. It also allows for operation deletion and unconstrained redefinition–not in accord with our desire for some form of compatibility in the class hierarchy.

Another feature of Object-Z which we have disregarded is the possibility of accessing variables directly . This operator ignores the defined interface and breaks down encapsulation of data.

As a result, the version of Object-Z we have used contains some modification to the one given in [4]. For further details, we refer the reader to [1].

3 Overview of C++

We give a very brief overview of C++. C++ has been described as "C plus classes", a rather harsh description based on the fact that C++ compilers will compile C. The class construct in C++ is an extension of the C struct to include such things as possible hiding of the data stored in class instantiations (i.e. objects), and a record of the operations that can be validly invoked on that data (the member functions).

The template construct in C++ is a relatively recent development and was not available to us at the time of this project. We used a version of C++ (supported by the GNU C++ compiler [14]) which lacks this template construct for classes. This was something of an inconvenience though we managed to work around it. C++ templates have an obvious correspondence in Object-Z and in our object model. In future work we would hope to have them at our disposal.

C++ supports inheritance, along the lines described above in the case of Object-Z. Moreover, in C++ there is a plethora of possible inheritance mechanisms which obtain from the large number of combinations of the associated keywords private, protected, and public. These can be applied not only to the contained data and member functions of a class definition but also in various combinations to the citations of these classes in other class definitions with no adequate rules [10]. However, in practice, only a few of these possibilities are actually used and we restrict our attention to an even smaller subset sufficient to support the expressiveness of Object-Z in the context of our model.

Similarly, C++ makes no distinction between attributes and states of objects, nor between the two forms of composition detailed in our model. The distinction is essential in visualising *what* the objects of a class look like, in order that a consistent mapping may be defined between the two languages. We use our model to first partition variables in Object-Z between attributes and state. In transformation to C++ only the attributes appear as arguments to the instantiation constructor (see section 4.1).

4 The Mapping

In this section we describe the mapping that has been found by means of the case studies. The approach has been highly pragmatic—we have made what we considered to be obvious identifications and proceeded from there. It is difficult to be fully formal as the semantics of Object-Z itself is not yet fully established. Full formality is not in fact our objective, rather we want to find something that works and looks useful.

The main case study which we completed has been to use the mapping to implement the shapes hierarchy as specified in [4, 2] to which we refer the reader for details of the specification. A subsequent and larger case study of part of a British Telecom office information system was also conducted.

We give the mapping below describing first the gross structural identifications and continuing with the treatment of Z predicates and invariants, operations and concluding with a discussion on types. This is then followed by an example.

4.1 Structures

The most obvious identification is that of Object-Z class with C++ class. Having done this then it is possible to map class structure as follows (from Object-Z to C++):

- class constants (object attributes) and state variables to **protected** class variables (but see later);
- inheritance to **public** inheritance in C++, in the case of multiple (fork-join) inheritance the base class is labelled **virtual**;
- composition carries over in the obvious way as variable declarations;
- the initialisation schema is absorbed into the instantiation constructor—null and copy constructors are also provided;
- operations to virtual member functions to allow for operation extensions;
- variable renaming (e.g. shape perimeter to circle circumference in the derivation of **Circle** from **Shape**) in Object-Z is achieved in C++ by declaring a reference variable of the new name initialised to the value of the old name.

The translation of class constants (object attributes) to C++ **protected** variables is not very satisfactory. Labelling them private would provide a safeguard against manipulation by subclasses, but equally it hides them from subclasses too—contrary to Object-Z and our model. However, part of the purpose of the mapping is to provide a framework of operation definitions which helps to prevent accidental abuse of these variables.

Virtual inheritance is necessary in order to support the fork-join inheritance mechanism where identically named variables are supposed to be identified when inherited from a common ancestor. Object-Z operations become virtual member functions in C++. Virtuality is needed in this case as in Object-Z operations that are inherited can always be extended in derived classes.

An *instantiation* constructor is provided. This corresponds to the notion of creating an object by giving values to the set V of class constants. It is the responsibility of the instantiation constructor to ensure that objects are created whose state configuration satisfies the requirements expressed as Object-Z initialisation schemas. Null and copy constructors are typically provided in C++ to allow ease of coding. `Class c;` and `Class c1 = c2;` declarations are very commonplace. The copy and null constructors can only be invoked in the cases where the initialisation schema permits if direct correspondence with the Object-Z is required. .Coding may, however, require the use of temporary variables which may be copies of existing variables and in these cases the copy constructor is very useful and can be invoked regardless of the strictures of Object-Z.

Composition provides for the invocation of operations of the composite objects and their combination into an interface of the super-object. This kind of structuring is referred to by the Z community as "promotion", and is a very typical object-oriented usage. An example could be a tree composed of menus where each menu object has an "update" operation. The tree object would like to present a "select-menu-then-update" interface which could be invoked on the tree level. This operation is achieved by promoting the update operation of the menu to an interface of the tree object together with a wrapping to achieve the desired selection. This separation of the menu local states from the global states greatly assists re-use. Our mapping provides for this directly.

In addition to the above, predicates and invariants in Object-Z are represented as C++ functions. We discuss these in the next section.

4.2   Predicates

Our mapping is *structural* and therefore we do not provide translation for predicates. It is here that the intelligence and creativity of the good programmer is required and where the difference is made between a proposal for a basis of a *translator* of Object-Z to C++, and our proposal for a *structural mapping*.

Predicates occur in Object-Z specifications in several contexts: as restriction of class attributes, as state invariants restricting state space, as operation pre- and post-conditions, and in initialisation schemas.

To represent the conjunction of the restrictions of class attributes and state space, we provide an invariant function in C++ which takes the attribute and state variable values of an object and returns a boolean (integer) verdict. The idea is that this can be invoked any time between object member function invocations and should return the value true if all is well. It is necessary that the operation pre- and post-conditions (also predicates coded in C++ member function bodies) should be correct in the sense that the invariant is preserved.

It is possible in principle to insist that the object invariant function is invoked before and after every member function invocation. This is an overhead that is patently unnecessary when the member functions are correctly specified and implemented.

The initialisation predicate is implemented in the C++ instantiation constructor and ensures that a newly-instantiated object is created in a valid initial state.

There is a complication in Object-Z associated with the state predicates (invariants). This is that in inheriting a class, a sub-class inherits the invariant of the super-class which then becomes conjoined with any additional invariant definition. This can correspond to the notion of *specialisation* in inheritance. This is still under discussion and we have not yet taken it into account in the mapping, but have left it as an issue for future work.

4.3 Operations

As mentioned above Object-Z operations are directly implemented as C++ virtual member functions. Virtuality is necessary to support the extension of operations that is a feature of our model. This Virtuality in C++ also permits complete redefinition which is not going to be used in our mapping. We insist that the constraints that are inherited from superclasses in Object-Z are correspondingly implemented in C++. If they are not then there is no guarantee that the state invariant (also inherited) would be preserved as operations are invoked during the lifetime of the object.

In order to compensate for the loss of direct variable access in Object-Z (see section 2), we provide standard C++ functions to retrieve these values as required. These functions are not labelled virtual as there is no intention to allow them to be redefined in derived classes. The keyword **const** indicates that they have no side-effects on the object's state.

4.4 Types

There are two kinds of types in Object-Z. We refer to these as basic types and class types.

Basic types are carried through to Object-Z from its foundations in Z. Class types are new in Object-Z and we have spent considerable discussion above on how they are managed in the context of our mapping.

However, we have noticed in the course of our case studies that the mismatch between what is provided by Object-Z basic types and those type definitions available in C++ has a significant effect on the mapping. This was particularly obvious in the case the office information system case study mentioned above.

We have found it necessary to implement some Object-Z basic types in C++ (we have not implemented a complete set, but those that we needed) in order that the mapping is not distorted from the clear correspondences that we have found. We have implemented the Z types of partial function and partial injection as C++ classes providing interfaces corresponding to the typical Z manipulations of data of these types.

This implementation was conducted on rather mathematical lines using the GNU library [6] **map** class definition as the basis. Instantiation of the pseudo-generic class definitions (no templates being available to us) provided in this library is a rather tortuous affair. We anticipate that availability of the template construct would make such matters easier, and moreover would provide a natural correspondence with Object-Z generic schemas and classes.

The approach that we took to implementing these types is not necessarily the most efficient in terms of the execution speed of the code that would be generated. We expect that performance gains could be made if required by ignoring the mathematical relationships that exist between Z relationship types, partial function types, and partial injection types and instead implementing them very directly.

4.5 Example

As an illustration, we give the Object-Z description of the *Shape* class[2].

```
┌─ Shape ──────────────────────────────────────────────
│  ┌───────────────────────────────────
│  │  perim : R
│  ├───────────────────────────────────
│  │  perim > 0
│  └───────────────────────────────────
│  ┌───────────────────────────────────────────────
│  │  position : Vector
│  └───────────────────────────────────────────────
│  ┌─ Move ─────────────────────────────────────────
│  │  Δ(position)
│  │  v? : Vector
│  ├───────────────────────────────────────────────
│  │  position' = position + v?
│  └───────────────────────────────────────────────
│  ┌─ Rotate ───────────────────────────────────────
│  │  Δ(position)
│  │  θ? : R
│  ├───────────────────────────────────────────────
│  │  position' = rotate(position, θ?)
│  └───────────────────────────────────────────────
└──────────────────────────────────────────────────────
```

The transformation of this Object-Z definition into C++ using the rules given above is as follows. For the sake of brevity, we give only the .h file.

```
#include "Global_defs.h"

class Shape {
 protected:
  RealAVec position;
  Real perim;
 public:
  // instantiation constructor
  Shape(Real p): position(2) {
    perim = p;
    Inv(perim); // Invariant test
  }
  // copy constructor
  Shape(const Shape& s) : position(2) {
```

---

[2]Notice the difference between our definition, in which attribute and state variables are being distinguished, and that given in[4].

```
  RealAVec the_position(2);
  Real the_perim;
  s.GetPosition(the_position);
  s.GetPerim(the_perim);
  position = the_position;
  perim = the_perim;
}
// null constructor
Shape() : position(2) {}
int Inv(Real the_perim);
virtual void Move(RealAVec& v_q);
virtual void Rotate(Real theta_q);
void GetPosition(RealAVec& get_pos_b) const;
void GetPerim(Real& get_per_b) const;
};
```

5 An Object Model

As mentioned earlier, the main motivation for defining an abstract model was to capture the common features of the two languages concerned, and then carry out the mapping in the context of this model. There have been several attempts at defining abstract models for object-oriented systems. Some, like [11], are cast in insufficiently formal terms for our purpose, and so are not capable of being used in the context of our mapping. On the other hand, some like [15] are so abstract that they have a very limited use in actually deriving practical rules for application in different languages. What we needed was a model specific enough to describe the main notions of object-oriented paradigm in a specific, consistent and formal manner and at the same time capable of being applied across language boundaries.

The model defined here is meant to serve this purpose. It also helps to clarify some of the features of Object-Z which we found to be confusing and suggest modifications, and to restrict our mapping to subsets of the two languages in which we can reasonably be confident of soundness.

We continue by presenting an outline of the model. Full details may be found in [1]. We begin with a brief look at some language-independent characteristics of class and object.

5.1 Objects

We require that objects have persistent identities. An object may have a set of states (state space) with the object at a single state at any given time. There may also be a set of operations associated with the object defining the possible and legal changes of state.

In other words, an object O is defined by a set of *(static) attributes*, a *state space* and a set of *operations*.

- The set of attributes is meant to remain constant during the life-cycle of the object. It may include a constant *id* (drawn from a given set *Id*) the value of which is unique to that object–its *identity*. Two distinct objects may share some of their attributes, but never their identities. For later convenience, in the case of a declaration $a : A$ for example, the identifier a can be regarded as the identity of the object.

- The object is at any time at some state (of its state space), and may move from one state to another as a result of some operation.

We make a point in distinguishing between the (fixed) attributes and states of an object. In the literature, the term "attributes" is used variably for either or both of the static and dynamic values (states) of objects. Here, we restrict it to the first, so as to differentiate between those characteristics of the object which remain constant and those which are susceptible to change by an (existing or future defined) operation. We find this distinction significant in the context of class inheritance and composition as will become clear later.

5.2 Classes

We define a class as an abstraction of objects with a common set of operations and a common type for their states. More specifically, assuming a global type Id, the definition of a class C consists of

- a set of typed variables V (corresponding to the object attributes), one of which may be the $id : Id$, and a predicate $P1$ defined on V,

- a set of typed variables S (corresponding to the object state space), and a predicate $P2$ defined on $V \cup S$,

- a set of operations Op none of which can effect any change in values of V.

As an abstraction, we represent a class C by a tuple $((V_C, P1_C), (S_C, P2_C), Op_C)$, or simply by (V_C, S_C, Op_C). This tuple characterises the objects which can be *created* using C, and corresponds to the notion of class *template* [5]. In line with C++ usage, we call any element of $V \cup S \cup Op$ a *member* of the class.

An object of such a class C is an *instantiation* of the template created in the following way. Values are given to the variables in the set V_C (subject to predicate $P1_C$ being satisfied) to represent the object's fixed attributes. The state space is the set of all values which the variable set S_C can take (i.e. values satisfied by the predicate $P2_C$), and the operation set the set Op_C.

Classes may be used as types for variables in the definition of another class. Such a use creates classes whose objects are composed of some other objects or have other objects as elements of their state space. These two variations will be dealt with later under the subsection *composition*.

5.3 Inheritance

Classes may be related to each other by an *inheritance* relation. We use inheritance for both code re-use and as a limited form of refinement. To satisfy the latter requirement, the inheritance should reflect some form of "is-a" relation. That is, we are wary of allowing features in inheritance which may result in defining subclasses entirely incompatible, in terms of *behaviour* with the superclass. Hence, we allow no operation redefinition, but only restriction or extension [3]. Then, syntactically, a class C inheriting another class D, is defined by giving the name of D and then listing the additional elements of V_C, S_C, Op_C and new predicates, with the semantic convention that all members of D are added to the corresponding sets of class C and all corresponding predicates are conjoined.

It is clear from this definition, that once a class inherits another class, it is legal to define operations affecting states as given in the inherited class. However, in no way may one do a similar thing affecting the fixed attributes. Our insistence right at the beginning on distinguishing between the two sets (V and S) guarantees that object integrity is maintained in the inheritance hierarchy.

5.4 Composition

Another relation formed between classes is that of *composition*. Here, objects of a class use objects of other classes as their building blocks or *sub-objects*. Let us call such a new class a *composite* class and the classes supplying its building blocks, its *source* classes. Two distinct possibilities arise:

1. An object of the composite class is a fixed configuration of a number of objects of the source class(es), and no operation of the super-object may cause a change in this configuration.

2. The composite object contains a variable number of sub-objects (one may add or delete objects), and/or the composite object may contain operations with the effect of changing its configuration.

In the first case, then the new object has a fixed configuration. This configuration then is declared in its attribute set V. The state space of the new object contains a composition of the state spaces of its sub-objects. We call this kind of composition a *product composition*.

In the second form of composition, one uses a collection of objects and/or the their configuration as state values of an object of another class. Then one may also define some extra operations to manipulate these sub-objects. So, in this case, variables whose types are derived from the source classes appear in the set S of the composite class. We call this kind of composition a *meta composition*.

Example. The distinction between the two forms of compositions become apparent by way of the following example.

Let the class of *Person* be defined (using Object-Z) as follows:

```
┌─ Person ────────────────────────────────────
│  ┌──────────────────────────────────────────
│  │ name : seq Char
│  │ sex : Male | Female
│  ├──────────────────────────────────────────
│  │ age : N
│  ├──────────────────────────────────────────
│  │ ┌─ Add_age ────────────────────────────
│  │ │ Δ(State)
│  │ ├──────────────────────────────────────
│  │ │ age' = age + 1
│  (other operations)
└────────────────────────────────────────────
```

Then a class of *MarriedCouple* may be defined to consist of objects each of which is a couple composed of two fixed persons (no spouse-swapping!). Now, the state space of a married couple is a Cartesian product of the state spaces of the two individuals: (*a.age, b.age*), where *a* and *b* represent the two individuals married to each other. This is a case of product composition.

On the other hand, a class of *Family* may be defined to consist of a (flexible) number of persons and operations for adding and removing members from the *Family*. Moreover, a state variable *head : Person* may be declared with an operation assigning a new person to this variable (say, at the death of the existing head). This operation effectively replaces a sub-object (as the value for the variable *head*) with another sub-object. This is a case of meta composition.

5.4.1 *Encapsulation*

We use encapsulation only in the context of composition. In inheritance, we allow unrestrained access to members of a superclass by its subclasses. But here, we require that objects are represented in the composition class by their interfaces, and that the interface contains only the set of (observable) operations defined in terms of input-output relations. Now, a composite class may contain two sets of state variables: one coming from the source classes, invisible and only accessed through the use of operations given in the interfaces, and the other (if any) defined explicitly in the composite class, and accessible by direct operations. This fact may be observed in the definitions given below.

For a class C with the operations set Op_C, let $c.Op_C$ denote the same set of operations represented as input-output relations for an arbitrary object $c : C$. Now, we define a class $D = (V_D, S_D, Op_D)$ to be a *product composition* of a class C with the set of observable operations Op_C if

- $c : C$ is included in V_D, and

- the set $c.Op_C$ is included in Op_D;

and the class D to be a *meta composition* of the class C if

- $c : C$ is included in S_D.

- the set $c.Op_C$ is included in Op_D;

Note that as classes in these notations are being used as (schema) types, one may also use derived types (such as power set types) of the source classes in the composite class in a similar manner.

6 Conclusions

We have produced a structural mapping from Object-Z to C++. We have not directly addressed use of the template construct in C++, nor have we completed all the work that would be necessary to support the type system of Object-Z in C++ terms.

In the course of this work, by using an object model that is an abstraction of the Object-Z and C++ sublanguages under consideration, we have had cognisance of accepted object-oriented concepts. We have restricted ourselves to sublanguages in each case mainly on the grounds of retaining what we regard as sound inheritance mechanisms. In particular we have discarded the operation deletion and redefinition possibilities of each language even though the mapping from one to the other is fairly obvious. The kind of inheritance that we acknowledge is incremental and encompasses both "specialisation" and "generalisation" [7].

In addition, the sublanguage of Object-Z excludes use of a potentially destructive variable access operator. This operator breaks down the requirements that data representation should not leak out of a class definition and that modifications to data should be controlled by interface functions that are trusted not to break invariants.

We have used a very simple sublanguage of C++–one that we think avoids many of the nasty pitfalls associated with the full panoply of keyword combinations allowed in C++.

The idea of a mapping provides an attack on the question of re-use. One of the major bugbears in this area is the question of knowing precisely what an implementation module is supposed to do. Formal specifications linked to matching code can help to answer this question [16]. Moreover, an implementation of a library of Z types is an implementation of standard entities whose properties can be well defined and held in common by anybody who understands elementary mathematical ideas.

We anticipate that this mapping will be used as an adjunct to creative programming. The concerns of system design and structuring (inheritance, composition, and interface definitions) will be separated from those of algorithm writing. Both of these activities still require human input, we hope to stabilise the connection between them.

6.1 Future Work

We need to investigate the properties of the C++ template construct now becoming available in terms of our object model to determine the extension of the mapping to include Object-Z generic type definitions.

The treatment of invariants needs to be resolved. This is as much an Object-Z language matter as a problem for the mapping, and it is for this reason that we have set this issue to one side for the time being.

The library of basic types needs to be completed in order that the basic support (in terms of richness of types) of Object-Z and C++ is brought into more close alignment. This completion will depend rather strongly on the template construct as essentially all Object-Z basic types (such as function, injection, list etc.) are generic.

Improvements to Object-Z will be considered in the light of supporting a smooth mapping of Object-Z constructs to constructs in C++ and possibly to other object-oriented programming languages.

Acknowledgement

We would like to acknowledge the work done by Thomas McNeilly, of Stirling University, Scotland, in implementing the case studies of this project, during a six-month placement with British Telecom.

References

[1] G-H. Bagherzadeh Rafsanjani, *An Abstract Object Model for Application to Mapping from Object Z to C++*, BT Group Technology Development and Procurement, Internal Report, 1991.

[2] D. Carrington, D. Duke, R. Duke, P. King, G Rose and G Smith, Object Z: An Object Oriented Extension to Z, in S. T. Vuong (ed.), *Formal Description Techniques II*, 281–297, North Holland 1990.

[3] E. Cusack, Inheritance in Object-Oriented Z, in Pierre America (ed.), *ECOOP '91, European Conference on Object-Oriented Programming*, 167–179, LNCS 512, Springer-Verlag 1991.

[4] R. Duke, P. King, G. Rose, G. Smith, *Technical Report No 91-1, The Object-Z Specification Language Version 1*, Software Verification Research Centre, Department of Computing Science, The University of Queensland, May 1991.

[5] J. Gallagher, Basic Concepts (Variations on a Theme), in G. Blair, J. Gallagher, D. Hutchinson and D. Shepherd (eds.), *Object-Oriented Languages, Systems and Applications*, 42–74, Pitman 1991.

[6] D. Lea, *User's Guide to GNU C++ Library*, Free Software Foundation Incremental, 1991.

[7] B. Meyer, *Object-Oriented Software Construction*, Prentice Hall, 1988.

[8] *OSI NM Forum 006 Library Supplement: DIS GDMO Translation Issue 1 Draft 4*, June 1990.

[9] S. Rudkin, Modelling information objects in Z, in J. de Meer, V. Heymer, R. Roth (eds.), *Open Distributed Processing*, 267–280, North Holland, 1992.

[10] M. Sakkinen, *A Critique of the Inheritance Principles of C++*, Computing Systems, Vol. 5 No. 1, 1992.

[11] A. Snyder, *An Abstract Object Model for Object-Oriented Systems*, Hewlett Packard Laboratories Technical Report, HPL-90-22, 1990.

[12] J. M. Spivey, *The Z Notation: A Reference Manual*, 2nd edition, Prentice-Hall, 1992.

[13] B. Stroustrup, *The C++ Programming Language*, Addison-Wesley, Reading, MA, 1986.

[14] M. Tiedemann, *User's Guide to Gnu C++*, Free Software Foundation Incremental, 1991.

[15] Y. Wand, A Proposal for a Formal Model of Objects, in (W. Kim, F. H. Lochovsky (eds.), *Object-Oriented Concepts, Databases and Applications*, 537–560, ACM Press, 1989.

[16] A. Wills, Capsules and Types in Fresco: Program Verification in Smalltalk, in Pierre America (ed.), *ECOOP '91, European Conference on Object-Oriented Programming*, 59–76, LNCS 512, Springer-Verlag 1991.

Deriving Tests for Objects Specified in Z

Elspeth Cusack and Clazien Wezeman

BT

Bibb Way, Ipswich IP1 2EQ, United Kingdom

Abstract

The OSI network management standards are expressed in terms of specifications of 'managed object definitions' to which implementations can claim conformance. This poses the problem of how to test such assertions. This paper reports our first steps towards the development of a testing theory for objects specified in object oriented Z. Our approach depends on the observation that Z class types can be viewed as labelled transition systems. This motivates the introduction into object oriented Z of definitions of internal action and conformance of an object specification to a class type. With these concepts in place, we suggest a test derivation procedure based on existing LOTOS technology.

1   Introduction

Object oriented Z has been the topic of a number of recent publications (for example, [4, 7, 9]) which have established that object orientation brings to Z useful ideas of modularity and design structuring. Rudkin [11] demonstrated that Z is a particularly suitable language in which to prepare formal descriptions of OSI managed objects in accordance with international standards [16]. This raises the question of how to check that an implementation does indeed conform to the intended managed object specification (which is actually a class type, in the usual object oriented Z terminology).

In particular we are interested in establishing whether an implementation possesses the functionality of its specification. This contrasts to robustness testing, which tries to assess whether only specified functionality is present. In addition to this we consider implementations to be *black boxes*–only their external behaviour can be examined.

This paper reports our first steps towards the solution of the problem. It presents a technique for deriving conformance tests from objects specified in Z.

Our notions of class type and instance are reviewed in Section 2. For a more complete description of our particular approach to object oriented Z we refer to [9].

We base our test derivation method on an existing method [14] for deriving conformance tests from labelled transition systems, the underlying semantic model for the international standard specification language LOTOS [1, 15]. This method is named the CO-OP method. We observe in Section 3 that instances of Z class types can be viewed as labelled transition systems. This link facilitates the formulation of object oriented Z definitions of *conformance of an object to a class type* and *internal actions* of objects. An introduction to labelled transition systems and LOTOS can be found in [3].

With the concept of conformance in place, we suggest in Section 4 a test derivation procedure. This depends on the translation into object oriented Z of the CO-OP method. The procedure produces from an object specification in Z a second specification which is the canonical tester for the original one. This canonical tester specifies all conformance tests of the original specification.

Object oriented specification can potentially lead to efficient testing. Since an instance of a type automatically conforms to each supertype, an object need only be tested against a specification derived from the class type of which it is claimed to be an instance. In order to realise this potential our definition of conformance is carefully related to the definition of subtyping. The object oriented concepts underlying this work were developed by ISO for modelling distributed systems, and are described in [8].

2 Concepts of object oriented Z

Types in conventional Z are disjoint sets of data values, primarily used for type checking. Object oriented Z, on the other hand, depends on an extended system of *class types*, primarily used as a means of efficiently structuring specifications [7]. A class type is written as a 'schemas of schemas', and determines a set of objects with a common behaviour pattern. All class types have a common syntactic form (or can be flattened into this form, in the case of class types defined using incremental inheritance [7, 8]). The generic syntax for a class type is as follows. The entries are Z schema boxes:

$$
\begin{array}{|l}
\hline
\ TYPE \underline{\hspace{4cm}} \\
\ Attributes \\
\ State \\
\ Initial\_State \\
\ Operation_1 \\
\quad . \\
\quad . \\
\quad . \\
\ Operation_n \\
\hline
\end{array}
$$

The schema *Attributes* declares a number of attributes – values or objects which are fixed when an instance of the class type *TYPE* is created and do not change (the *constants* of the Australian dialect Object-Z [4, 9]). At least one attribute is declared in each class type, corresponding to the persisting identity of each instance of the type. The schema *State* (a formal name) declares a number of state variables and the invariant relationships between them. *State* therefore determines a state space STATENAME. The schema *Initial_State* declares the valid initial states of a newly-created instance of the class type (the initial state space). All attributes and state variables are declared to have a type in the extended type system.

Each schema *Operation_i* (a formal name) declares ways in which state or attribute values can be accessed by the environment. Each operation schema must include at least one of the following schema declarations

- $\Xi Attributes$, where the operation permits the reading of an attribute value, or depends in some way on an attribute value

- $\Xi State$, where the operation permits some observation of the current state of the object, or depends in some way on the current state, but does not cause a state change

- $\Delta State$, where the operation leads to a change in the state of the object.

An *instance* of a class type is an object specification formed from the class type by setting the values of the attributes declared in *Attributes*, fixing a valid initial state and giving actual names to the operations, their inputs and their outputs[1]. Each object has a unique identity *object.name* as one of its attributes. We can therefore use this name to create actual names for the state and operation schemas, and inputs and outputs. This is done in the following schema, which specifies an instance with initial state s_0 . The specification can be turned into conventional Z by removing the outside schema box.

$$
\begin{array}{|l}
\hline
\text{— } object.name \bullet TYPE \text{———————————} \\
\hline
object.name \\
attribute_1 \\
\quad . \\
\quad . \\
attribute_m \\
state(object.name) \\
s_0 \\
operation_1(object.name) \\
\quad . \\
\quad . \\
operation_n(object.name) \\
\hline
\end{array}
$$

We interpret the instance *object.name* $\bullet$ *TYPE* as a partial specification of an implemented object with identity *object.name*.

   If each instance of a class type A is also an instance of a class type B then we say that A is a *subtype* of B (equivalently, B is a *supertype* of A). This implies that subtyping is a preorder on class types, indicating behavioural compatibility or type conformance.

   If A is a subtype of B then any instance *object.name* $\bullet$ A of A can be perceived as an object of type B. In the terminology of Ehrich and Sernadas [10] it possesses a behavioural aspect *object.name* $\bullet$ B of type B (a partial specification of the object which suppresses all detail not defined in the class type B). This constitutes our formal interpretation of the informal requirement that 'instances of a type are also instances of each supertype', the foundation of substitutability in object oriented modelling.

3   A labelled transition system interpretation

We introduce two conventions which will simplify our discussion of object oriented Z:

---

[1]The term instance is sometimes also used to denote an implementation of an object specification. Our concern with conformance testing makes a distinction essential.

1. Unless an operation corresponds to a spontaneous state change of an object, an input or output variable must be declared. So operations which use $\Delta State$ but have neither input nor output variables are internal (unobservable) actions, corresponding to the internal event in LOTOS. All other operations can be thought of as interactions with the environment, or external operations.

2. An external operation corresponds to exactly one point of interaction between an object and its environment. The actions to which the operation corresponds are denoted by the operation name together with the values of the input and output variables (if they exist – and at least one of them must).

Conventional Z makes no distinction between observable and internal operations. The conditions above are therefore intended to give the specifier the expressive power to indicate whether or not an operation is observable.

With these conditions in place, we observe that a class type possesses

- a set of fixed attributes.

- a state space STATENAME

- a set of initial states

- a set of operation names OPERATIONNAME

- a set of actions EVENT*, such that

  - each member of EVENT* corresponds to a member of OPERATIONNAME, together with input or output values in the case of external actions

  - there is at least one member of EVENT* corresponding to each member of OPERATIONNAME

- a mapping from EVENT* into $\mathbf{P}(\text{STATENAME} \times \text{STATENAME})$, which assigns a set of state transitions to each action. An action a maps onto a pair of states (s_1, s_2) only is there exists an operation which can bring an instance of the class from state s_1 into state s_2 by performing action a.

We conclude that the instances defined by a class type are simply labelled transition systems[2] in which the labels of transitions are selected from the set EVENT*. We can therefore think of the instances of a class type P as 'template processes' which can be implemented. If s_0 is an initial state of P and A is a valid set of attribute values let $P(s_0, A)$ denote the corresponding instance. The environment of an implemented instance may be able to make observations of the state of the process, and to read attribute values, in addition to engaging in interactions which cause the state to change.

The theory of behavioural equivalences for labelled transition systems may now be used to compare class types and their instances. We found particularly valuable the concepts of *conformance* and *extension* defined for these systems

---

[2]Schumann et al [12] showed previously that behaviour trees could help understand the behaviour of class types, but did not pursue a process calculus interpretation.

184

by Brinksma et al [1]. Below we give an informal definition of these concepts for labelled transition systems Q and P. The definitions use *trace* to be a finite sequence of actions recording the behaviour of a labelled transition system from its initial state to another state. Also *traces(P)* denotes the set of possible traces of P:

- *Q conforms to P* exactly when Q contains no unexpected deadlocks with respect to traces of P;
  i.e. Q may not refuse to perform, after having executed a trace of P, any actions that P can not refuse after performing that trace.

- *Q extends P* if Q conforms to P and $traces(P) \subseteq traces(Q)$

Extension is a preorder on processes, and was suggested in [5, 6] as a suitable subtyping relationship for processes, with conformance as the type membership relation. This yields the result that an instance of a subtype always conforms to each supertype, satisfying the requirement of Section 2.

In earlier work on object oriented Z, it was assumed that any state variable or attribute could be read at any time by the environment without causing a state change [7]. The approach of this paper permits the expression of a wider range of possibilities for access to state variables and attributes, which affect the behavioural relationships between processes.

Example 1 Let P and Q be labelled transition systems described by the LOTOS processes $P = input?a; input?b; P$ and $Q = input?a; Q [] input?b; Q$. Then Q extends P. But if the environment wants to exploit the fact that P is a two-state process (for example, to store 1 bit of data) then Q is not an acceptable substitute.

More precisely, suppose we have $P' = P_0$, where P_0 is recursively defined as $P_0 = input?a; P_1 [] read!0; P_0$ and $P_1 = input?b; P_0 [] read!1; P_1$ and $Q' = input?a; Q'[]input?b; Q'[]read!c; Q'$. Then P' and Q' correspond to P and Q with a state observation interaction available at a gate called *read*:

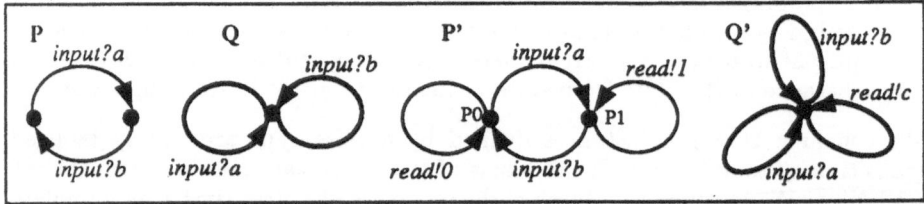

Since Q' can output only a constant value c at gate *read*, $traces(P')$ contains traces not in $traces(Q')$. So Q' does not extend P'. The process P' can be represented as a Z class type as follows, assuming given basic types *IDset* and *Inputset*:

P'
name : IDset
a, b : Inputset

```
┌─ State ─────────────────────────────────────────────────────────
│  s : {0, 1}
└──────────────────────────────────────────────────────────────────

┌─ Init ──────────────────────────────────────────────────────────
│  s = 0
└──────────────────────────────────────────────────────────────────

┌─ read ──────────────────────────────────────────────────────────
│  ΞState
│  s! : {0, 1}
│ ─────────────────────────────────────
│  s! = s
└──────────────────────────────────────────────────────────────────

┌─ input ─────────────────────────────────────────────────────────
│  ΔState
│  x? : {a, b}
│ ─────────────────────────────────────
│  x? = a ∧ s = 0 ∧ s' = 1
│  x? = b ∧ s = 1 ∧ s' = 0
└──────────────────────────────────────────────────────────────────
```

It is simple matter to define a subtyping preorder on class types, based on extension:

Definition 1 Let Q and P be class types. Q is a *subtype* of P if and only if

- each possible initial state $s_{0,Q}$ of Q can be mapped to a valid initial state $s_{0,P}$ of P

- if $s_{0,Q}$ is an initial state of Q and B is a set of attribute values defined in Q, then the template process $Q(s_{0,Q}, B)$ extends the template process $P(s_{0,P}, A)$ for some set of attribute values A defined in P.

This definition is clearly transitive, as required for preorders, and is closely related to the definition of subtyping used in our earlier work on object oriented Z [7]. If Q and P are class types, such that Q is a subtype of P in the sense of Definition 1, but with the extra condition that any state variable or attribute can be read at any time by the environment without causing a state change, then Q can be shown to be a subtype of P in the sense of [7]. A proof is sketched in the appendix.

Definition 2 An object implementation u with an initial state u_0 *conforms* to a class type P (synonymously, has a behavioural aspect of type P) if and only if u_0 can be mapped to a permitted initial state s_0 of P, and the behaviour of u conforms as a labelled transition system to $P(s_0, A)$ for some set of attribute values A.

It is easy to show that an object implementation conforms to a class type exactly when it is an instance of some subtype of the class type. It is immediate that an object specification conforming to a class type also conforms to each supertype, satisfying the requirement of Section 2. In addition, this definition formalises our earlier definition of the instance – type relationship [7].

The specification of a system in object oriented Z involves three activities. First, the desired class types are identified, defined (using incremental inheritance techniques as appropriate) and arranged in a type hierarchy. Secondly, the required instances of these types are created. The third and final step is to specify how these instances may interact. We have identified operations defined in class types with actions. The third step is thus a simple check that external actions with the same name are indeed intended to be potential synchronisation points.

This means that we regard inter-object communication as synchronisation on shared events. The suggestion of Carrington et al [4] fits our requirements: input and output values of operations are identified where the names are identical, save for the '?' or '!' decorations. This forces the situation that operations whose inputs and outputs are linked in this way must occur simultaneously.

Other implications are that communication between objects specified in Z is synchronous and that operations are atomic in the sense of being indivisible in time. In other words, all inputs, outputs and state changes are assumed to happen at the same time.

4   Deriving testers from class types

Brinksma established that corresponding to each process is a 'canonical tester' process, loosely the most general environment with which the process can successfully interact [2]. The canonical tester is a process that runs concurrently and communicating with an implementation under test. It tests whether the external behaviour of the implementation conforms to the specification. The basic ideas of a canonical tester are firstly that it is capable of exploring all traces in the specification, but will not explore any others; and secondly, the concurrent composition of the canonical tester and any given process can reach an unexpected deadlock if and only if the process does not conform to the specification.

We may use the same idea for Z testers. We have already used a notion of traces of object specifications in Z derived from our labelled transition system interpretation. We have given notions of interaction and conformance with respect to object oriented Z specifications. These notions coincide with the notions defined for labelled transition systems on which the canonical tester is based. This allows us to take the canonical tester as a model for a conformance tester for object oriented Z specifications. The CO-OP method [14] provides an algorithm for deriving canonical testers from non-deterministic labelled transition systems. It is summarised in the next subsection. Following that subsection the main building blocks of a new version of the method which can derive canonical testers from object oriented Z specifications are presented.

4.1   Derivation of testers from labelled transition systems

The CO-OP method is named after two sets, called *Compulsory* and *Options*. *Compulsory* is a set of sets of actions and *Options* is a set of actions. They are used to express the behaviour of the tester.

To understand how the tester is constructed by the CO-OP method we must distinguish *unstable states* from *stable states*: unstable states are states from which at least one internal transition (that is, transitions corresponding to an internal action) can be performed; stable states are states from which no internal transitions can be performed. The method maintains the following invariant which holds for each state that can be reached by the tester after performing some trace σ: 'Each element in *Compulsory* corresponds to a stable state that can be reached by the object specification after performing σ and contains exactly those actions that the specification can perform from that state. *Options* contains all actions that the specification can perform from the unstable states it can reach after performing σ'.

Consider a canonical tester that has interacted with an implementation under test performing σ. The tester cannot force the implementation to perform actions that may occur from unstable states which the specification can reach after performing σ, since the implementation may internally have moved to a state where these actions are not possible. Some force may be applied by the tester to make an implementation perform actions that can be done from stable states which the specification can reach after performing σ. The tester must then offer to participate in at least one action for each of these stable states. A conforming process must interact: ultimately it must move to one of the stable states, from where it must be able to perform at least one of the actions selected by the tester.

The CO-OP method describes this behaviour of a tester that performed σ by a LOTOS expression:

$$T(B \text{ after } \sigma) =$$
$$\sum_{op \epsilon Options(B after \sigma)} op; \; T(B \text{ after}(\sigma \; ; \; op))$$
$$[] \; (\sum_{V \epsilon Orth(Compulsory(B after \sigma))} i; \; (\sum_{a \epsilon V} (a; \; T(B \text{ after } (\sigma \; ; \; a)))))$$

where, for $A = \{A_1, \ldots, A_n\}$ a set of sets, $Orth(A)$ stands for $\{ \{x_1\} \cup \ldots \cup \{x_n\} \mid x_1 \epsilon A_1, \ldots, x_n \epsilon A_n. \}$; and where, for $V = \{v_1, \ldots, v_n\}$ a set of actions, $\sum_{a \epsilon V} a; \; B(a)$ stands for LOTOS choice expression $v_1; \; B(v_1)[] \ldots []v_n; \; B(v_n)$. Expression $T(B \text{ after } (\sigma; \; a))$ describes the behaviour of the tester that performed trace σ followed by transition a. This behaviour is produced recursively: the sets Compulsory and Options are re-evaluated, while maintaining the invariant. The above expression is then applied again. This process is repeated until no new tester states are encountered.

4.2 Derivation of testers from Z specifications

We can produce canonical testers from Z specifications describing objects in a way that is very similar to that used in the CO-OP method described above.

The basic types of the object's specification are also used in the tester's specification. In addition to this the tester will use three basic types, which are used to store information extracted from the specification of the object under test: OPERATIONNAME defines the set of operations in use in the object specification; STATENAME is the set of states which together form the statespace of the object; EVENT is the set of external actions used in the object's specification. So EVENT is a subset of the set of actions EVENT* introduced in Section 3. In addition to the free types of the object's specification, the tester specification uses one free type : TESTERSTATUS. It can be set to NODE, or to contain a set of OPERATIONNAMEs. The tester uses the same global constants which are also used by the object's specification.

4.2.1 State definition

The tester's state is described by the TesterState schema:

```
┌─ TesterState ──────────────────────────────────
│  unstablestatespace : P(STATENAME)
│  stablestatespace : P(STATENAME)
│  status : TESTERSTATUS
└────────────────────────────────────────────────
```

Variable *status* defines the behaviour of the tester. It is used in the precondition of each tester operation, enabling or disabling that operation. With this state definition we give an invariant relationship which must be true in every state of the tester and which is maintained by every operation on it: 'if the tester has performed a trace σ, then its *unstablestatespace* and its *stablestatespace* must contain respectively all unstable states and all stable states which can be reached by the specification that performed σ'.

4.2.2 Tester functions

Six functions are assumed to be available and they are not formally defined here:

Function *events* produces the set of external actions that can be performed during execution of a given operation. At the moment we assume that each operation involves exactly one action. An action may be built from one or more variables that are decorated with ? or ! symbols.

The functions *establish_unstablestatespace* and *establish_stablestatespace* map states to sets of respectively unstable object states and stable object states. A state is in the set if the object specification can move from the given state to that state by performing zero or more internal actions. Functions *unstablestatespacereachedafter* and *stablestatespacereachedafter* produce the new unstablestatespace and stablestatespace variables of a tester that has interacted with a process under test. The results will depend on the values of the variables before the event happened, and on the nature of the event itself.

We assume *satisfies_precondition* to be an existing relation. A combination of a state and an operation are in the relation if the operation can be performed from that state (that is, if the precondition of the operation is satisfied by the state.)

In addition we define a function *opns* that maps a state to a set of external operations. An external operation is in the set if it can be performed from the state.

```
│  opns : STATENAME → P(OPERATIONNAME)
├────────────────────────────────────────────────
│  ∀ s : STATENAME •
│      opns (s) = { op : OPERATIONNAME |
│                  (s, op) ∈ satisfies_precondition ∧ events(op) ≠ ∅}}
```

We define a function *compulsoryopns* to build a set of sets of operations. Each of its elements corresponds to a state in a given statespace. It contains exactly those operations which are possible from that state.

$$compulsoryopns : \mathbf{P}(STATENAME) \rightarrow \mathbf{P}(\mathbf{P}(OPERATIONNAME))$$

$$\forall \, statespace : \mathbf{P}(STATENAME) \bullet$$
$$compulsoryopns \, (statespace) = \{s : statespace \bullet opns(s)\}$$

The function is used to build the equivalent of the *Compulsory* set of the CO-OP method. It is applied to the stablestatespace variable. By replacing the operations in the result by the actions that can be performed in those operations, we obtain the set *Compulsory*. We do not apply this replacement. Instead we first apply Orth to this set of operations, and then replace operations by corresponding actions. Since we assume that each operation corresponds to one action only, this gives exactly the set *Orth(Compulsory)*.

Function *optionalopns* builds a set of operations:

$$optionalopns : \mathbf{P}(STATENAME) \rightarrow \mathbf{P}(OPERATIONNAME)$$

$$\forall \, statespace : \mathbf{P}(STATENAME) \bullet$$
$$optionalopns \, (statespace) =$$
$$\{op : OPERATIONNAME \mid \exists \, s : statespace \bullet op \in opns(s)\}$$

An operation is in the set if and only if it can be performed from a state in the given statespace. The function is used to build an equivalent of the *Options* set of the CO-OP method. It is applied to the unstablestatespace variable. By replacing in the result the operations by the actions that can be performed from those operations, we obtain the set Options.

The invariant of the conventional CO-OP method tester is equal to that of the Z tester when operationnames are replaced by actions that can occur during these operations.

4.2.3   Behaviour

Initially the tester *status* must be set to *NODE*. From the object's specification we may derive the initial *unstablestatespace* and *stablestatespace* variables. If *s* is defined as the initial state of the object specification, then the tester is initialised as:

```
┌─ InitializeTester ────────────────────────────────
│ TesterState
├────────────────────────────────────────────────────
│ status = NODE
│ unstablestatespace = establish_unstablestatespace(s)
│ stablestatespace = establish_stablestatespace(s)
```

The tester's behaviour is captured in three schemas. From the NODE status, the tester may wish to test operations that can be performed from states in the unstablestatespace. The TryTestOfOptionalOperation schema gives the tester's behaviour for testing these optional operations. After performing the operation, the tester will update the unstablestatespace and stablestatespace variables. This behaviour corresponds to testing *Options* in the CO-OP method for labelled transition systems.

$$
\begin{array}{|l}
\hline
\_\_ TryTestOfOptionalOperation _____ \\
\Delta TesterState \\
out! : EVENT \\
\hline
status = NODE \\
\exists\, y : optionalopns(unstablestatespace) \bullet out! \in events(y) \\
unstablestatespace' = unstablestatespacereachedafter(out!, \\
\qquad\qquad\qquad\qquad stablestatespace, unstablestatespace) \\
stablestatespace' = stablestatespacereachedafter(out!, \\
\qquad\qquad\qquad\qquad stablestatespace, unstablestatespace) \\
status' = NODE \\
\hline
\end{array}
$$

Alternatively when the status is NODE the tester may select a set of operations which can be performed from states in the stablestatespace. It must select this set so that from each state in the stablestatespace there is at least one operation in the set that can be performed from that state. The tester will set its status to be that set. This behaviour corresponds to the internal action which is used in the CO-OP method for labelled transition systems to precede behaviour testing elements of Orth(Compulsory):

$$
\begin{array}{|l}
\hline
\_\_ SelectOrthCompulsoryElement _____ \\
\Delta TesterState \\
\hline
stablestatespace' = stablestatespace \\
unstablestatespace' = unstablestatespace \\
status = NODE \\
status' \in Orth(compulsoryopns(stablestatespace)) \\
\hline
\end{array}
$$

Once the tester has selected an element of *Orth(Compulsory)* it can perform TestOrthCompulsoryElementOperations. It must offer participation in any operation which name is included in the status. After performing the operation the tester will reset its status to NODE, and update its stablestatespace and unstablestatespace variables. This behaviour corresponds to the test of elements of *Orth(Compulsory)* in the CO-OP method for labelled transition systems.

$$
\begin{array}{|l}
\hline
\_\_ TestOrthCompulsoryElementOperations _____ \\
\Delta TesterState \\
out! : EVENT \\
\hline
\exists\, y : OPERATIONNAME;\ z : \mathbf{P}(OPERATIONNAME) \mid \\
\qquad status = opset\ (z) \bullet (y \in z) \wedge (out! \in events(y)) \\
unstablestatespace' = unstablestatespacereachedafter(out!, \\
\qquad\qquad\qquad\qquad stablestatespace, unstablestatespace) \\
stablestatespace' = stablestatespacereachedafter(out!, \\
\qquad\qquad\qquad\qquad stablestatespace, unstablestatespace) \\
status' = NODE \\
\hline
\end{array}
$$

Grouped together in a class type, the Z schemas above describe a generic canonical tester for instances of a class type with state space STATENAME, a set of actions OPERATIONNAME and a set of external actions EVENT.

4.3 Test derivation algorithm

The above schemas describe the behaviour of the tester in general terms. Now we wish to define the tester for a given specification, by a process of automatic derivation. To do this we need to actualise the schemas with real values that are related to the object's specification. First the initial state of the tester needs to be derived from the object specification following the InitializeTester schema. For the state thus found, the three operation schemas need to be actualised. For each new tester state thus found again actualisation of the operations is needed. This process is repeated until no new tester states are encountered.

This algorithm has been applied to the specification P' of Section 3. The resulting tester is given below. Since P' does not use any unstable states, the unstablestatespace of the tester state is always empty and is not used in any of the operations. We have left it out of the tester specification.

```
┌─ TesterForP' ──────────────────────────────────
│ ┌─ TesterState ─────────────────────────────────
│ │ stablestatespace : P(STATENAME)
│ │ status : TESTERSTATUS
│ └───────────────────────────────────────────────
│
│ ┌─ InitializeTester ────────────────────────────
│ │ TesterState
│ │ ───────────────────────────────────────────────
│ │ status = NODE
│ │ stablestatespace = {0}
│ └───────────────────────────────────────────────
│
│ ┌─ SelectOrthCompulsoryElement0 ────────────────
│ │ Δ TesterState
│ │ ───────────────────────────────────────────────
│ │ stablestatespace = {0}
│ │ status = NODE
│ │ status' ∈ {{read}, {input}}
│ │ stablestatespace' = stablestatespace
│ └───────────────────────────────────────────────
│
│ ┌─ SelectOrthCompulsoryElement1 ────────────────
│ │ Δ TesterState
│ │ ───────────────────────────────────────────────
│ │ stablestatespace = {1}
│ │ status = NODE
│ │ status' ∈ {{read}, {input}}
│ │ stablestatespace' = stablestatespace
│ └───────────────────────────────────────────────
│
```

$$
\begin{array}{|l}
\hline
\_\,TestOrthCompulsoryElement00\_\! \\
\Delta\,TesterState \\
out!:EVENT \\
\hline
stablestatespace = \{0\} \\
status = \{read\} \\
out! = (s! = 0) \\
status' = NODE \\
stablestatespace' = stablestatespace \\
\hline
\end{array}
$$

$$
\begin{array}{|l}
\hline
\_\,TestOrthCompulsoryElement01\_ \\
\Delta\,TesterState \\
out!:EVENT \\
\hline
stablestatespace = \{0\} \\
status = \{input\}. \\
out! = (x? = a) \\
status' = NODE \\
stablestatespace' = \{1\} \\
\hline
\end{array}
$$

$$
\begin{array}{|l}
\hline
\_\,TestOrthCompulsoryElement11\_ \\
\Delta\,TesterState \\
out!:EVENT \\
\hline
stablestatespace = \{1\} \\
status = \{read\} \\
out! = (s! = 1) \\
status' = NODE \\
stablestatespace' = stablestatespace \\
\hline
\end{array}
$$

$$
\begin{array}{|l}
\hline
\_\,TestOrthCompulsoryElement10\_ \\
\Delta\,TesterState \\
out!:EVENT \\
\hline
stablestatespace = \{1\} \\
status = \{input\} \\
out! = (x? = b) \\
status' = NODE \\
stablestatespace' = \{0\} \\
\hline
\end{array}
$$

The algorithm has also been applied to the Z specification of the Sieve managed object [11]. The Sieve specification was slightly altered to make some internal transitions explicit. The canonical tester was then produced following the above method. This resulted in a specification of the tester that used 276 operations. Each operation was presented by a schema. The tester specification could be made more concise. It appeared that it could be rewritten to 12 operations only. The concise tester has equivalent testing power to the much larger one. They are both canonical testers and describe the same behaviour. Current work aims to improve the above algorithm to produce concise testers.

5 Conclusions

We have shown that class types and instances can be represented in Z in a way that has a natural operational semantics expressed in terms of labelled transition systems or processes. This paper is intended to be an overview to demonstrate the feasibility of our approach. Definitions of subtyping and of the conformance of an object to a type definition have been formulated within this framework and are consistent with earlier work on object oriented LOTOS and Z. This new interpretation of object oriented Z makes possible the application to object oriented Z specifications of the CO-OP method of conformance test derivation. This technique will let us derive conformance tests from Z specifications of OSI managed objects.

Acknowledgements This work has been considerably improved by the suggestions and criticism of our colleagues Hossein Rafsanjani, Steve Rudkin and Jeremy Wilson.

References

[1] Ed Brinksma, Giuseppe Scollo and Chris Steenbergen, *LOTOS specifications, their implementations and their tests*, in G Bochmann, B Sarikaya (Eds) *Protocol Specification, Testing and Verification VI*, North Holland, 1987

[2] Ed Brinksma, *A theory for the derivation of tests*, S Aggarwal, K Sabnani (Eds) *Protocol Specification, Testing and Verification VIII*, North Holland, 1989

[3] Ed Brinksma and Tommaso Bolognesi, *Introduction to the ISO specification language LOTOS*, Computer Networks and ISDN Systems, Vol 14 Number 1, 1987

[4] D Carrington, D Duke, R Duke, P King, G Rose and G Smith, *Object-Z: An object oriented extension to Z*, in S Vuong (Ed), *Formal Description Techniques, 1989*, North Holland, 1990

[5] Elspeth Cusack, *Refinement, conformance and inheritance*, Formal Aspects of Computing Vol 3 No 2, April – June 1991

[6] E Cusack, S Rudkin and C Smith, *An object oriented interpretation of LOTOS*, in S Vuong (Ed), *Formal Description Techniques, 1989*, North Holland, 1990

[7] Elspeth Cusack, *Inheritance in object oriented Z*, in P America (Ed), *Proc. European Conference on Object Oriented Programming, 1991*, Lecture Notes in Computer Science 512, Springer-Verlag, 1991

[8] Elspeth Cusack, *Object oriented modelling in Z*, in J de Meer (Ed) *International Workshop on ODP, October 1991*, North Holland, 1992

[9] Elspeth Cusack and G H B Rafsanjani, *ZEST*, in S Stepney, R Barden and D Cooper (Eds), Object Orientation in Z, Workshops in Computing, Springer-Verlag, 1992

194

[10] H-D Ehrich and A Sernadas, *Fundamental Object Concepts and Construc-tions*, in Technische Universität Braunschweig Report 91-03 (Workshop IS-CORE 91, London)

[11] Steve Rudkin, *Modelling information objects in Z*, in J de Meer (Ed) *International Workshop on ODP, October 1991*, North Holland, 1992

[12] S A Schumann, D H Pitt and P J Byers, *Object oriented process speci-fication*, in C Rattray (Ed), *Specification and Verification of Concurrent Systems*, BCS/Springer-Verlag, 1990

[13] J M Spivey, *The Z Notation: A Reference Manual*, Prentice Hall Interna-tional Series in Computer Science, 1989

[14] Clazien D Wezeman, *The CO-OP method for compositional derivation of canonical testers*, in E Brinksma, G Scollo, C A Vissers (Eds), *Protocol Specification, Testing and Verification, IX*, North Holland, 1990

[15] ISO IS 8807, *LOTOS – a formal description technique based on the tem-poral ordering of observational behaviour*, 1989

[16] ISO/IEC DIS 10165 (Parts 1–4) *Management Information Services – Structure of Management Information*, June 1990

Appendix: Definition 1 implies subtyping in the sense of Cusack [7]

In [7], attributes of a class type, like state variables, are declared as compo-nents of the state schema. Initial state schemas are omitted to avoid clutter – we can simply assume that any valid state may be an initial state. Space con-siderations prevent the definition of subtyping from [7] being repeated here: it depends on a mapping which coerces each value in the statespace of the subtype to a corresponding in the state space of the supertype. Corresponding to each operation in the supertype there must be an operation in the subtype. The coercion permits the comparison of corresponding operations – roughly, we re-quire that any state change or output produced by the operation on an instance of the subtype could have been produced by the operation on an instance of the supertype.

Let Q and P be class types, such that Q is a subtype of P in the sense of this paper. In particular, suppose that $Q(s_{0,Q}, B)$ extends $P(s_{0,P}, A)$ for some initial state $s_{0,Q}$ mapping to initial state $s_{0,P}$ and sets of attribute values A and B. Suppose further that there are *read* operations by which every state variable and attribute declared in P and Q can be read at any time without causing any state changes. Then Q can be shown to be a subtype of P in the sense of [7]. The proof is sketched below.

First of all, we define a mapping f from the statespace X_Q of $Q(s_{0,Q}, B)$ into the statespace X_P of $P(s_{0,P}, A)$. We then need to establish that whenever e is the name of an action in EVENT*, the set Y of transitions associated with e in $Q(s_{0,Q}, B)$ is related to the set Z of transitions associated with e in $P(s_{0,P}, A)$ by $dom\, Z \subseteq dom\, Y^{f \times f}$ and $(dom Z \lhd Y^{f \times f}) \subseteq Z$.

Let $\sigma \in traces(P(s_0, A))$ and consider the values of state variables or attributes in $Q(s_{0,Q}, B)$ after σ. Since traces$(P(s_{0,P}, A)) \subseteq traces(Q(s_{0,Q}, B))$, any value that can be obtained from $P(s_{0,P}, A)$ – that is, the value of *any* state variable or attribute defined in P – can also be obtained from $Q(s_{0,Q}, B)$. A consequence of this is that Q must declare at least the attributes and state variables of P, and that attributes and state variables declared in both P and Q have the same type. This implies that states in X_Q can be mapped to states in X_P by discarding the 'extra' components , giving a natural mapping f from X_Q to X_P.

Using the notation set out in [1] for labelled transition systems, suppose $P(s_0, A) = \sigma \Rightarrow P(s_0, A)' - e \rightarrow$ for some process $P(s_0, A)'$ and action e. Then $\sigma. < e > \in traces(Q(s_0, B))$, which implies that $Q(s_0, B) = \sigma \Rightarrow Q(s_0, B)' - e \rightarrow$ for some process $Q(s_0, B)'$. This establishes that e can be performed by $Q(s_0, B)$ whenever it could be performed by $P(s_0, A)$, and so $dom Z \subseteq dom\ Y^{f \times f}$.

Finally, we need to show that any transition labelled with action e in the process $Q(s_{0,Q}, B)$ after σ can be mapped by f into a transition associated with e in the process $P(s_{0,P}, A)$ after σ. Let *read* denote some operation by which a state or attribute value defined in P can be read. If there exists a process $Q(s_{0,Q}, B)''$ such that $Q(s_{0,Q}, B) = \sigma \Rightarrow Q(s_0, B)' - e \rightarrow Q(s_0, B)''$, but which then deadlocks with every possible action *read!a*, then the definition of extension ensures that there must exist a $P(s_{0,P}, A)''$ such that $P(s_{0,P}, A) = \sigma \Rightarrow P(s_{0,P}, A)' - e \rightarrow P(s_{0,P}, A)''$ but which then deadlocks with every possible action *read!a*. This contradicts the definition of *read*. We conclude that $(dom Z \lhd Y^{f \times f}) \subseteq Z$, where Y and Z are the sets of transitions associated with e in $Q(s_0, B)$ and $P(s_0, A)$ respectively.

.

Using Z in Communications Engineering (Invited Talk)

Elspeth Cusack

BT

Bibb Way, Ipswich IP1 2EQ,

United Kingdom

1 Introduction

A team at BT Labs has been using Z to tackle problems in telecommunications engineering for the last 3 years. We have increasingly found Z to be more satisfactory for use in some application areas than already standardised formal description techniques.

In this talk, I explain the motivation for BT's involvement. This is not just a formality. The company's development effort is focussed on topics which have a real chance of increasing the company's profitability, and the work programme described is strongly driven by the needs of internal customers.

I will need to explain some background about the application areas, and I also want to say a little about why we have been drawn to *object oriented* Z.

2 Structure of the talk

First of all I will mention the major areas of communication engineering to which our work relates, and then I will touch on the history of formal description in this field. Next, I will tell you a little more about OSI Network Management. Databases of network management information are constructed from building blocks called "managed objects" [17]. We now use ZEST, our own dialect of object oriented Z, to specify managed objects. ZEST is a close cousin of the Australian dialect Object Z.

Finally, I will touch on the use of Z by the ISO[1] Open Distributed Processing project (ODP) [18], as that is very relevant to the current ISO New Work Item ballot on Z.

3 Important programmes and issues

The emphasis in communications engineering is shifting from raw technology such as OSI and ISDN towards architectures designed for ease of introduction of new services (as in the intelligent network) or for the integration of support for distribution, interworking, interoperability and portability (as in Open Distributed Processing systems.)

---

[1] International Organisation for Standardisation

Network management is already with us – to give an idea of complexity, current network operations units in BT manage 2–3 million access lines, deal with thousands of event reports per day, and control the work of several thousand maintenance people. "Management" means performance management, security management, maintenance, access management, layer management and so on. BT, via a subsidiary based in Atlanta, is now competing in the global private network management market.

We need pre-competitive international standards to open up markets. Standards specify *what* is required, not *how* the specification is implemented. This paves the way for competing implementations of the same standard. The standardisation process shares the load of conceptual development. We need ways of testing that implementations actually conform to the standards they claim to implement. Such conformance testing is once-only, black box testing. Test suites, or ways of deriving them, need to be standardised to make sure that the test process is repeatable. Current practice in this area depends on engineering heuristics.

Finally, the success story in modelling of the last five years in all of the areas mentioned has been object oriented, with objects forming natural units of storage, distribution, management, failure and so on.

4 Formal description techniques

Z is not the specification language traditionally thought of in the context of communications engineering. There are three *formal description techniques (FDTs)* recognised by ISO and CCITT[2] for specifying protocols and services [13]. Each of them is already an international standard, and Z is not on the list.

LOTOS combines a process calculus with algebraic datatyping using ACT-ONE [15]. It is most applicable to protocols with complex behaviour. It has given rise to a powerful theory of conformance testing.

SDL has been under development since the early 70s. Datatyping (in ACT-ONE, lifted wholesale from LOTOS) was added in SDL88. The latest version, SDL92, contains a description of "Object SDL" [16]. SDL has a healthy user community centred round ISDN and signalling protocols.

Estelle is a PASCAL derivative, and has never attracted as much attention as LOTOS and SDL[3].

So, is there a role for Z in this field? I believe so, and in the remainder of this talk, I would like to explain why.

---

[2] International Consultative Committee on Telephony and Telegraphy

[3] Was the effort of standardising the FDTs worthwhile? Well, there is no normative text for protocol standards written in any of them – basically, the languages took too long to develop. But, the languages have contributed a much greater awareness of modelling and specification issues, and a pool of experts throughout the world who are now seeded into many corporate and collaborative telecommunications development projects. For example, the modelling concepts of the ODP Reference Model, though expressed in English, have obvious roots in formal methods. There has been no revolution, but degree of evolution.

5 Specification techniques for OSI management standards

A *managed object* is an abstraction of a real-world entity – perhaps a modem, or a circuit, or a PC, or a customer. The Management Information Base, a collection of *instances* of managed objects, is a potentially enormous database.

ISO has standardised an informal specification technique in a document called the Guidelines for the Definitions of Managed Objects (GDMO) [8, 17]. One problem with the GDMO is that it provides only English for the specification of managed object behaviour. Another problem is that the GDMO allows inheritance, via superclass declarations in a managed object definition, but offers no guidance on the intended meaning.

My team first became involved in this area to help our network management colleagues with these problems. Our first experiment used LOTOS in a case study specification of a managed object. We were not happy with the results for various reasons. Firstly, the style of algebraic specification was very cumbersome for what was essentially an information object. This was particularly offputting for management people who were not LOTOS experts. Secondly, although we had done some research in object oriented LOTOS, we had failed to find an easy mechanism for incremental inheritance [3, 10]. Thirdly, as managed objects do not communicate directly with each other, LOTOS process calculus offered rather too rich a model.

The issue of algebraic specification was clearly also going to be a problem with SDL (although SDL is successfully used in BT to develop specifications of networking protocols, where datatypes are inherently relatively simple.)

By mid-1990, stimulated by the publication of work on Object-Z by the University of Queensland [2], we were forming some opinions of our own on object oriented Z [4, 5]. So we repeated the case study, using first conventional Z, and then an object oriented version. We found that Z's emphasis sat very well with the GDMO, with GDMO attributes fitting into state schemas and actions, and notifications and pre- and post-conditions fitting into operation schemas.

With object oriented Z, there was an immediate correspondence between "managed object" and "class type". The behaviour of a managed object, including inherited behaviour, was much easier to articulate. Our own investigation [11] resulted in some preliminary ways of reasoning about behaviour, especially verifying subtype relationships (subtyping in the sense of behavioural compatibility, not just signature compatibility).

Later work demonstrated that we could use specifications in our own object oriented Z dialect ZEST [6] as a basis for rigorous derivation of conformance tests, and as a starting point for implementation.

6 Specifying managed objects

In 1992 we have been specifying several managed objects in ZEST. Some engineers who specialise in network management – and who have not even managed to go on a Z training course – are involved in this work, which is greatly adding to its credibility within the company.

The choice of objects let us exercise inheritance techniques and subtyping relationships. The objects are taken from a simple hierarchy centred on the *event reporting sieve*, an object that accepts notifications and selectively transforms them into event reports which are output; another is the *temporal correlator*, a proprietary BT managed object which inherits from the *event reporting sieve*, adding functionality. We are feeding back from this exercise into the continuing development of ZEST.

These specifications have been implemented in C^{++} using the informal technique described in the paper in these proceedings by Hossein Rafsanjani and Steve Colwill [9]. The code appears to be as efficient as code prepared directly from the informal GDMO specifications. The degree of correspondence between the ZEST specifications and the implementations depends on the C^{++} class libraries used (because the library provides the level of abstraction.) Also, the ZEST specifications reduce the amount of documentation required.

The need to improve the GDMO by seeking a formalism for managed object specification has of course been recognised by other organisations. BNR, for example, published research on a VDM approach in 1991 [12]. The CCITT is considering in early 1993 a work item to standardise on a single formalism. An initial UK position will be assembled over the next couple of months. There is thus no consensus on the best choice of language for specifying managed objects. And indeed, how could there ever be an objectively "best" language! Any decision taken will be seen in some quarters as bold; but I think that a bold choice which allows timely and innovative developments to continue is preferable to "analysis paralysis".

7 Deriving tests for managed objects

About a year ago, BT's Conformance Test Lab was asked to look at the problem of testing managed object implementations for conformance to their specifications. As I mentioned earlier, existing best practice is largely heuristic. However, we are also exploring an approach based on LOTOS technology. The *Co-Op Method* derived by Clazien Wezeman provides a way to derive a canonical test process from a given process, or *labelled transition system* [14]. (The method realises the theory of Ed Brinksma published in 1988 [1].) The canonical tester can be separated into test cases, and a realistic number of tests selected for use.

This work is reported in a paper in these proceedings [7]. The paper outlines a way of transferring the Co-Op Method into an object oriented Z environment. In order to do this, we had to introduce various sophistications – or complications – into our object oriented Z concepts. I will summarise the main points. We interpret class types as processes. We find we have to distinguish operations involving interaction with the environment from internal operations (essentially, spontaneous changes of state – like the internal event in LOTOS or CCS.) This leads us to strengthen our subtyping definition, and to define the *conformance* of an implementation to a class type. The definitions of subtyping and conformance interwork to ensure that an implementation which conforms to a class type also conforms to each supertype, as we would expect.

A small example using the Co-Op Method is calculated in the paper. The method was tried on the *sieve* managed object (which has 10 operations) and it generated a canonical tester with 256 operations! This number was reduced on inspection to 12 – this explains why test selection, as well as test derivation, is an important issue.

The canonical tester approach is theoretically sound, automatable[4] and repeatable, but it remains to be seen if implementations suitable for practical industrial use can be found.

8 Open Distributed Processing

The ODP Reference Model standards are due in 1994 and will provide an integrated framework for the specification and design of distributed systems. The ODP Reference Model describes five *viewpoints* which form the *framework of abstractions*. The *Information Viewpoint* is concerned with the structure and manipulation of the information content of an enterprise[5]. Object oriented modelling is used within each viewpoint, using a specific set of ODP modelling concepts. These concepts are interpreted in LOTOS, Z and SDL in a separate ISO working document [19].

The Trader [20] is the first ODP object to be standardised. The Trader enables servers to advertise their services and clients to find suitable servers. It therefore supports dynamic reconfiguration of applications during run-time, with consequent benefits of flexibility. The latest working draft on the Trader includes a Z specification prepared by BT – it was selected by ISO delegates in preference to other submitted specifications in LOTOS and SDL. There is also an annex containing an Object Z description, interesting because it explicitly displays the interaction between the Trader and objects with which the Trader communicates. But the Z specification of the Trader itself is basically an Object Z specification with the class schema removed.

Since it is ISO policy that formal techniques used in standards must themselves be standards, the ODP Working Group strongly supports the current New Work Item ballot on Z.

9 Concluding remarks

My conclusions are that Z is good for specifying information objects, and sometimes object oriented Z is even better. Z is relatively accessible to nonspecialists, which is a significant factor in industry. Finally, an international standard for Z would be helpful.

Our Z work will be continuing in 1993, and probably expanding into new and important topics such as service feature interaction. The year will be crucial for the future of Z, with the ISO ballot and ongoing discussions on a standard technique for specifying managed objects.

Acknowledgements The following people directly contributed to work mentioned in this paper: Graeme Anderson, Rob Booth, Jon Legh-Smith, Tony Judge, Hossein Rafsanjani, Steve Rudkin, Clazien Wezeman and Jeremy Wilson. Other people have contributed to closely related work, and yet others

---

[4] It has been implemented in the latest LOTOS toolset.
[5] In ODP jargon, managed objects are information viewpoint specifications.

- including some whose main areas of expertise are conformance testing and network management - are helping to take the whole programme forward.

References

[1] Ed Brinksma, *A theory for the derivation of tests*, in S Aggarwal, K Sabnani (Eds), *Protocol Specification, Testing and Verification VIII*, North Holland, 1989

[2] D Carrington, D Duke, R Duke, P King, G Rose and G Smith, *Object-Z: An object oriented extension to Z*, in S Vuong (Ed), *Formal Description Techniques 1989*, North Holland, 1990

[3] Elspeth Cusack, Steve Rudkin and Chris Smith, *An object oriented interpretation of LOTOS*, in S Vuong (Ed), *Formal Description Techniques 1989*, North Holland, 1990

[4] Elspeth Cusack, *Inheritance in object oriented Z*, in P America (Ed), Proc. European Conference on Object Oriented Programming, 1991, Lecture Notes in Computer Science 512, Springer, 1991

[5] Elspeth Cusack, *Object oriented modelling in Z*, in J de Meer (Ed) *International Workshop on ODP, October 1991* North Holland, 1992

[6] Elspeth Cusack and G H B Rafsanjani, *ZEST*, in S S Stepney, R Barden and D Cooper (Eds), *Object Orientation in Z*, Workshops in Computing, Springer 1992

[7] Elspeth Cusack and Clazien Wezeman, *Deriving tests for objects specified in Z*, these Proceedings

[8] Tony Jeffree, *GDMO: Tools for defining OSI managed objects*, in *Advanced Networking Week*, Blenheim Online, 1992

[9] G H B Rafsanjani and Steve Colwill, *From Object-Z to C++ - a structural mapping*, these Proceedings

[10] Steve Rudkin, *Inheritance in LOTOS*, in K R Parker and G A Rose (Eds), *Formal Description Techniques 1991*, North Holland, 1992

[11] Steve Rudkin, *Modelling information objects in Z*, in J de Meer (Ed) *International Workshop on ODP, October 1991*, North Holland, 1992

[12] Linda Simon and Lynn S Marshall, *Using VDM to specify OSI managed objects*, in K R Parker and G A Rose (Eds), *Formal Description Techniques 1991* North Holland 1992

[13] K J Turner, *Using Formal Description Techniques*, Macmillan 1992

[14] Clazien D Wezeman, *The CO-OP method for compositional derivation of canonical testers*, in E Brinksma, G Scollo, C A Vissers (Eds), *Protocol Specification, Testing and Verification, IX*, North Holland, 1990

[15] ISO IS 8807, *LOTOS – a formal description technique based on the temporal ordering of observational behaviour*, 1989

[16] CCITT Com X-R 17-E, Rec Z.100 *Functional Specification and Description Language (SDL)*, 1992

[17] CCITT Rec X.720 – X.722 — ISO/IEC IS 10165 (Parts 1–4) *Management Information Services – Structure of Management Information*, 1992

[18] CCITT Rec X.902 — ISO/IEC CD 10746-2.1 *Basic Reference Model of Open Distributed Processing – Part 2: Descriptive Model*, 1992

[19] CCITT Rec X.905 — ISO/IEC SC21 WG7 N752 *Basic Reference Model of Open Distributed Processing – Part 5: Architectural Semantics*, November 1992

[20] ISO/IEC SC21 WG7 N743 *Working Document of the ODP Trader*, November 1992

Information Systems

Using Formal Specification in the Acquisition of Information Systems Educating Information Systems Professionals

Paul A. Swatman

Department of Computer Science, Curtin University of Technology
Perth, Western Australia

Abstract

Research into the industrial application of formal methods has concentrated almost exclusively on the specification of software systems in high-risk or safety critical applications—thus, attention has been directed to technical problems with technical systems. The Formal Methods Research Group at Curtin University has, however, been addressing the potential practical application of Z and Object-Z in the development of information systems within a "real-world" commercial context.

In this paper, I discuss educational issues associated with the use of formal specification, in particular Z and Object-Z, within the commercial Information Systems (IS) domain. From an educational perspective, I report three specification case studies undertaken by means of action research: one in an artificial setting, two in a commercial setting; and the development of a training and technology transfer programme applicable within the IS domain.

1 Introduction

A formal specification provides a precise medium for communication:

- between the specifier on the one hand and the designers and implementors on the other

- between the specifier and the client(s).

Further, if the specification language is designed for *human* analysis, a precise specification in that language forms a basis for:

- the identification of errors, omissions and inconsistencies

- validation against the needs of the client(s)

Consequently, formal specification offers the potential for the early identification of specification problems so that such problems may be resolved both early and relatively cheaply. The Formal Methods Research Group at Curtin University is currently addressing the potential practical application of formal specification using the languages Z [40] and Object-Z [17] in the development of (management) information systems within a "real-world" commercial context.

In [46] we:

- described a framework appropriate for the development of information systems within a commercial context

- described a method within that framework:

  - which accepts the principle of multiple *Weltanschauungen* of information systems and the subjectivity of information systems requirements

  - within which information systems requirements may be determined using, *inter alia*, formal modelling (in Object-Z) as an analytic tool

  - in which a formal specification, structured on the basis of the Object-Oriented approach, forms the interface between requirements definition and solution design and which, consequently, supports Object-Oriented design and implementation within the framework of Henderson-Sellers and Edwards' Fountain Model [27, 26].

- presented a "simulated" case study of the development of a formal specification of an essentially representative information system.

This work was extended:

- in [48] in which early results were reported from industrial trials of this method within Western Australia; and

- in [47] in which a project management structure was described which supports the application of the method for software acquisition within the Information Systems (I.S.) domain.

In this paper, I discuss educational issues associated with the use of formal specification (in particular, Z and Object-Z) within the commercial IS domain. I:

- analyse the learning experiences of three students who have chosen to undertake their project in the domain of formal methods.

- describe the evolution of an introductory course in formal specification in Z and Object-Z which we have offered to undergraduate and graduate diploma students within the Department

- describe a strategy for transferring formal specification methods to organisations for use within the IS domain

2 Research Methodology

In considering the education of Information Systems professionals in formal methods of system specification it became apparent that theory was poorly developed. In consequence, I accepted Banville and Landry's [1, page 58] exhortation for the use of pluralistic research methods and adopted a three-part, essentially qualitative, research strategy utilising complementary, case study based research methods:

descriptive/interpretive analysis In the first round of case studies, an undergraduate student, under my supervision specified a fragment of a computer-aided software engineering (CASE) tool, with the researcher providing consultancy services on demand. A project diary was kept and the student's experiences analysed and fed back into the specification process by means of the hermeneutic circle (after Boland [3]). Following analysis, the results of this study formed input to an education programme which preceded a second round of case studies, this time conducted by

action research within a real-world context in collaboration with an industrial partner. The results of this second round of case studies, in turn, fed back into the development of an educational programme which, itself, is investigated by

action research In parallel with the second round of case studies, I prepared a unit offered as part of tertiary studies in computing and presented it, first at the honours level, then at the undergraduate level. I observed and analysed the educational process, feeding these results and the results of an ongoing analysis of the specification case studies back into the educational programme which evolved over a number of iterations.

I rejected a more quantitative approach to the investigation of this problem as being premature since theory in this area is poorly developed. Bonoma [4, page 201] notes that although quantitative methods produce results which are high in data integrity, they are not suitable for situations where information and theory/hypothesis building is required. Benbaset et al. concur and summarise the views of a number of researchers in the Information Systems field, supporting the use of the case study approach to investigate:

> "[problems] *in which research and theory are at their early, formative stages; and sticky, practice-based problems where the experiences of the actors are important and the context of action is critical"* [2, page 369].

I decided to develop, for the first study round, a simulated case which is largely representative—it does not exhibit any special characteristics which would suggest otherwise. The simulated case can also be considered revelatory, though possibly not in the strict sense suggested by Yin [52]. In general, Chatfield [8] supports the use of simulation under these circumstances, that is, for the investigation of problems which are difficult or impossible to solve analytically and Galliers [19, 18] adds weight to the applicability of these techniques within the IS domain.

I then explored the educational process from two entirely different perspectives, both of which made use of the action research approach, an "interventionist" research method recommended for use in *"evolving criteria by which to articulate and appraise actions taken in organisational contexts..."* [41, page 559]:

- I undertook two further case studies in which I initially trained research students in the application of the method described in [46] and then acted as expert consultant during their subsequent collaborative (pilot) information systems acquisition projects.

- I also undertook action research directed at the education of undergraduate level students within the Department in formal specification techniques. The course was offered and evolved over five iterations.

3 Case Study—1990: KOH Kian Hwee

In late 1989, Koh Kian Hwee, an undergraduate student who had done quite well in software engineering, agreed to fulfil his undergraduate project obligations while participating in research into learning to apply formal methods of software specification. From Koh's perspective the project involved learning to write specifications in the formal language Z and preparing a specification of a rudimentary Computer Aided Software Engineering (CASE) tool, in fact, a Structure Chart [53] editor. From the perspective of this programme of research, however, the project formed a case study of the learning and application of formal methods and, in particular, Z.

Care must be taken when extrapolating from the results of this case study, since the project on which it is based is not representative of applications in industry in three important ways:

- It is not realistically scaled. It could reasonably be anticipated that the specification would be completed by a novice within the relatively short time available for an undergraduate project—nominally 240 hours over 9 months. The problems of structuring large specifications did not, therefore, arise

- It took place within an "artificial" environment

- There was only one view of the requirement—Koh did not have to contend with the multiple *Weltanschauungen* [9] which typically exist in problem situations within the IS domain. The coverage of this case study in relation to the development method described in [46] and depicted in Figure 1 is restricted to the formal modelling phase.

Koh began the project with the following background, he:

- was familiar with Structure Charts

- was familiar with the mathematics underlying Z

- had received a brief introduction to the Object-Oriented paradigm

- had been introduced to formal methods in principle and to the ideas of axiomatic specification

I was able to offer him an introduction and guide to the literature, in particular [40, 39, 28, 29, 21, 24] and was prepared to be active in assisting him to learn and apply formal methods. It is important to be clear that, at that time, my own experience of formal specification and Z was limited and exclusively derived from the literature, although I did have many years professional experience as a systems analyst and project manager. There are striking similarities between this project and a commercial pilot project having the primary aim of evaluating the potential of new technology.

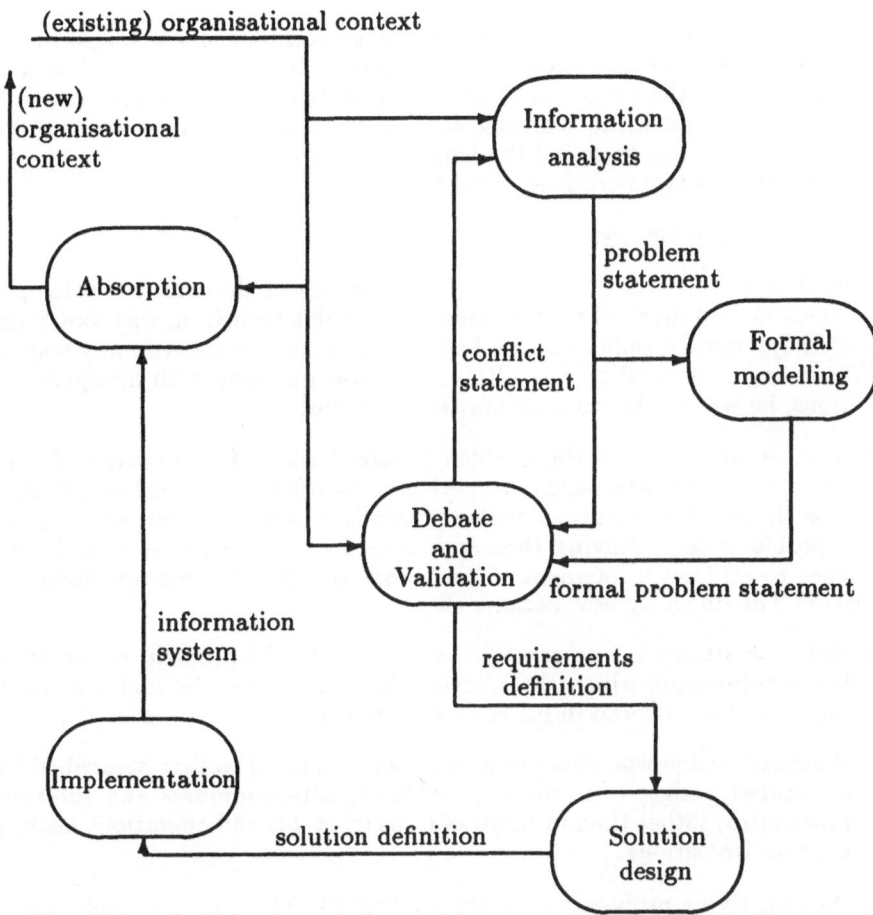

Figure 1: A Suggested Information Systems Development Process Model

The first difficulty which we encountered was particularly interesting in the way in which it initially presented—as a specification problem. Over the long vacation preceding the project, Koh had read the literature which I provided and, in March 1990, when he returned at the beginning of first semester he appeared to have made sound progress in learning the underlying theory. As semester progressed, he appeared to make little *practical* progress although he devoured any worked case studies which I could provide or he could locate by literature search.

By the middle of the year, he had still not presented any Z fragments of his own and, although the project is designed to be split between first and second semester in the ratio 1:3, I began to be concerned. In discussions, Koh indicated that although he was able to read, analyse and understand quite complex specifications, he found the language difficult to *write*.

Koh pointed to two perceived difficulties:

- with the mathematics

- with style—he was unwilling to show me any of the abortive attempts which he had made at specification since he felt their form was contrived. Perhaps more significantly, he had not been able to identify any way of assessing their quality—i.e. although he was unhappy with his specifications, he was unable to pinpoint the problems.

My first attempt to address this problem involved asking Koh to attempt a set of small exercises in specification at varying levels of mathematical complexity. Within 24 hours, Koh returned with essentially correct, elegant solutions to all the problems set. Solving these problems had also given Koh sufficient confidence to attempt a fragment of the CASE tool specification and show me the result. The difficulty now became clear:

- Koh was attempting to specify the solution to the problem rather than the requirements which the solution must meet, i.e. he had too much implementation detail in his early specification

- the specification was structured in a manner similar to that prescribed by structured design, in terms of procedures, sub-procedures and sub-sub-procedures, rather than in terms of objects, states and operations leading to state transitions

- the underlying problems were not mathematical but, rather, problems of abstraction. The decomposition paradigm which he had adopted and the consequent mechanism for communication between modules (procedures, in this case) led to very unnatural representation in Z.

The difficulty arose as a consequence of a lack of *methodological* literature specifically related to abstraction and modelling for representation in Z. Spivey [40] provides a language syntax definition; Ince [28] and Woodcock and Loomes [50] and, more recently, others [14, 36] give an introduction to the mathematical underpinnings (set theory and formal logic) specifically linked to Z. Hayes [24] has collected a number of case studies in which software systems are presented both informally and formally specified in Z. It should, perhaps, be emphasised that none of the case studies in [24] are concerned with developing the conceptual model but, rather, with specifying a fixed (presumably obvious) conceptual model in Z. Our immediate problem, then, was not how to write a Z specification for the CASE tool but, rather, how to structure the (informal) conceptual abstraction of the problem in such a way that the resulting model could be represented both precisely and naturally in Z.

As Svoboda [42] indicates, if we are to succeed in requirements specification, we need a (more or less) prescriptive method to lead us to a conceptual model of the problem. Since, in practice, it is this conceptual model (rather than the problem itself) which is specified, the model should be expressed in terms of abstract data types [32], the natural structure for Z specification. The methodological literature on the Object-Oriented approach (at that time, principally [34, 5, 11]), together with sessions in which we reviewed informal Object-Oriented models of the CASE tool developed by Koh, assisted us to address that problem.

The natural process model for the specification phase, the evolutionary model, was adopted for this project:

1. sketch out an appropriate conceptual model

2. examine and criticise the conceptual model by means of a conventional walkthrough, on the basis of:

   - syntactic and semantic error
   - clarity
   - style

Following the walkthrough, one of three possible courses of action can be taken:

   - if satisfactory, then the specification may be considered complete
   - if unsatisfactory, then either:
     - further refine and develop the specification prior to repeating this step; or
     - return to the first step and repeat the process of deriving the underlying model of the system.

As modelling (both formal and informal) progressed, the importance of the review process became evident and I was able to make the following observations:

- In his third year of an undergraduate course throughout which (in some units explicitly, in others implicitly) structured programming and design was the "good practice" paradigm presented, Koh tended to fall back on the principles of functional decomposition suggested within the structured model whenever he found himself in difficulty.

- Given an appropriately expressed conceptual model, it remains possible to specify that model in Z in a number of ways. At this time the only significant generally accepted style guideline which we were able to deduce from the literature was the observation that operations are most understandably specified as the disjunction of a "correct" operation and a set of "error" operations with distinct pre- and post-conditions (informally, erroneous for various reasons and with various results)[1].

Perhaps the most important consequence of these observations is the difficulty of learning to use a formal specification language (in particular, Z) in isolation from collegiate discussion or, ideally, expertise in the practical use of the language within the structure of some appropriate development method. Indeed, the iterative nature of the process and the difficulty which Koh found in criticising his own specification (a difficulty which was evident in all subjects studied, including myself) suggested that walkthroughs/specification reviews are so important that it may be difficult to apply formal specification in isolation. This discussion is extended in Section 9 below.

In his project report [31, page 28], Koh indicated that, in retrospect, he perceived his most significant difficulties to be seeing the problem from a specifier's rather than an implementor's perspective; and modelling the system in an appropriate form and at the "right" level of abstraction. It is interesting to note that, by the end of the project, Koh no longer considered the mathematics as worthy of significant comment.

I set out below an analysis of the problems which I observed during this project.

3.1   Modelling—Abstraction

Koh encountered two distinct categories of difficulty within this general classification:

- The problem of *what to abstract*. Koh experienced difficulty in differentiating between the requirements of the system, on the one hand and mechanisms for fulfilling an underlying requirement on the other. This is not a problem specific to the language Z, or even to formal specification in general but, rather, a key issue in systems analysis, described and analysed in detail by Davis in [12, pages 12–23] and elsewhere.

- The problem of deriving an *appropriate conceptual modelling structure* for use with Z, then resisting the temptation to fall back on the familiar functional decomposition techniques when under pressure (or, often, without realising that one is doing so).

In other words, in attempting to derive a conceptual model of a situation, it is necessary: firstly, to determine and discard those aspects of the situation which are irrelevant; and secondly to organise the remainder (the necessary aspects) in an appropriate way. This case study offers **no support** for the assertions:

- that deriving an appropriate conceptual model of a situation is easy

- that a structure based on abstract data types or objects is in any way "natural" to those who have been trained in analysis, design and/or programming primarily on the basis of functional decomposition

---

[1]Gravell [22] and Macdonald [33] have since published useful papers on style issues in Z

3.2 Modelling—Syntactic Style

For the duration of Koh's project, few explicit guidelines existed within the literature. The style which we adopted was derived:

- partially, by induction from the published case studies—a difficult process since the literature covered the period in which a good "standard" Z style was evolving (and, consequently, many styles were represented); and

- partially, by reference to the literature on object-oriented analysis and design

The *philosophy* which underlies our evolving style is based on the importance of formal specification as a communications medium, a position supported by Hayes and Jones' insightful argument in favour of non-executable specification languages [25]. In the IS domain, this perspective is particularly important, since:

- as we have argued in [46], an important contribution of formal specification is to assist the client(s) to *understand* the complex situation in which we are to intervene

- it is unreasonable to anticipate or require that a significant proportion of users or clients will ever be mathematically literate

Although [22, 33] now fill the important "syntactic style" vacuum in the Z literature, they did not, unfortunately, appear in time to contribute to this case study.

3.3 Modelling—Process

Within the formal modelling phase, the task of the specifier is to translate an informal requirements statement[2] into a formal specification. I have described the iterative process which we adopted for this phase above.

The single most significant problem uncovered in this case study is the difficulty of getting started (a difficulty which, in a general context, is widely recognised within the problem solving literature). Nominally, Koh had spent 60 hours man-time over almost 4 months before he was willing to begin to write a specification. Underlying this problem were:

- the issues which are described in Section 3.1 above

- a belief that the conceptual model must be expressed in Z initially

- an expectation that an appropriate conceptual model could be described initially

- an inability to assess the quality of the conceptual model or its formal representation

These four sub-problems appear to be mutually supportive and, in this case, led to the inability to make any practical progress. We only began to make progress when each of these sub-problems was attacked in isolation:

---

[2]which may or may not be for the entire problem situation

- As I have discussed in Section 3.1, it is important to define an appropriate modelling philosophy, one which may be translated into the formal language in an intuitive manner.

- There is no reason why the conceptual model must be expressed in Z initially. Formal representation is dependent on the conceptual model but not *vice versa*. In a manner analogous to that by which we teach students to program (by first writing structure charts and pseudocode or Nassi-Schneiderman Diagrams, then coding the design in their chosen programming language), we can teach students to write formal specifications by modelling the problem using an informal technique with an appropriate underlying philosophy, then specifying the conceptual model in a formal specification language.

- Understanding problem situations is difficult, but models of the situation *as currently understood* can help to clarify them. Clearly, in these circumstances early models, while useful are most unlikely to be accurate. Further, even in the relatively simple case represented in this study, there are a number of syntactically and semantically "correct" problem representations which conform to the underlying modelling philosophy. A "correct" model may, however, be "awkward" and difficult to analyse and understand. Once Koh had a specification to work with, he found that he was able to refine it, even rework it from scratch—but until he put his initial specification down on paper he made no progress.

- Evaluating the quality of the conceptual model is not a formal specification problem *per se*, but an evaluation of the model structure against the problem situation and the modelling philosophy which underlies the formal language being used (in the case of Z, abstract data types and state machines). The evaluation (once the underlying philosophy is identified) can occur whether or not the conceptual model is expressed in Z.

Once expressed in Z, the model representation may be syntactically checked automatically using one of number of tools—we used $fuzz$ [38]—but the problems of stylistic and semantic checking remain. Stylistic checking was undertaken throughout this project during walkthroughs conducted in an informal manner. This process was recursive in that the style standards against which we measured the specification were developed (within our underlying philosophy) throughout the project as a result of our analysis of "awkwardness" within the specification. Initially, semantic checking was totally informal, but as the project progressed towards a final specification we began to formulate and prove theorems—standard theorems such as initialisation and applicability to show that the specification was generally sound; and application-specific theorems to ensure that particular required properties did, in fact, follow from our specification. We did not begin to prove theorems about the system until late in the project because:

  - we were making significant progress by means of informal analysis

  - my primary concern was not the *product* but the learning exercise. During the project, it became clear that an important difficulty ex-

isted purely because of the perceived interplay between a set of unfamiliar techniques—consequently, I did not want to introduce a
further technique while we could manage without doing so.

Since we began this process late, we ran out of time before completing
the standard proofs—the following observations are, therefore, tentative.
The formal conduct of proofs is a laborious process and, in the case of this
relatively simple project, the standard proofs offered no unexpected insight into either the specification or the problem. The application-specific
proofs which we carried out did, however, provide us with more confidence
of the specification's soundness in areas that we considered particularly
important (by definition—we only conducted such proofs when we were
unconvinced by our informal argument, or when we considered that the
issue was sufficiently important to warrant the additional effort involved).

Two further process related questions were raised:

- *How can we tell whether we are making (satisfactory) progress?*

- *How do we know when to stop refining our specification?*

These difficulties are not specific to formal specification, but to any task with
goals which cannot be stated precisely and which, consequently, require the
application of professional judgement. Progress can only evaluated by reference
to a set of criteria against which the evolving specification can be measured.
I have discussed syntactic, stylistic and semantic-consistency criteria above,
but we are still faced with the problem that the specification itself can never
be compared formally against the unstructured, contradictory and ambiguous
problem context typical within the IS domain. I suggest that we are making
progress whenever we are learning more about the problem situation, whether
the specification is being expanded to encompass new facts, modified to resolve
misunderstanding, or redesigned (and, normally, reduced in size) to reflect a
new appreciation of the problem structure.

Hall [23] has suggested that, typically, once a structure for the model has
been defined, progress in developing and extending that model is rapid. As
progress slows, the *structure* of the model is re-evaluated and changed, then
the new model tightened and improved. This case study supports that view in
general—though as novice specifiers, we progressed through three representations of the problem before we felt satisfied that we had captured the essence
of the problem in an acceptable and useful way. At a point in the process
of refining our representation of the problem, we found that we had begun to
"tinker" with a representation of the problem with which we were essentially
satisfied. I hypothesise that such a point may occur in the general case—an
hypothesis which is supported by the other case studies reported in this paper.

4   A Second Round of Case Studies

By February 1991, my experience and understanding of applying the techniques
was greatly enhanced. I had:

- attended a course in formal specification offered by Roger Duke of the
University of Queensland [15]

- developed a significant specification of an Information System during which process Dr. Duke, who has extensive experience in specification using Z and Object-Z within the technical and scientific domains, acted as "expert consultant"

- conducted interviews with representatives of organisations which had extensive experience of the application of formal specification within the software development process[3]

- begun to develop a method within which formal specification could be applied in the IS domain[4]

- gained the experience described in Section 3 above

It was at this time that I decided to use the specification language Object-Z rather than Z within my system development method. There were a number of reasons for doing so:

- Possibly the most significant difficulty experienced by Koh resulted from the lack of a well developed set of guidelines for deriving an appropriate underlying conceptual mode. The structure of an Object-Z specification closely matches the Object-Oriented model, allowing me to rely on a large body of research (both published and in progress) as a basis for the modelling process within my method.

- Object-Z specifications seem to be more *intuitively* structured than their Z equivalents and therefore seem easier to read. Interviews with students within the Department who have been taught both languages provides overwhelming support for this statement. This is a rather surprising result since the students have a text (in 1991 [14], in 1992 [36]) covering Z while Object-Z is supported only by a Technical Report [17]. The ability to communicate formal specifications successfully to non-technical users is a primary factor in the transfer of this "technology" to the IS domain.

- Object-Z offers improved structuring facilities, important for large and complex systems [7, 16, 17].

- The close structure match with the Object-Oriented model allows a smooth transition between problem and solution models—an important benefit of the Object-Oriented approach.

In the two case studies which follow, I do not attempt to replicate the conditions described in Section 3. Instead, I attempt to apply the knowledge gained from the experiences of 1990 in a search for further insight. In 1991, two research students, Michael Gan and Danielle Fowler, were to begin projects under my supervision in which they would apply the systems development method I had devised within a commercial IS environment. Before they began their

---

[3]Interviews were conducted by the author in January 1991 with Anthony Hall of Praxis PLC., John Wordsworth of IBM's Hursley Laboratories and Paul Robinson of Rolls Royce and Associates

[4]A description of the method as it stood at the beginning of this project may be found in [48]. The method as developed to date is set out in [46]

projects proper, I taught a short course covering the essentials of specification in Z and Object-Z (derived from [15], extended with material covering the Object-Oriented Approach [27, 43] and the development method of [46] as it then stood [48] in which formal specification is used both as an analytic and communication tool).

The course introduced the specification language, its mathematical basis, the underlying modelling paradigm and a system development method within which formal specification could be applied. This introduction was not *thorough*—the students were not "experts" at the end of the course—but they were presented with the most significant issues which had affected Koh in the previous year and with sketches of the solutions which we had found. The final issue which I wanted to address by means of this course was the problem which Koh had encountered in "getting started". I was particularly interested in whether this problem would arise at the beginning of each analysis/specification exercise, or only in the first instance.

At the conclusion of the course, therefore, the students were encouraged to work together and asked to complete a specification of a simplified telephone system, a problem which was suggested in [50, 15]. As a consequence of the results of the case study involving Koh, I recommended that students model the problem informally before beginning their Object-Z specification. In particular, I advised them to identify the class(es) of object concerned and to consider the use of state transition diagrams as a means of describing the potential "life history" of each object class. I made myself available as a "reactive" consultant—that is, I attempted to restrict my help to answering the particular question asked—so that any issue raised during the specification process was identified by the students rather than by the "expert".

The problem is a relatively simple one and was undertaken successfully. Consequently, there is little to be gained by a detailed exposition of the specification process followed in this case—my primary involvement was in intermediate walkthroughs and the primary purpose which I served was to give the specifiers confidence to proceed. There was, however, one significant and unexpected result. The problem is expressed in a rather physical (implementation dependent) way—in terms of telephones connected to a central exchange. Having produced a specification structured on this basis, the students began to discuss the level of abstraction at which the specification had been written and to address the question:

> *To what extent is this a specification of* how to satisfy *requirements rather than a specification of the requirements themselves?*

After consulting me to confirm that this was an appropriate question to ask, the students re-examined the underlying representation of the model and concluded that the idea of a central exchange was implementation detail. Consequently the specification was redeveloped purely as a network of telephones. These students were therefore able to incorporate and make use of formal specification within the overall analytic process.

An analysis of this specification exercise suggests that the students had little problem in "steeling themselves" to write the specification. *Post hoc* discussions with the students disclosed a number of reasons why the problem did not surface in this instance:

- the short time allowed for completion of the exercise (two weeks) offered limited scope for procrastination

- development and informal specification of a conceptual model provided a useful start

- evaluation of the conceptual model as a basis for a formal specification in Object-Z promoted collegiate discussion which, at times, became intense and which, in turn, promoted "sketched" solutions in Object-Z to illustrate preferred conceptual structures

In the first specification within each of the following case studies, where the student worked alone, the problem of starting recurred—though to a very much reduced degree. In later specifications within these case studies, the degree of the problem became negligible.

5   Case Study—1991: Michael C.Y. GAN

Michael Gan was an honours student in the Department of Computer Science in 1991, having completed his pass degree within the Department in 1990. He had shown no special interest in, or aptitude for mathematics during his undergraduate career, though his performance in the core mathematics units had been adequate. Gan had some experience of the Object-Oriented approach since his undergraduate project, undertaken in 1990, had applied that approach to the development of a CASE tool. Otherwise, Gan began the project with a background similar to that of Koh (see Section 3).

This case study offers a more secure basis for extrapolation than that involving Koh, since the project on which it is based has the following characteristics:

- the project was modestly, but realistically scaled

- the problem situation was relatively unstructured and poorly understood by the actors within the situation

- multiple *Weltanschauungen* existed within the problem domain

- the project was "real-world" and undertaken in collaboration with the Western Australian Government Department of State Services.

5.1   High-Level Specification of the Problem Context

Gan developed two specifications during his project. The first, a high-level specification of the interactions between a set of information systems, was intended to serve three (educationally-oriented) purposes:

1. to introduce him to the technical and organisational context in which the system which he would next specify (the focus of his project) would be installed

2. to address a problem which had surfaced during Koh's project: the temptation to fall back on functional decomposition and "programmer thinking"

3. to expose a problem highlighted by Macdonald [33]: the importance of adopting a consistent level of abstraction

I had stressed to Gan the importance, at least in the first instance, of developing a conceptual model in some informal manner before attempting to write a formal specification. I had suggested that the most suitable modelling paradigm, given a target specification in Object-Z, was Object-Oriented. However, after some discussion both between Gan and myself and between Gan and the end-users, Gan suggested that an initial model be developed using Dataflow Diagrams (DFDs) [13]. Both Gan and the users felt more comfortable with this technique.

This approach was adopted and, once Gan and the users were happy that the DFDs described the problem adequately, Gan began the process of developing a formal specification. Before this could be done, the informal model was restructured in an object-oriented manner. Although this process was undertaken in an *ad hoc* fashion, no problems were encountered arising from the change in modelling paradigm. I suggest that while this process is not ideal—there is clear redundancy—it need not be discouraged in the early stages of adoption by an organisation of the method [46] and/or Object-Z.

The conversion to Object-Z highlighted a problem of language maturity—the lack of any support tools. In view of this, Gan chose first to convert the specification into Z, using *fuzz* to help in the process of identifying syntax errors, then to complete the conversion to Object-Z. This problem also arose in Fowler's project (see Section 6) and has arisen in my own work. The availability of tools is often raised as an issue when I give presentations on this research to IS professionals—I discuss this further in Section 9.

The formal specification was extended, revised and improved by the natural, evolutionary process described in Section 3 and was evaluated by means of walkthroughs conducted by Gan and myself and (towards the end of the specification process) by Gan and the users[5]. The specification's evolution proceeded smoothly and, as in the previous case study, the specification was restructured a number of times during the process.

Gan [20, page 56] commented that undertaking, as his first "solo" formal specification, a high-level representation of a complex problem context helped to differentiate specification from implementation and highlighted the issue of level-of-abstraction.

5.2   Knowledge-Based System Specification

Having completed the high-level contextual specification, Gan began the analysis of the tender evaluation process.

It quickly became apparent that, amongst the domain experts, there were different views of the problem context and different views of the sort of action which was appropriate in response to that situation—and that realisation led to my eventual incorporation of ideas from Soft Systems Methodology within the systems development method described in [46]. During the project, however, Gan used techniques of knowledge elicitation drawn from the domain of Knowledge-based (Expert) Systems.

---

[5]This case study, viewed as a pilot specification within an industrial context, is described in [45].

By this time, Gan was sufficiently familiar with the Object-Oriented approach that he didn't feel the need to develop an informal *functional* model of the problem situation before assembling the information which he had elicited into an object-oriented, but informal representation. The remainder of the process leading to eventual specification in Object-Z was similar to that described in relation to the previous specifications discussed in this paper. That is, an initial specification in Z (in order to make use of the type/syntax checker ƒUZZ) and finally to Object-Z. The resulting Object-Z specification was extended, revised and improved through the natural evolutionary process already described, the evolving specification being evaluated by means of walkthroughs conducted by Gan and myself and, later, Gan and the system users.

The principal difficulties which Gan experienced during specification were problems of conceptual modelling:

- identifying the key elements to be included in the model and the most appropriate level of abstraction

- the problem of choosing amongst the various possible ways of structuring the specification

- identifying opportunities to factor out general properties. In the case of the contextual specification, for example, the sub-systems which make up the problem context may be represented as objects. It is possible, within the scope of our interest in this problem, to:

  - specify a general class (say, Application) of which each particular sub-system may be considered an instance; or
  - specify a general (but incomplete) class (say, Application); then, for each sub-system, use inheritance and extend that general class into a dedicated class (which, at any time, will contain a single instance)
  - consider each sub-system simply as an instance of a dedicated class

Some problems which related specifically to the formal specification process or to Gan's understanding of the underlying mathematics were, however, identified:

- the lack of support tools—in particular, a syntax/type checker—for Object-Z prompted us to produce an intermediate specification in Z. In the second specification, that of the knowledge-based system, Gan's confidence had grown sufficiently to allow him to conduct the evolutionary process directly in Object-Z (though he did specify and type-check his first-cut specification in Z).

- the need for third-party discussion and analysis of his specification, particularly in relation to intuitive representation of the problem and other issues of style. Initially, the need was for a novice-expert relationship, but the required level of expert advice soon reduced and was replaced by a need for collegiate discussion.

- the concept of infinite sets was initially troublesome. Although Gan was familiar with the concept of (say) an infinite set of integers, he found reasoning about infinite sets of relationships between infinite sets of concrete objects and infinite sets of abstract objects extremely unfamiliar.

As the project progressed, problems of expression—how to state a concept clearly, elegantly and correctly in the formal language—arose and were resolved relatively easily. The primary means of resolution were (in the order of importance which applied at the beginning of the case study):

1. a type/syntax checker ($f$uzz)

2. expert assistance

3. collegiate discussion and evolving style "standards"

Collegiate discussion, initially the least important of these "tools", retained its significance while expert assistance became much less important[6]. The rôle of the type/syntax checker changed as the project progressed from that of a tutor—which (in the extreme case) could be used to arrive at a syntactically correct statement by "trial and error"—to that of a cheap, fast, partial substitute for a walkthrough (i.e. a tool to detect silly errors of expression quickly, cheaply and effectively). Although the type/syntax checker remained a useful and valuable tool for the *economical* application of formal specification, it did not remain strictly necessary.

5.3   The User's View of Formal Specification

In describing the project so far, I have concentrated on the learning experiences of the specifier. Since the project was undertaken in collaboration with the Western Australian Department of State Services (DoSS), I was able to examine (albeit in an informal, unstructured manner) the interaction of the users both with the specifiers and with the formal specifications themselves.

The principal users received no formal training in Object-Z nor the method of [46], although Gan discussed the method and the aims of the pilot with them before starting work. The users were aware that a second, longer-term pilot project was in progress in parallel (reported in Section 6).

Although initial analysis and specification was undertaken informally, once an Object-Z specification had been derived that (evolving) specification formed the basis for all discussions with the users. No attempt was made to insulate the users from the mathematics. In informal discussions and walkthroughs, the Object-Z specification was supported by discussion and by diagrams drawn to illustrate particular points. The final specification was presented to the users in a manner typical of the Z/Object-Z literature—surrounded by explanatory text.

I do not suggest that the users could be said fully to understand the specification to the extent, for example, that they could derive consequent properties. I identified two sub-levels of understanding applicable to users as *specification readers*:

statement level Even in the early stages of the project the users were able to achieve an understanding of the specification at a statement level with

---

[6]This reflects the experience reported during interviews conducted at three organisations in the scientific and technical application domain which have adopted formal specification. While expert consultants are initially necessary to the successful application of the techniques, the importance of the external experts diminishes as a core of experienced specifiers develops within the organisation.

the help of the specifier—some statements they could understand very quickly, some statements they could understand after explanation. During the first walkthrough, the users were able to identify issues which required clarification within the specification and errors which had passed undetected during the informal analysis and specification process. In one case, an error was detected which required Gan to consult me (in my rôle as specification expert) before he could satisfy the users.

system level As the project progressed, the principal user rapidly became familiar with the structure of a Object-Oriented specification and consequently was able to:

- lead a discussion and criticism of the specification as a system of objects

- declare (informally) properties which he considered *should* follow and criticise formal translations of those statements suggested by the specifier

Towards the end of the project, the principal user became unavailable and final walkthroughs were conducted with other users within the Department. Although these users had been involved with some earlier specifications, their understanding was essentially at the statement level. As a consequence, although the users claimed to understand the specification, Gan was concerned that the full implications of the specification had not been exposed to criticism[7]. This step backward highlighted the need for user training particularly in the underlying modelling paradigm if the maximum benefit is to be obtained from the use of formal specification. Although it is the conventional wisdom within the IS domain that the difficulty with the application of formal specifications is a consequence of the mathematics, this case study suggests that from the perspective of the reader, as from the perspective of the specifier, conceptual modelling is the crucial issue.

6 Case Study—1991: Danielle C. Fowler

Danielle Fowler is a PhD student within the Department of Computer Science at Curtin University, researching under my direction. Fowler's first degree (awarded with 1st class honours) was in Information Systems. Although her experience of mathematics was limited to Maths I at TEE level and she had no previous exposure to the Object-Oriented approach, she did have considerable familiarity with (other) informal and semi-formal systems and information analysis techniques. This case study extends the basis for extrapolation provided by the studies reported in Sections 3 and 5. It can be differentiated from both studies since the project on which it is based is:

- substantial

- multi-organisational, in terms of both clients (user organisations) and developers; and

---

[7]In this instance the problem was resolved by seconding the project controller from the project discussed in Section 6 to sit in on the final walkthroughs.

- geographically distributed

Consequently, this project highlights the problems of communication within the project team: between the team and clients; and between client organisations themselves. The extended basis for extrapolation is made more secure (though still, of course, merely indicative):

- since the specifier has an educational and experiential background which is more closely comparable with that of IS professionals; and

- because of the following underlying project characteristics, shared with the project reported in Section 5:

  - multiple *Weltanschauungen* exist within the problem domain

  - the project is "real-world", in this case undertaken in collaboration primarily with the Department of State Services and, secondarily, with Telecom Plus

6.1 Understanding Formal Specification

Like Gan, Fowler began the project proper after completing the course and the "exercise" specification of the telephone system discussed in Section 4. I interviewed Fowler to discuss her reaction to the course and specification exercise.

It was not surprising that, given her IS background, Fowler found the mathematics (particularly predicate logic and the schema calculus) unfamiliar. She did not, however, find the necessary mathematics conceptually difficult. She reported that she gained the ability to read and understand specifications without difficulty, but found their practical application rather harder. Supporting the results reported in the other cases discussed within this paper, Fowler found that the problem of writing specifications had two important dimensions:

- while the *concept* of a system as a set of objects undergoing state transitions was relatively easy to grasp (and, indeed, seemed an intuitively obvious representation once specified—either formally or otherwise), actually *creating* such a representation (except in the most superficial of cases) was found rather difficult.

- representation of objects within the formal language was hampered by a lack of familiarity with the underlying mathematics. Fowler was familiar with relatively few *combinations* of constructs—while her toolkit was reasonably extensive and while, at the statement level, she could express herself successfully, she found it difficult to derive a set of statements which expressed a more complex idea. She commented that, initially, her limited experience of Z/Object-Z constructs *tended to determine* the structure of her design.

Undertaking the example specification of the telephone system was particularly important in this case, in that:

- it exposed, clearly, the difference between understanding the specification as a reader and being able to construct such a specification

- it provided Fowler with confidence that she was capable of writing specifications

- it provided an understanding of the evolutionary nature of the specification process and the importance of defining a suitable representation of the system state

Since Stage I of the project which underlies this case study had already been implemented and since the project and its context is both complex and substantial, a significant information gathering exercise was needed before it was appropriate to begin formal specification to any significant degree. During the period of this information gathering exercise, a particular problem arose concerning the definition of the "standard" to which messages transmitted between the various Supplynet user organisations should conform. This problem and the contribution which Object-Z made to its satisfactory resolution is described in [45].

Fowler's application of Object-Z within this context helped to build her confidence in her own ability to use formal specification effectively as an analytic tool and a medium for precise communication. In essence, this exercise required Fowler to:

- fully understand the specification set out in [46] and the corresponding system

- represent desirable properties of the system within the formal language

- argue by means of the underlying logical calculus that these desirable properties are indeed consequences of the specification; and

- identify (and communicate to the Supplynet team) key properties of the specification (and the corresponding properties of the underlying system) which give rise to these desirable properties

It is interesting to note that this aspect of the application of formal specification requires the use of its mathematical basis—but does *not* require modelling skills. Fowler, however, reports that she found this exercise of intermediate difficulty—harder than simply reading a specification but easier than writing one. Given Fowler's IS background and her low-level mathematical background, this observation gives support to the suggestion that the key factor in the application of formal specification by IS professionals is not mathematics but, contrary to the IS literature, conceptual modelling.

Fowler has since completed a high-level Object-Z specification of the problem context and is now working on a specification of the issues (technical and organisational) associated with connecting a new client organisation to the system. In our discussions during the course of Fowler's research project, she has reported difficulties similar to those experienced by Gan (see Section 5)—though she did not report Gan's specific difficulty with infinite sets. The most significant (apparently) mathematically based problem reported by Fowler initially presented as a difficulty with the concepts of domain and range of relations. This problem is often reported by the less mathematically-oriented students in my introductory specification classes and has been a regular topic discussed by novice specifiers who contribute to the AARnet news group, comp.specification.z.

At a syntactic level the students seem to understand the idea, but in practice there is often confusion. I began to be successful in my explanation when I treated the problem, not as a mathematical one, but as one connected to conceptual modelling. The principal cause of the difficulty appears to be the concept of a connection between two sets of "concrete" objects being itself treated as an object (albeit an abstract one). While the idea of a system as a set of interacting "concrete" objects seems to be intuitive, the concept of an interacting set of "concrete" *and* "abstract" objects in a model which does not differentiate between these categories appears to require a conceptual leap on the part of the student.

As in Gan's case, a syntax/type checker, expert assistance (decreasing in importance as the project progresses) and collegiate discussion (increasing in importance as the project progresses) have been the primary means of resolution of these difficulties. This case study clearly does not support the conventional wisdom within the IS domain that the mathematical difficulty of formal specification techniques renders them beyond the scope of IS professionals—indeed, it adds weight to the argument that the mathematics is a secondary issue from an educational perspective.

6.2 The User's View of Formal Specification

In describing this case study I have concentrated on the learning experiences of the specifier. Since the project is being undertaken in collaboration with the Western Australian Department of State Services (DoSS), I have been able to examine (albeit in an informal, unstructured manner) the interaction of the users both with the specifiers and with the formal specifications themselves.

A number of members of the Supplynet team and IS management associated with the system, although given no formal training, have been exposed to specifications in Object-Z as a part of the project.

Senior IS Managers within DoSS have been able to follow specifications to the degree necessary to monitor progress and manage the project effectively. The technical project leader, a practising systems analyst, has been able to understand and evaluate the implications of specifications presented by Fowler. Although the modelling paradigm underlying the representation was not familiar to her, her general analytic and modelling skills provided a sound basis from which to approach the problem.

The central member of the Supplynet team, from the point of view of this research project, was the Project Controller. Originally, it was agreed that the Controller would attend the training course described in Section 4. Unfortunately, due to pressure of work within DoSS, he was able to attend only about 30% of the course—covering the method of [46] an introduction to the mathematical basis underlying Object-Z and an example of an Object-Z specification.

Irrespective of the reduced training, the Controller has been able to follow specifications presented to him and quickly understand the specifications at the "system" as opposed to the "statement" level—see Section 5.3. A number of factors appear to have contributed to this speedy understanding:

- attendance at the introductory course (see Section 4), abbreviated though it was, helped to remove any component of "fear of mathematics". Many of the students who have attended my course in formal specification as a part of their first degree in Computer Science have reported the mathematics as a "hurdle" to be overcome. Although the mathematics rapidly ceases to be a problem once the initial "hurdle" is overcome, almost all non-mathematically-oriented students (and, many of the mathematically oriented ones) are initially taken aback by the use of symbols in this context.

- commitment to the underlying project provided an incentive to try hard to make the most of the potential benefits offered by the method and the language. As in the case study reported in Section 5, the committed user was able to make effective use of the tool.

- the Controller's enthusiasm for the solution (whose potential benefits he saw) and his predisposition to want to understand the situation in detail combined with his commitment to the underlying project to allow him to put in the necessary effort to understand **thoroughly** the first specification he was exposed to.

- having once been able to understand a specification thoroughly and in detail, he was willing to put the same effort into understanding each subsequent specification to which he was exposed.

This suggests that, for a pilot project, it is important that:

- the user really wants the problem solved

- an early success *apparent to the user* be achieved—even if the success is relatively minor

- every effort be made to get the user over the initial mathematical "hurdle"

7 An Undergraduate Course in Formal Specification

The course described in Section 4 formed the basis of the course which was offered to second year undergraduates and to students in the one-year graduate diploma course during 1991.

In 1991, I reorganised the order of presentation of material within the pair of software engineering units which, together, are within the core of both the Department's undergraduate degree and graduate diploma. After revision, the first semester unit was concerned primarily with a methodological overview, systems analysis and specification while the second unit was concerned primarily with system design issues. *Inter alia*:

- an introduction to abstract modelling within an Object-Oriented paradigm and the formal specification language Z and its application were taught within the first unit; and

- Object-Z and its application; and further material on the Object-Oriented approach (particularly the interface to Design and Programming) were taught within the second unit.

The material is not divided between two units on pedagogical grounds—I perceive the two units as a single year-long software engineering component—the formal material simply happens to be presented in the middle of the syllabus.

The reorganisation of material caused a minor administrative difficulty. A number of students had completed the first unit in a previous year—at a time when the unit did not contain material on formal specification or appropriate abstraction and modelling methods—but had not studied the second unit. Consequently, these "out-of-phase" students did not have the prerequisite knowledge to attempt the study of Object-Z (which is presented by extension from an (assumed) understanding of Z). In 1991, therefore, I repeated the relevant new material from the first unit during weeks 2–5 of the second unit as an alternate stream specifically for those out-of-phase students. The study of Object-Z began for all students in week 7.

The division between the two units provided a benefit from a research perspective—I was able to compare the effects of two variations on the teaching of the material covered in the first semester unit. Lectures and tutorials were as similar as possible in both presentations—the same overhead slides were used, the same references provided, the same tutorial questions were set. The variation was in the assessment method—in first semester, assessment was purely by means of question in the final examination while, in second semester, the students were assessed by a combination of a take-home assigned specification and a question on the final examination paper. This difference in assessment pattern, as expected, led to a variation in study pattern. Over three[8] presentations of the first section and one presentation of the remainder of the material to undergraduate level students interviews with tutors indicate a consistent result—that only 30% of students attempt tutorial questions if their answers to such questions do not directly impact their semester mark. All students, however, *do* (actually, they *must*) attempt assignments which directly contribute to their semester mark. Consequently, while only 30% of students in first semester had completed a specification, all students in second semester had done so.

The comparison was not quantitative—it was considered unreasonable to assume that students in semester 2 would be unable to gain access to assignment/test/examination materials used in semester 1. A qualitative evaluation of the results (observation, review of examination answers, interviews with the tutors, interviews with the students) resulted in a **strongly** indicative result supporting the benefits gained by students from actually writing a specification—while not *directly* comparable, it is interesting to note that all students who completed the assignment specification satisfactorily (42 of 45 students) gained at least 40% of the available marks relating to Z on the final examination, while only 60% of the students in first semester gained 40% or more on the Z question in the final examination.

An assignment was set for all students in second semester in relation to the Object-Z material. Observation and interviews with the tutors indicated that students who had studied Z in first semester had more difficulty with the Object-Z assignment—i.e., they required more time and assistance from the tutor during the course of the assignment—than those students who had

---

[8]including first semester, 1992 in which I was on study leave and the material was presented on my behalf by Paula Swatman who is a Lecturer in Information Systems within the Department

studied Z in second semester. There was, however, only a slight difference between the two groups in final performance in the Object-Z assignment— and no significant difference in the relative performance of these groups in the Object-Z question on the final examination. This suggests that actually *writing the first specification* is the critical factor in making progress in learning to apply formal specification techniques—and supports the results of the case studies set out above.

In 1992, I suggested that a slightly different approach be taken. Students were given four weeks to prepare the specification of an Oil Terminal (originally described in [51]) at a very simplistic level. The students were informed that this specification was to form the basis of a test—they would be required to extend the specification (in some way) under examination conditions. They would not be allowed to bring their specification into the examination, but they were warned that if they had not thought the problem through and written the basic specification, there would be insufficient time for them to complete the test in the time allocated.

The results of this test were interesting in three ways:

- since they needed not only to write the specification but also to understand it (so that they could later extend it) each student was *committed* to solving the problem. Interviews with the tutors support this—one tutor reported that she could not appear on campus in the week before the test without being approached by students wishing to discuss the specification; while another reported that groups of students could be seen in the coffee-shop at all hours during the week before the test, working on and arguing about the specification.

- all tutors reported that the most important issue on which advice was sought was "conceptual structure" followed by "specification style". Although syntactic issues were discussed, they were reported to be relatively trivial. All tutors agreed that access to a syntax/type checker such as ƒuzz would be beneficial and I hope to make ƒuzz available to students in 1993[9].

- the pass rate was approximately 85%

These results support the case studies discussed above in recognising the importance of:

- abstraction and modelling

- actually writing a specification

- collegiate discussion

- expert advice; and

- commitment to solving the problem

In the following section, I apply the experience gained in creating an educational programme for undergraduate students in the development of an approach to technology transfer.

---

[9]unfortunately, we only have a single copy within the Department at present

8   A Technology Transfer Strategy

Socio-technical approaches to information systems requirements determination and an Object-Oriented approach to software development are increasingly being applied successfully by organisations within the IS domain. The principal challenge faced by an IS domain organisation when evaluating the potential benefit of the method suggested in [46] is the application of Object-Oriented formal specification within the information elicitation/analysis/debate/specification process. Two issues must be addressed in developing a strategy for such evaluation:

- potentially, can IS professionals within the organisation be trained to use the techniques effectively—and does such training lead to their eventual ability to apply the techniques independently of expert consultants? If so

- how should the organisation approach the evaluation process?

I address each of these issues in turn.

8.1   Can IS Professionals be Trained in Formal Specification

Five of the seven members of the Formal Methods Research Group at Curtin University have backgrounds in Information Systems:

Paul Swatman More than 12 years commercial experience of developing information systems before considering formal methods. I am unusual within the group in also having a strong mathematical background.

Paula Swatman More than 10 years experience as an IS professional specialising in IS management before considering formal methods, but no previous significant mathematical background. After studying formal methods in early 1991, Paula successfully lectured the first of the software engineering units in which we teach formal methods to undergraduate level students in 1992.

Jocelyn Armarego Jocelyn has 8 years experience as an IS professional specialising in Systems Analysis but no previous significant mathematical background. After attending a training course in late 1990, Jocelyn has been successfully tutoring into the Department's formal methods units for two years.

Danielle Fowler See Section 6—Danielle had a purely IS background before commencing her PhD project in 1991. Danielle, in addition to her research, has successfully tutored into the Department's formal methods units for two years.

Michael Johnstone Michael has 8 years experience as an IS professional in a software development rôle and had a very limited mathematical background before embarking on his MSc proposal in mid-1991.

Five IS professionals within the Department have participated in the research programme and all have been successful in gaining a sound understanding of and ability to apply formal specification in Object-Z. While not conclusive, this supports the findings of the case studies reported in [45] and earlier in this paper in indicating that IS professionals may be trained in the application of the techniques.

8.2 Evaluating the Recommended Method

In order for an organisation (which already makes use of socio-organisational analysis and Object-Oriented design and programming techniques) to evaluate the method for the acquisition of information systems described in [46]:

- access to expert consultants must be arranged

- a pilot project must be identified. The choice of pilot project is important—user commitment and enthusiasm was a significant factor in the successful initial application of formal specification within the Department of State Services

- the pilot project must be staffed, and the project staff must be trained—ideally by those who will be acting as expert consultants during the project. The background and skills necessary to fulfil these rôles covers a wide spectrum. In this paper, I have identified, informally, a number of distinct rôles within what is, ideally, a multi-disciplinary development team:

  specification specialists The specification specialist is an essentially technical rôle requiring the ability to write formal specifications. In view of the importance of collegiate discussion in the process of learning and becoming independent, at least two specification specialists should be selected. The experience of educating and training such specialists, discussed above, suggests that an ability to abstract, analyse and model problem situations conceptually is considerably more important to the successful use of formal specification techniques than is any previous mathematical training or level of mathematical sophistication. At least one specification specialist should be chosen from amongst the analyst/specifiers within the organisation considered to be committed to high-quality information systems, but all may be chosen without regard for their mathematical ability—they should, however, have an understanding of the Object-Oriented approach. These members of the team will, initially, work closely with the expert consultants

  business/systems analyst The critical rôle of this team member is to elicit information from the user/client and to assist in communication between the user/client and the specifier. Olle et al. have stated:

  > "Feedback from the user acceptor [the representative of the users or the executive responsible or both] and from other users is important, especially during the analysis stage.

Users should not be expected to react to specifications expressed in some highly mathematical form, however rigid and complete this may be" [35, page 17]

Whether or not we accept that view[10], we need members of our team who are skilled readers of formal specifications (but who need not have the additional skills necessary for specification writing) and who can translate the formal specification into a form acceptable for communication with users unfamiliar with the notation. Such a form may be wholly or partly textual, diagrammatic, or by means of an animated prototype; and may replace or (preferably) support the formal specification in discussions with users. Even if we decide to insulate the user from the symbolic specification, enormous benefits of increased understanding may still be gained in the process of specification writing and translation. While business/systems analyst(s) may be chosen without regard for their mathematical ability, they should already be familiar with socio-organisational analysis and the Object-Oriented approach.

user (or client) and project manager In my analysis of the case studies reported in this paper, commitment to the development of the information system chosen as the subject of the pilot—and to the development of a high-quality product—has been identified as a potentially significant success factor. The potential benefit of the application of formal specification in this context is a consequence of the clarity with which the problem context may be represented and, therefore, perceived. That clarity must be recognised by both the user/client and the project manager as being important. While these members of the team do not require the ability to read formal specifications directly, the case studies reported in this paper and in [45] suggest that additional benefit may accrue if both the user/client and the project manager are prepared to consider a formal specification as one of the media by means of which the specifier and business/systems analyst may communicate.

system designer and system builder (programmer) Those members of the team responsible for implementing the formal information system will be required to design and build a solution to specification. Since I suggest an Object-Oriented systems development approach, these members of the team should be familiar with Object-Oriented Design and Programming techniques. A specific study of the educational needs of these team members is beyond the scope of this paper, although the results of interviews conducted in January 1991 with representatives of organisations which have used formal specification within the technical domain suggest that the level of training in formal specification required is similar to that required of business/systems analysts. System designers and builders, then, should be able to read a formal specification analytically, but need

---

[10]Further industrial research reported in [45] in which a formal specification was used as a means of direct communication with users of information systems at all managerial levels, has produced encouraging results and has led to doubt concerning the general applicability of Olle et al.'s assertion.

not have any specification writing skills.

All members of the pilot development team with the exception of the project manager and the user/client should attend a training course based upon that which I have developed for our undergraduate students. The project manager and the user/client need attend only a much reduced training course in which the principles of the method are discussed and in which Object-Z is introduced. Jones has reported the beneficial effects of undertaking a case study drawn from the context of course participants as the capstone of an industry training program (in that case, in the formal method, VDM) [30] as has Hall[11]. Following those examples, I recommend that the two courses should flow smoothly into the pilot project—both groups should come together with the expert consultants and the pilot project should commence as if it were simply an educational case study. During the course of the pilot project, the expert consultants will take a progressively less active role.

9 Conclusions

9.1 Summary

The Case studies reported in this paper, supported by my experience of developing and teaching an introductory course in formal specification to students studying for their first degree in Computer Science, highlight the following issues:

- There are special problems to be faced by the student writing a first specification in Z or Object-Z. It is clear that specification writing is more difficult than specification reading. Additional difficulties may be categorised:

  - abstraction and modelling
  - expressing the model symbolically
  - the modelling process
  - evaluation of the model and the process

  the least important of which (though it may not be so perceived by the student at the time) being that of expressing the model symbolically.

  The need to address the syntax and syntactic style issues is well accepted within the literature, but the experience reported in Sections 5 and 6 suggests that abstraction, modelling and the modelling process may and should also be addressed directly within an introductory Z/Object-Z course. Evaluation of the developing model cannot be addressed so easily, but group specification exercises supported by inter- and intra-group specification walkthroughs have been found beneficial.

  A number of authors including [10, 27, 49, 6, 37] discuss the process of conceptual modelling within the Object-Oriented paradigm, though none offers more than guidelines and a framework within which they may

---

[11] Interview conducted January 1991.

be applied. These modelling methods are, therefore, non-prescriptive—indeed, since there are many alternate classification structures for any given problem context, there seems little prospect of any prescriptive technique being applicable within a sufficiently wide problem domain to be useful. Nor is there any suggestion within the literature that this problem is in any way peculiar to the Object-Oriented paradigm. Consequently, the finding of these case studies, that conceptual modelling issues are more significant than issues relating to the expression of a model in a formal language (in particular, Object-Z), while not currently acknowledged within the research literature or reflected in currently available text books [28, 50, 40, 14, 36], should not be considered surprising.

- While this study does not preclude the possibility that formal specification can be applied by an isolated analyst within an organisation, it provides substantial evidence of advantages to be gained from developing specifications in a situation in which access to other specifiers is available. Specification walkthroughs appear to offer significant benefits in terms of clarity and elegance of representation, as well as of simple correspondence with the perceived problem context. An important benefit of formal specifications within the IS domain is the basis which they provide for meaningful and precise analysis of and debate about the problem situation—communication between interested parties is therefore central to the realisation of the potential benefits.

- If formal specifications are to contribute to the effective analysis of an unstructured and poorly understood problem context, there should be a strong correspondence between the structure of the conceptual models which form the basis of thinking about the problem context and the formal specification—that is, a structural correspondence between the theory and what amounts to the model of the theory. If both informal model and formal specification share an underlying modelling paradigm—in the case considered within this paper, the Object-Oriented paradigm—analysts may freely swap between formal and informal systems as they attempt to gain an understanding of the problem context, since:

  - it is simpler to formulate and prove theorems within the formal representation which represent (desired) properties of the context

  - it is easier to see the effect within the problem context of a property of the formal system

- The lack of tools for Object-Z is an impediment to its commercial use. Probably the most important tools from the perspective of the IS domain are:

  Specification creation The only currently available method of creating Object-Z specifications is, with the help of the "oz" macros from the University of Queensland, by means of LaTeX. Such a techno-centric solution is likely to be unacceptable within the commercial IS domain except during the current early experimental period. Some tools for specification in Z are currently available (e.g. Forsite, CADiZ, Formaliser)

Specification checking There are currently no tools available which will syntax or type check an Object-Z specification, though there are a number of tools including *f*uzz and the three specification creation tools mentioned above which will syntax and type check Z specifications. At the present stage of technology transfer, a tool of this kind is probably the most pressing need.

CASE When presenting the ideas arising from this research programme to the professional IS community at conferences (e.g. [44]), within action research studies or as part of the Australian Computer Society's Certificate in Software Quality Assurance programme in Western Australia, I am *always* asked:

- whether a tool exists which will automatically create diagrammatic documentation from the Object-Z specification; and if so
- whether the user of such a CASE tool may interact at the diagrammatic level (to some extent at least) to generate or alter the Object-Z specification

While such a tool is not the most critical need at present, it is probably required before we can expect to see widespread independent commercial use of Object-Z within the IS domain.

9.2 Conclusion

The case studies presented within this paper highlight the following issues underlying the effective use of formal methods:

Abstraction Identifying the significant issues within a problem situation

Conceptual Modelling Structuring relevant information in a manner appropriate for understanding and analysis

Specification Representing the structured abstraction within a formal medium

Analysis Analysis of the situation at both formal and informal levels:

- the capacity to frame assertions concerning the system within the formal language and argue whether such assertions hold
- the capacity to deduce consequent properties of the formal representation of the system and understand the implications within the system of those deductions (i.e. the implications within the "model" of properties of the "theory")

The studies indicate that the key issues are those concerned with abstraction and conceptual modelling. A number of textbooks including [14, 36] provide a satisfactory coverage of typed set theory, predicate logic and the Z schema calculus (which may be easily extended within a training course for Object-Z) for the specification of information systems which, as one might expect, seem to be technically less complex than systems within the technical and scientific domain. In none of our case studies has it been necessary to exercise any but the most basic results of the underlying mathematics. Certainly, the formal specification language and its mathematical basis have to be learned but, in all three cases studied in depth, the research students (and, indeed, the committed users—at a "reading" level) were able to confront this necessity successfully. An understanding-in-principle was achieved and a basic specification "toolkit" assembled by both Fowler and Gan (irrespective of the student's mathematical background) during the introductory course. From this point, both students were able to extend their "toolkit" and become more practiced in the use of the available constructs without further formal training.

While Fowler was slower than Gan to become comfortable with Object-Z, her previous experience and relatively wide-ranging undergraduate education in analysis and specification within the IS domain gave her a head start in abstraction and modelling. Even though, prior to the projects' start, Gan had met the Object-Oriented paradigm and Fowler had not, Fowler was soon able to develop Object-Oriented conceptual models of more complex problem environments and to employ Object-Z productively within an organisationally complex IS environment. In 1990, Koh had also been able to build up a conceptual specification "toolkit" fairly easily, but his lack of experience, education and training in abstract modelling made it difficult for him to conceptualise the model to be specified.

These studies suggest that if the initial hurdle of "fear of mathematics" can be overcome—and in all cases studied, whether Computer Science or Information Systems educated research student, user within the IS domain, IS professional or academic staff member specialising in IS or Software Engineering, that hurdle *was* overcome—skill, experience, education and training in (informal) modelling and analysis within an organisational context are the most significant factors affecting the successful use of formal specification within the IS domain.

There are two obvious sources of IS professionals educated and trained in formal specification:

- graduates from tertiary courses which include formal specification within the curriculum

- existing IS professionals who have received retraining

Within Australia, Curtin University's Department of Computer Science, the University of Queensland's Department of Computer Science and other institutions include formal specification within the undergraduate curriculum; and both Curtin and Queensland offer public courses on Z and Object-Z. In Western Australia, I teach a segment on Object-Z and its application in the Australian Computer Society's Certificate in Software Quality Assurance programme.

I have described in Sections 4 and 7 the subject matter of my introductory course and shown that the course can be completed successfully by students irrespective of their prior background in discrete mathematics. In the case studies reported in Sections 5 and 6 and in the argument presented in Section 8.1, I have presented evidence that such a course provides a sufficient basis (given access to expert consultation in the early stages of adoption) for further self-education and the development of specifications of realistic software systems in a commercial context. An organisation may, therefore, evaluate formal specification by means of a pilot project for the following cost:

- a six-day training course attendance by each member of the pilot project team

- a one-day overview course attendance by a user representative and the pilot project manager

- a contract for expert consultation

all of which, in Western Australia, can be provided by the Formal Methods Research Group within the Department of Computer Science at Curtin University.

The case studies reported here support the (unsurprising) experience reported[12] from the technical domain, that expert consultation decreases in importance as the organisation builds its own skills base. This paper, therefore, supports the assertion that:

> there are cost-effective ways of making formal methods available to industry within the IS domain by some combination of educational and training programmes

References

[1] Banville C, Landry M. Can the field of MIS be disciplined? Communications of the ACM, 32(1), 1989.

[2] Benbasat I, Goldstein DK, Mead M. The case research strategy in studies of information systems. MIS Quarterly, 11(3):369–386, 1987.

[3] Boland RJ. Phenomenology: A preferred approach to research on IS. In Mumford E, Hirschheim R, Fitzgerald G, Wood-Harper A (eds), Research Methods in Information Systems, pp 193–201. Elsevier Science Publishers B.V., Amsterdam, 1985.

[4] Bonoma TV. Case research in marketing: Opportunities, problems and a process. Journal of Marketing Research, 22:199–208, 1985.

[5] Booch G. Software Engineering with Ada. Benjamin Cummings, Menlo Park, second edition, 1987.

[6] Booch G. Object-Oriented Design with Applications. Addison-Wesley, 1990.

[7] Carrington D, Duke D, Duke R, King P, Rose G, Smith G. Object-Z: An object-oriented extension to Z. In Vuong S (ed), Formal Description Techniques, II (FORTE'89), pp 281–296. North-Holland, 1990.

[8] Chatfield C. Problem Solving: A Statistician's Guide. Chapman & Hall, London, 1988.

[9] Checkland PB. Systems Thinking, Systems Practice. Wiley, Chichester, 1981.

---

[12] Interviews conducted at Praxis PLC.; IBM, Hursley; and Rolls Royce and Associates, January 1991

[10] Coad P, Yourdon E. Object-Oriented Analysis. Prentice Hall, Englewood Cliffs, N.J., 1990.

[11] Cox BJ. Object Oriented Programming. Addison Wesley, Reading, Mass, 1986.

[12] Davis AM. Software Requirements: Analysis and Specification. Prentice Hall, Englewood Cliffs, 1990.

[13] DeMarco T. Structured Analysis and System Specification. Yourdon Press, New York, 1979.

[14] Diller A. Z: An Introduction to Formal Methods. John Wiley and Sons, 1990.

[15] Duke R. Writing formal specifications for high quality software development. Seminars, 1990.

[16] Duke R, Duke D. Aspects of object-oriented formal specification. In Proc. 5th Australian Software Eng. Conf. (ASWEC'90), pp 21–26, Sydney, 1990.

[17] Duke R, King P, Rose G, Smith G. The Object-Z specification language: Version 1. Technical Report 91-1, Software Verification Research Centre, Dept. of Computer Science, Univ. of Queensland, Australia, 1991.

[18] Galliers RD. Choosing appropriate Information Systems research approaches: A revised taxonomy. In Nissen HE, Klein H, Hirschheim R (eds), Proc. Conf. The Information Systems Research Arena of the 90's: Challenges, Perceptions, and Alternative Approaches – ISRA-90, Copenhagen, 1990.

[19] Galliers RD, Land FF. Choosing appropriate information systems research methodologies. Communications of the ACM, 30(11):900–902, 1987.

[20] Gan MCY. Using Object-Z in the specification phase of a commercial knowledge based system development. Honours thesis, Depertment of Computer Science, Curtin University, 1991.

[21] Gibbins PF. What are formal methods. Information and Software Technology, 30(3), 1988.

[22] Gravell A. What is a good formal specification. In Proceedings of the 5th Annual Z User Meeting, Lady Margaret Hall, Oxford, 1990.

[23] Hall A. Seven myths of formal methods. IEEE Software, 7(5):11–19, 1990.

[24] Hayes I (ed). Specification Case Studies. Prentice Hall International (UK), London, 1987.

[25] Hayes I, Jones C. Specifications are not (necessarily) executable. Software Eng. Journal, 4(6):330–339, 1989.

[26] Henderson-Sellers B, Edwards J. The O-O-O methodology for the object-oriented life cycle. submitted for publication, 1992.

[27] Henderson-Sellers B, Edwards JM. The object-oriented systems life cycle. Communications of the ACM, 33(9):142–159, 1990.

[28] Ince DC. An Introduction to Discrete Mathematics and Formal System Specification. Clarendon Press, Oxford, 1988.

[29] Jones CB. Systematic Software Development Using VDM. Prentice Hall International (UK) Ltd., London, 1986.

[30] Jones CB. Formal methods and their role in industry. Tutorial Presentation at 6th Australian Software Engineering Conference—ASWEC'91, 1991.

[31] Koh KH. The applicability of formal specification. Undergraduate Project Report, 1990.

[32] Liskov B, Zilles S. Programming with abstract data types. ACM SIGPLAN Notices, 9(4):50–59, 1974.

[33] Macdonald R. Z usage and abusage. Technical Report 91003, R.S.R.E., Malvern, 1991.

[34] Meyer B. Object-oriented Software Construction. Prentice Hall International (UK) Ltd, Hemel Hempstead, Herts, 1988.

[35] Olle T, Hagelstein J, Macdonald I, Roland C, Sol H, Assche FV, Verrijn-Stuart A. Information Systems Methodologies: A Framework for Understanding. Addison Wesley, Wokingham, 1988.

[36] Potter B, Sinclair J, Till D. An Introduction to Formal Specification and Z. Prentice Hall International Series in Computer Science. Prentice Hall International, Hemel Hempstead, 1991.

[37] Rumbaugh J, Blaha M, Premerlani W, Eddy F, Lorenson W. Object-Oriented Modelling and Design. Prentice Hall, Englewood Cliffs, N.J., 1991.

[38] Spivey JM. The *f*UZZ Manual. Computing Science Consultancy, 2 Willow Close, Garsington, Oxford OX9 9AN, UK, 1988.

[39] Spivey JM. An introduction to Z and formal specifications. Software Engineering Journal, 4(9), 1989.

[40] Spivey JM. The Z Notation: A Reference Manual. International Series in Computer Science. Prentice Hall, Hemel Hempstead, Hertfordshire HP2 4RG, UK, 1989.

[41] Susman GI, Evered RD. An assessment of the scientific merit of action research. Administrative Science Quarterly, 23:582–603, 1978.

[42] Svoboda CP. Structured Analysis, pp 218–243. Tutorial. IEEE Computer Society Press, 1990.

[43] Swatman PA, Swatman PMC. The software reusability issue: Perspectives from software engineering and information systems. In Proceedings of the 1st Australian Conference on Information Systems, 1990.

[44] Swatman PA, Swatman PMC. Is the Information Systems community wrong to ignore formal specification methods? In Clarke R, Cameron J (eds), 2nd Shaping Organisations, Shaping Technology Conference (SOST'91), pp 219–240, 1991.

[45] Swatman PA, Swatman PMC. Applying formal specifications in IS development—two case studies. Technical report, School of Computing, Curtin University, 1992. In Preparation.

[46] Swatman PA, Swatman PMC. Formal specification: An analytic tool for (management) information systems. Journal of Information Systems, 2(2):121–160, 1992.

[47] Swatman PA, Swatman PMC. Managing the formal specification of information systems. In Proceeding of the International Conference on Organization and Information Systems, Bled, Slovania, 1992.

[48] Swatman PA, Swatman PMC, Duke R. Electronic Data Interchange: A high-level formal specification in Object-Z. Technical Report 1991/4, School of Computing, 1991.

[49] Wirfs-Brock R, Wilkerson B, Wiener L. Designing Object-Oriented Software. Prentice Hall, Englewood Cliffs, N.J., 1990.

[50] Woodcock JCP, Loomes M. Software Engineering Mathematics: Formal Methods Demystified. Pitman Publishing Ltd., London, UK, 1988.

[51] Wordsworth J. Teaching formal specification methods in an industrial environment. In Software Engineering 86, pp 43–51. Peter Perigrinus, London, 1986.

[52] Yin RK. Case Study Research: Design and Methods, vol 5 of Applied Social Research Methods Series. Sage Publications, Newbury Park, California, 1989.

[53] Yourdon E, Constantine LL. Structured Design: Fundamentals of a Discipline of Computer Program and Systems Design. Yourdon Press Computing Series. Prentice hall, Englewood Cliffs, N.J., 1979.

Practical Experiences of Z and SSADM

Christine Draper
Secure Information Systems Limited
Fleet, England.

Abstract

This paper describes an industrial approach to the use of formal and structured methods. It investigates the extent to which formal and structured methods may be integrated, in both technical and methodological terms. The conclusions presented are based on practical experiences in the development of secure systems products.

1   Introduction

At Secure Information Systems Limited (SISL), we use the Z notation to define secure systems products, in support of their development using structured methods. Z is used to specify the critical part of the product and to prove that it meets the required security properties.

Section 2 identifies the particular requirements on SISL's development process that lead to the integration of formal and structured methods. One important feature of our process is the use of a "dual-team" approach, in which formal methods activities are performed by formal methods specialists, working in collaboration with SSADM [1] analysts and designers. In Section 3, this approach is examined in an industrial context, and the implications are discussed.

The use of specialists contrasts with the multi-disciplinary approach of reported work [2,3,4], where the aim has been to provide appropriate transformation tools so that a system developer may work with both formal and diagrammatic representations. Section 4 describes in more detail how Z specifications are produced from an SSADM design, and explores the degree of correspondence that may in practice be achieved between elements of the design and the formal specification.

Section 5 presents some of our results in applying this integrated process. Some concluding remarks are made in Section 6.

2   Process Requirements

2.1   Introduction

This section describes two important requirements on SISL's development process, namely the requirement to use formal methods and the need to integrate this with a structured development methodology. These requirements arise from standards for developing secure systems to the highest levels of assurance, which are mandated by sources such as the Department of Defense "Orange Book" [5], CESG Memo 3 [6] and ITSEC [7].

2.2   Use of Formal Methods

The development of secure systems to the highest levels of assurance (e.g. A1, UKL6) requires the use of formal methods to specify the critical parts of the system, and to prove that the specification satisfies a formal model of the required security properties, known as the formal security policy model. It is also necessary to provide confidence that the specification is implementable by discharging consistency proof obligations (e.g., the absence of contradiction in the specification). A proof of the correctness of implementation (i.e. formal refinement) is not required; indeed, previous studies [8] indicate that formal refinement is currently impractical on an industrial scale.

The security policy model is specified by viewing an abstract secure system as a state transition machine [9]. The policy model constrains the transitions that a secure system may make, and the states it may occupy.

In contrast, the system specification is written in the standard Z style, with the system state and operations specified as schemas. The specification must therefore be mathematically interpreted as a state transition machine before the security proof can be undertaken. The specification of a system, its interpretation and proof against a formal policy model, is illustrated in [10,11].

2.3   Integration with Structured Methods

A methodology such as SSADM is required to provide the following:

- a structured approach to the specification, design and implementation of the system;
- traceability of functional and security requirements throughout the design and into code;
- a clear separation of critical and non-critical parts of the system.

Parts of the system that are less critical are developed entirely using structured methods. For critical parts of the system, the use of formal methods as described in the previous section must be integrated with the structured methodology, in such a way that the correspondence between the structured design and the formal specification is clearly demonstrable.

The exclusive use of formal methods, which is described in [12] for a small system, is not considered viable for the much larger products under development at SISL. Two significant reasons why this approach is not considered feasible are discussed below.

2.3.1   Process Maturity

To replace the use of structured methods with formal methods would require the complete restructuring of the development process. The scale of this task would be difficult to justify in the short term.

Even if a suitable process were developed, it would be immature and would therefore have a high attendant risk. A critical requirement in the development of secure systems is that the process should be well defined, stable and controllable. This is unlikely to be achieved in a newly developed process, using techniques that do not benefit from the wealth of practical experience gained on projects using structured methods.

2.3.2   Applicability

Despite the wide range of potential applications for formal methods, particular notations are limited in both the aspects of systems that can be easily described, and their suitability for describing a system at different levels of abstraction (i.e., their use from analysis through design to implementation).

Formal methods are highly effective during the early stages of secure system development, where the effects of basic design decisions on system security can be analysed and coarse security flaws detected. The assurance gained from analysing the security at this level is far greater than the marginal increase in assurance from demonstrating the correctness of translation between two design representations. The lack of pragmatic methods for developing systems from formal specification to code means that there is no obvious replacement for the detailed design aspects of structured methods.

3   Our Approach

3.1   Overview

In the development process used by SISL, each secure systems product is developed by a design team and supported by a formal methods team which is drawn from a dedicated formal methods group. This section concentrates on the implications of this "dual-team" approach.

The formal methods team is responsible for all of the formal specification and proof work for that product, and is independent from the design team in a way analogous to the Verification, Validation and Testing (VV&T) team required by Defence Standard 00-55 ([13]).

This requires the formal methods team to work closely with the design team, both to understand the design and to ensure that the requirements of the formal security policy model are fully understood.

Section 3.2 discusses the reasons for the dual-team approach. The communication that arises between the two teams is detailed in Section 3.3, and the need to ensure correspondence between the formal and informal specifications is discussed in Section 3.4.

3.2   Use of Specialist Team

The use of a dedicated formal methods team, rather than training design staff to use formal methods, is influenced by the following considerations:

- formal proof
- design expertise
- training
- focus
- risk management

These aspects are discussed in the following sections.

3.2.1   Formal Proof

Although formal specification is arguably accessible to most software engineers, given suitable training, formal proof requires a far greater understanding of the mathematical theory behind the formal notation and therefore requires the use of specialists. This inevitably leads to the conclusion that there must be an interface between the design team and the specialists who will perform the proof.

The only alternative to that described above would be to use specialists for the proof activity but not the formal specification. This would be highly undesirable, as the provers would have a limited understanding of the design and would be relatively unfamiliar with the formal specification; the designers would also have no feel for the requirements imposed by the proof tool and limited appreciation of the formal security policy model. It would also serve to weaken communications between the designers and formal methods team when discussing how the design is to meet the security policy.

3.2.2   Design Expertise

Design teams also contain specialists, for example in user interfaces, systems software, hardware and communications. It is unreasonable to expect all engineers to be experts in all subjects. The use of a specialist formal methods group avoids the need to compromise on expertise in other areas.

3.2.3 Training

The pervasive use of formal methods would require a fundamental shift in the skills profile of development staff. This would require a continuous programme of education and training, even assuming designers are willing and able to use formal methods. The relatively long learning curve for formal methods also needs to be considered.

3.2.4 Focus

With the described arrangement, the formal specification can be produced without the influence of design constraints such as performance, reliability, and hardware configurations. It is therefore easier to focus on the abstract security requirements and how they will be met. Having a specialist formal methods group from which formal methods teams are formed also helps knowledge and experience to be shared more easily.

3.2.5 Risk Management

The use of formal methods on this scale is still relatively immature, and the concentration of responsibility for the formal methods activities in a dedicated group assists in the management of the associated risk to timescales and budgets.

3.3 Communication

Strong communication between the formal methods team and the design team is a critical factor in the success of our approach. Communication is carried out through both controlled and informal mechanisms. The controlled mechanisms include:

- technical notes clarifying design decisions agreed between the formal methods and design teams
- problem reports raised on design and formal methods documents
- objective reviews of design documents by the formal methods team
- reviews of the compliance of the formal specification to the top-level design
- reviews of the lower-level design documents and code against the formal specification

A carefully controlled system of configuration management and quality assurance ensures that all review comments and problem reports are acted upon promptly and satisfactorily.

All Z is written according to a prescribed standard, which requires a thorough English description of all elements of the Z specification. Although most communication is oral or via English documents, the formal specifications are intended to be accessible at a reasonable level to an engineer with no Z training.

The separation of the formal methods and design teams requires extra effort to ensure that a common understanding is reached. It does however have an additional benefit in that design documents are subject to scrutiny by the formal methods team, who can concentrate on the security of the system objectively, without being unduly influenced by design decisions and implementation constraints.

3.4   Correspondence

In any approach using two notations to represent the same design, it will be necessary to demonstrate the correspondence between the two representations. One of the implications of the dual-team approach is an increased emphasis on ensuring this correspondence. This is achieved through a series of review procedures that check the compliance between the formal specification and design documents, as illustrated in Figure 1.

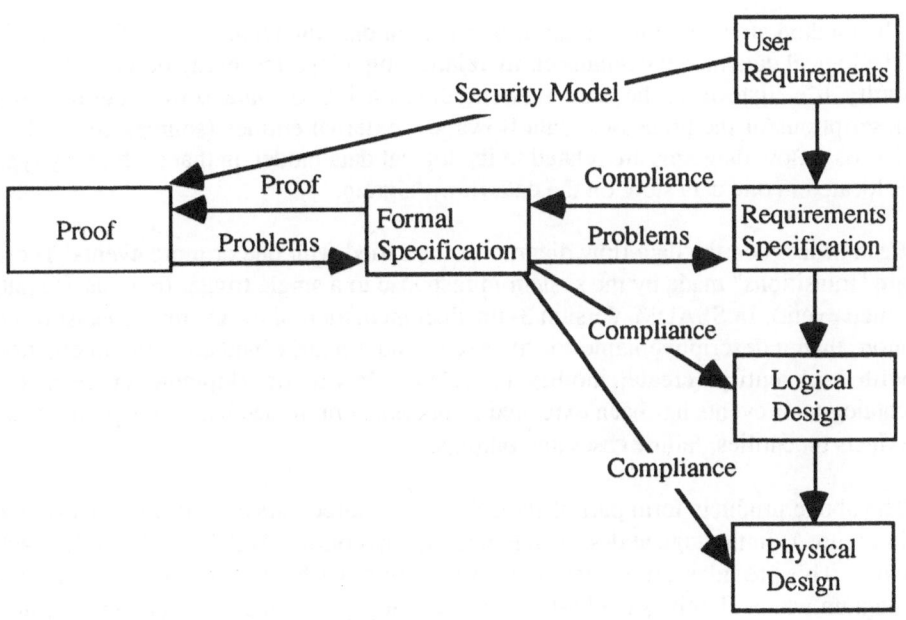

Figure 1: Correspondence to SSADM products

The customer's requirements are used as a basis for the SSADM requirements specification, which contains products such as data flow diagrams and entity-relationship diagrams. Formal specifications are developed from these top-level design products, and proofs are performed on these formal specifications. Any problems discovered during the specification or proof activities are used to drive changes to the informal design.

The subsequent logical and physical design are shown to uphold the security of the formal specification, although the design may contain more implementation detail than the formal specification.

4   Z and SSADM

4.1   Overview of SSADM

The development process used by SISL is based on a tailored version of SSADM. For the purposes of this paper, a subset of the SSADM method is presented in an abstract form.

The method starts with the creation of a logical data model and a data flow model. The logical data model contains entity relationship diagrams, entity descriptions and entity life histories. The data flow model consists of data flow diagrams and descriptions of the processes, data flows and external entities (sources and sinks). The data flow diagrams are related to the logical data model, in that each entity type is located in one data store on the data flow diagram.

Each process on the data flow diagram is identified with one or more events. These are "transitions" made by the system in response to a single trigger (e.g., user input, timed event). In SSADM Version 3, the documentation of events may consist of no more than a descriptive name for the event, and a matrix indicating the interaction with each entity (create, modify or delete). In our development process, the catalogue of events has been extended to provide a more detailed description of the effects on entities, failure cases and outputs.

The above products form part of the SSADM requirements specification, as shown in Figure 1. In the logical design, a logical process outline is then produced for each event. This provides a more detailed description of each event, using a Jackson-like diagram which identifies the basic processing steps to be taken. The process outlines and logical data model are subsequently developed into a physical design.

4.2   Identification of Critical Parts

As noted in Section 2.2, the formal specification describes only the security-critical parts of the system. One way in which the SSADM methodology has been tailored is to identify and separate the security-relevant aspects of the design. As an example, the catalogue of events is divided into those events necessary to uphold the security of the system, and those that have no effect on its security. This division is maintained and refined throughout the design process.

4.3   Relationship to Z

The main point of correspondence between the Z and SSADM is chosen at the level of events. In general, one Z operation is chosen to correspond to one SSADM event in the security-critical part of the requirements specification. Other products in the data flow model and logical data model are used to support the specification, but detailed correspondence with these products is not demonstrated.

The choice of correspondence is made because the response of a system to an SSADM event most closely matches the idea of a transition in a state machine.

4.3.1   State

The system state in the Z specification is chosen to support the specification of the events. It will contain the information in the entity descriptions and entity relationship diagrams, but may differ from a mechanical translation for the following reasons:

- redundancy is eliminated from the entity relationship diagram (note that in SSADM, redundancy may not be eliminated from the entity relationship diagrams until the logical design stage)
- redundancy is added to simplify the Z specification (i.e. derived variables or abbreviations)
- certain entities may be eliminated by the use of relations in Z (n:m relations are not permitted in SSADM and are removed by the use of link entities)
- abstraction is used to simplify the data structures
- state variables may be introduced to specify sequencing constraints
- the organisation of the data is changed to simplify the Z specification

SSADM entity descriptions and entity relationship diagrams are relatively formal and produced at an early stage in the development, hence a mechanical translation into a Z system state is a possibility. This approach is rejected because the formal specification must facilitate both informal understanding of the system, and formal reasoning about its security and consistency. [4] suggests that a direct translation into Z is more difficult to read than a Z specification written directly, and our experience indicates that the above simplifications are necessary both for readability and to facilitate proof.

4.3.2   Input/Output

The input and output variables of a Z operation will usually contain the same information as the data flows that cross the system boundary on the data flow diagram. This correspondence again is not exact because:

- I/O descriptions often contain control information, rather than pure data

- I/O descriptions may be at a lower level of abstraction (e.g. specifying a range by two boundary values rather than a set)

- a single I/O description may contain information for more than one logical operation

The direct translation of I/O descriptions is rejected for the reasons described in Section 4.3.1 and because the inputs and outputs need to be exactly those corresponding to the logical operation, not the complete I/O description.

4.3.3   Operations

As stated previously, there is usually a one-to-one mapping between Z operations (transitions in the system state machine) and SSADM events. There are cases, however where this is not possible:

- Common processing may not be identified in the high-level SSADM products. The formal specification may specify the events at a lower level of granularity to take advantage of logically similar operations on the system.

- An SSADM event represents the system's response to a single trigger. This trigger may actually cause a sequence of actions, which could potentially be specified individually.

- Often, several different triggers can cause identical processing (e.g. a system alarm may be triggered by different sources). These triggers would each give rise to a separate event, which can be specified by a single Z operation.

The operations in the formal specification will show the overall effect on entities and not the individual processing steps on the logical process outline. Furthermore, although the failure cases, effects and outputs of an event should be matched in the corresponding operations, this match cannot be mechanical, because:

- The description of the failure cases and effects is entirely informal, beyond the identification of which entity types are affected.

- The description of the processing is often procedural even within an event, and becomes more so as the design progresses.

- An SSADM event may include concepts that cannot easily be expressed in Z (e.g., wait until something happens).

- The structure of the Z state may differ from the SSADM state, and the processing must be adjusted accordingly.

For these reasons, it can be seen that the correspondence between the events catalogue and Z operations is necessarily informal. The correspondence with subsequent design products remains informal, because although the description becomes more detailed, it remains informal and becomes increasingly procedural.

5   Results

The results from using our approach have been encouraging. As explained in Section 5.1, the close communication between the formal methods and design teams make it hard to isolate the effect of the formal methods activities on the project, however some illustration of the impact is given in Section 5.2.

5.1   Measuring Impact

The problem of gathering meaningful metrics is ironically hampered by the success of integrating the formal and structured methods. Because of the variety of communication mechanisms, it is not possible to take account of issues raised by any single mechanism. Further, as a significant part of the communication is informal and therefore not recorded, the total impact of the formal methods activities can only be determined via a subjective assessment.

Due to the configuration management procedures, however, it is possible to isolate the impact of formal methods on the design via the controlled communications mechanisms identified in Section 3.3. The first example in Section 5.2 is drawn from a review of compliance between a formal specification and a top-level design document. The second example provides a more subjective illustration of the impact of formal methods, but is supported by the number of technical notes and review comments arising from communication with the formal methods team.

5.2   Illustration of Impact

The first example concerns the first version of a design specification, containing approximately 25 events. The design specification had passed a full informal review by the design team and a review of an early draft by the corresponding formal methods team (before formal specification had been completed). During the formal specification and outline proof activities, the following problems were found in the design specification:

wrong/omitted failure case	15
incorrect state change	2

missing outputs	3
other security problems	5

In addition, there were 20 details which required further clarification. The first category of problems were mainly missing security checks, or failure cases that breached the security policy. The second and third categories were largely a failure to meet functional requirements, and were detected either as a lack of logical consistency or through an inconsistency within the design documentation. The fourth category included situations where the functional requirements apparently contradicted the security policy.

Most of the discovered security problems were not obvious until subjected to the rigorous analysis provided by formal methods. The example also illustrates that formal methods are not simply a tool for analysing security, but also lend precision and completeness to the definition process.

The second example is of a specification which had again been fully reviewed by the design and formal methods teams. A number of security problems had apparently been addressed satisfactorily. It was only when work commenced on interpreting the formal specification that it became apparent that the intuitively secure behaviour that the informal specification upheld was not sufficient to meet the strict view of security required by the formal security policy model. This resulted in the need for significant rework to the design which, without formal methods, may have been overlooked until late in the development process.

6   Conclusions

This paper has presented an approach to integrating the use of formal and structured methods, in which two key factors are:

- a dual-team approach, where formal methods specialists work with SSADM designers
- the crafting of formal specifications to facilitate analysis and proof, rather than a mechanical translation of the structured design into a formal notation

Currently, this methodology is being used successfully in the development of secure systems products, although it could be applied wherever it is desirable to integrate formal methods into an established development process.

Looking to the future, our approach is sufficiently flexible that the role of formal methods within the development process might be modified, for example by replacing top-level design documents with formal specifications, or by increasing the involvement of the design team in the formal specification activities.

References

1. NCC. SSADM Version 4 Reference Manual. NCC, 1990

2. Randell G. Data Flow Diagrams and Z. Z User Workshop 1990, Springer-Verlag 1990

3. Semmens L, Allen P. Using Yourdon and Z: an Approach to Formal Specification. In: Nicholls JE (ed) Z User Workshop 1990. Springer-Verlag 1990

4. Polack F, Whiston M, Hitchcock P. Structured Analysis - A Draft Method for Writing Z Specifications. In: Nicholls JE (ed) Z User Workshop 1991. Springer-Verlag 1991

5. DoD. DoD Trusted Computer System Evaluation Criteria (Orange Book)

6. CESG. UK Systems Confidence Levels, CESG Computer Security Memorandum No. 3

7. EC. Information Technology Security Evaluation Criteria (ITSEC). EC 1991, ISBN 92-826-3004-8

8. Smith P, Keighley R. The Formal Development of a Secure Transaction Mechanism. In: Prehn S, Toetenel WJ (eds) VDM '91. Springer-Verlag, LNCS 551

9. Goguen J, Meseguer J. Security Policies and Security Models. Procs IEEE Symposium on Computer Security and Privacy, 1982

10. Arthan RD. Formal Specification of a Proof Tool. In: Prehn S, Toetenel WJ (eds) VDM '91. Springer-Verlag, LNCS 551

11. Jones RB. Methods and Tools for the Verification of Critical Properties. In: Morris JM, Shaw RC (eds) Procs. 5th Refinement Workshop. Springer-Verlag 1992

12. Kemmerer RA. Integrating Formal Methods into the Development Process. IEEE Software, Sept. 1990

13. Interim Defence Standard 00-55, The Procurement of Safety-Critical Software in Defence Equipment. April 1991

Methods, Quality and Animation

Support for using Z

Rosalind Barden and Susan Stepney *

Logica Cambridge Ltd
Betjeman House
104 Hills Road
Cambridge
CB2 1LQ
0223 – 66343
email: rosalind@logcam.co.uk

Abstract

This paper provides guidance for those who are looking for support in their use of Z. It points out that you should decide the *why*, *what* and *how* of using Z, and provides areas to consider in making those decisions. A method is needed to support the 'how' of Z. Z in its raw state is not a method, it is a notation. The paper looks at the various aspects which help to make up an effective method, and discusses how these combine together. It provides an overview of existing approaches to Z specification and describes their usefulness in general, and in light of the aspects of method. The paper goes on to describe, briefly, a handbook on Z being produced as part of the ZIP project[1] and concludes with some thoughts on how Z may develop.

1 Using Z

Z is not a panacea — there is often little point in trying to specify everything formally. Some things are not amenable to formal specification (for instance, non-functional requirements), some aspects are already well understood and in any case have their own, special purpose, notations (for example, parsing) and as formal treatment is a lengthy process it is rarely appropriate to apply formal notations in a blanket way. Nonetheless significant benefits arise from specification in Z in terms of better communication between team members,

---

*This paper is copyright ©Logica UK Ltd
[1] ZIP is a collaborative project under the United Kingdom's Department of Trade and Industry IED initiative

and between specifiers and client. For a more detailed discussion of the benefits of formal methods see [Hal90a].

[Bro90] reports on a project in which Z used for specification alone, led to eventual rate code of production which was one and a half times the standard rate for the type of system in question. In the CICS project a 9% gain in productivity as a result of using Z, is reported in [HK91]. This paper also records the increase in accuracy of the finished code, in the first months of the release of the software there are approximately $2\frac{1}{2}$ fewer errors in the parts which were specified in Z than in those which were not. Another noted success in using Z is that of the T800 transputer chip which we discuss in section 4.7.1.

You should keep things under control by carefully defining your own development rules. Before you start your project you should decide why you are using Z, you should also decide what you are going to specify, to what level of formality, and in what manner you are going to use Z.

Decide why you are using Z: Z will not solve all system development problems. However, it can make a significant contribution in, for example, the following areas

- project management (visibility of progress, support for design reviews)

- requirements capture and validation

- design (as a thinking tool, to verify the captured design, and to help document the design)

- documentation (not only design documentation but also for use during maintenance).

Z may be used for any, or all, of these purposes. However, in order to work out how to fit Z into the life-cycle it is necessary for you to know *why* you are using Z.

Decide what Z will be used for: Z can be used for a variety of purposes and different techniques will be suitable in each context. In deciding what you are going to specify you need to consider the style in which you intend to use Z (for instance state and operations, functional, object oriented).

You need to resist the temptation to rush into symbols, you cannot begin to express ideas formally until you have an understanding of what it is you are trying to say. You also need to resist sirens calling for code before the specification is finished. Formal specification can take longer, but the time taken to produce working code is usually reduced.

Although you may review your decision about what to use Z to specify, do not alter it in an ad hoc manner

Decide how far you will go: you need to decide how formal to be, this will help to provide an environment for your formal specification work. Many formal specifications specify the system at an abstract level only.

Performing a complete formal proof would be very expensive, although a few sketch proofs of key properties could be carried out without incurring too great a cost. The more important it is that the system be reliable and the more expensive it would be if a mistake were to occur, the more likely it is that you want to satisfy yourself that the system you have specified behaves correctly, and hence the more proof work you can justify.

Beyond the specification stage come considerations of refinement towards code and the proof of that refinement.

Don't run too fast: a very important factor in choosing your approach to Z specification is the existing knowledge of your project team. If they are already familiar with object oriented design or structured methods then there is a smaller step to take if these structuring techniques continue to be used.

Specifiers require an appropriate level of fluency with the Z notation, this can be acquired through training courses, reading case studies and practising. It is helpful if an expert advisor is available to advise the project team.

Use a tool: for any industrial project the use of a tool to support editing Z specifications, type checking, and configuration management is essential. A list of Z tools is given by [Par91].

You should be aware that the tools you choose may have an effect on the method which you use to write your specification. Tools may support only a subset of the notation, and they may force a particular style of use for example some tools will enforce declaration before use, and this may have an effect on whether to follow a top-down or a bottom-up process.

If you do not use a type checker then you will need to allocate additional resources to reviewing, since you will have to do this 'proof reading' visually.

Consider all points again: these decisions cannot be made in isolation, as each one affects the others. For example there are no tools which support type checking of the object oriented variants of Z

Having decided why you are using Z, you will need assistance with the *how*, in other words you will need a method.

2 Is Z a method?

People often reach for their dictionaries in answer to such a question. We are no exception. [Cha72] defines 'method' as follows

> **method** *n.* the mode or rule of accomplishing an end: orderly procedure: manner: orderly arrangement: classification: system, rule: manner of performance: an instructional book systematically arranged.

Many so-called 'formal methods', such as Z, are nothing of the sort. Currently [Spi92] is regarded as a de facto standard for Z. It provides the notation for Z together with laws that govern the manner in which the aspects of the language behave. This is an invaluable reference manual which most Z specifiers keep by their sides. At the time of writing, a new standard is being devised for Z to be submitted to the British Standards Institution [BN92]. However, neither of these provide a method in the sense defined above.

There are many approaches to the use of Z, and we present an overview of them in this paper, which should serve as an introductory guide and survey for those who are looking for assistance with their Z specifications. In section 3 we discuss the components that go towards making up a method. In subsequent sections we review various known approaches to Z and relate them to the components of a method.

3   Three ingredients of a method

The most obvious users of Z are the people who write Z specifications. However, many different people will need to read these specifications, for example reviewers, evaluators, assessors, designers, and programmers. Without support for *all* users of Z, any realistic size specification will be difficult to write and impossible to read.

Assistance in structuring a specification is required, this helps writers to assemble their thoughts in a sensible manner. Moreover it helps the readers of the specification immensely — an unstructured document is practically useless. To write a Z specification you also require a process that provides support for producing it. As with a document in any language, both reader and writer need to be fluent.

Each of these three aspects — structure, process and fluency — is discussed in the following sections.

3.1   Structure

'Structure' is that part of method concerned with 'orderly arrangement and classification'.

A simple system can be understood as a whole. But for any realistically sized system, a specifier needs to structure the specification in such a way that it can be understood in parts. Approaches that help to gain an initial understanding can also lead specifiers to a good structure for the eventual specification. [Woo89] shows how Z's schema language can be used to help structure a specification. [MS87] show how the technique of promotion can be used to partition the system specification into local and global concerns. However, a survey of Z users [BSC92] showed that many specifiers feel the need for additional support for structuring their specifications.

Two approaches that can help with understanding and structuring a Z specification of a large system are structured analysis (discussed in section 4.3) and object orientation (section 4.4 describes approaches to using this with Z).

3.2   Process

'Process' is the aspect of method concerned with 'orderly procedure or manner'. A process provides users with a staged approach to specification development; a refinement process guides how the specification is turned into code. Details of each stage in the process are provided and there are checkpoints to assist with monitoring of the process.

An approach based around the ideas of state based specifications with operations has been developed largely at the Programming Research Group at the University of Oxford (PRG); and introduced into industry notably at IBM United Kingdom Laboratories Ltd at Hursley Park for use on the CICS system. We have dubbed this 'the Established Strategy'. This describes an approach to systems specification (see section 4.1 for more details) and also the production of the system design with its refinement to code.

Another approach, for developing Z specifications of secure systems, has been developed principally by the Government Communications Headquarters (described in section 4.2). In section 4.5 we look at examples of Z used in a functional style. Other organisations have begun to develop processes, and we provide summaries of these in section 4.6.

All processes should recognise the need for an iterative approach, although often they are presented as 'one-pass'. [Gui90] reports experiments showing that the focus of software designers' attention does not follow a fixed path, but makes opportunistic shifts as insight is gained into various aspects of the problem. [Wor91] argues that the process of refinement of a specification equally does not follow a smooth path from abstraction to code, but that the designer moves back and forth as if moving along a 'saw-tooth' until the refinement is eventually reached. The same argument is readily applied to the process of producing a fairly abstract specification, from a highly abstract partial description given by the abstract state and global variables. Review stages in the process are an important part of this iteration.

The order of the final presentation of the specification may differ from the order in which it was constructed. Certain items may be introduced as the specification is written (for example, reports from operations and global variables), but these may well be presented all together at the beginning of a specification document. It is important to realise the distinction between presentation and production. Do not expect specifications which you read to tell the development story, and do not present your specifications in the way in which you first wrote them!

3.3 Fluency

'Fluency' addresses the 'manner of performance' aspects of method. Fluency with Z is directly comparable with fluency in any other language. The user is able to express ideas clearly without stumbling, constructions are neat, and the meaning is apparent to anyone else conversant in the language. Good use is made of the language — the appropriate notation is used. There is a difference between the fluency required to *read* a specification, and the familiarity with and understanding of the notation that enables the writer to choose a good way of *expressing* that which is required.

Many introductory texts for Z encourage users in their first take-up of the language. Such books usually concentrate on explaining the notation, and Z's features are illustrated through the use of small examples. These books play a valuable rôle in providing users with an explanation of the notation. For example [Lig91] and [Imp91] provide an introduction to the principal parts of the Z notation, [WL88] and [Dil90] introduce the mathematics of Z and include some small case studies. [PST91] and [Wor92], as well as providing an introduction to the notation, also describe the Established Strategy for writing Z specifications.

For the more experienced user there are some brief guides for enhancing one's facility with the notation. [Gra91] provides some guide-lines for writing a good Z specification (for example, 'prefer clarity to brevity' and 'choose the state to simplify the description of the operations'). [Mac91] gives useful tips about writing succinct and readable Z. There are a number of published case studies in Z. These do not provide the reader with any direct instruction about Z, but by studying them the reader can learn from the style adopted by the authors. Notable amongst such case studies is the collection [Hay87b].

Notice that most of the texts mentioned in this section are not exclusively concerned with fluency, they may include some pointers to process and structure.

3.4 Putting it all together

To write good Z specifications, you need all three ingredients to be present. You need a way of structuring the system. You need a process which provides steps to follow and checkpoints in building the system. And you need to be fluent with the notation, to ensure that the eventual specification can be written clearly and concisely. Together these three describe what is required from a method for Z.

We have not dealt with the aspect of method covering 'the mode or rule of accomplishing an end: system, rule'. Although 'process' can give some guidelines for the steps through which a development should go, it is not appropriate to give a *rule* applicable to all Z projects.

4 Available Z approaches

In this section we describe the principal approaches to Z specification and provide a short discussion on each one.

4.1 The Established Strategy

The Established Strategy covers the whole cycle of development from specification through to code. Below we describe only the parts relating to specification. The method we present is distilled from [Wor89a], [Wor89b] and [Woo92]. The Established Strategy produces a 'state and operations' style of specification, and has the following steps

Perform preliminary analysis: the requirements are analysed in order to identify the important concepts of the problem. These concepts are represented by sets and constants; some sets may have additional structure, for example, sequences. Any relationships between the sets and constants are ascertained; not all sets need be related to others.

Record the given sets and global constants: a record is made of the given sets that are to be used as types, and of the global variables for the specification, along with an explanation of their purpose. This is an important part of the process of modelling the requirements.

Develop application-oriented theory: often some special purpose theory has to be developed when writing a specification. Since the theory is important for the specification it should be given an early position in the specification document.

Specify the abstract state: the abstract state is described using one or more schemas (which are combined to give the complete description).

Specify the initial state: a schema that describes the initial state of the system is stated, and a proof given that it is implementable. 'Creation of the initial state' is regarded as an operation, the result of which is the initial state. Note that there may be more than one possible initial state of the system.

Specify the successful case of the operations: Each operation is specified, ignoring any error conditions for now. This results in partial operations.

Calculate the operation preconditions: the preconditions of the partial operations are calculated. The description of the abstract operation is checked to ensure that the precondition is explicit in the operation schema; if not, it is added. It is helpful to provide a summary of the preconditions of the partial operations. This assists in the description of the error cases, and forms the basis for the complete operation table (see later).

Specify the error cases: the schemas which describe the operation exceptions are described. The preconditions of the partial operations tell us where to start in describing the errors, but discussion with the user is essential to ensure that the errors are handled in the appropriate way.

Make the operations total: the partial operations that describe the successful cases and the various errors are combined to give a total description. This is usually achieved using schema disjunction. Sometimes it may be necessary to prove that this interface is total. A table is produced that shows the inputs for, and precondition of, each of the partial operations which make up the total ones. This table helps to support the understanding of the operations.

[Wor92] enhances the Established Strategy by providing a useful guide to reviewing Z specifications. The approach helps to structure the specification to an extent, for example by encouraging the description of the successful case of operations first, followed by calculation of preconditions, and thence to specification of exceptions.

4.1.1 Applications of the Established Strategy

One application of the Established Strategy is described by [Spi90] in which Z is used to specify the real-time kernel for a diagnostic X-ray machine. The starting point for the specification was the documentation and source code of an existing system. Interestingly this, like the much of the CICS work, is an example of using Z in a reverse engineering context. The aim of the specification was to provide a description of an existing system for a new implementation on different hardware.

The various aspects of the state (for example, interrupt handlers, background processes) are described as separate schemas which are then conjoined. Operations describe the processes. By calculating the operation preconditions the author uncovered an error in one of the kernel's operations which could sometimes lead to deadlock. This has interesting implications for those who say that Z is not suited to applications with timing aspects.

The Established Strategy has been used successfully in a number of contexts, notably in applications concerning transaction processing. It is followed, to varying degrees, in [Bly90], [Kin90], [HW90] and [MW90] which all describe aspects of CICS.

4.1.2 Discussion

The steps of the Established Strategy represent both the order used to present the finished specification, and the order in which the specification is to be developed. However, the development process may well involve one or more iterations, as unhappy consequences discovered later may require the model that was developed earlier to be modified.

As summarised here, the Established Strategy appears not to be hierarchical. One means to add hierarchy is through the use of promotion, a technique which is often used heavily with this strategy.

If you prefer a functional approach to specification, this style is not well suited to it. The only place where global functions are specified is when the application-oriented theory is developed

The approach to errors means that they tend to be treated as exceptions in which nothing changes and an error report is given. There are other approaches, for instance it may be necessary to record that the errors have occurred or recovery action may be needed before further operations can occur (for example, in the case of underflow or overflow). A further problem is that this approach makes it more likely that proper consideration of how the system behaves in error cases will be postponed until implementation.

The Established Strategy is the best documented process with the most published examples based around it. It provides steps which should be performed in order to produce a specification. Some guidance is given on to how to structure the specification document, and the state and operations style with the Established Strategy promotes provides a way of structuring the specification itself.

4.2 The process of developing a security specification

The method adopted for security specification is rather different from the Established Strategy of 'state and operations' style described above, because of the requirement for proof. The proofs needed are that a particular property (of being secure) holds. Although it is particularly suitable for proving *security* properties, it can be used for any properties described by a formal model. This approach is described in detail in [CES91], which also includes a worked example.

The approach uses two models: an abstract Security Model that defines the security policy, and a functional FTLS (Formal Top Level Specification) that defines the actual operations on the system. A proof is needed to show that the operations satisfy the security policy. The point of the method is to end up with a single, clear proposition to be proved. The method for specifying and proving a secure system is summarised below.

Construct a generic Security Model and its security policy: the abstract security model is generic, with parameters such as objects, users, classification, and data. It has the following components

- generic definitions of the system's state, inputs, and outputs
- a generic definition of the abstract system, in terms of a total state transition function and possibly other components
- a security policy, as an extra constraint on the abstract system.

The security policy includes such things as a *clearance* property (saying that users cannot receive outputs that they are not cleared to receive) and information flow properties (that objects with low classification are not affected by, and hence cannot deduce the existence of, objects or inputs of higher classification). This policy defines what is meant by security in the system.

Construct an FTLS: the functional FTLS is a 'state and operations' style specification. This has the advantage that the operations can be split up into success and failure components, and combined in the classic manner to give a total operation. These operations are combined and recast as a total state transition function.

Instantiate the Security Model: the generic security model is instantiated using concepts from the FTLS. For example, generic objects might be instantiated in terms of FTLS files and applications. A (necessarily informal) justification is given that each of these instantiations is reasonable. An instantiated system and instantiated secure system are just the generic abstract system and generic abstract secure system with these instantiations.

Define and justify interpretation functions from the FTLS to the instantiated security model: various interpretation functions are defined. These give the mapping from the components of the FTLS (its state, inputs, outputs, and state transition function as constructed from its operations) to the corresponding concepts in the instantiated security model.

Prove the totality and functionality of the state transition functions and interpretation functions: again, the justification for the reasonableness of these interpretation functions is necessarily informal. One good criterion (though it is neither necessary nor sufficient) is that the interpretation functions be injective (one-to-one). Hence nothing that might potentially be compromising security at the FTLS level is lost when being interpreted at the Security Model level.

Prove the consistency of the specifications: since it is possible to prove anything, including the security property, of an inconsistent specification, it is important to prove the specification is consistent. This is not possible in general, but it is possible if certain, recommended, restrictions are imposed.

Prove the security property holds for the FTLS under the interpretation, to an appropriate level of assurance: the technique of formal partial proof is available if there is insufficient resource for a full proof. Instead of proving the goal as it stands, it is proved under certain assumptions or hypotheses. The least plausible hypothesis is then proved under a new set of assumptions. If all the hypothesis are obvious enough for the required level of assurance, stop. Otherwise, choose the least plausible remaining one, and repeat the process.

4.2.1 Discussion

As with the Established Strategy, this method is mainly a description of a process through which a specifier should step in order to produce a proven-secure specification. It does provide some structure in the state and operations part, which also need to be translated into state transition functions. Thus we feel that it has slightly more structure in it than the Established Strategy.

Notice that owing to the style restrictions used to make proof more tractable, little use is made of schemas. At first sight this might suggest that the fluency exhibited is not as great as in a more general systems case. However, extensive use is made of parts of notation such as μ, which is considered esoteric by some. Many of the restrictions on the way in which Z is written are because of the limited support offered by current proof tools. Once tools become more mature, a more natural style of developing secure system specifications will become possible.

This approach has been published comparatively recently, and hence there is little available experience on which to base comments.

4.3 Structured methods and Z

Structured methods provide a process for analysing a system and for structuring it into smaller subsystems. Structured methods are based on informal text and diagrams, are typically well documented, and offer a methodical process. Many organisations already use structured methods with their Z. The ZIP survey [BSC92] discovered instances of Z being used with a variety of structured methods.

Several groups are working on integrating of Z with a structured method, where the method provides the process and the Z provides the formalism (and, additionally, increases the opportunity for mechanical verification of the structured analysis).

4.3.1 Z and SSADM

The SAZ project [PWH92b], [PWH92a] is investigating combining Z with SSADM version 4 [SSA90]. The draft SAZ method is used after the requirements specification module of SSADM, to guide the development of a Z specification from the outcome of the SSADM analysis. The Z specification is guided by the systems analysis, rather than being exclusively derived from it, in order that the process of formalisation can help detect errors and omissions in the informal analysis. SAZ recommends that the formalisation be focussed on the most critical or complex areas of the system. The draft SAZ method consists of the following three stages

Specify the state: the Z state specification is based on the SSADM 'logical data model' which consists of entities, attributes, data constraints and (conditional) relationships.

Specify the control structure: a Z specification of the control structure — constraints on the order in which operations are performed — is based on the SSADM 'effect correspondence diagram' and 'entity life histories'. For information systems these control structures are usually fairly straightforward.

Specify individual operations: the internal details of the operations identified in the control structure specification are specified as Z operation schemas. A simple operation may be specified by a single schema, a more complex one may be broken down into a series of piped, more simple, schemas.

4.3.2 Z and Yourdon

[SA91] describe a method of using Z and Yourdon together to produce a specification. The Entity Relationship model is used as the basis for a formal model of the system state. An Entity Relationship diagram provides a clear overall picture of the structure and relationships of a system; the corresponding Z provides a formal basis, and can be used to capture constraints that cannot be easily expressed on a diagram. Processes in the Data Flow model are mapped onto operation schemas. The paper describes how to perform this mapping, giving some specific guidance which shows how parts of the diagrams are converted into Z.

4.3.3 Other work

Other work in this area includes [Bry90] who gives a report of a structured and Formal Methods workshop, and [vHV91] on Z and Petri nets.

Z can be used for more than making a particular structured analysis technique formal. For example, work on enriching structured methods is discussed in [RPJ92].

4.3.4 Combining Z with structured analysis

Structured methods themselves provide a process for writing specifications. The work which has looked at how to integrate Z into such processes has concentrated upon slotting Z in at a specific point. Typically, the principal use of the structured method is to use it to provide an overall structure of the system and then use Z within this framework. Thus, these approaches can mainly be assigned to the structural side of method. The relatively routine translation into Z used by this approach does not demand a higher than average fluency.

There is a tension when combining a structured analysis method with Z. If the form of the Z is kept close to the informal analysis, it tends to result in a verbose and cluttered specification that lacks the elegance that is essential for understanding. But a more concise and elegant form of the Z is further removed from the informal analysis, and it is less clear that the correspondence between the two forms is correct. However, it is important that Z and any accompanying structured method being used should each be applied where they can benefit the development process most. For example [Dra93] describes a way of developing and proving secure systems that uses both Z and SSADM. SSADM is used in the requirements specification and design stages, while Z is used to formalise the requirements, and as a basis for the formal proof of security. The Z corresponds closely to the SSADM, but it is not produced by some merely mechanical translation. Components may be removed or added to the specification, in order to make the Z form more appropriate for its task.

Although structured methods themselves provide a process for writing specifications, the work which has looked at how to integrate Z into such processes has concentrated upon slotting Z in at a specific point. Typically, the principal use of the structured method is to use it to provide an overall structure of the system and then use Z to specify within this framework. Thus, these approaches can mainly be assigned to the structural side of method. The relatively routine translation into Z used by this approach does not demand a higher than average fluency.

4.4 Object orientation and Z

Object orientation is a way of structuring software [Mey88], [Boo91], and promises many benefits, including the elusive one of *reuse*. An 'object' can be thought of as something that encapsulates a piece of state together with some behaviour (the operations that access and modify that state). Objects provide a way to structure a system specification by partitioning an otherwise global state space into meaningful chunks. In addition, objects are instances of classes, which are arranged in inheritance hierarchies. Classes can inherit properties from their parents, as well as defining new state and behaviour of their own. Inheritance is an abstraction mechanism that can be used to structure a specification — properties of similar objects are described once, in the specification of a common superclass, and hence complex classes can be specified, and understood, in stages. Also necessary for an object oriented system specification is a way of describing how various objects are composed in the framework that defines the system in question.

Object oriented concepts can be used to provide a structure for Z specifications. There are also benefits in reuse: existing class specifications can be reused in new contexts, and any associated proofs (for example, of refinement) should also be reusable. If an object oriented implementation is intended, an object oriented specification is appropriate, in order to use a consistent paradigm during development.

Z can be used to specify state and behaviour. However, Z provides no construct to group operations on a particular state, to apply these operations to different instances, or to inherit these properties. Following Wegner's classification [Weg87a], [Weg87b], we might say that Z is object *based* (it supports objects), but not object *oriented* (it does not support classes or inheritance).

4.4.1 Object based usage of Z

Two approaches that use Z in an object-based manner are Hall's style [Hal90b], [SBC92, chapter 3], and ZERO — Z Expression of Refinable Objects [WM91a], [WM91b], [Why92]. An object-based approach that requires some small changes to Z scope rules, in order to integrate Z with HOOD (an object-based development method) is described in [GI90], [SBC92, appendix A].

4.4.2 Object oriented extensions to Z

There are many object oriented extensions to Z being developed that include support for classes and inheritance. [SBC92] is a collection of the same case studies written in various object oriented dialects of Z; papers documenting various individual approaches include

- Object-Z [CDD+90], [DD90a], [DD90b], [DRL90], [DKRS91], [Ros92]

- MooZ — Modular object oriented Z [MC91], [MC92b], [MCS92], [MC92a]

- OOZE — Object Oriented Z Environment [AG91], [AG92]

- Z++ [Lan91], [Lan92]

- ZEST — Z Extended with Structuring [CR92].

Of all these, Object-Z is probably the best known, because of the many case studies that have been published.

4.4.3   Discussion

Only average fluency is required to read or write a specification in any one of these languages (Hall's style is peppered with μ and θ, but they are confined to a few clichéd usages). Most of the extended notations provide extra constructs for defining classes and some for composing objects into systems.

Most of these object oriented approaches to Z offer plenty of help with structure — using objects to carve up a system's state space, and inheritance to build up complexity in stages. They offer little help with the process; they all implicitly assume the use of some existing object oriented analysis and design process.

Care has to be taken when using an object oriented approach: the temptation to write 'code' can be strong. But if this is avoided, it is possible to write clear, abstract specifications of classes and inheritance hierarchies that are readily comprehensible. Framework specifications (the way in which the various objects are composed in a particular system) can be expressed, but be warned that this is still an active research area in object orientation, see for example [HHG90], [Joh92]. Also be warned that these object oriented variants have a long way to go before they can match the maturity of Z in language stability, formal semantics, and tool support. However, they offer promise in the areas of structuring specifications of large, complex systems, and for reusing specifications and proofs. We watch their development with interest.

4.5   Functional development

Although the form of the specification does not necessarily dictate the eventual form of the program which is derived from it, if you plan to use a functional language to implement your system it helps if the specification is written in a similar style.

4.5.1   Examples of functional specification

An example of re-organisation of a specification into a more functional style is given by [MLH91] in which the flexitime specification of [Hay87a] is used as an example.

[DG90] describe how they use Z to gain an insight into the system architecture of an oscilloscope. Their approach is a functional one. Complex functions are broken down into composition of simpler ones, each of which describes part of the oscilloscope process. These help to provide a user's view point of the system. This helps to make the system more usable since it is the user who will have to understand the operations (in order to configure the machine). The specification is fairly abstract which helps to avoid the complexities which might occur at a lower level, for instance a model of time as a ticking clock suffices at this level.

[GD90] discusses this approach further. The 'framework' approach used means that they obtain a resuable specification that can be applied to a family of instruments. The advantages of a resuable framework include

- producers share specification and component manufacturing costs

- users will be aided by the consequent uniformity of system behaviour

- designers can devote effort to producing an elegant and abstract specification

- highly skilled engineers can be used to write the specification (making good use of this rare resource).

The underlying approach is to focus on models that can serve as reusable components. The aim is to find 'regularities' across the system and to abstract away from them. Making the specification modular helps to ameliorate configuration problems.

4.5.2 Discussion

The oscilloscope work provides useful ideas on the development of generic frameworks, and is worthy of attention whether you are interested in functional programming, or not. The process here is very much to do with abstraction and looking ahead to reuse. Quite a high level of fluency is demanded by this approach, although the real test of skill comes in the approach to modelling required. The structure of the specification comes from making the system as generic as possible. This presents some problems in using Z as currently defined, but the paper offers ways of side-stepping the type-checking problems which arise.

4.6 Other approaches

4.6.1 Large system specification

Some early ideas for using Z to describe large systems, described in [Nas90], are summarised here.

A high level abstract specification is produced, which provides an overview of the system. The system is then split into a number of sub-systems which are each specified fully in Z. Each sub-system specification is a specification in its own right — in order to understand the relationship of the sub-system to the rest of the system the high level document should be read.

Describe abstract requirements for system: the requirements document is the users' view of the system, 'users' means both other parts of the system as well as end-users.

Produce abstract specification of system: the higher level specification provides an overview of the system and the rules by which the subsystems should be combined and the way in which they interact.

Write the subsystem specifications: each subsystem contains some part of the state together with the basic operations on that part of the state ('basic' can be thought of as schemas which are atomic rather than made up of a number of component operations).

Re-examine subsystems against abstract requirements: as we pointed out earlier, the process of producing a specification is not rigidly top-down. It is necessary to look again at the abstract requirements and make additions and changes to them arising from the design decisions which have been made in subsequence steps.

The full specification produced by this approach is in the form of a tree of specifications, each containing a description of some part of the system to a particular level of abstraction.

4.6.2 Discussion

This approach, which was developed with transaction processing in mind, offers considerable help with structuring specifications; as the author says, it 'demands rather than encourages a modular style'. Nash provides a process whereby this structuring may be achieved. The paper gives some assistance with what might be described as the fluency of refinement, and at the specification level discourages the use of some parts of the schema calculus (for instance, schema negation). The level of fluency in Z required to write specifications using this approach may be less than with plain Z.

We have not come across any other examples of this approach in use; it is promising and merits further attention.

4.7 Hardware development

There are many published uses of Z being used to develop hardware, we have already cited some examples. [Ger90] suggests some reasons for this preponderance of hardware specifications such that hardware may be an area where there are the best returns for using formal methods; and techniques already exist for checking circuit designs, thus such systems are more amenable to the application of formal methods.

4.7.1 Transputer floating point unit

The use of Z for the development of the floating point unit of the T800 trans-puter chip is well documented, some papers which describe this experience are: [SW89], [inm], [May90] and [Bar89].

The development of the chip proceeded in three main phases

1. a high level specification of what the chip should do was produced in Z

2. this was then translated, using mathematical techniques, into a descrip-tion of how the chip would perform the operations

3. the commands in these procedures were then translated into the low level micro-instructions which control the individual components of the chip.

Using formal techniques the initial design of the floating point unit, there were significant time savings and the formally specified parts of the hardware worked first time. Each step was proved correct. The last two steps were carried out semi-mechanically using an occam source transformation tool written in ML (although not itself proven). Much of the process of producing the floating point unit was concerned with the refinement aspects and the proof of the refinement.

4.7.2 Further reading

Other sources of information on hardware specifications may be found in [SD89] which gives an Object-Z specification involving a substantial amount of proof, [Bow87a] and [Bow87b] on microprocessor instruction sets, [Kem88a] and [Kem88b] on the Viper work, and [WBJ92] which discusses a pelican crossing specification.

5 A Z methods handbook

From the beginning, the ZIP project has intended to make available a handbook which would guide users in applying Z in industrial situations. We have been involved in the production of this handbook. The handbook is aimed at people who have understood the basics of the language and now wish to become *users* of Z.

Often people attend a short course (typically a week) and once returned to their offices are required to sit down and start using Z. No matter how good the tuition on the course, this is a tall order. Z specifiers require more support than this.

As part of the process of defining the Z handbook we explicitly asked users of Z what they would like to see in a Z handbook [BSC92]. The general feeling of the participants of the survey was that we should not provide a prescriptive method for Z, but instead provide suggestions and guide-lines. They demanded more advice for the Z practitioner, and requested the provision of rationale for, and good illustrations of, various parts of the notation.

The handbook consists of a series of case studies of varying sizes, each specification is accompanied by the normal explanatory text plus some 'meta-commentary' which helps to illustrate a particular language feature or specification technique. Each of these comments is tagged with a label, and the labels are gathered together into a glossary of definitions. Thus the reader may consult the glossary for an explanation of a particular notion, and from there be directed to examples of that idea in use. Alternatively, the case studies may be studied and the commentary read to elucidate various points — for instance the effect of using that piece of notion in this context, or the reason why the specification has been written in a particular way.

It illustrates, through the case studies, approaches to structuring the specifications. The principal case studies show examples of

- questioning the amount of detail *really* required and hence reducing the complexity of the specification by increasing the abstraction

- breaking down a system using the different rôles played by various actors in the system

- employing entity relationship diagrams to help decide the structure

- considering the local and global states separately and using promotion to describe their connections

- use of refinement to show the relationship between abstract and concrete specifications.

Some ideas for the process of building a Z specification are also pursued, both through exposition and through the commentary given on the case studies.

This handbook requires a reasonable degree of fluency with Z, and aims to increase greatly the fluency of its readers. Plenty of tips are presented for neater specification, and explanations to encourage understanding and exploitation of the whole of the Z notation.

6   Concluding remarks

In order to use Z successfully you must know 'why' you are doing so, 'what' you will use it for and 'how' you will do so. The why and the what need to be considered carefully and decisions taken. These will help you to decide how you will use Z, but these matters are not independent of each other. The decision of what you will use Z for relies on there being available methods to support the *how* of Z's application.

Z in its raw state is not a method. Nonetheless the various approaches to Z specification which have been developed provide considerable help for users of Z. We have looked at three ingredients which characterise a method for Z. None of the approaches provides *the* method for Z, rather each offers assistance with aspects of the structure-process-fluency view. This choice of approach will depend on the particular requirements of the project in question and the project team's initial knowledge of Z and other techniques.

The ZIP project Z handbook which we have described in this paper helps by enhancing its readers' fluency, by looking at different structuring techniques, and by examining various processes by which Z specifications may be built.

Better techniques for integrating Z with various structuring techniques will come to the fore as these approaches are applied to more examples in industry. This will mean that tool support for Z and extensions to it will improve; which in turn will lead to a greater take up of the Z notation. We believe that the object oriented approaches to Z (especially Object-Z) exhibit particular promise and we look forward to the development of more rigorous underpinnings for them, as well as larger examples of their use.

Z is being taken up increasingly and there are many published examples of its use. Such papers offer users support with techniques for using Z. Work within the ZIP project as described above, and also in standards and tools described elsewhere in these proceedings provide further assistance for and help with using Z. The future of Z as a leading industrial formal notation is bright.

References

[AG91]   Antonio J. Alencar and Joseph A. Goguen. OOZE: An Object Oriented Z Environment. In Pierre America, editor, *ECOOP'91: European Conference on Object-Oriented Programming*, volume 512 of *Lecture Notes in Computer Science*, pages 180–199. Springer Verlag, 1991.

[AG92]   Antonio J. Alencar and Joseph A. Goguen. OOZE. In Stepney et al. [SBC92], chapter 7, pages 79–94.

[Bar89]   Geoff Barrett. Formal methods applied to a floating-point number system. *IEEE Transactions on Software Engineering*, SE-15(5):611–621, May 1989.

[BHL90]   Dines Bjørner, C. A. R. Hoare, and H. Langmaack, editors. *VDM'90: VDM and Z — Formal Methods in Software Develop-*

ment, Kiel, volume 428 of *Lecture Notes in Computer Science.* Springer Verlag, 1990.

[Bly90]   David Blyth. The CICS application programming interface: Temporary storage. IBM Technical Report TR12.301, IBM UK, Hursley Park, December 1990.

[BN92]   Stephen M. Brien and John E. Nicholls. Z base standard, version 1.0. ZIP document ZIP/PRG/92/121, SRC D-132, Oxford University PRG, November 1992.

[Boo91]   Grady Booch. *Object Oriented Design with Applications.* Benjamin-Cummings, 1991.

[Bow87a]   Jonathan P. Bowen. Formal specification and documentation of microprocessor instruction sets. In H. Schumny and J. Mølgaard, editors, *Proceedings of Euromicro '87, Microcomputers: Usage, Methods and Structures. Volume 21(1-5) of Microprocessing and Microprogramming*, pages 223–230. Elsevier North-Holland, August 1987.

[Bow87b]   Jonathan P. Bowen. The formal specification of a microprocessor instruction set. Technical Monograph PRG-60, Programming Research Group, Oxford University Computing Laboratory, January 1987.

[Bro90]   David Brownbridge. Using Z to develop a CASE toolset. In Nicholls [Nic90], pages 142–149.

[Bry90]   A. Bryant. Structured methodologies and formal notations: Developing a framework for synthesis and investigation. In Nicholls [Nic90], pages 229–241.

[BSC92]   Rosalind Barden, Susan Stepney, and David Cooper. The use of Z. In Nicholls [Nic92b], pages 99–124.

[CDD+90]   David A. Carrington, David Duke, Roger Duke, Paul King, Gordon A. Rose, and Graeme Smith. Object-Z: An object-oriented extension to Z. In S. Vuong, editor, *Formal Description Techniques II, FORTE'89*, pages 281–296. North-Holland, 1990.

[CES91]   CESG. A formal development methodology for high confidence systems. CESG Computer Security Manual F, Communications-Electronics Security Group (L7), Government Communications Headquarters, Cheltenham, U.K., February 1991.

[Cha72]   *Chambers Twentieth Century Dictionary.* W & R Chambers, new edition, 1972.

[CR92]   Elspeth Cusack and G. H. B. Rafsanjani. ZEST. In Stepney et al. [SBC92], chapter 10, pages 113–126.

[DD90a]   David Duke and Roger Duke. Towards a semantics for Object-Z. In Bjørner et al. [BHL90], pages 244–261.

[DD90b]   Roger Duke and David Duke. Aspects of object-oriented formal specification. In *Australian Software Engineering Conference*, 1990.

[DG90]   Norman Delisle and David Garlan. A formal specification of an oscilloscope. *IEEE Software*, pages 29–36, September 1990.

[Dil90]   Antoni Diller. *Z: An Introduction to Formal Methods*. Wiley, 1990.

[DKRS91]   Roger Duke, Paul King, Gordon A. Rose, and Graeme Smith. The Object-Z specification language version 1. Technical Report 91-1, Software Verification Research Centre, Department of Computer Science, University of Queensland, May 1991.

[Dra93]   Christine Draper. Practical experiences of Z and SSADM. In Jonathan P. Bowen and John E. Nicholls, editors, *Proceedings of the 7th Annual Z User Meeting, London*, Workshops in Computing. Springer Verlag, 1993.

[DRL90]   Roger Duke, Gordon A. Rose, and Anthony Lee. Object-oriented protocol specification. In L. Logrippoo, R. L. Probert, and H. Ural, editors, *Protocol Specification, Testing and Verification 10*, pages 325–338. North-Holland, 1990.

[GD90]   David Garlan and Norman Delisle. Formal specifications as reusable frameworks. In Bjørner et al. [BHL90], pages 150–163.

[Ger90]   Susan L. Gerhart. Applications of formal methods: Developing virtuoso software. *IEEE Software*, pages 7–10, September 1990.

[GI90]   R. Di Giovanni and P. Luigi Iachini. HOOD and Z for the development of complex systems. In Bjørner et al. [BHL90], pages 262–289.

[Gra91]   Andrew M. Gravell. What is a good formal specification? In Nicholls [Nic91], pages 137–150.

[Gui90]   R. Guindon. The knowledge exploited by experts during software system design. *International Journal of Man-Machine Studies*, 33:279–304, 1990.

[Hal90a]   J. Anthony Hall. Seven myths of formal methods. *IEEE Software*, pages 21–28, September 1990.

[Hal90b]   J. Anthony Hall. Using Z as a specification calculus for object-oriented systems. In Bjørner et al. [BHL90], pages 290–318.

[Hay87a]   Ian J. Hayes. Flexitime specification. In *Specification Case Studies* [Hay87b].

[Hay87b] Ian J. Hayes, editor. *Specification Case Studies*. Prentice Hall, 1987.

[HHG90] Richard Helm, Ian M. Holland, and Dipayan Gangopadhyay. Contracts: Specifying behavioral compositions in object-oriented systems. *OOPSLA/ECOOP'90 Proceedings, ACM SIGPLAN Notices*, 25(10):169–180, 1990.

[HK91] Iain S. C. Houston and Steve King. CICS project report: Experience and results from the use of Z in IBM. In Prehn and Toetenel [PT91], pages 588–596.

[HW90] Iain S. C. Houston and John B. Wordsworth. A Z specification of part of the CICS file control API. IBM Technical Report TR12.272, IBM UK, Hursley Park, February 1990.

[Imp91] Michael Imperato. *An Introduction to Z*. Chartwell-Bratt, 1991.

[inm] inmos. IMS T800 architecture. Technical Note 6.

[Joh92] Ralph E. Johnson. Documenting frameworks using patterns. *OOPSLA'92 Proceedings, ACM SIGPLAN Notices*, 27(10):63–76, October 1992.

[Kem88a] Duncan H. Kemp. Specification of Viper1 in Z. RSRE Memorandum 4195, Royal Signals and Radar Establishment, September 1988.

[Kem88b] Duncan H. Kemp. Specification of Viper2 in Z. RSRE Memorandum 4217, Royal Signals and Radar Establishment, October 1988.

[Kin90] Steve King. The CICS application programming interface: Program control. IBM Technical Report TR12.302, IBM UK, Hursley Park, December 1990.

[Lan91] Kevin C. Lano. Z++, an object-orientated extension to Z. In Nicholls [Nic91], pages 151–172.

[Lan92] Kevin C. Lano. Z++. In Stepney et al. [SBC92], chapter 9, pages 105–112.

[Lig91] David Lightfoot. *Formal Specification Using Z*. Computer Science series. Macmillan, 1991.

[Mac91] Ruaridh Macdonald. Z usage and abuse. RSRE Memorandum 91003, Royal Signals and Radar Establishment, February 1991.

[May90] David May. Use of formal methods by a silicon manufacturer. In C. A. R. Hoare, editor, *Developments in Concurrency and Communication*, University of Texas at Austin Year of Programming series, pages 107–129. Addison-Wesley, 1990.

[MC91] Silvio Lemos Meira and Ana Lúcia C. Cavalcanti. Modular object oriented Z specifications. In Nicholls [Nic91], pages 173–192.

[MC92a]   Silvio Lemos Meira and Ana Lúcia C. Cavalcanti. MooZ case stud-
          ies. In Stepney et al. [SBC92], chapter 5, pages 37–58.

[MC92b]   Silvio Lemos Meira and Ana Lúcia C. Cavalcanti. The MooZ spec-
          ification language. Technical report, Universidade Federal de Per-
          nambuco, Departamento de Informática, Recife - PE, 1992.

[MCS92]   Silvio Lemos Meira, Ana Lúcia C. Cavalcanti, and C. S. Santos. The
          Unix filing system: A MooZ specification. Technical report, Uni-
          versidade Federal de Pernambuco, Departamento de Informática,
          Recife - PE, 1992.

[Mey88]   Bertrand Meyer. *Object-oriented Software Construction*. Prentice
          Hall, 1988.

[MLH91]   Richard Mitchell, Martin Loomes, and John Howse. Organising
          specifications: a case study. Technical Report BPC 91/1, Brighton
          Polytechnic, Department of Computing, January 1991.

[MS87]   C. Carroll Morgan and Bernard A. Sufrin. Specification of the Unix
          filing system. In Hayes [Hay87b].

[MS91]   Joseph M. Morris and Roger C. Shaw, editors. *4th Refinement
          Workshop*. Workshops in Computing. Springer Verlag, 1991.

[MW90]   P. Mundy and John B. Wordsworth. The CICS application pro-
          gramming interface: Transient data and storage control. IBM Tech-
          nical Report TR12.299, IBM UK, Hursley Park, October 1990.

[Nas90]   Trevor C. Nash. Using Z to describe large systems. In Nicholls
          [Nic90], pages 150–178.

[Nic90]   John E. Nicholls, editor. *Z User Workshop: Proceedings of the 4th
          Annual Z User Meeting, Oxford*, Workshops in Computing. Springer
          Verlag, 1990.

[Nic91]   John E. Nicholls, editor. *Proceedings of the 5th Annual Z User
          Meeting, Oxford*, Workshops in Computing. Springer Verlag, 1991.

[Nic92a] John E. Nicholls. Domains of application for formal methods. In
          Proceedings of the 6th Annual Z User Meeting, York [Nic92b], pages
          145–156.

[Nic92b] John E. Nicholls, editor. *Proceedings of the 6th Annual Z User
          Meeting, York*, Workshops in Computing. Springer Verlag, 1992.

[Par91]   Colin E. Parker. Z tools catalogue. ZIP document ZIP/BAe/90/020,
          British Aerospace, Warton, May 1991.

[PST91]   Ben Potter, Jane Sinclair, and David Till. *An Introduction to For-
          mal Specification and Z*. Prentice Hall, 1991.

[PT91]   S. Prehn and W. J. Toetenel, editors. *VDM'91: Formal Soft-ware Development Methods, Noordwijkerhout, Volume 1: Confer-ence Contributions*, volume 551 of *Lecture Notes in Computer Sci-ence*. Springer Verlag, 1991.

[PWH92a]   Fiona Polack, Mark Whiston, and Peter Hitchcock. The SAZ method – version 0.1. Technical report, Department of Computer Science, University of York, May 1992.

[PWH92b]   Fiona Polack, Mark Whiston, and Peter Hitchcock. Structured analysis — a draft method for writing Z specifications. In Nicholls [Nic92b], pages 287–328.

[Ros92]   Gordon A. Rose. Object-Z. In Stepney et al. [SBC92], chapter 6, pages 59–77.

[RPJ92]   David Redmond-Pyle and Mark B. Josephs. Enriching a structured method with Z. In *Proceedings of the Conference on Integrating Structured and Formal Methods, Leeds, 1991*, Workshops in Com-puting. Springer Verlag, 1992.

[SA91]   Lesley Semmens and Pat Allen. Using Yourdon and Z: An approach to formal specification. In Nicholls [Nic91], pages 228–253.

[SBC92]   Susan Stepney, Rosalind Barden, and David Cooper, editors. *Object Orientation in Z*. Workshops in Computing. Springer Verlag, 1992.

[SD89]   Graeme Smith and Roger Duke. Specification and verification of a cache coherence protocol. Technical Report 126, Department of Computer Science, University of Queensland, August 1989.

[Spi90]   J. Michael Spivey. Specifying a real-time kernel. *IEEE Software*, pages 21–28, September 1990.

[Spi92]   J. Michael Spivey. *The Z Notation: a Reference Manual*. Prentice Hall, 2nd edition, 1992.

[SSA90]   Manchester NCC. *SSADM Manual Version 4*, 1990.

[SW89]   David Shepherd and Greg Wilson. Making chips that work. *New Scientist*, 1664:61–64, May 1989.

[vHV91]   K. M. van Hee and L. J. Somers M. Voorhoeve. Z and high level Petri nets. In Prehn and Toetenel [PT91], pages 204–219.

[WBJ92]   Margaret M. West, T. F. Buckley, and P. H. Jesty. Pelican safety study. Research Report 92.4, University of Leeds, School of Com-puter Studies, March 1992.

[Weg87a]   Peter Wegner. Dimensions of object-based language design. *OOP-SLA '87 Proceedings, ACM SIGPLAN Notices*, 22(12):168–182, 1987.

[Weg87b] Peter Wegner. The object-oriented classification paradigm. In Bruce Shriver and Peter Wegner, editors, *Research Directions in Object-Oriented Programming*. MIT Press, 1987.

[Why92] Peter J. Whysall. Z Expression of Refinable Objects. In Stepney et al. [SBC92], chapter 4, pages 29–35.

[WL88] James C. P. Woodcock and Martin Loomes. *Software Engineering Mathematics*. Pitman, 1988.

[WM91a] Peter J. Whysall and John A. McDermid. An approach to object oriented specification using Z. In Nicholls [Nic91], pages 193–215.

[WM91b] Peter J. Whysall and John A. McDermid. Object oriented specification and refinement. In Morris and Shaw [MS91], pages 150–184.

[Woo89] James C. P. Woodcock. Structuring specifications in Z. *IEE Software Engineering Journal*, 4(1):51–66, 1989.

[Woo92] James C. P. Woodcock. *Using Standard Z*. Prentice Hall, 1992. to appear.

[Wor89a] John B. Wordsworth. Practical experience of formal specification: a programming interface for communications. In *Proceedings of ESEC'89*, number 387 in Lecture Notes in Computer Science. Springer Verlag, 1989.

[Wor89b] John B. Wordsworth. A Z development method. Draft version 0.11, IBM UK, Hursley Park, January 1989.

[Wor91] Robert Worden. The process of refinement. In Morris and Shaw [MS91], pages 1–5.

[Wor92] John B. Wordsworth. *Software Development with Z*. Addison-Wesley, 1992.

Acknowledgements

CICS is a trademark of the IBM Corporation.

This work was carried out as part of the ZIP project which is a United Kingdom Department of Trade and Industry IED initiative, project number IED4/1/1639. The part funding by the DTI is gratefully acknowledged.

We would like to thank Sam Valentine of the University of Brighton, Fiona Polack of the University of York, Paul Smith of SISL, and anonymous referees for advice and helpful suggestions.

Cleanroom and Z

Glyn Normington

IBM United Kingdom Laboratories Ltd
Hursley Park, WINCHESTER, Hampshire SO21 2JN

Abstract

This paper describes an approach to developing software which combines aspects of Cleanroom Software Engineering with the Z formal specification language and the style of design documentation known as "literate programming".

Introduction

The aim of combining Cleanroom and Z is to enable the production of software with very few defects. This is achieved by writing a formal specification of the product and then refining the specification into code in provably correct steps.

However, three problems with this approach must be solved:

1. How to construct a specification which captures the customer's requirements.

2. How to ensure that refinement steps really are correct.

3. How to translate the lowest level refinement into code. If this is done manually, errors may be introduced and the lowest level of refinement and code tend to get out of step.

The first problem applies to informal as well as formal specifications and is not dealt with further here.

Cleanroom software engineering provides solutions to problems 2 and 3. A review process is used to check the correctness of each refinement step. Also, the refinement is documented using a subset of the programming language and so no translation is necessary.

The Z specification language improves on Cleanroom's solution to problem 2 by increasing the precision with which correctness criteria may be stated and checked.

Since the Cleanroom review process concentrates on program fragments it is inefficient if these fragments are lost in a morass of detail as the refinement proceeds. This is especially the case when the program is maintained or enhanced since it is then necessary to extract the fragments so that the changes can be verified. Literate programming solves this problem by keeping the refinement steps separate and combining them only for compilation.

The rest of this paper deals with the following three topics in more detail: Cleanroom, Z, and literate programming. A process is outlined and some tools to assist the process are described. Then a tiny example of the notation is presented and, finally, some conclusions are drawn.

Cleanroom

Cleanroom software engineering is a way of developing software which includes:

1. Specification of the product function,
2. Prediction of the relative frequency of use of each function by customers,
3. Correct refinement of specification (into a subset of the programming language[1]) supported by a review process,
4. No unit testing or function verification testing,
5. Statistical testing of code based on the prediction of customer use,

and

6. Estimation of the mean time to failure of the shipped product.

Case studies show that Cleanroom is capable of producing high quality code with few defects and a long mean time to failure.

The use of Z and literate programming with Cleanroom builds on items 1 and 3. The other aspects of Cleanroom software engineering may be applied independently of the notation used for specification and design (see [1] for more information).

Z

Z was chosen for specification and refinement in place of the notations normally used with Cleanroom for a number of reasons which are dealt with below. For more information on Z, see [4], [5], and [8].

---

[1] See, for instance, [2] and [7].

Specification

Cleanroom and Z specifications both consist of formal specifications of abstract data types. An abstract data type is some data and a collection of operations which are the only way of accessing and updating the data. The data persists across calls to the operations and so is known as state data since it carries the state of the abstract data type.

Z specifications are written in terms of an abstract model of the state data.

Cleanroom specifications say what effect any sequence of operations (known as a "stimulus history") has in terms of the response to the last operation.

Both types of specification are abstract in that they do not expose the choice of concrete data representation used to implement the abstract data type. However, Cleanroom specifications tend towards one of two styles: state-based or axiomatic.

A state-based style is seen when functions are provided on the stimulus history to determine the state of the abstract data type. For instance, given a complete sequence of database add and delete operations, a particular database record exists if and only if it has been added but not subsequently deleted. A function may therefore be written which extracts this information from any such sequence.

The state-based style has been used successfully in software projects. For an account of the use of Z to restructure the CICS/ESA product, see [6].

An axiomatic style is seen when operations are defined by the relationships between them and the effects of certain combinations of operations. For instance, the effect of a pop operation on a stack is the same as the effect of a push followed by a pop followed by another pop. This is because a push operation does not destroy information already in the stack. This style of specification is difficult to use since it is hard to judge when the task of specification is finished.

So Cleanroom and Z specifications appear to offer equivalent facilities for the superior state-based style. But Z is much better at handling state-based specifications since it was designed for that purpose.

Z also has the advantage that it is a powerful and expressive language which enables specifications to be constructed from small pieces using, for example, conjunction ("and") and disjunction ("or"). These constructs apply both to state data and operations and so it is easy to specify large abstract data types in terms of smaller abstract data types.

Refinement

Refinement is the process of moving from a specification to code in a number of steps. Intermediate steps implement a specification using code and lower level specifications. Where the specification is formal and the step has some correctness criteria, it is possible to verify the correctness of the step by checking that the criteria have been satisfied.

In Cleanroom, it appears that the correctness criteria are often informally stated, whereas Z enables theorems to be written down which are precise and unambiguous. In addition to a sound basis for proof, this precision also means the proofs are capable of machine assistance.

Non-determinism

Since Z is based on a relational model, it handles non-determinism. Stimulus history specifications are based on a functional model and require generalisation to enable them to include non-determinism. Non-determinism is important even when the implementation is completely deterministic. It enables the specifier to say explicitly that there is a choice of behaviour which is unimportant (i.e. there is no requirement to behave one way or the other).

Refinement in Z also handles non-determinism.

Other Factors

Another factor which led to the choice of Z was the experience and skills in using it for specification in CICS and also because of its use outside IBM and the working relationship with the Oxford Programming Research Group - the centre of Z research. Z was already part of the CICS/ESA development process for new, encapsulated code (see [6]). Also, there has been significant investment in tools for Z. These tools will be discussed later.

Literate Programming

A literate program is a textual document containing a collection of named program fragments. A program fragment may invoke other program fragments by name. Program fragments are introduced in the order which best help the reader to understand the program. In this way, a program is like a piece of literature. The program fragments are reorganised to produce compilable output files.

For more information on literate programming refer to [9], [10], and [11].

Verification

Verification of programs applies to particular program fragments known as "prime" programs. Each prime can be checked for correctness when it is introduced. Nesting of primes does not facilitate such checking as this makes it more difficult to focus on each one in turn. Verification reviews then need to be tied closely to the process of writing the code and subsequent changes to the code become difficult to re-verify.

Literate programming allows refinement steps to be kept separate in the program text and gathered together only for compilation. When the name of a code fragment is also the name of a piece of Z which specifies what the code fragment does, then there is a natural relationship between verifiable fragments of code and literate programming code fragments.

Interleaving of Text and Formal Notation

The normal style of a Z specification is interleaved formal and informal text. Typically each Z schema is explained and augmented by text preceeding it and following it. So there is a synergy between this style of specification and the literate style of programming which interleaves code and informal text.

Literate programming also encourages the programmer to keep the design documentation up to date since it is in the same document as the code.

Literate programming also matches the Cleanroom approach of using a programming language subset for refinement. Both avoid a translation step between the design documentation and the code and hence reduce maintenance problems.

Hybrid Approaches

Literate programming is also applicable when no formal specification exists. In such cases, it is possible to use peer reviews more effectively by concentrating attention on one code fragment at a time. So literate programming is useful when some code is being developed formally and the remainder informally. It allows the formal and informal fragments to coexist.

Process

An outline process is as follows:

1. Write a Z specification to capture the customer requirements.
2. Prove properties of the system before it is implemented. These properties may be checked against the original customer requirements.

Refine the Z specification into code as follows:

3. Choose refinement steps in consultation with other developers.

4. Document the steps in terms of code, lower-level specifications, and theorems which imply the correctness of the steps.

5. Prove the theorems.

6. When all the refinement steps are complete, collect the code into compilable units.

Other aspects of the process, such as testing, may follow Cleanroom practice or traditional methods and are not addressed here.

Tools

Short term

The following tools will be used in the short term:

- Z editor with integrated syntax and type checker.
- Schema expander for expanding both sides of a theorem for verification. This is necessary for certain specifications which are constructed from many small parts.
- Code collector for gathering code fragments into compilable units.
- Inspection recording tool for tracking the number and progress of verification reviews.
- BookMaster for text formatting.
- PL/X compiler.

Longer term

The following tools will be investigated in the longer term:

- Theorem proving assistant to enable correctness proofs to be guaranteed correct.
- Proof obligation generator to calculate the theorems which need to be proved to ensure a refinement step is correct.

An Example of the Notation

The following specification (or "schema") simply states that x is an input binary(31) variable and that y' and z' are output variables[2] of the same type which must be set to the value of x.

$$
\begin{array}{|l}
\hline
\,S \\\\
\quad x,\ y',\ z'\ :\ Bin31 \\
\hline
\quad x = y' = z' \\
\hline
\end{array}
$$

Next we describe a single refinement step as an example of the notation.

Set y to the value of x and then set z to the value of y.[3]

$S \leqslant$

$$
\begin{array}{ll}
\text{do;} & \\
\quad T & \qquad (8) \\
\quad U & \qquad (9) \\
\text{end do;} &
\end{array}
$$

Used on page(s): Not used.

The two specifications T and U are combined using sequential composition (do/end in PL/X). They are defined as follows:

$$
\begin{array}{|l}
\hline
\,T \\\\
\quad x,\ y'\ :\ Bin31 \\
\hline
\quad x = y' \\
\hline
\end{array}
$$

$$
\begin{array}{|l}
\hline
\,U \\\\
\quad y,\ y',\ z'\ :\ Bin31 \\
\hline
\quad y = y' = z' \\
\hline
\end{array}
$$

The step is correct provided the following theorems are true.[4] See [7] for the

---

2 The use of a prime (') to "decorate" output variables is a Z convention. Decorating a schema corresponds to decorating all its free variables.

3 The symbol $\leqslant$ means "is refined by".

4 The symbol **pre** means the precondition of an operation, i.e. the condition which must hold if the operation is to terminate and satisfy the relation between inputs and outputs. In these

theorems which need to be proved for other refinement steps.

$$pre \ S \vdash pre \ T$$

$$(pre \ S) \wedge T \vdash (pre \ U)'$$

$$(pre \ S) \wedge T \wedge U' \vdash S[y''/y',z''/z']$$

An expanded form of the last theorem is shown below.

$$[x, \ y', \ y'', \ z'': \ Bin31 \ |$$
$$x = y' \wedge y' = y'' = z''] \vdash x = y'' = z''$$

This theorem is easily proved by eliminating y' from the equations in the hypothesis.

Code collection

Suppose that T and U were refined as follows.

Assign x to y.

$$T \leqslant$$

```
y = x;
```

Used on page(s): 7.

---

examples, the preconditions are effectively true.

The symbol $\vdash$ denotes a theorem with hypotheses on the left and conclusions on the right.

The operator $\wedge$ denotes conjunction ("and") of specifications.

The expression $S[y''/y',z''/z']$ denotes S with a substitution of new variable names for old, i.e. y'' is substituted for y' and z'' for z'.

Assign *y* to *z*.

$U \leqslant$

```
z = y;
```

Used on page(s): 7.

Then the code collector would produce the following code to implement *S*.
Notice that some of the text relating to the refinement steps has been
included as comments.

```
*/**Source File: CLEANZ Refstep: S Line: 1680 ******/
*/*                                                  */
*/* Set y to the value of x and then set z to the   */
*/* value of y.                                      */
*/*                                                  */
*/****************************************************/
 do;
*/**Source File: CLEANZ Refstep: T Line: 1741 ******/
*/*                                                  */
*/* Assign x to y .                                  */
*/*                                                  */
*/****************************************************/
    y = x;
*/**Source File: CLEANZ Refstep: U Line: 1746 ******/
*/*                                                  */
*/* Assign y to z .                                  */
*/*                                                  */
*/****************************************************/
    z = y;
 end do;
```

Conclusions

The general conclusion is that it is not cost-effective in a commercial software environment to do even semi-formal refinement without machine assistance. This is due to a number of factors.

There are many unspecified interfaces in commercial software such as interfaces to existing pieces of code and interfaces to other products. These inter-

faces pose a problem when it is necessary to call them from a refinement of a Z specification. Either a risk must be taken or a relatively large investment made in specifying the interface.

The approach of specifying program fragments using schemas results in many unwieldy proofs. The proofs are often not difficult from a mathematical point of view, but are large because they involve expanding the schemas involved.

The semantics of a subset of a commercial programming language such as PL/X are unpleasant particularly for datatypes such as pointers. These semantics are explored further in [3] and [7].

There is no simple way to separate concurrency concerns and yet produce an efficient implementation.

A more positive conclusion is that there are many similarities between the usual style of writing a Z specification and literate programming. For instance, both Z specifications and literate programs can be viewed and used as documents. The use of interleaved formal and informal notations in both cases gives a good balance between precision and comprehensibility. These similarities make the use of literate programming natural in implementing a Z specification.

Acknowledgements

I would like to thank the following people for their help:

My colleagues on the "100x Quality" task force which examined the use of Cleanroom and Z:

Peter Collins, Peter Lambros, Peter Lupton, and John Wordsworth,

For help on Cleanroom:

Merle Beghtel, Laurie Griffiths, Kim Hathaway, Mike McMorran, Mark Pleszkoch, Steve Rosen, and Alan Spangler,

For help in research and training, the following members of the Oxford University Programming Research Group:

Steve King, Jane Sinclair, and Jim Woodcock,

For help on the process for Cleanroom and Z:

Ann Dalton, Alan Flint, and Abul Rahman,

For help with tools:

Gaz Bloxsidge, Bob Buxton, Tracy Firth, Simon Gregory, Jonathan Hoare, and Paul Mundy.

References

Cleanroom:

[1] *Developing Defect-Free Software with Cleanroom Software Engineering* by Mark Pleszkoch and Alan Spangler of the Cleanroom Software Technology Center (CSTC) in Gaithersburg

[2] *The Design PL/X Language* by Kim Hathaway and Steve Rosen of the CSTC

[3] *An Approach to a Weakest Precondition Semantics for Design PL/X* by Jane Sinclair, Steve King, and Jim Woodcock (unpublished paper)

Z:

[4] *The Z Notation - A Reference Manual* by Mike Spivey (ISBN 0-13-983768-X)

[5] *Specification Case Studies* by Ian Hayes (ISBN 0-13-832544-8)

[6] *CICS project report: Experiences and results from the use of Z in IBM* by Iain Houston and Steve King (pages 588-596 of *VDM '91: Formal Software Development Methods*, volume 551 of Lecture Notes in Computer Science published by Springer-Verlag)

[7] *Using Z and Design PL/X for Software Development* by John Wordsworth (unpublished IBM Technical Report)

[8] *Software Development with Z* by John Wordsworth (Addison-Wesley)

Literate programming:

[9] *The WEB System of Structured Documentation* by Donald Knuth (Stanford University report number STAN-CS-83-980)

[10] *Programming Pearls* in Communications of the ACM of May and June 1986 (volume 29 numbers 5 and 6) edited by Jon Bentley

[11] A literate programming mailing list on the Internet which may be joined by sending a message containing only the line

```
SUBSCRIBE LITPROG "Your Real Name In Quotes"
```

to LISTSERV@SHSU.EDU. You will receive an email acknowledgment with further information about the list.

Productivity of Cleanroom with and without Z

This appendix addresses the apparent difference between our experience of Cleanroom with Z in CICS and that of Cleanroom (without Z) in the COBOL/SF project. This was raised during the question time at the Z User Meeting.

The discrepancy was in the area of cost-effectiveness. I maintain that using Cleanroom with the Z language is not generally cost-effective in a commercial environment whereas the COBOL/SF project documented by Dan Craigen showed a reasonable productivity.

Of course, it is impossible to compare productivity levels on different projects with any accuracy especially given the differences between the two projects and the teams which worked on them. However, the differences are significant, so I will try to offer an explanation.

Where we have been able to apply Cleanroom techniques. our productivity has been reasonable and we met our target dates. In other areas, we have written Z specifications but have found the process of refinement, documenting correctness criteria, and proving them correct in a team review to be unachievable for a number of reasons:

1. CICS/ESA is a 20-year old software product. To restructure a component requires equivalent function to be maintained otherwise much other old code needs to be reworked, at a large cost.

   This makes the interfaces between restructured components and the old code more complex than would have been the case in a newer, better structured product such as COBOL/SF.

2. CICS/ESA depends very much on other complex software products such as MVS, VTAM, RACF, VSAM, etc. There are no formal specifications of the interfaces to these products which greatly increases the cost of formal refinement down onto these interfaces.

   I suspect that similar problems in COBOL/SF are on a much smaller scale. COBOL/SF transforms a Cobol program into another equivalent program with better structure, so its main external interfaces are for file input and output. This is an order of magnitude simpler than a transaction processor's requirements on other products.

3. The performance of a transaction processor such as CICS is critical to its customers' businesses whereas the performance of COBOL/SF is not. So CICS cannot avoid heavy use of features of a programming language, such as pointers, which enable good performance. This increases the proof burden considerably.

   We found the proof rules for the assignment statement complex and difficult to apply in the presence of pointers, aliasing, and other complexities inherent in our target language (a subset of a systems programming flavour of PL/1).

In contrast, Mark Pleszkoch of the Cleanroom Software Technology Center comments:

> In the COBOL/SF project specifically, the use of pointers and arrays was quickly encapsulated, so that the vast majority of the code dealt in terms of higher-level abstract data types such as stacks and queues.

4. CICS code has to deal with concurrency; COBOL/SF is a sequential program.

5. Our approach with Z was fairly formal. We wrote formal specifications in Z. Our refinement approach, which we were unable to afford on a large scale, was to document data and operation refinements in Z and to write down the correctness criteria as mathematical theorems. In addition, we worked on a denotational semantics of the implementation language subset which gave us an understanding of some of the underlying complexities of this language.

Mark Pleszkoch comments:

> In terms of formality, we are definitely much less formal than typical Z users. There is a formal basis for Cleanroom, and we at the CSTC have worked to derive formal proof rules for the complications that you mentioned, but we find that most of the teams (especially the U.S. based teams) don't apply verification at the level of formality where these issues surface. Instead, we concentrate in the Cleanroom education on the intuitive level, so that people know a correct intended function when they see one.
>
> I believe that the key to applying Cleanroom in a cost-effective, highly productive manner is to not force developers to go to a level of formality beyond their needs (and abilities), while at the same time not losing the benefits of precise documentation that makes clear what each piece of code is designed to do.

Animating Z specifications in SQL*Forms3.0

Matthew Love
School of Computing and Management Sciences
Sheffield Hallam University, Sheffield S11 8HD, UK

Abstract

This paper outlines the role of animation when developing formal specifications of computer software, and presents a method for animating Z specifications in the CASE product SQL*Forms3.0   The method includes a novel way of grouping the Z predicates in such a way that schema composition and inclusion are supported.   A worked example is given.

1   Introduction

For well over a decade computer scientists have been searching for methods of developing trustworthy software systems. There is an obvious need for reliability in safety critical systems, but even data processing systems would benefit if emergency maintenance costs could be avoided.

One approach to greater reliability is through the use of "Formal Methods". Here a suitably rigorous mathematical language [1], [2], [3] is used to draw up an initial systems level specification, which may be analysed through theorems and proofs until the developers are sure that it is sound. Then, by following well-founded rules [4] that map abstract specifications to detailed designs, it may be 'reified' or rewritten in more and more concrete terms.

One of the more obvious difficulties in the whole Formal Methods approach lies in deriving an initial systems specification that is at once both valid (describes a system that will be useful to the end user) and verifiably correct (is self-consistent, whose logic works etc). It is widely recognised [5] [6] that the people in the best position to have a 'feel' for the validity of the specification are the domain experts. But pilots, doctors, engineers and pension advisors are unlikely to be able to read even small parts of the formal specification. The mathematics that enables verification acts to prevent validation.

The Formal Method process model MoD Draft 00-55 (Safety Critical Software Systems) [7] recognises this and requires two documents to be written. First a *"Software Requirements Specification"* is written in natural language, then a Formal Methods based *"Software Specification"* . An *"executable prototype"* is made of the Software Specification, bearing "the minimum number of changes" from the original[1]. The design team is then required to test the prototype to ensure that it behaves as described in the Software Requirements Specification document.

If the user interface is sufficiently clear the end-user / domain expert can play a full part in this testing. Unexpected test results are likely to traced back to one of two sources : the domain expert has requested something (or a combination of somethings) but has not appreciated the consequences, or the Formal Methods experts have found an alternative meaning for the original request. Either way the problem has been spotted, and one or both of the specifications can be revised at an early stage.

All of this assumes that it is possible to generate a useful animation of the formal Software Specification. It is essential that the production process is itself reliable, otherwise test results cannot be trusted. It is also highly desirable that the generation is very quick, so as to allow an interactive exploration of ideas at this very early stage of requirements elicitation.

This paper describes a method for animating Z specifications in the proprietary product SQL*Forms3.0. The method is suitable for automation.

2   SQL*Forms3.0

The animation method outlined below transforms Z specifications into executable PL/SQL as supported by the Oracle Corp's product SQL*Forms version 3.0 [8]. The principles of the method could, however, be transferred to other host environments. SQL*Forms was chosen for rather pragmatic reasons:- this particular case tool is very well known, so support and advice is available; runs on all sizes of machines from laptop to mainframe; and is already installed at very many sites, so following this paper manually is 'free'. Against this, the animation is designed to fit the tool. A bottom up approach of "design the tool to fit the animation" would produce more elegant internal code [9].

SQL*Forms is a front-end user interface to tables stored in a relational database. Suppose, for example, that a table had been created by the line
            create table telephoneDir(name char(20), phone number) ;
then a screen can be created merely by giving the table name (ie telephoneDir) and the number of lines to be displayed (eg 5). The Forms product retrieves the definition of the table and automatically generates a user interface form:

----

1.   Footnote

In 00-55 terminology an *animation* is an *executable prototype* plus a *discussion* document covering those areas of the Software Specification that the prototype does not attempt to cover. This paper uses the terms animation and executable prototype interchangeably.

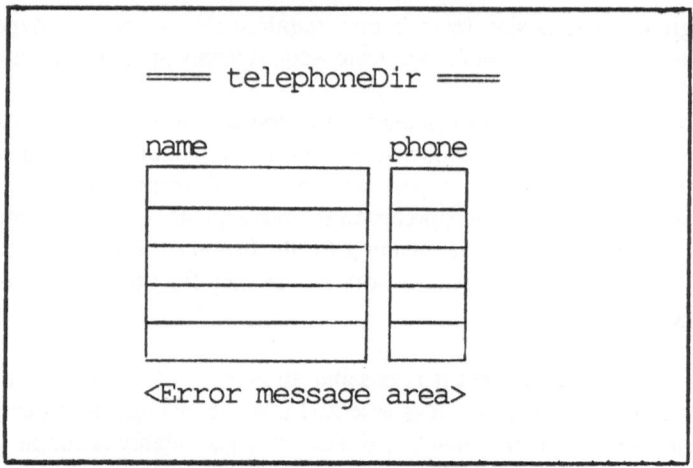

Figure 1.   Default screen generated by SQL*Forms

SQL*Forms has in-built keystrokes to display ("query") the current database values onto the screen. Values may then be altered, entered or deleted as the user chooses, and saved ("committed") to the database.

The package has some powerful data validation facilities, foremost of which are so called "triggers", which associate SQL predicates with fields, lines, tables or whole forms. Whenever one of these is manipulated in a particular way (eg insert, alter, delete, read) the associated trigger(s) fire, and only if all evaluate to *true* does the data get saved into the database. Should any trigger fail then the whole transaction is rolled back to the beginning, and an error message (system supplied unless the designer gives a more appropriate one) is displayed. In this way the state of the database remains inviolate.

Triggers may be written in the language PL/SQL as a procedural list of SQL predicates followed by an exception block, which is executed only if one of the predicates fails. For example, the extract of code in Figure 2 prevents a person's name being entered into the telephone directory if it was already listed.

```
procedure precondition is
begin
    select .... from ....
        where person not in (select name from telephoneDir) ;
exception
    when .... then
        message('Name is already listed in directory') ;
        raise form-trigger-failure ;
end ;
```

Figure 2.   Extract of PL/SQL procedure code

In PL/SQL procedures may call other procedures and may pass parameters.The exact type of failure in a subroutine's predicate may be signalled to the outer procedures via a specific Exception clause. Exception errors may be cascaded through to outer levels, permitting them to be handled as the designer chooses.

The end-user / domain expert need know nothing of all this - all they see is a form inviting data entry. They may visit fields and enter data in any order. When they press the 'commit' key their data is saved to the database, or they see an error message explaining which predicate failed to operate.

3 Relating Z and SQL*Forms

The basic construction of the animation can now be explained.

3.1 Data Structures

SQL, being a relational language, demands that all data structures are represented by tables. For the Z structures **functions** and **relations** the representation is simple : a table, of the same name as the function or relation, has columns for the domain and range values. A predicate is used to check that function domain does not contain duplicates.

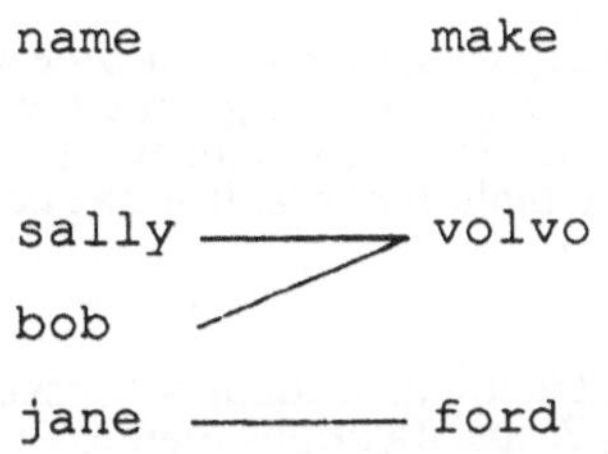

car_type :

name	make
sally	volvo
bob	volvo
jane	ford

Figure 3a. A partial function car_type : name ⇸ make

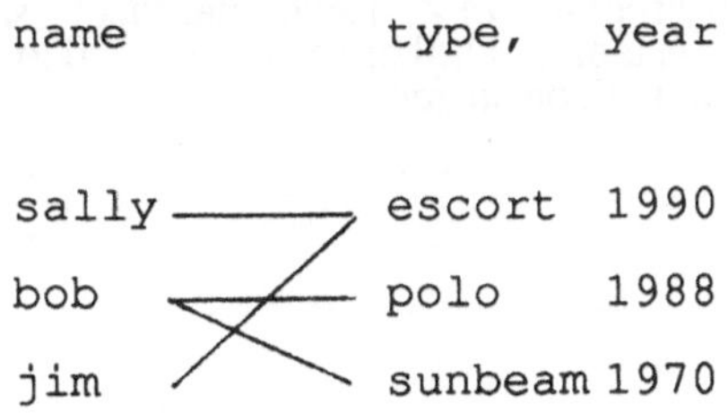

owners :

name	type	year
sally	escort	1990
bob	polo	1988
bob	sunbeam	1970
jim	escort	1990

Figure 3b. A relation owns : name ⟷ (type X year)

Powersets can also be represented by a single table. For example, in
(X ⟼ set of Y's)   each Y could be listed beside its key X.

X	⟼	{1,2,3}	X	1
Y	⟼	{7,5}	X	2
			X	3
			Y	7
			Y	5

It turns out to be useful, however, if an additional (albeit redundant) table is created which holds a list of the current key values. This is because the SQL*Forms interface has a facility to display a single entry from the key table together with the associated non-key values from the data table, meaning that as the user scrolls though the domain/key values the system will display all the range/powerset values for that key. (It is of course necessary for the system to keep the key table up to date with the base table. This is programmed via the trigger steps already described.)

Sequence tables have a 'position' column. The Forms package can display data in sequence via an ORDER BY <POSITION-COL-NAME> command. The internal storage order of rows does not affect the results of processing.

seq : [q, w, e, r, t, y]	seq : position	value
	1	q
	2	w
	4	r
	6	y
	3	e
	5	t

Inverse functions could be programmed as tables that are updated each time the master function table is updated. It is easier, though, to access the original table by column name, so redundancy is removed. It is possible to tell Forms to display tables with the columns in other than the normal order, so the table *looks* as if it has been reversed.

The **base data types** provided by SQL are those often found in data processing applications :- integer, time, date, character etc. Most Z specifications map to these with ease. The normal due caution has to be taken over the use of Decimal. Finite sets may be enumerated in a table, and the SQL*Forms system can check that each time an enumerated set value is used it is "IN" this table.

The above discussion covers the principle data structures of Z. Relational theory says that all finite data structures can be represented via tables. Further work is needed to find the most pragmatic representations for structures not considered above.

3.2 Z Predicates

Z predicates are represented by SQL predicates. SQL is, of course, already designed to work with multi-row tables, so a major component of Z, set logic, is easy to encode. It further helps that UNION, INTERSECTION, set MINUS and IN are provided as SQL keywords.

Examples :-   (Further examples are found in Section 5)

  setA   U   setB   select * from setA
                                      UNION select * from setB ;

  x $\in$ dom(setA)   select .... from ....
                                      where x IN (select dom from setA) ;

  y' = 3   insert into <y-table> value (3) ;

The new value of y' is intended to replace any older one (nb see Section 4 for an expansion of this), so the step
                    delete y-table ;
would be placed before the insert. This illustrates that some Z predicates involve more than one SQL substep. This causes no problems. The sequence of executing substeps is described in Section 4.

3.3 Schema Calculus

An important feature of Z is its calculus for combining subschemas into composites.

Schema **inclusion,** including the Δ and Ξ conventions, are coded as subroutine calls to the included schema's predicates / procedures. If the included Z schema made use of input (?) or output (!) variables screen fields for data entry or display need creating on the including schema's display area.

Schema **conjunction** (AND) are sequences of calls. Schema **disjunction** (OR) is programmed by calling the second schema as an exception should (any part of) the first schema fail. It is noted that this gives a deterministic implementation of OR. It is possible to give a non-deterministic implementation, but at the expense of extra coding.

As well as having SQL tables to represent pre-state data structures, tables are declared to represent post-state (ie primed) tables. Since SQL does not allow primes in table names a '1' is used instead, eg telephoneDir1. As the last action of a successful operation 'Housekeeping' procedures copy primed values to their unprimed counterparts areas.

4   Grouping of predicates

Consider what would happen if the following specification were translated into SQL and executed in the order as written :-

silly ————————	Partial SQL translation
x : N	create table silly (x number) ;
y' : N	create table silly1(y number) ;

1	x < 10	select .... from silly where x < 10 ; exception ..."not less than 10" .... ;
2	y' = x + x	delete silly1 ; insert into silly1 (select x + x from silly) ;
3	y' > 0	select ... from silly1 where y > 0 ; exception .... ;
4	y' = x * x	delete silly1 ; insert into silly1 (select x * x from silly) ;

Line 1 would check that the initial value of x was less than 10. If not the exception mechanism would halt the animation with the given error message. X could then be set to less than 10 and the whole predicate series started again.

Line 2 would set y' to x + x.

LIne 3 would check that the value of y' was greater than 0 (exception .....)

Line 4 would then set y' to x * x.   This would be saved to the database.

The reader will have observed that there are two assignments to y'. These are compatible for some values of input (ie x = 2) but not others (x = 1 and x = 3 to 9, for example)[2]. Also, the predicate y' > 0 comes before the second assignment. The final value of y' is left unchecked.

----

2 Footnote

Incompatible "assignment" such as the examples shown is one of the key things that the animation is trying to detect. Extensive use of schema inclusion - much encouraged by Z users - may bring together assignments that were written in remote parts of the specification.   For the same reason there may be a great jumble in the order of statements involving any given variable.

It is also worth noting that testing the specification by animation in no way replaces the need for a full proof. As noted above, the specification of Silly gives behaves in a different way for x = 2 than for other values. Testing shows behaviour for chosen cases. Proofs are needed to establish that the desired results hold for all cases.   The reader might work out what happens for x = 0.

So, an important and, as far as the author is aware, a novel step in transforming the Z specification into executable code is to arrange the executable code into groups, where the groups are to be executed in sequence but inside a group individual statements may be executed in any order. The groups are based on whether the Z predicate is a precondition, a state change, or postcondition. A fourth group does some housekeeping tasks.

Group 1 :   All *preconditions* .
             These predicates refer only to constants and unprimed variables. Since these do not alter values the statements may be executed in any order.

Group 2 :   All "*assignments*" (Nb - see below)
             These Z predicates are of the form
             primed-var = expression of constants and unprimed variables

Group 3 :   All *postconditions*
             These predicates may refer to primed and/or unprimed values but do not change them. Again, any order.

Group 4 :   Housekeeping.
             Z often uses delta tables, that is 'before' and 'after' views of the same structure. The housekeeping copies after-values (primed tables) into before-values (unprimed) prior to the next user operation.

In fact each Group 2 predicate is encoded as two substeps :

Group 2a :   *Actual assignment*
             a Delete + Insert sequence as explained earlier.
             <u>All</u> such sequences, wherever they occur, are executed before ....

Group 2b :   *Confirmation of success* of assignments
             Reevaluate each assignment and check that the result corresponds to the final stored value of the target variable.

Hence the sequence of executable statements for the specification of Silly would be :-

Group 1 :	precondition	check	$x < 10$
Group 2a :	assignments	set	$y' := x + x$
		set	$y' := x * x$
Group 2b :	confirmation	check	$y' == x + x$
		check	$y' == x * x$
Group 3 :	postcondition	check	$y' > 0$
Group 4 :	housekeeping	copy	[none in this example]

The allocation to these groups can be made on a syntactic examination of the Z predicates, and has successfully been automated for a number of Z constructs.

302

The method, though, must prohibit the use of one form of assignment :- where the right hand side refers to primed variables, eg $y' = x' + 5$. This is because the variable x' may not yet have its value. It is, however, always possible to rewrite such expression in terms of unprimed values.

5 A Worked Example

The following example is taken from Diller's excellent tutorial book "Z : An Introduction to Formal Methods" [11]. He gives a full exposition of a simple internal telephone directory system, which can be summarised as follows :

"A university maintains a list of members, who are entitled to have telephone extensions. A Very Important Person might have two or more extensions, but mere mortals may even have to share an extension. It is required [amongst other things] to be able to *add* new directory entries - or get replies 'Person not a member' or 'Entry already exists' - *remove* entries, and *update* existing entries."

5.1 DoAddEntry

Right at the top level of the specification, this operation either adds a new entry to the directory or produces messages 'Not Member' or 'Entry Exists'.

Z: DoAddEntry $\hat{=}$ (AddEntry $\land$ Success) $\lor$ NotMember $\lor$ EntryExists

The specification shows examples of AND and OR constructs. AND is coded as a sequence of "call AddEntry group 1, call Success group 1, AddEntry2, Success2" etc. The ORs are coded as exception blocks, should any one of the above procedures fail. If no specification component applies (ie the whole specification is logically 'false') a system error message is automatically supplied.

SQL: procedure DoAddEntry is begin
              AddEntry_1 ; Success_1 ;
              AddEntry_2a ; Success_2a ; ....
              AddEntry_4 ; Success_4 ;
              exception ....
                  NotMember_1 ... NotMember_4 ;
                  exception
                      EntryExists_1 ..... 4 ;
         end ;

5.2 AddEntry

AddEntry adds a new *name?* and *newnumber?* to the directory. In PL/SQL these are denoted as screen fields by prefixing the names with a colon.

The annotation to the right of the Z schema shows the coding group(s) for the PL/SQL translations. Eg the predicate (name? members) will be allocated to procedure AddEntry_1.

```
AddEntry _____
    Δphone                                                          1 - 4
    name?         : Person
    newnumber? : Phone
  _____
    name? ∈ members                                                 1
    (name? ⟼ newnumber?) ∉ telephoneDir                             1
    telephoneDir' = telephoneDir U {name? ⟼ newnumber?}             2a/b
    members' = members                                              2a/b
  _____
```

procedure AddEntry_1 is ....
    Δphone_1 ;   *-- ie call subprocedure Δphone_1*
    select .... from .... where :name in (select member from members) ;
    select .... from .... where :name, :newnumber not in
                                        (select * from telephoneDir) ;

procedure AddEntry_2a is ....
    Δphone_2a ;
    delete telephoneDir1;
    insert into telephoneDir1   select * from telephoneDir
                  UNION   select (:name, :newnumber from ....) ;

    delete members1 ;
    insert into members1   select * from members ;

procedure AddEntry_2b is ....
    Δphone_2b ;
    isSetEqual(telephoneDir1,   select * from telephoneDir
                                  UNION select :name,:newnumber from ....) ;
    isSetEqual(members1, members) ;
                                        (Nb - abbreviated syntax.)
procedure AddEntry_3 is
    Δphone_3 ;

procedure AddEntry_4 is
    Δphone_4 ;

5.3 △phone

This Z schema defines the member and telephoneDir data structures. These are created as SQL tables. The schema has no predicates, so the precondition, assignment and postcondition procedures are all *NULL* . However the housekeeping procedure copies the post- table values to the pre- tables.

△phone_____
　　members, members'　　　: Person
　　telephoneDir , telephoneDir'　 : Person ↦ Phone
|_____

create table members, members1　　　 (member char(20)) ;
create table telephoneDir, telephoneDir1 (name char(20), phone number) ;

procedure △phone_1, 2a, 2b, 3 are all NULL ;

procedure △phone_4 is
　　delete members ;
　　insert into members select * from members1 ;

　　delete telephoneDir ;
　　insert into telephoneDir select * from telephoneDir1 ;

6　Using the Animator to Demonstrate Specified Behaviour

In the book Diller goes on to specify a RemoveEntry operation, and constructs an **UpdateExistingEntry** out of **RemoveEntry** ; **AddEntry**. He then muses as to what might happen if this operation were to be applied to a VIP. Observe that though a VIP may have several extensions, each extension could be shared with several other people. Does UpdateExistingEntry change just a single VIP-Extension mapping, or do all related mappings change as well? Diller takes some five pages and four interim schemas to show how the composed UpdateExistingEntry can be rationalised into a single schema that is sufficiently simple for an easy theorem and proof analysis.

In cases such as this animation could be used to explore the effect of the composition through test cases. Only when the user agrees that the specification appears to have the right behaviour, and thus can be assumed to be fairly stable, would a full, expensive, proof be attempted.

7   State of the Research

The animation method has been developed by applying it by hand to a number of specifications found in the published literature. The largest example so far involves some 50 schemas with a maximum nested depth of seven. Response time for queries against tables containing 100+ items is a few seconds (running on HP 4000 workstations).

A pilot translation program has been written in C which translates a subset of Z into PL/SQL. The program has several restrictions :- the input interface is 'Z text' rather than maths based, data structures are translated by hand, and some set operations have yet to be implemented. However, the pilot does show that the method can be automated.

The choice of SQL*Forms3.0 has been moderately successful. Other researchers will be interested in the use of relational tables, the trigger mechanisms and the exception handling. The screen based user interface is also noteworthy.   Two significant weaknesses are that it is not possible to report which line of a query caused an exception (sets might overlap -- but which elements ?) and the procedure parameter passing is not sufficiently expansive to cope with query parametrisation. The author does note that SQL*Forms was not written with Z animation applications in mind !

8. Summary and Conclusions

This paper has described a method of interpreting Z specifications such that they can be animated in a relational system. This has been illustrated by using PL/SQL to encode and to control of activation of the Z predicates.

The method contains a novel way of grouping the Z predicates into batches of preconditions, "assignments", postconditions and housekeeping predicates, and shows how the effects of assignment can be mutually cross-checked. A pilot implementation has shown that all this may be automated and that the stylistic restrictions placed upon the specifier are not severe.

The end-user / domain expert need know nothing of the internal workings of either the translation method or of the animation itself. S/he is presented with a screen containing named data entry fields and may fill these in in any order desired. When she presses the Commit key text messages appear stating which line, if any, of the schema failed to execute. Successful operations update the database, so sequences of operations can be tested.

The advantages of fast and automatic translation and of a clear user interface are obvious, especially when looking back at the project's original aim of providing a tool that can enable domain experts and specification experts to communicate through the shared use of an interactive tool. The Oracle SQL*Forms3.0 tool has been found adequate in supporting the method, though there may well be other 4GL environments which make coding easier.

References

1. Gallimore R.M. , Coleman D. ; *Introduction to Abstract Data Type Specifications using OBJ.* Umist. 1984

2. Spivey J.M. ; *The Z notation : a reference manual.* Prentice Hall 1989.

3. Dawes J ; *The VDM-SL Reference Guide.* Pitman Publishing, 1991.

4. Jones C B ; *Systematic Software Development using VDM.* Prentice Hall, 1991

5. *IEEE Guide to Software Requirements Specifications.* IEEE Inc, New York, 1984

6. *DoD - STD - 2167A   Military Standard, Defense Systems Software Development.* Dept of Defense, Washington DC 20301. 1988

7. *Interim Defence Standard 00-55 ; The Procurement of Safety Critical Software in Defence Equipment.* Ministry of Defence (Part1 : Requirements; Part2 : Guidance). 1991

8. Oracle Corporation ; *SQL*Forms 3.0 User's Guide and Reference* 1991

9. Morrey I et al; *Case Studies in the animation of formal specifications.* Internal Paper, School of Computing and Management Sciences, Sheffield Hallam University, Sheffield S11 8HD. 1992

10. Jabry Z, Austin S ; *An experiment in VDM to SQL Translation.* NPL Report DITC 193/91, National; Physical Laboratory, Teddington, Middx. UK. 1991

11. Diller A ; *Z : An Introduction to Formal Methods.* Wiley 1990.

Appendices

Select Z Bibliography

Jonathan Bowen *

Oxford University Computing Laboratory
Programming Research Group
11 Keble Road, Oxford OX1 3QD, UK
Email: <Jonathan.Bowen@comlab.ox.ac.uk>

Abstract

This bibliography contains a list of Z references that are either available as published papers, books or technical reports from institutions, or from the author, the Programming Research Group (PRG) librarian or via electronic mail. The bibliography is in alphabetical order by author name(s).

Introduction

The list of references is maintained in electronic form, in BIBTEX bibliography database format, which is compatible with the widely used LATEX document preparation system [175]. It is intended to keep the bibliography up to date and to issue it to coincide with the regular Z User Meetings. The BIBTEX source file used for this bibliography [37] is available via electronic mail by sending a message containing the command "send z z92.bib" to the address <archive-server@comlab.ox.ac.uk>. The Z bibliography is also available via anonymous FTP on the Internet. For more information on accessing the bibliography electronically from the Z archive, see [333].

To add new references concerned with Z to this list, please send details via electronic mail to the address <zforum-request@comlab.ox.ac.uk> or post them to Jonathan Bowen (address above). It is helpful if you can give as much information as possible so the entry could be included as a reference in future papers concerning Z.

Acknowledgements

Ruaridh Macdonald of RSRE, Malvern, initiated the idea of a Z bibliography and helped maintain it for several years. Joan Arnold at the PRG has assisted in maintaining the bibliography as part of her work as secretary to the UK Information Engineering Directorate (IED) ZIP project, a collaborative research project concerned with Z standards, methods and tools.

---

*Funded by the UK SERC under the Information Engineering Directorate SAFEMOS project (IED3/1/1036).

References

[1] G.D. Abowd. Agents: Communicating interactive processes. In D. Diaper, D. Gilmore, Gilbert Cockton, and Brian Shackel, editors, *Human-Computer Interaction: INTERACT'90*, pages 143–148. Elsevier Science Publishers B.V. (North-Holland), 1990.

[2] G.D. Abowd. *Formal Aspects of Human-Computer Interaction*. DPhil thesis, Oxford University Computing Laboratory, 11 Keble Road, Oxford, UK, 1991.

[3] G.D. Abowd, J.P. Bowen, A. Dix, M.D. Harrison, and R. Took. User interface languages: a survey of existing methods. Technical Report PRG-TR-5-89, Oxford University Computing Laboratory, 11 Keble Road, Oxford, UK, October 1989.

[4] J-R. Abrial. The B tool. In G. Goos and J. Hartmanis, editors, *VDM – The Way Ahead. Proc. 2nd VDM-Europe Symposium*, volume 328 of *Lecture Notes in Computer Science*, pages 86–87. VDM-Europe, Springer-Verlag, 1988.

[5] J-R. Abrial. The B method for large software, specification, design and coding (abstract). In S. Prehn and W.J. Toetenel, editors, *VDM'91: Formal Software Development Methods*, volume 552 of *Lecture Notes in Computer Science*, pages 398–405. Springer-Verlag, 1991.

[6] J-R. Abrial, S.A. Schuman, and B. Meyer. Specification language. In R.M. McKeag and A.M. Macnaghten, editors, *On the Construction of Programs: An Advanced Course*, pages 343–410. Cambridge University Press, UK, 1980.

[7] J-R. Abrial and I.H. Sørensen. KWIC-index generation. In J. Staunstrup, editor, *Program Specification: Proceedings of a Workshop*, volume 134 of *Lecture Notes in Computer Science*, pages 88–95. Springer-Verlag, 1981.

[8] A.J. Alencar and J.A. Goguen. OOZE: An object-oriented Z environment. In P. America, editor, *Proc. ECOOP'91 European Conference on Object-Oriented Programming*, volume 512 of *Lecture Notes in Computer Science*, pages 180–199. Springer-Verlag, 1991.

[9] A.J. Alencar and J.A. Goguen. Two examples in OOZE. Technical Report PRG-TR-25-91, Oxford University Computing Laboratory, 11 Keble Road, Oxford, UK, 1991.

[10] D.B. Arnold, D.A. Duce, and G.J. Reynolds. An approach to the formal specification of configurable models of graphs systems. In G. Maréchal, editor, *Proc. EUROGRAPHICS'87, European Computer Graphics Conference and Exhibition*, pages 439–463. Elsevier Science Publishers B.V. (North-Holland), 1987.

The paper describes a general framework for the formal specification of modular graphics systems. The approach is illustrated by an example taken from the Graphical Kernel System (GKS) and uses the Z specification notation.

[11] D.B. Arnold and G.J. Reynolds. Configuring graphics systems components. *Software Engineering Journal*, 3(6):248–256, November 1988.

[12] R.D. Arthan. Formal specification of a proof tool. In S. Prehn and W.J. Toetenel, editors, *VDM'91: Formal Software Development Methods*, volume 551 of *Lecture Notes in Computer Science*, pages 356–370. Springer-Verlag, 1991.

[13] R.D. Arthan. On free type definitions in Z. In J.E. Nicholls, editor, *Z User Workshop, York 1991*, Workshops in Computing, pages 40–58. Springer-Verlag, 1992.

[14] P.B. Austin, K.A. Murray, and A.J. Wellings. File system caching in large point-to-point networks. *Software Engineering Journal*, 7(1):65–80, January 1992.

[15] C. Bailes and R. Duke. The ecology of class refinement. In J.M. Morris and R.C. Shaw, editors, *Proc. 4th Refinement Workshop*, Workshops in Computing, pages 185–196. Springer-Verlag, 1991.

[16] M. Bailey. Formal specification using Z. In *Proc. Software Engineering anniversary meeting (SEAS)*, page 99. SEA, 1987.

[17] J. Bainbridge, R.W. Whitty, and J.B. Wordsworth. Obtaining structural metrics of Z specifications for systems development. In J.E. Nicholls, editor, *Z User Workshop, Oxford 1990*, Workshops in Computing, pages 269–281. Springer-Verlag, 1991.

[18] J-P. Banâtre. About programming environments. In J-P. Banâtre, S.B. Jones, and D. de Métayer, editors, *Prospects for Functional Programming in Software Engineering*, volume 1 of *Research Reports*, chapter 1, pages 1–22. Springer-Verlag, 1991. ESPRIT Project 302.

[19] R. Barden, S. Stepney, and D. Cooper. The use of Z. In J.E. Nicholls, editor, *Z User Workshop, York 1991*, Workshops in Computing, pages 99–124. Springer-Verlag, 1992.

[20] G. Barrett. Formal methods applied to a floating-point number system. *IEEE Transactions on Software Engineering*, 15(5):611–621, May 1989.

This paper presents a formalization of the IEEE standard for binary floating-point arithmetic in Z. The formal specification is refined into four components. The procedures presented form the basis for the floating-point unit of the Inmos IMS T800 transputer. This work resulted in a joint UK Queen's Award for Technological Achievement for Inmos Ltd and the Oxford University Computing Laboratory in 1990. It was estimated that the approach saved a year in development time compared to traditional methods.

[21] L.M. Barroca and J.A. McDermid. Formal methods: Use and relevance for the development of safety-critical systems. *The Computer Journal*, 35(6):579–599, December 1992.

[22] M. Benjamin. A message passing system: An example of combining CSP and Z. In J.E. Nicholls, editor, *Z User Workshop, Oxford 1989*, Workshops in Computing, pages 221–228. Springer-Verlag, 1990.

[23] M. Benveniste. Operational semantics of a distributed object-oriented language and its Z formal specification. Rapport de recherche 1230, INRIA, France, May 1990.

[24] M. Benveniste. Writing operational semantics in Z: A structural approach. In S. Prehn and W.J. Toetenel, editors, *VDM'91: Formal Software Development Methods*, volume 551 of *Lecture Notes in Computer Science*, pages 164–188. Springer-Verlag, 1991.

[25] S. Bera. Structuring for the VDM specification language. In G. Goos and J. Hartmanis, editors, *VDM – The Way Ahead. Proc. 2nd VDM-Europe Symposium*, volume 328 of *Lecture Notes in Computer Science*, pages 2–25. VDM-Europe, Springer-Verlag, 1988.

[26] P.G. Bishop, editor. *Fault Avoidance*, chapter 3, pages 56–140. Applied Science. Elsevier Science Publishers Ltd, 1990.

Section 3.88 (pages 94–96) provides an overview of Z. Other sections describe related techniques.

[27] D. Bjørner, C.A.R. Hoare, and H. Langmaack, editors. *VDM and Z – Formal Methods in Software Development*, volume 428 of *Lecture Notes in Computer Science*. VDM-Europe, Springer-Verlag, 1990.

Proc. Third International Symposium of VDM-Europe, 17–21 April 1990, Kiel, Germany. A number of papers concerned with Z were presented [57, 87, 102, 111, 112, 117, 169, 251, 278, 302, 325].

[28] D. Blyth. The CICS application programming interface: Temporary storage. IBM Technical Report TR12.301, IBM United Kingdom Laboratories Ltd., Hursley Park, Winchester, Hampshire SO21 2JN, UK, December 1990.

One of a number of reports on the CICS application programming interface. See also [139, 168, 213].

[29] J.P. Bowen. Formal specification and documentation of microprocessor instruction sets. In H. Schumny and J. Mølgaard, editors, *Proc. EUROMICRO'87, Microcomputers: Usage, Methods and Structures*, volume 21, pages 223–230. Elsevier Science Publishers B.V. (North-Holland), August 1987.

[30] J.P. Bowen. The formal specification of a microprocessor instruction set. Technical Monograph PRG-60, Oxford University Computing Laboratory, 11 Keble Road, Oxford, UK, January 1987.

The Z notation is used to define the Motorola M6800 8-bit microprocessor instruction set.

[31] J.P. Bowen, editor. *Proc. Z Users Meeting, 1 Wellington Square, Oxford*, 11 Keble Road, Oxford, UK, December 1987. Oxford University Computing Laboratory.

The 1987 Z Users Meeting was held on Friday 8 December at the Department of External Studies, Rewley House, 1 Wellington Square, Oxford, UK. The LaTeX [175] source of the Proceedings is available by sending the command "`send z proc87.tex`" to the address <`archive-server@comlab.ox.ac.uk`> via e-mail [333].

[32] J.P. Bowen. Formal specification in Z as a design and documentation tool. In *Proc. Second IEE/BCS Conference on Software Engineering*, volume 290, pages 164–168. IEE/BCS, July 1988.

[33] J.P. Bowen, editor. *Proc. Third Annual Z Users Meeting*, 11 Keble Road, Oxford, UK, December 1988. Oxford University Computing Laboratory.

The 1988 Z Users Meeting was held on Friday 16 December at the Department of External Studies, Rewley House, 1 Wellington Square, Oxford, UK. Issued with *A Miscellany of Handy Techniques* by R. Macdonald, RSRE, *Practical Experience of Formal Specification: a programming interface for communications* by J.B. Wordsworth, IBM, and a number of posters. This is available from the Librarian at the Oxford University Computing Laboratory. The LaTeX [175] source file for the main part of the document is available by sending the command "`send z proc88.tex`" via e-mail to the PRG archive server on <`archive-server@comlab.ox.ac.uk`> [333].

[34] J.P. Bowen. Formal specification of window systems. Technical Monograph PRG-74, Oxford University Computing Laboratory, 11 Keble Road, Oxford, UK, June 1989.

Three existing window systems, X from MIT, WM from Carnegie-Mellon University and the Blit from AT&T Bell Laboratories are covered.

[35] J.P. Bowen. POS: Formal specification of a UNIX tool. *Software Engineering Journal*, 4(1):67–72, January 1989.

[36] J.P. Bowen. Formal specification of the ProCoS/safemos instruction set. *Microprocessors and Microsystems*, 14(10):631–643, December 1990.

This article is part of a special issue on *Formal aspects of microprocessor design*, edited by H. Zedan. See also [263].

[37] J.P. Bowen. Z bibliography. Oxford University Computing Laboratory, 1990–1993.

This bibliography is maintained in BibTeX database format at the PRG. It is available via electronic mail, together with a LaTeX [175] file for printing the bibliography, by sending a message containing the command "`send z z.bib z.tex`" to the PRG archive server on <`archive-server@comlab.ox.ac.uk`> [333]. Note that the source of the bibliography is about 150 Kbytes in size. If your mailer has a limit of 100 Kbytes (and many do), and you have access to the UNIX utilities *uncompress* and *uudecode*, please access the compressed uuencoded version instead using the command "`send z z.uu`" The *Z bibliography* is also available electronical via anonymous FTP on the Internet. See [333] for further details. To add entries, please send as complete information as possible to <`zforum-request@comlab.ox.ac.uk`>.

[38] J.P. Bowen. X: Why Z? *Computer Graphics Forum*, 11(4):221–234, October 1992.

This paper asks whether window management systems would not be better specified through a formal methodology and gives examples in Z of X11.

[39] J.P. Bowen, R.B. Gimson, and S. Topp-Jørgensen. The specification of network services. Technical Monograph PRG-61, Oxford University Computing Laboratory, 11 Keble Road, Oxford, UK, August 1987.

[40] J.P. Bowen, R.B. Gimson, and S. Topp-Jørgensen. Specifying system implementations in Z. Technical Monograph PRG-63, Oxford University Computing Laboratory, 11 Keble Road, Oxford, UK, February 1988.

[41] P.T. Breuer. Z! in progress: Maintaining Z specifications. In J.E. Nicholls, editor, *Z User Workshop, Oxford 1990*, Workshops in Computing, pages 295–318. Springer-Verlag, 1991.

[42] S.M. Brien, J.E. Nicholls, et al. Z base standard. ZIP Project Technical Report ZIP/PRG/92/121, SRC Document: 132, Version 1.0, Oxford University Computing Laboratory, 11 Keble Road, Oxford, UK, November 1992.

The first publicly available version of the proposed BSI Z Standard, obtainable from the Secretary, ZIP Standards, Oxford University Computing Laboratory (address above). See also [277] for the current most widely available Z reference manual.

[43] C. Britton, M. Loomes, and R. Mitchell. Formal specification as constructive diagrams. In A. Nú nez and D. Fay, editors, *Special Volume: Short Notes EUROMICRO'92*, volume 37, pages 175–178. Elsevier Science Publishers B.V. (North-Holland), January 1993.

[44] D.J. Brown and J.P. Bowen. The Event Queue: An extensible input system for UNIX workstations. In *Proc. European Unix Users Group Conference*, pages 29–52. EUUG, May 1987.

[45] D. Brownbridge. Using Z to develop a CASE toolset. In J.E. Nicholls, editor, *Z User Workshop, Oxford 1989*, Workshops in Computing, pages 142–149. Springer-Verlag, 1990.

[46] T. Bryant. Structured methodologies and formal notations: Developing a framework for synthesis and investigation. In J.E. Nicholls, editor, *Z User Workshop, Oxford 1989*, Workshops in Computing, pages 229–241. Springer-Verlag, 1990.

[47] A. Burns and I.W. Morrison. A formal description of the structure attribute model for tool interfacing. *Software Engineering Journal*, 4(2):74–78, March 1989.

[48] A. Burns and A.J. Wellings. Occam's priority model and deadline scheduling. In *Proc. 7th Occam User Group Meeting, Grenoble*, 1987.

[49] A. Burns and A.J. Wellings. A formal description of Ada tasking in Z. Computer Science Report YCS122, University of York, Heslington, York YO1 5DD, UK, 1989.

[50] A. Burns and A.J. Wellings. Priority inheritance and message passing communication: A formal treatment. Computer Science Report YCS116, University of York, Heslington, York YO1 5DD, UK, 1989.

[51] J.S. Busby and D. Hutchison. The practical integration of manufacturing applications. *Software Practice and Experience*, 22(2):183–207, 1992.

[52] P. Butcher. A behavioural semantics for Linda-2. *Software Engineering Journal*, 6(4):196–204, July 1991.

[53] M.J. Butler. Service extension at the specification level. In J.E. Nicholls, editor, *Z User Workshop, Oxford 1990*, Workshops in Computing, pages 319–336. Springer-Verlag, 1991.

[54] D. Carrington. ZOOM workshop report. In J.E. Nicholls, editor, *Z User Workshop, York 1991*, Workshops in Computing, pages 352–364. Springer-Verlag, 1992.

This paper records the activities of a workshop on Z and object-oriented methods held in August 1992 at Oxford. A comprehensive bibliography is included.

[55] D. Carrington, D. Duke, R. Duke, P. King, G.A. Rose, and G. Smith. Object-Z: An object-oriented extension to Z. In S. Vuong, editor, *Formal Description Techniques, II (FORTE'89)*, pages 281–296. North-Holland, 1990.

[56] D. Carrington and G. Smith. Extending Z for object-oriented specifications. In *Proc. 5th Australian Software Engineering Conference (ASWEC'90)*, pages 9–14, 1990.

[57] P. Chalin and P. Grogono. Z specification of an object manager. In D. Bjørner, C.A.R. Hoare, and H. Langmaack, editors, *VDM and Z – Formal Methods in Software Development*, volume 428 of *Lecture Notes in Computer Science*, pages 41–71. VDM-Europe, Springer-Verlag, 1990.

[58] S.J. Clarke, A.C. Combes, and J.A. McDermid. The analysis of safety arguments in the specification of a motor speed control loop. Computer Science Report YCS136, University of York, Heslington, York YO1 5DD, UK, 1990.

This report describes some timing extensions to Z.

[59] B. Cohen. Justification of formal methods for system specifications & A rejustification of formal notations. *Software Engineering Journal*, 4(1):26–38, January 1989.

[60] B.P. Collins, J.E. Nicholls, and I.H. Sørensen. Introducing formal methods: the CICS experience with Z. In B. Neumann et al., editors, *Mathematical Structures for Software Engineering*. Oxford University Press, UK, 1991.

[61] J. Cooke. Editorial – formal methods: What? why? and when? *The Computer Journal*, 35(5):417–418, October 1992.

An editorial introduction to two special issues on *Formal Methods*. See also [21, 62, 199, 258, 322] for papers relevant to Z.

[62] J. Cooke. Formal methods – mathematics, theory, recipes or what? *The Computer Journal*, 35(5):419–423, October 1992.

[63] A. Coombes and J.A. McDermid. A tool for defining the architecture of Z specifications. In J.E. Nicholls, editor, *Z User Workshop, Oxford 1990*, Workshops in Computing, pages 77–92. Springer-Verlag, 1991.

[64] A. Coombes and J.A. McDermid. Specifying temporal requirements for distributed real-time systems in Z. Computer Science Report YCS176, University of York, Heslington, York YO1 5DD, UK, 1992.

[65] D. Cooper. Educating management in Z. In J.E. Nicholls, editor, *Z User Workshop, Oxford 1989*, Workshops in Computing, pages 192–194. Springer-Verlag, 1990.

[66] S. Craggs and J.B. Wordsworth. Hursley Lab wins another Queen's Award & Hursley and Oxford – a marriage of minds & Z stands for quality. *Developments, IBM Hursley Park*, 8:1–2, 21 April 1992.

[67] I. Craig. *The Formal Specification of Advanced AI Architectures*. AI Series. Ellis Horwood, September 1991.

This book contains two rather large (and relatively complete) specifications of AI systems using Z. The architectures are the blackboard and Cassandra architectures. As well as showing that formal specification *can* be used in AI at the architecture level, the book is intended as a case-studies book, and also contains introductory material on Z (for AI people). The book assumes a knowledge of Z, so for non-AI people its primary use is for the presentation of the large specifications. The blackboard specification, with explanatory text, is around 100 pages.

[68] D. Craigen, S. Gerhart, and T. Ralston. An international survey of industrial applications of formal methods. Technical report, Atomic Energy Control Board of Canada, US National Institute of Standards and Technology, and US Naval Research Laboratories, 1993. To appear.

[69] D. Craigen, S. Kromodimoeljo, Irwin Meisels, Bill Pase, and Mark Saaltink. EVES: An overview. In S. Prehn and W.J. Toetenel, editors, *VDM'91: Formal Software Development Methods*, volume 551 of *Lecture Notes in Computer Science*, pages 389–405. Springer-Verlag, 1991.

[70] S. Croxall, P. Lupton, and J.B. Wordsworth. A formal specification of the CPI communications. IBM Technical Report TR12.277, IBM United Kingdom Laboratories Ltd., Hursley Park, Winchester, Hampshire SO21 2JN, UK, 1990.

[71] E. Cusack. Inheritance in object oriented Z. In P. America, editor, *Proc. ECOOP'91 European Conference on Object-Oriented Programming*, volume 512 of *Lecture Notes in Computer Science*, pages 167–179. Springer-Verlag, 1991.

[72] E. Cusack. Object oriented modelling in Z for open distributed systems. In J. de Meer, editor, *Proc. International Workshop on ODP*. North Holland, 1992.

[73] E. Cusack and M. Lai. Object oriented specification in LOTOS and Z (or my cat really is object oriented!). In J.W. de Bakker, W.P. de Roever, and G. Rozenberg, editors, *REX/FOOL School/Workshop on Foundations of Object-Oriented Languages*, volume 489 of *Lecture Notes in Computer Science*, pages 179–202. Springer-Verlag, 1990.

[74] R.S.M. de Barros and D.J. Harper. A method for the specification of relational database applications. In J.E. Nicholls, editor, *Z User Workshop, York 1991*, Workshops in Computing, pages 261–286. Springer-Verlag, 1992.

[75] A.M.L. de Vasconcelos and J.A. McDermid. Incremental type-checking in Z. Computer Science Report YCS185, University of York, Heslington, York YO1 5DD, UK, 1992.

[76] N. Delisle and D. Garlan. Formally specifying electronic instruments. In *Proc. Fifth International Workshop on Software Specification and Design*. IEEE Computer Society, May 1989. Also published in ACM SIGSOFT Software Engineering Notes 14(3).

[77] N. Delisle and D. Garlan. A formal specification of an oscilloscope. *IEEE Software*, pages 29–36, September 1990.

Unlike most work on the application of formal methods, this research uses formal methods to gain insight into system architecture. The context for this case study is electronic instrument design.

[78] A.J.J. Dick, P.J. Krause, and J. Cozens. Computer aided transformation of Z into Prolog. In J.E. Nicholls, editor, *Z User Workshop, Oxford 1989*, Workshops in Computing, pages 71–85. Springer-Verlag, 1990.

[79] A. Diller. Specifying interactive programs in Z. Research Report CSR-90-13, School of Computer Science, University of Birmingham, UK, August 1990.

[80] A. Diller. *Z: An Introduction to Formal Methods*. Wiley, Chichester, UK, June 1990.

This book offers a comprehensive tutorial to Z from the practical viewpoint. Many natural deduction style proofs are presented and exercises are included.

[81] A. Diller. Z and Hoare logics. In J.E. Nicholls, editor, *Z User Workshop, York 1991*, Workshops in Computing, pages 59–76. Springer-Verlag, 1992.

[82] V. Doma and R. Nicholl. EZ: A system for automatic prototyping of Z specifications. In S. Prehn and W.J. Toetenel, editors, *VDM'91: Formal Software Development Methods*, volume 551 of *Lecture Notes in Computer Science*, pages 189–203. Springer-Verlag, 1991.

[83] D. Duke. Structuring Z specifications. In *Proc. 14th Australian Computer Science Conference*, 1991.

[84] D. Duke. Enhancing the structures of Z specifications. In J.E. Nicholls, editor, *Z User Workshop, York 1991*, Workshops in Computing, pages 329–351. Springer-Verlag, 1992.

[85] D. Duke. *Object-Oriented Formal Specification*. PhD thesis, Dept. of Computer Science, University of Queensland, Australia, 4072, 1992.

[86] D. Duke and R. Duke. A history model for classes in Object-Z. Technical Report 120, Department of Computer Science, University of Queensland, Australia 4072, 1989.

[87] D. Duke and R. Duke. Towards a semantics for Object-Z. In D. Bjørner, C.A.R. Hoare, and H. Langmaack, editors, *VDM and Z – Formal Methods in Software Development*, volume 428 of *Lecture Notes in Computer Science*, pages 244–261. VDM-Europe, Springer-Verlag, 1990.

[88] R. Duke and D. Duke. Aspects of object-oriented formal specification. In *Proc. 5th Australian Software Engineering Conference (ASWEC'90)*, pages 21–26, 1990.

[89] R. Duke, I.J. Hayes, P. King, and G.A. Rose. Protocol specification and verification using Z. In S. Aggarwal and K. Sabnani, editors, *Protocol Specification, Testing, and Verification VIII*, pages 33–46. North-Holland, 1988.

[90] R. Duke, P. King, G.A. Rose, and G. Smith. The Object-Z specification language. In T. Korson, V. Vaishnavi, and B. Meyer, editors, *Technology of Object-Oriented Languages and Systems: TOOLS 5*, pages 465–483. Prentice Hall, Hemel Hempstead, Hertfordshire, UK, 1991.

[91] R. Duke, P. King, G.A. Rose, and G. Smith. The Object-Z specification language. Technical Report SVRC 91-1, Version 1, Software Verification Research Center, University of Queensland, St. Lucia, Queensland 4072, Australia, May 1991.

This has been reprinted by ISO JTC1 WG7 as document Number 372.

[92] R. Duke and G.A. Rose. A complete Z specification of an interactive program editor. Technical Report 71, Department of Computer Science, University of Queensland, Australia, 4072, 1986.

[93] R. Duke, G.A. Rose, and A. Lee. Object-oriented protocol specification. In L. Logrippo, R.L. Probert, and H. Ural, editors, *Protocol Specification, Testing, and Verification X*, pages 325–338. North-Holland, 1990.

[94] R. Duke and G. Smith. Temporal logic and Z specifications. *Australian Computer Journal*, 21(2):62–69, May 1989.

[95] N.E. Fenton and D. Mole. A note on the use of Z for flowgraph transformation. *Information and Software Technology*, 30(7):432–437, 1988.

[96] E. Fergus and D.C. Ince. Z specifications and modal logic. In P.A.V. Hall, editor, *Proc. Software Engineering 90*, volume 1 of *British Computer Society Conference Series*. Cambridge University Press, July 1990.

[97] C.J. Fidge. Specification and verification of real-time behaviour using Z and RTL. In J. Vytopil, editor, *Formal Techniques in Real-Time and Fault-Tolerant Systems*, Lecture Notes in Computer Science, pages 393–410. Springer-Verlag, 1992.

[98] M. Flynn, T. Hoverd, and D. Brazier. Formaliser – an interactive support tool for Z. In J.E. Nicholls, editor, *Z User Workshop, Oxford 1989*, Workshops in Computing, pages 128–141. Springer-Verlag, 1990.

[99] I. Fogg, B. Hicks, A. Lister, T. Mansfield, and K. Raymond. A comparison of LOTOS and Z for specifying distributed systems. *Australian Computer Science Communications*, 12(1):88–96, February 1990.

[100] P.H.B. Gardiner, P.J. Lupton, and Jim C.P. Woodcock. A simpler semantics for Z. In J.E. Nicholls, editor, *Z User Workshop, Oxford 1990*, Workshops in Computing, pages 3–11. Springer-Verlag, 1991.

[101] D. Garlan. The role of reusable frameworks. *ACM SIGSOFT Software Engineering Notes*, 15(4):42–44, September 1990.

[102] D. Garlan and N. Delisle. Formal specifications as reusable frameworks. In D. Bjørner, C.A.R. Hoare, and H. Langmaack, editors, *VDM and Z – Formal Methods in Software Development*, volume 428 of *Lecture Notes in Computer Science*, pages 150–163. VDM-Europe, Springer-Verlag, 1990.

[103] D. Garlan and D. Notkin. Formalizing design spaces: Implicit invocation mechanisms. In S. Prehn and W.J. Toetenel, editors, *VDM'91: Formal Software Development Methods*, volume 551 of *Lecture Notes in Computer Science*, pages 31–45. Springer-Verlag, 1991.

[104] S. Gerhart, D. Craigen, and T. Ralston. Observations on industrial practice using formal methods. In *Proc. 15th International Conference on Software Engineering (ICSE), Baltimore, Maryland, USA*, May 1993. To appear.

[105] S.L. Gerhart. Applications of formal methods: Developing virtuoso software. *IEEE Software*, pages 6–10, September 1990.

This is an introduction to a special issue on Formal Methods with an emphasis on Z in particular. It was published in conjunction with special Formal Methods issues of *IEEE Transactions on Software Engineering* and *IEEE Computer*. See also [77, 116, 214, 275, 308].

[106] S. Gilmore. Correctness-oriented approaches to software development. Technical Report ECS-LFCS-91-147 (also CST-76-91), University of Edinburgh, UK, 1991.

This is a PhD thesis providing a critical evaluation of Z, VDM and algebraic specifications.

Copies available from: Dorothy McKie, Laboratory for Foundations of Computer Science, Department of Computer Science, The James Clerk Maxwell Building, The King's Buildings, University of Edinburgh, Edinburgh EH9 3JZ, UK.

[107] R.B. Gimson. The formal documentation of a Block Storage Service. Technical Monograph PRG-62, Oxford University Computing Laboratory, 11 Keble Road, Oxford, UK, August 1987.

[108] R.B. Gimson and C.C. Morgan. Ease of use through proper specification. In D.A. Duce, editor, *Distributed Computing Systems Programme*. Peter Peregrinus, London, UK, 1984.

[109] R.B. Gimson and C.C. Morgan. The Distributed Computing Software project. Technical Monograph PRG-50, Oxford University Computing Laboratory, 11 Keble Road, Oxford, UK, July 1985.

[110] J. Ginbayashi. Analysis of business processes specified in Z against an E-R data model. Technical Monograph PRG-103, Oxford University Computing Laboratory, 11 Keble Road, Oxford, UK, December 1992.

[111] R. Di Giovanni and P.L. Iachini. HOOD and Z for the development of complex systems. In D. Bjørner, C.A.R. Hoare, and H. Langmaack, editors, *VDM and Z – Formal Methods in Software Development*, volume 428 of *Lecture Notes in Computer Science*, pages 262–289. VDM-Europe, Springer-Verlag, 1990.

[112] R. Gotzhein. Specifying open distributed systems with Z. In D. Bjørner, C.A.R. Hoare, and H. Langmaack, editors, *VDM and Z – Formal Methods in Software Development*, volume 428 of *Lecture Notes in Computer Science*, pages 319–339. VDM-Europe, Springer-Verlag, 1990.

[113] A.M. Gravell. Minimisation in formal specification and design. In J.E. Nicholls, editor, *Z User Workshop, Oxford 1989*, Workshops in Computing, pages 32–45. Springer-Verlag, 1990.

[114] A.M. Gravell. What is a good formal specification? In J.E. Nicholls, editor, *Z User Workshop, Oxford 1990*, Workshops in Computing, pages 137–150. Springer-Verlag, 1991.

[115] F. Halasz and M. Schwartz. The Dexter hypertext reference model. In *NIST Hypertext Standardization Workshop*, January 1990.

[116] A. Hall. Seven myths of formal methods. *IEEE Software*, pages 11–19, September 1990.

Formal methods are difficult, expensive, and not widely useful, detractors say. Using a case study and other real-world examples, this article challenges such common myths.

[117] A. Hall. Using Z as a specification calculus for object-oriented systems. In D. Bjørner, C.A.R. Hoare, and H. Langmaack, editors, *VDM and Z – Formal Methods in Software Development*, volume 428 of *Lecture Notes in Computer Science*, pages 290–318. VDM-Europe, Springer-Verlag, 1990.

[118] P.A.V. Hall. Towards testing with respect to formal specification. In *Proc. Second IEE/BCS Conference on Software Engineering*, volume 290, pages 159–163, Liverpool, UK, July 1988, July 1988. IEE/BCS.

[119] M. Harrison. Engineering human-error tolerant software. In J.E. Nicholls, editor, *Z User Workshop, York 1991*, Workshops in Computing, pages 191–204. Springer-Verlag, 1992.

[120] C.L. Harrold. Formal specification of a secure document control system for SMITE. Report no. 88002, RSRE, Ministry of Defence, Malvern, Worcestershire, UK, February 1988.

[121] W.T. Harwood. Proof rules for Balzac. Technical Report WTH/P7/001, Imperial Software Technology, Cambridge, UK, 1991.

[122] W. Hasselbring. A formal Z specification of ProSet-Linda. Technical report, University of Essen, Fachbereich Mathematik und Informatik – Software Engineering, Schuetzenbahn 70, 4300 Essen 1, Germany, 1992.

Available via anonymous FTP from hp06c.informatik.uni-essen.de (132.252.61.3) under "pub/Informatik-Berichte".

[123] H.P. Haughton. Using Z to model and analyse safety and liveness properties of communication protocols. *Information Software Technology*, 33(8):575–580, October 1991.

[124] H.P. Haughton and K.C. Lano. Three dimensional maintenance. In M. Munro and P. Carroll, editors, *Fourth Software Maintenance Workshop Notes, 18–20 September 1990*. Centre for Software Maintenance, Durham, UK, 1990.

This paper presents an object-oriented extension to Z with the aim to aid software maintenance.

[125] I.J. Hayes. Applying formal specification to software development in industry. *IEEE Transactions on Software Engineering*, 11(2):169–178, February 1985.

[126] I.J. Hayes. Specification directed module testing. *IEEE Transactions on Software Engineering*, 12(1):124–133, January 1986.

[127] I.J. Hayes. Using mathematics to specify software. In *Proc. First Australian Software Engineering Conference*. Institution of Engineers, Australia, May 1986.

[128] I.J. Hayes, editor. *Specification Case Studies*. International Series in Computer Science. Prentice Hall, Hemel Hempstead, Hertfordshire, UK, 1987.

This book, the first published on Z, contains material from PRG Technical Monographs 46–50, edited by I.J. Hayes and written mainly by members of the PRG. The contributors are I.J. Hayes, L.W. Flinn, R.B. Gimson, C.C. Morgan, I.H. Sørensen and B.A. Sufrin. The book forms a varied collection of case studies using Z. See also [133] for the second edition of this book.

[129] I.J. Hayes. A generalisation of bags in Z. In J.E. Nicholls, editor, *Z User Workshop, Oxford 1989*, Workshops in Computing, pages 113–127. Springer-Verlag, 1990.

[130] I.J. Hayes. Specifying physical limitations: A case study of an oscilloscope. Technical Report 167, Department of Computer Science, University of Queensland, Australia, 4072, July 1990.

[131] I.J. Hayes. Interpretations of Z schema operators. In J.E. Nicholls, editor, *Z User Workshop, Oxford 1990*, Workshops in Computing, pages 12–26. Springer-Verlag, 1991.

[132] I.J. Hayes. Multi-relations in Z: A cross between multi-sets and binary relations. *Acta Informatica*, 29(1):33–62, February 1992.

[133] I.J. Hayes, editor. *Specification Case Studies*. International Series in Computer Science. Prentice Hall, Hemel Hempstead, Hertfordshire, UK, 2nd edition, 1992. In press.

This is the 2nd edition of the first ever published book on Z [128]; it contains substantial revisions to every chapter. The notation has been revised to be consistent with *The Z Notation: A Reference Manual* by Mike Spivey [277]. The CAVIAR chapter has been extensively changed to make use of a form of modularization.

Divided into four sections, the first provides examples of specifications, the second is devoted to the area of software engineering, the third covers distributed computing, analyzing the role of mathematical specification, and lastly, the fourth part covers transaction processing. The book will be of interest to the professional software engineer involved in designing and specifying large software projects.

[134] I.J. Hayes. VDM and Z: A comparative case study. *Formal Aspects of Computing*, 4(1):76–99, 1992.

[135] He Jifeng, C.A.R. Hoare, and J.W. Sanders. Data refinement refined. In B. Robinet and R. Wilhelm, editors, *Proc. ESOP 86*, volume 213 of *Lecture Notes in Computer Science*, pages 187–196. Springer-Verlag, 1986.

[136] B. Hepworth. ZIP: a unification initiative for Z standards, methods and tools. In J.E. Nicholls, editor, *Z User Workshop, Oxford 1989*, Workshops in Computing, pages 253–259. Springer-Verlag, 1990.

[137] B. Hepworth and D. Simpson. The ZIP project. In J.E. Nicholls, editor, *Z User Workshop, Oxford 1990*, Workshops in Computing, pages 129–133. Springer-Verlag, 1991.

[138] M.G. Hinchey. Formal methods for system specification. *IEEE Potentials Magazine*, 1993. To appear.

[139] I.S.C. Houston. The CICS application programming interface: Automatic transaction initiation. IBM Technical Report TR12.300, IBM United Kingdom Laboratories Ltd., Hursley Park, Winchester, Hampshire SO21 2JN, UK, December 1990.

One of a number of reports on the CICS application programming interface. See also [28, 168, 213].

[140] I.S.C. Houston and S. King. CICS project report: Experiences and results from the use of Z in IBM. In S. Prehn and W.J. Toetenel, editors, *VDM'91: Formal Software Development Methods*, volume 551 of *Lecture Notes in Computer Science*, pages 588–596. Springer-Verlag, 1991.

[141] I.S.C. Houston and J.B. Wordsworth. A Z specification of part of the CICS file control API. IBM Technical Report TR12.272, IBM United Kingdom Laboratories Ltd., Hursley Park, Winchester, Hampshire SO21 2JN, UK, 1990.

[142] A.D. Hutcheon and A.J. Wellings. Specifying restrictions on imperative programming languages for use in a distributed embedded environment. *Software Engineering Journal*, 5(2):93–104, March 1990.

[143] P.L. Iachini. Operation schema iterations. In J.E. Nicholls, editor, *Z User Workshop, Oxford 1990*, Workshops in Computing, pages 50–57. Springer-Verlag, 1991.

[144] M. Imperato. *An Introduction to Z*. Chartwell-Bratt, 1991.

[145] D.C. Ince. *An Introduction to Discrete Mathematics and Formal System Specification*. Oxford Applied Mathematics and Computing Science Series. Oxford University Press, UK, 1988.

[146] D.C. Ince. Z and system specification. In D.C. Ince and D. Andrews, editors, *The Software Life Cycle*, chapter 12, pages 260–277. Butterworths, UK, 1990.

[147] Inmos Ltd. Specification of instruction set & Specification of floating point unit instructions. In *Transputer Instruction Set – A compiler writer's guide*, pages 127–161. Prentice Hall, Hemel Hempstead, Hertfordshire, UK, 1988.

Appendices F and G use a Z-like notation to give a specification of the instruction set of the IMS T212 and T414 transputers, and the T800 floating-point transputer.

[148] A. Jack. It's hard to explain, but Z is much clearer than English. *Financial Times*, page 22, 21 April 1992.

[149] J. Jacky. Formal specifications for a clinical cyclotron control system. *ACM SIGSOFT Software Engineering Notes*, 15(4):45–54, September 1990.

[150] J. Jacky. Specifying a safety-critical control system in Z. In J.C.P. Woodcock, editor, *Proc. Formal Methods Europe Symposium (FME'93), Odense, Denmark*, Lecture Notes in Computer Science. Springer-Verlag, 19–23 April 1992. To appear.

[151] J. Jacob. The varieties of refinements. In J.M. Morris and R.C. Shaw, editors, *Proc. 4th Refinement Workshop*, Workshops in Computing, pages 441–455. Springer-Verlag, 1991.

[152] C.W. Johnson. Applying temporal logic to support the specification and prototyping of concurrent multi-user interfaces. In D. Diaper and N. Hammond, editors, *People and Computers VI: Usability Now*, pages 145–156. Cambridge University Press, UK, 1991.

[153] C.W. Johnson and M.D. Harrison. Declarative graphics and dynamic interaction. In F.H. Post and W. Barth, editors, *Proc. EUROGRAPHICS'91*, pages 195–207. Elsevier Science Publications, North Holland, Netherlands, 1991.

[154] M. Johnson and P. Sanders. From Z specifications to functional implementations. In J.E. Nicholls, editor, *Z User Workshop, Oxford 1989*, Workshops in Computing, pages 86–112. Springer-Verlag, 1990.

[155] P. Johnson. Using Z to specify CICS. In *Proc. Software Engineering anniversary meeting (SEAS)*, page 303. SEA, 1987.

[156] C.B. Jones. Interference revisited. In J.E. Nicholls, editor, *Z User Workshop, Oxford 1990*, Workshops in Computing, pages 58–73. Springer-Verlag, 1991.

[157] D. Jordan, J.A. McDermid, and I. Toyn. CADiZ – computer aided design in Z. In J.E. Nicholls, editor, *Z User Workshop, Oxford 1990*, Workshops in Computing, pages 93–104. Springer-Verlag, 1991.

See also [300].

[158] L.E. Jordan. The kernel Z type checking rules. Technical Report LEJ/-TC3/001, Imperial Software Technology, Cambridge, UK, 1991.

[159] L.E. Jordan. The Z syntax supported by Balzac-II/1. Technical Report LEJ/S1/001, Imperial Software Technology, Cambridge, UK, 1991.

[160] M.B. Josephs. The data refinement calculator for Z specifications. *Information Processing Letters*, 27(1):29–33, 1988.

[161] M.B. Josephs. A state-based approach to communicating processes. *Distributed Computing*, 3:9–18, 1988.

A theoretical paper on combining features of CSP and Z.

[162] M.B. Josephs. Specifying reactive systems in Z. Technical Report PRG-TR-19-91, Oxford University Computing Laboratory, 11 Keble Road, Oxford, UK, July 1991.

[163] M.B. Josephs and D. Redmond-Pyle. Entity-relationship models expressed in Z: A synthesis of structured and formal methods. Technical Report PRG-TR-20-91, Oxford University Computing Laboratory, 11 Keble Road, Oxford, UK, July 1991.

[164] M.B. Josephs and D. Redmond-Pyle. A library of Z schemas for use in entity-relationship modelling. Technical Report PRG-TR-21-91, Oxford University Computing Laboratory, 11 Keble Road, Oxford, UK, August 1991.

[165] D.H. Kemp. Specification of Viper1 in Z. Memorandum no. 4195, RSRE, Ministry of Defence, Malvern, Worcestershire, UK, October 1988.

[166] D.H. Kemp. Specification of Viper2 in Z. Memorandum no. 4217, RSRE, Ministry of Defence, Malvern, Worcestershire, UK, October 1988.

[167] P. King. Printing Z and Object-Z LaTeX documents. Department of Computer Science, University of Queensland, May 1990.

A description of a Z style option "oz.sty", an extended version of Mike Spivey's "zed.sty" [274], for use with the LaTeX document preparation system [175]. It is particularly useful for printing Object-Z documents [55, 87]. The style file and the guide are available electronically by sending an e-mail message containing the command "send z oz.sty oz.tex" to <archive-server@comlab.ox.ac.uk> [333].

[168] S. King. The CICS application programming interface: Program control. IBM Technical Report TR12.302, IBM United Kingdom Laboratories Ltd., Hursley Park, Winchester, Hampshire SO21 2JN, UK, December 1990.

One of a number of reports on the CICS application programming interface. See also [28, 139, 213].

[169] S. King. Z and the refinement calculus. In D. Bjørner, C.A.R. Hoare, and H. Langmaack, editors, *VDM and Z – Formal Methods in Software Development*, volume 428 of *Lecture Notes in Computer Science*, pages 164–188. VDM-Europe, Springer-Verlag, 1990.

Also published as Technical Monograph PRG-79, Oxford University Computing Laboratory, February 1990.

[170] S. King and I.H. Sørensen. Specification and design of a library system. In *The Theory and Practice of Refinement: Approaches to the Formal Development of Large-Scale Software Systems*. Butterworths, London, UK, 1989.

[171] S. King, I.H. Sørensen, and J.C.P. Woodcock. Z: Grammar and concrete and abstract syntaxes. Technical Monograph PRG-68, Oxford University Computing Laboratory, 11 Keble Road, Oxford, UK, 1988.

[172] P. Knaggs. Formal descriptive languages (student reports), MSc Software Engineering 1990/91. Technical report, School of Computing and Mathematics, Teesside Polytechnic, Middlesbrough, Cleveland TS1 3BA, UK, 1991.

This is a collection of reports, written by the students on the MSc in Software Engineering course. These reports were written after a 20 hour introduction to Z and were collected and produced by Peter Knaggs.

[173] R.D. Knott and P.J. Krause. The implementation of Z specifications using program transformation systems: The SuZan project. In C. Rattray and R.G. Clark, editors, *The Unified Computation Laboratory*, volume 35 of *IMA Conference Series*, pages 207–220, Oxford, UK, 1992. Clarendon Press.

[174] M.K.F. Lai. A formal interpretation of the MAA standard in Z. Technical Report DITC 184/91, National Physical Laboratory, Teddington, Middlesex, UK, June 1991.

[175] L. Lamport. LaTeX *User's Guide & Reference Manual*. Addison-Wesley Publishing Company, Reading, Massachusetts, USA, 1986.

Z specifications may be produced using the document preparation system LaTeX together with a special LaTeX style option. The most widely used style files are fuzz.sty [276], zed.sty [274] and oz.sty [167].

[176] K.C. Lano. Z++: An object-orientated extension to Z. In J.E. Nicholls, editor, *Z User Workshop, Oxford 1990*, Workshops in Computing, pages 151–172. Springer-Verlag, 1991.

[177] K.C. Lano and P.T. Breuer. From programs to Z specifications. In J.E. Nicholls, editor, *Z User Workshop, Oxford 1989*, Workshops in Computing, pages 46–70. Springer-Verlag, 1990.

[178] K.C. Lano and H.P. Haughton. An algebraic semantics for the specification language Z++. In *Proc. Algebraic Methodology and Software Technology Conference (AMAST '91)*. Springer-Verlag, 1992.

[179] K.C. Lano and H.P. Haughton. Reasoning and refinement in object-oriented specification languages. In *Proc. ECOOP'92 European Conference on Object-Oriented Programming*, Lecture Notes in Computer Science. Springer-Verlag, 1992.

[180] K.C. Lano and H.P. Haughton. *The Z++ Manual*. Lloyd's Register of Shipping, 29 Wellesley Road, Croydon CRO 2AJ, UK, 1992.

[181] K.C. Lano, H.P. Haughton, and P.T. Breuer. Using object-oriented extensions of Z for maintenance and reverse-engineering. Technical Report PRG-TR-22-91, Oxford University Computing Laboratory, 11 Keble Road, Oxford, UK, 1991.

[182] D. Lightfoot. *Formal Specification using Z*. Macmillan, 1991.

[183] R.L. London. Specifying reusable components using Z: Sets implemented by bit vectors. Technical Report CR-88-14, Tektronix Laboratories, P.O. Box 500, MS 50-662, Beaverton, Oregon 97077, USA, November 1988.

[184] R.L. London and K.R. Milsted. Specifying reusable components using Z: Realistic sets and dictionaries. *ACM SIGSOFT Software Engineering Notes*, 14(3):120–127, May 1989.

Presented at the *5th International Workshop on Software Specification and Design*, Pittsburgh, Pennsylvania, 19–20 May 1989. A longer version entitled *Specifying and Verifying Reusable Components Using Z: Sets and Dictionaries* appeared as Technical Report CR-88-10, Tektronix Laboratories, P.O. Box 500, MS 50-662, Beaverton, Oregon 97077, USA, October, 1988.

[185] P.J. Lupton. Promoting forward simulation. In J.E. Nicholls, editor, *Z User Workshop, Oxford 1990*, Workshops in Computing, pages 27–49. Springer-Verlag, 1991.

[186] R. Macdonald. Z usage and abusage. Report no. 91003, RSRE, Ministry of Defence, Malvern, Worcestershire, UK, February 1991.

This paper presents a miscellany of observations drawn from experience of using Z, shows a variety of techniques for expressing certain class of idea concisely and clearly, and alerts the reader to certain pitfalls which may trap the unwary.

[187] B.P. Mahony and I.J. Hayes. A case-study in timed refinement: A mine pump. *IEEE Transactions on Software Engineering*, 18(9):817–826, September 1992.

[188] A. Martin. Encoding W: A logic for Z in 2OBJ. In J.C.P. Woodcock, editor, *Proc. Formal Methods Europe Symposium (FME'93), Odense, Denmark*, Lecture Notes in Computer Science. Springer-Verlag, 19–23 April 1992. To appear.

[189] D. May. Use of formal methods by a silicon manufacturer. In C.A.R. Hoare, editor, *Developments in Concurrency and Communication*, University of Texas at Austin Year of Programming Series, chapter 4, pages 107–129. Addison-Wesley Publishing Company, 1990.

[190] D. May, G. Barrett, and D. Shepherd. Designing chips that work. In C.A.R. Hoare and M.J.C. Gordon, editors, *Mechanized reasoning and hardware design*, International Series in Computer Science, pages 3–19. Prentice Hall, 1992.

[191] D. May and D. Shepherd. Verification of the IMS T800 microprocessor. In *Proc. Electronic Design Automation*, pages 605–615, London, UK, September 1987.

[192] J.A. McDermid. Special section on Z. *Software Engineering Journal*, 4(1):25–72, January 1989.

A special issue on Z, introduced and edited by Prof. J.A. McDermid. See also [35, 273, 318].

[193] J.A. McDermid, editor. *The Theory and Practice of Refinement: Approaches to the Formal Development of Large-Scale Software Systems*. Butterworths, London, UK, 1989.

Papers from the Refinement Workshop at the University of York, held on 7–8 January 1988, including several on Z.

[194] J.A. McDermid. Formal methods: Use and relevance for the development of safety critical systems. In P.A. Bennett, editor, *Safety Aspects of Computer Control*. Butterworth-Heinemann, Oxford, UK, 1991.

This paper discusses a number of formal methods and summarizes strengths and weaknesses in safety critical applications; a major safety-related example is presented in Z.

[195] M.A. McMorran and J.E. Nicholls. Z user manual. Technical Report TR12.274, IBM United Kingdom Laboratories Ltd., Hursley Park, Winchester, Hampshire SO21 2JN, UK, July 1989. Version 1.0.

[196] S.L. Meira and A.L.C. Cavalcanti. Modular object-oriented Z specifications. In J.E. Nicholls, editor, *Z User Workshop, Oxford 1990*, Workshops in Computing, pages 173–192. Springer-Verlag, 1991.

[197] S.L. Meira and A.L.C. Cavalcanti. The MooZ specification language. Technical report, Universidade Federal de Pernambuco, Departamento de Inforática, Recife – PE, Brasil, 1992.

This report can be obtained via anonymous FTP from the machine gctc.itep.br (150.161.1.2) under "pub/MooZ/MooZ.ps.Z" or by e-mailing a request to Ana Lucia Cavalcanti on <alcc@DI.UFPE.BR>.

[198] B. Meyer. On formalism in specifications. *IEEE Software*, 2(1):6–26, January 1985.

[199] V. Mišić, D. Velašević, and B. Lazarević. Formal specification of a data dictionary for an extended ER data model. *The Computer Journal*, 35(6):611–622, December 1992.

[200] J.D. Moffett and M.S. Sloman. A case study representing a model: to Z or not to Z? In J.E. Nicholls, editor, *Z User Workshop, Oxford 1990*, Workshops in Computing, pages 254–268. Springer-Verlag, 1991.

[201] B.Q. Monahan. Book review. *Formal Aspects of Computing*, 1(1):137–142, January–March 1989.

A review of *Understanding Z: A Specification Language and Its Formal Semantics* by Mike Spivey [272].

[202] B.Q. Monahan and R.C. Shaw. Model-based specifications. In J.A. McDermid, editor, *Software Engineer's Reference Book*, chapter 21. Butterworth-Heinemann, Oxford, UK, 1991.

This chapter contains a case study in Z, followed by a discussion of the respective trade-offs in specification between Z and VDM.

[203] C.C. Morgan. Data refinement using miracles. *Information Processing Letters*, 26(5):243–246, January 1988.

Also reprinted in [209].

[204] C.C. Morgan. Procedures, parameters, and abstraction: Separate concerns. *Science of Computer Programming*, 11(1), October 1988.

Also reprinted in [209].

[205] C.C. Morgan. The specification statement. *ACM Transactions on Programming Languages and Systems (TOPLAS)*, 10(3), July 1988.

Also reprinted in [209].

[206] C.C. Morgan. Types and invariants in the refinement calculus. In *Proc. Mathematics of Program Construction Conference*, Twente, June 1989.

[207] C.C. Morgan. *Programming from Specifications*. International Series in Computer Science. Prentice Hall, Hemel Hempstead, Hertfordshire, UK, 1990.

[208] C.C. Morgan and K.A. Robinson. Specification statements and refinement. *IBM Journal of Research and Development*, 31(5), September 1987.

Also reprinted in [209].

[209] C.C. Morgan, K.A. Robinson, and P.H.B. Gardiner. On the refinement calculus. Technical Monograph PRG-70, Oxford University Computing Laboratory, 11 Keble Road, Oxford, UK, October 1988.

A collection of papers including [203, 205, 204, 208].

[210] C.C. Morgan and J.W. Sanders. Laws of the logical calculi. Technical Monograph PRG-78, Oxford University Computing Laboratory, 11 Keble Road, Oxford, UK, September 1989.

This document records some important laws of classical predicate logic. It is designed as a reservoir to be tapped by *users* of logic, in system development.

[211] C.C. Morgan and B.A. Sufrin. Specification of the Unix filing system. *IEEE Transactions on Software Engineering*, 10(2):128–142, March 1984.

[212] C.C. Morgan and J.C.P. Woodcock. What is a specification? In D. Craigen and K. Summerskill, editors, *Formal Methods for Trustworthy Computer Systems (FM89)*, Workshops in Computing, pages 38–43. Springer-Verlag, 1990.

[213] P. Mundy and J.B. Wordsworth. The CICS application programming interface: Transient data and storage control. IBM Technical Report TR12.299, IBM United Kingdom Laboratories Ltd., Hursley Park, Winchester, Hampshire SO21 2JN, UK, October 1990.

One of a number of reports on the CICS application programming interface. See also [28, 139, 168].

[214] K.T. Narayana and S. Dharap. Formal specification of a look manager. *IEEE Transactions on Software Engineering*, 16(9):1089–1103, September 1990.

[215] K.T. Narayana and S. Dharap. Invariant properties in a dialog system. *ACM SIGSOFT Software Engineering Notes*, 15(4):67–79, September 1990.

[216] T.C. Nash. Using Z to describe large systems. In J.E. Nicholls, editor, *Z User Workshop, Oxford 1989*, Workshops in Computing, pages 150–178. Springer-Verlag, 1990.

[217] D. Neilson. Hierarchical refinement of a Z specification. In J.A. McDermid, editor, *Theory and Practice of Refinement*. Butterworth Scientific, 1989.

[218] D. Neilson. Machine support for Z: the zedB tool. In J.E. Nicholls, editor, *Z User Workshop, Oxford 1990*, Workshops in Computing, pages 105–128. Springer-Verlag, 1991.

[219] D. Neilson and D. Prasad. zedB: A proof tool for Z built on B. In J.E. Nicholls, editor, *Z User Workshop, York 1991*, Workshops in Computing, pages 243–258. Springer-Verlag, 1992.

[220] J.E. Nicholls. Working with formal methods. *Journal of Information Technology*, 2(2):67–71, June 1987.

[221] J.E. Nicholls, editor. *Z User Workshop, Oxford 1989*, Workshops in Computing. Springer-Verlag, 1990.

Proceedings of the Fourth Annual Z User Meeting, Wolfson College & Rewley House, Oxford, UK, 14–15 December 1989. Published in collaboration with the British Computer Society. For the opening address see [230]. For individual papers, see [22, 45, 46, 65, 78, 98, 113, 129, 136, 154, 177, 216, 233, 266, 279, 305].

[222] J.E. Nicholls. A survey of Z courses in the UK. In J.E. Nicholls, editor, *Z User Workshop, Oxford 1990*, Workshops in Computing, pages 343–350. Springer-Verlag, 1991.

[223] J.E. Nicholls, editor. *Z User Workshop, Oxford 1990*, Workshops in Computing. Springer-Verlag, 1991.

Proceedings of the Fifth Annual Z User Meeting, Lady Margaret Hall, Oxford, UK, 17–18 December 1990. Published in collaboration with the British Computer Society. For individual papers, see [17, 41, 53, 63, 100, 114, 131, 137, 143, 156, 157, 176, 196, 200, 218, 222, 229, 242, 257, 306, 330]. The proceedings also includes an *Introduction and Opening Remarks*, a *Selected Z Bibliography*, a selection of posters and information on Z tools.

[224] J.E. Nicholls. Domains of application for formal methods. In J.E. Nicholls, editor, *Z User Workshop, York 1991*, Workshops in Computing, pages 145–156. Springer-Verlag, 1992.

[225] J.E. Nicholls, editor. *Z User Workshop, York 1991*, Workshops in Computing. Springer-Verlag, 1992.

Proceedings of the Sixth Annual Z User Meeting, York, UK. Published in collaboration with the British Computer Society. For individual papers, see [13, 19, 74, 54, 81, 84, 119, 219, 224, 236, 250, 267, 294, 301, 323, 335] The proceedings also includes an *Introduction and Opening Remarks*, a *Select Z Bibliography* and a section answering *Frequently Asked Questions*.

[226] J.E. Nicholls et al. Z in the development process. Technical Report PRG-TR-1-89, Oxford University Computing Laboratory, 11 Keble Road, Oxford, UK, June 1989.

Proceedings of a discussion workshop held on 15 December 1988 in Oxford, UK, with contributions by Peter Collins, David Cooper, Anthony Hall, Patrick Hall, Brian Hepworth, Ben Potter and Andrew Ricketts.

[227] C.J. Nix and B.P. Collins. The use of software engineering, including the Z notation, in the development of CICS. *Quality Assurance*, 14(3):103–110, September 1988.

[228] A. Norcliffe and G. Slater. *Mathematics for Software Construction*. Series in Mathematics and its Applications. Ellis Horwood, 1991.

[229] A. Norcliffe and S. Valentine. A video-based training course in reading Z specifications. In J.E. Nicholls, editor, *Z User Workshop, Oxford 1990*, Workshops in Computing, pages 337–342. Springer-Verlag, 1991.

[230] B. Oakley. The state of use of formal methods. In J.E. Nicholls, editor, *Z User Workshop, Oxford 1989*, Workshops in Computing, pages 1–5. Springer-Verlag, 1990.

A record of the opening address at the meeting.

[231] C. O'Halloran. The software repeater (an exercise in Z specification). Report no. 4090, RSRE, Ministry of Defence, Malvern, Worcestershire, UK, 1987.

[232] C.E. Parker. Z tools catalogue. Technical Report ZIP/BAe/90/020, British Aerospace, Warton, UK, May 1991.

[233] M. Phillips. CICS/ESA 3.1 experiences. In J.E. Nicholls, editor, *Z User Workshop, Oxford 1989*, Workshops in Computing, pages 179–185. Springer-Verlag, 1990.

[234] M. Pilling, A. Burns, and K. Raymond. Formal specifications and proofs of inheritance protocols for real-time scheduling. *Software Engineering Journal*, 5(5):263–279, September 1990.

[235] P.R.H. Place and W. Wood. Formal development of Ada programs using Z and Anna: A case study. CMU Technical Report CMU/SEI-91-TR-1, ADA235698, Carnegie-Mellon University, Software Engineering Institute, Pittsburgh, Pennsylvania, USA, February 1991.

Copies available from: Research Access Inc., 3400 Forbes Avenue, Suite 302, Pittsburgh, PA 15213, USA. Telephone: +1-800-685-6510. Fax: +1-412-682-6530.

[236] F. Polack, M. Whiston, and P. Hitchcock. Structured analysis – a draft method for writing Z specifications. In J.E. Nicholls, editor, *Z User Workshop, York 1991*, Workshops in Computing, pages 261–286. Springer-Verlag, 1992.

[237] F. Polack, M. Whiston, and K. Mander. The SAZ project: Integrating SSADM and Z. In J.C.P. Woodcock, editor, *Proc. Formal Methods Europe Symposium (FME'93), Odense, Denmark*, Lecture Notes in Computer Science. Springer-Verlag, 19–23 April 1992. To appear.

[238] B.F. Potter, J.E. Sinclair, and D. Till. *An Introduction to Formal Specification and Z*. International Series in Computer Science. Prentice Hall, Hemel Hempstead, Hertfordshire, UK, 1990.

[239] S. Prehn and W.J. Toetenel, editors. *VDM'91: Formal Software Development Methods*, volume 551 of *Lecture Notes in Computer Science*. Springer-Verlag, 1991. Volume 1: Conference Contributions.

Papers with relevance to Z include [12, 24, 69, 82, 103, 140, 303, 309, 334].

[240] S. Prehn and W.J. Toetenel, editors. *VDM'91: Formal Software Development Methods*, volume 552 of *Lecture Notes in Computer Science*. Springer-Verlag, 1991. Volume 2: Tutorials.

Papers with relevance to Z include [5, 321].

[241] G.P. Randell. Translating data flow diagrams into Z (and vice versa). Report no. 90019, RSRE, Ministry of Defence, Malvern, Worcestershire, UK, 1990.

[242] G.P. Randell. Data flow diagrams and Z. In J.E. Nicholls, editor, *Z User Workshop, Oxford 1990*, Workshops in Computing, pages 216–227. Springer-Verlag, 1991.

[243] A.P. Ravn, H. Rischel, and V. Stavridou. Provably correct safety critical software. In *Proc. IFAC Safety of Computer Controlled Systems 1990 (SAFECOMP'90)*. Pergamon Press, 1990.

Also available as Technical Report No. CSD-TR-625 from Dept. of Computer Science, Royal Holloway, University of London, Egham, Surrey TW20 0EX, UK.

[244] K. Raymond, P. Stocks, and D. Carrington. Using Z to specify distributed systems. Technical Report 181, Key Centre for Software Technology, University of Queensland, Australia 4072, 1990.

[245] J.N. Reed. Semantics-based tools for a specification support environment. In *Mathematical Foundations of Programming Language Semantics*, volume 298 of *Lecture Notes in Computer Science*. Springer-Verlag, 1988.

[246] J.N. Reed and J.E. Sinclair. An algorithm for type-checking Z: A Z specification. Technical Monograph PRG-81, Oxford University Computing Laboratory, 11 Keble Road, Oxford, UK, March 1990.

[247] K.A. Robinson. Refining Z specifications to programs. In *Proc. Australian Software Engineering Conference*, pages 87–97, 1987.

[248] G.A. Rose and P. Robinson. A case study in formal specifications. In *Proc. First Australian Software Engineering Conference*, May 1986.

[249] P. Rudkin. Modelling information objects in Z. In J. de Meer, editor, *Proc. International Workshop on ODP*. North Holland, 1992.

[250] M. Saaltink. Z and Eves. In J.E. Nicholls, editor, *Z User Workshop, York 1991*, Workshops in Computing, pages 223–242. Springer-Verlag, 1992.

[251] A.C.A. Sampaio and S.L. Meira. Modular extensions to Z. In D. Bjørner, C.A.R. Hoare, and H. Langmaack, editors, *VDM and Z – Formal Methods in Software Development*, volume 428 of *Lecture Notes in Computer Science*, pages 211–232. VDM-Europe, Springer-Verlag, 1990.

[252] P. Sanders, M. Johnson, and R. Tinker. From Z specifications to functional implementations. *British Telecom Technology Journal*, 7(4), October 1989.

[253] S.A. Schuman and D.H. Pitt. Object-oriented subsystem specification. In L.G.L.T. Meertens, editor, *Program Specification and Transformation*, pages 313–341. North Holland, 1987.

[254] S.A. Schuman, D.H. Pitt, and P.J. Byers. Object-oriented process specification. In *Specification and Verification of Concurrent Systems*, Workshops in Computing, pages 21–70. Springer-Verlag, 1990.

[255] L.T. Semmens and P.M. Allen. Using entity relationship models as a basis for Z specifications. Technical Report IES1/90, Leeds Polytechnic, Faculty of Information and Engineering Systems, Leeds, UK, 1990.

[256] L.T. Semmens and P.M. Allen. Using Yourdon and Z to specify computer security: A case study. Technical Report IES4/90, Leeds Polytechnic, Faculty of Information and Engineering Systems, Leeds, UK, 1990.

[257] L.T. Semmens and P.M. Allen. Using Yourdon and Z: An approach to formal specification. In J.E. Nicholls, editor, *Z User Workshop, Oxford 1990*, Workshops in Computing, pages 228–253. Springer-Verlag, 1991.

[258] L.T. Semmens, R.B. France, and T.W.G. Docker. Integrated structured analysis and formal specification techniques. *The Computer Journal*, 35(6):600–610, December 1992.

[259] C.T. Sennett. Review of type checking and scope rules of the specification language Z. Report no. 87017, RSRE, Ministry of Defence, Malvern, Worcestershire, UK, November 1987.

[260] C.T. Sennett. Formal specification and implementation. In C.T. Sennett, editor, *High-Integrity Software*. Pitman, 1989.

[261] C.T. Sennett. Demonstrating the compliance of Ada programs with Z specifications. In *BCS/FACS Refinement Workshop*, January 1992.

[262] C.T. Sennett and R. Macdonald. Separability and security models. Report no. 87020, RSRE, Ministry of Defence, Malvern, Worcestershire, UK, November 1987.

[263] D.E. Shepherd. Verified microcode design. *Microprocessors and Microsystems*, 14(10):623–630, December 1990.

This article is part of a special issue on *Formal aspects of microprocessor design*, edited by H. Zedan. See also [36].

[264] D.E. Shepherd and G. Wilson. Making chips that work. *New Scientist*, 1664:61–64, May 1989.

A general article containing information on the formal development of the T800 floating-point unit for the transputer including the use of Z.

[265] L.N. Simcox. The application of Z to the specification of air traffic control systems: 1. Memorandum no. 4280, RSRE, Ministry of Defence, Malvern, Worcestershire, UK, April 1989.

[266] A. Smith. The Knuth-Bendix completion algorithm and its specification in Z. In J.E. Nicholls, editor, *Z User Workshop, Oxford 1989*, Workshops in Computing, pages 195–220. Springer-Verlag, 1990.

[267] A. Smith. On recursive free types in Z. In J.E. Nicholls, editor, *Z User Workshop, York 1991*, Workshops in Computing, pages 3–39. Springer-Verlag, 1992.

[268] G. Smith and R. Duke. Specification and verification of a cache coherence protocol. Technical Report 126, Department of Computer Science, University of Queensland, Australia 4072, 1989.

[269] G. Smith and R. Duke. Modelling a cache coherence protocol using Object-Z. In *Proc. 13th Australian Computer Science Conference (ACSC-13)*, pages 352–361, 1990.

[270] I. Sommerville. *Software Engineering*, chapter 9, pages 153–168. Addison-Wesley, 4th edition, 1992.

A chapter entitled *Model-Based Specification* including examples using Z.

[271] I.H. Sørensen. A specification language. In J. Staunstrup, editor, *Program Specification: Proceedings of a Workshop*, volume 134 of *Lecture Notes in Computer Science*, pages 381–401. Springer-Verlag, 1981.

[272] J.M. Spivey. *Understanding Z: A Specification Language and its Formal Semantics*, volume 3 of *Cambridge Tracts in Theoretical Computer Science*. Cambridge University Press, UK, January 1988.

Published version of 1985 DPhil thesis.

[273] J.M. Spivey. An introduction to Z and formal specifications. *Software Engineering Journal*, 4(1), January 1989.

[274] J.M. Spivey. A guide to the zed style option. Oxford University Computing Laboratory, December 1990.

A description of the Z style option "zed.sty" for use with the LaTeX document preparation system [175]. The style file and the guide are available electronically by sending an e-mail message containing the command "send z zed.sty zguide.tex" to the PRG archive server [333] on <archive-server@comlab.ox.ac.uk>.

[275] J.M. Spivey. Specifying a real-time kernel. *IEEE Software*, pages 21–28, September 1990.

This case study of an embedded real-time kernel shows that mathematical techniques have an important role to play in documenting systems and avoiding design flaws.

[276] J.M. Spivey. *The fUZZ Manual.* Computing Science Consultancy, 2 Willow Close, Garsington, Oxford OX9 9AN, UK, 2nd edition, 1992.

A Z type-checker and "fuzz.sty" style option for LaTeX documents [175]. The package is compatible with the book, *The Z Notation: A Reference Manual* by the same author [277]. Technical enquiries can be sent to Mike Spivey at 2 Willow Close, Garsington, Oxford OX9 9AN, UK, or by e-mail at <Mike.Spivey@comlab.ox.ac.uk>. An order form is available via electronic mail by sending a message containing the command "send z fuzz" to the PRG archive server [333] on <archive-server@comlab.ox.ac.uk>.

[277] J.M. Spivey. *The Z Notation: A Reference Manual.* International Series in Computer Science. Prentice Hall, Hemel Hempstead, Hertfordshire, UK, 2nd edition, 1992.

This is the 2nd edition of the first widely available reference manual on Z originally published in 1989. The Reference Manual provides a complete and definitive guide to the use of Z in specifying information systems, writing specifications and designing implementations. See also the new draft Z standard [42].

[278] J.M. Spivey and B.A. Sufrin. Type inference in Z. In D. Bjørner, C.A.R. Hoare, and H. Langmaack, editors, *VDM and Z – Formal Methods in Software Development*, volume 428 of *Lecture Notes in Computer Science*, pages 426–438. VDM-Europe, Springer-Verlag, 1990.

See also [279].

[279] J.M. Spivey and B.A. Sufrin. Type inference in Z. In J.E. Nicholls, editor, *Z User Workshop, Oxford 1989*, Workshops in Computing, pages 6–31. Springer-Verlag, 1990.

[280] S. Stepney, R. Barden, and D. Cooper, editors. *Object Orientation in Z.* Workshops in Computing. Springer-Verlag, 1992.

This is a collection of papers describing various OOZ approaches – Hall, ZERO, MooZ, Object-Z, OOZE, Schuman & Pitt, Z++, ZEST and Fresco (an OO VDM method) — in the main written by the methods' inventors, and all specifying the same two examples. The collection is a revised and expanded version of a ZIP report distributed at the 1991 Z User Meeting at York.

[281] S. Stepney, R. Barden, and D. Cooper. A survey of object orientation in Z. *Software Engineering Journal*, 7, March 1992.

[282] S. Stepney and S.P. Lord. Formal specification of an access control system. *Software – Practice and Experience*, 17(9):575–593, September 1987.

[283] P. Stocks, K. Raymond, and D. Carrington. Representing distributed system concepts in Z. Technical Report 180, Key Centre for Software Technology, University of Queensland, Australia 4072, 1990.

[284] P. Stocks, K. Raymond, D. Carrington, and A. Lister. Modelling open distributed systems in Z. *Computer Communications*, 15(2):103–113, March 1992.

In a special issue on the practical use of FDTs (Formal Description Techniques) in communications and distributed systems, edited by Dr. Gordon S. Blair.

[285] B. Stoddart and P. Knaggs. The event calculus (formal specification of real time systems by means of diagrams and Z schemas). In *5th International Conference on putting into practice methods and tools for information system design*, University of Nantes, Institute Universitaire de Technologie, 3 Rue du Maréchal Joffre, 44041 Nantes Cedex 01, France, September 1992.

[286] B.A. Sufrin. Formal system specification: Notation and examples. In D. Neel, editor, *Tools and Notations for Program Construction*. Cambridge University Press, UK, 1982.

An example of a filing system specification, this was the first published use of the schema notation to put together states.

[287] B.A. Sufrin. Towards formal specification of the ICL data dictionary. *ICL Technical Journal*, August 1984.

[288] B.A. Sufrin. Formal methods and the design of effective user interfaces. In M.D. Harrison and A.F. Monk, editors, *People and Computers: Designing for Usability*. Cambridge University Press, UK, 1986.

[289] B.A. Sufrin. Formal specification of a display-oriented editor. In N. Gehani and A.D. McGettrick, editors, *Software Specification Techniques*, International computer science series, pages 223–267. Addison-Wesley Publishing Company, 1986.

[290] B.A. Sufrin. A formal framework for classifying interactive information systems. In *IEE Colloquium on Formal Methods and Human-Computer Interaction*, number 09 in IEE Digest, pages 4/1–14. IEE, 1987.

[291] B.A. Sufrin. Effective industrial application of formal methods. In *Proc. 11th IFIP Computer Congress*. North-Holland, 1989.

[292] B.A. Sufrin and He Jifeng. Specification, analysis and refinement of interactive processes. In M. Harrison and H. Thimbleby, editors, *Formal Methods in Human-Computer Interaction*, volume 2 of *Cambridge Series on Human-Computer Interaction*, chapter 6, pages 153–200. Cambridge University Press, UK, 1990.

A case study on using Z for process modelling.

[293] B.A. Sufrin and J.C.P. Woodcock. Towards the formal specification of a simple programming support environment. *Software Engineering Journal*, 2(4):86–94, July 1987.

[294] P.A. Swatman, D. Fowler, and C.Y.M. Gan. Extending the useful application domain for formal methods. In J.E. Nicholls, editor, *Z User Workshop, York 1991*, Workshops in Computing, pages 125–144. Springer-Verlag, 1992.

[295] P.A. Swatman, P.M.C. Swatman, and R. Duke. Electronic data interchange: A high-level formal specification in Object-Z. In *Proc. 6th Australian Software Engineering Conference (ASWEC'91)*, 1991.

[296] P.F. Terry and S.R. Wiseman. On the design and implementation of a secure computer system. Memorandum no. 4188, RSRE, Ministry of Defence, Malvern, Worcestershire, UK, June 1988.

[297] S. Thompson. Specification techniques [9004-0316]. *ACM Computing Reviews*, 31(4):213, April 1990.

A review of *Formal methods applied to a floating-point number system* by Geoff Barrett [20].

[298] D. Till and B.F. Potter. The specification in Z of gateway functions within a communications network. In *Proc. IFIP WG10.3 Conference on Distributed Processing*, Amsterdam, The Netherlands, October 1987. Elsevier Science Publishers B.V. (North-Holland).

[299] B.S. Todd. A model-based diagnostic program. *Software Engineering Journal*, 2(3):54–63, May 1987.

[300] I. Toyn. *CADiZ Quick Reference Guide*. York Software Engineering Ltd., University of York, York YO1 5DD, UK, 1990.

A guide to the CADiZ (Computer Aided Design in Z) toolkit. This makes use of the UNIX *troff* family of text formatting tools. Contact David Jordan at the address above or on <yse@minster.york.ac.uk> via e-mail for further information on CADiZ. See also [157] for a paper introducing CADiZ. Support for LaTeX [175] is now available.

[301] S.H. Valentine. Z^{--}, an executable subset of Z. In J.E. Nicholls, editor, *Z User Workshop, York 1991*, Workshops in Computing, pages 157–187. Springer-Verlag, 1992.

[302] M.J. van Diepen and K.M. van Hee. A formal semantics for Z and the link between Z and the relational algebra. In D. Bjørner, C.A.R. Hoare, and H. Langmaack, editors, *VDM and Z – Formal Methods in Software Development*, volume 428 of *Lecture Notes in Computer Science*, pages 526–551. VDM-Europe, Springer-Verlag, 1990.

[303] K.M. van Hee, L.J. Somers, and M. Voorhoeve. Z and high level Petri nets. In S. Prehn and W.J. Toetenel, editors, *VDM'91: Formal Software Development Methods*, volume 551 of *Lecture Notes in Computer Science*, pages 204–219. Springer-Verlag, 1991.

[304] M.M. West and B.M. Eaglestone. Software development: two approaches to animation of Z specifications using Prolog. *Software Engineering Journal*, 7(4):264–276, July 1992.

[305] R.W. Whitty. Structural metrics for Z specifications. In J.E. Nicholls, editor, *Z User Workshop, Oxford 1989*, Workshops in Computing, pages 186–191. Springer-Verlag, 1990.

[306] P.J. Whysall and J.A. McDermid. An approach to object-oriented specification using Z. In J.E. Nicholls, editor, *Z User Workshop, Oxford 1990*, Workshops in Computing, pages 193–215. Springer-Verlag, 1991.

[307] P.J. Whysall and J.A. McDermid. Object-oriented specification and refinement. In J.M. Morris and R.C. Shaw, editors, *Proc. 4th Refinement Workshop*, Workshops in Computing, pages 151–184. Springer-Verlag, 1991.

[308] J.M. Wing. A specifier's introduction to formal methods. *IEEE Computer*, 23(9):8–24, September 1990.

[309] J.M. Wing and A.M. Zaremski. Unintrusive ways to integrate formal specifications in practice. In S. Prehn and W.J. Toetenel, editors, *VDM'91: Formal Software Development Methods*, volume 551 of *Lecture Notes in Computer Science*, pages 545–570. Springer-Verlag, 1991.

[310] S.R. Wiseman and C.L. Harrold. A security model and its implementation. Memorandum no. 4222, RSRE, Ministry of Defence, Malvern, Worcestershire, UK, September 1988.

[311] A.W. Wood. A Z specification of the MaCHO interface editor. Memorandum no. 4247, RSRE, Ministry of Defence, Malvern, Worcestershire, UK, November 1988.

[312] K.R. Wood. The elusive software refinery: a case study in program development. In J.M. Morris and R.C. Shaw, editors, *Proc. 4th Refinement Workshop*, Workshops in Computing, pages 281–325. Springer-Verlag, 1991.

[313] W.G. Wood. Application of formal methods to system and software specification. *ACM SIGSOFT Software Engineering Notes*, 15(4):144–146, September 1990.

[314] J.C.P. Woodcock. Teaching how to use mathematics for large-scale software development. *Bulletin of BCS-FACS*, July 1988.

[315] J.C.P. Woodcock. Calculating properties of Z specifications. *ACM SIGSOFT Software Engineering Notes*, 14(4):43–54, 1989.

[316] J.C.P. Woodcock. Mathematics as a management tool: Proof rules for promotion. In *Proc. 6th Annual CSR Conference on Large Software Systems*, Bristol, UK, September 1989.

[317] J.C.P. Woodcock. Parallel refinement in Z. In *Proc. Workshop on Refinement*. Butterworths, 1989.

[318] J.C.P. Woodcock. Structuring specifications in Z. *Software Engineering Journal*, 4(1):51–66, January 1989.

339

[319] J.C.P. Woodcock. Transaction refinement in Z. In *Proc. Workshop on Refinement*. Butterworths, 1989.

[320] J.C.P. Woodcock. Z. In D. Craigen and K. Summerskill, editors, *Formal Methods for Trustworthy Computer Systems (FM89)*, Workshops in Computing, pages 57–62. Springer-Verlag, 1990.

[321] J.C.P. Woodcock. A tutorial on the refinement calculus. In S. Prehn and W.J. Toetenel, editors, *VDM'91: Formal Software Development Methods*, volume 552 of *Lecture Notes in Computer Science*, pages 79–140. Springer-Verlag, 1991.

[322] J.C.P. Woodcock. The rudiments of algorithm design. *The Computer Journal*, 35(5):441–450, October 1992.

[323] J.C.P. Woodcock and S.M. Brien. W: A logic for Z. In J.E. Nicholls, editor, *Z User Workshop, York 1991*, Workshops in Computing, pages 77–96. Springer-Verlag, 1992.

[324] J.C.P. Woodcock and M. Loomes. *Software Engineering Mathematics: Formal Methods Demystified*. Pitman Publishing Ltd., London, UK, 1988.

[325] J.C.P. Woodcock and C.C. Morgan. Refinement of state-based concurrent systems. In D. Bjørner, C.A.R. Hoare, and H. Langmaack, editors, *VDM and Z – Formal Methods in Software Development*, volume 428 of *Lecture Notes in Computer Science*, pages 340–351. VDM-Europe, Springer-Verlag, 1990.
Work on combining Z and CSP.

[326] J.B. Wordsworth. Teaching formal specification methods in an industrial environment. In *Proc. Software Engineering '86*, London, UK, 1986. IEE/BCS, Peter Peregrinus.

[327] J.B. Wordsworth. Specifying and refining programs with Z. In *Proc. Second IEE/BCS Conference on Software Engineering*, volume 290, pages 8–16. IEE/BCS, July 1988.
A tutorial summary.

[328] J.B. Wordsworth. Refinement tutorial: A storage manager. In *Proc. Workshop on Refinement*. Butterworths, January 1989.

[329] J.B. Wordsworth. A Z development method. In *Proc. Workshop on Refinement*. Butterworths, January 1989.

[330] J.B. Wordsworth. The CICS application programming interface definition. In J.E. Nicholls, editor, *Z User Workshop, Oxford 1990*, Workshops in Computing, pages 285–294. Springer-Verlag, 1991.

[331] J.B. Wordsworth. *Software Development with Z*. Addison-Wesley, 1992.
This book provides a guide to developing software from specification to code, and is based in part on work done at IBM's UK Laboratory that recently won the UK Queen's Award for Technological Achievement in 1992.

[332] W.D. Young. Comparing specifications paradigms: Gypsy and Z. Technical Report 45, Computational Logic Inc., 1717 W. 6th St., Suite 290, Austin, Texas 78703, USA, 1989.

Presented at the *12th National Computer Security Conference*, Baltimore, Maryland, USA, 10–13 October 1989.

[333] Z archive. Oxford University Computing Laboratory, 1993.

A computer-based archive server at the Programming Research Group in Oxford is available for use by anyone with access to electronic mail. This allows people interested in Z (and other things) to access various archived files. In particular, messages from the Z FORUM electronic mailing list [336] and a Z bibliography [37] are available. To access the archive server, send e-mail to `<archive-server@comlab.ox.ac.uk>`; the "`Subject:`" line and/or the body of the message should contain lines such as the following:

`help`	help on using the PRG archive server
`index`	general index of categories (e.g., "`z`")
`index z`	index of Z-related files
`send z z.bib`	send the Z bibliography in BIBTEX format
`send z 5.2 5.3`	send issues 5.2 and 5.3 of Z FORUM
`path name@site`	specify return e-mail address (optional)

The Z archive is also available via anonymous FTP on the Internet. Type the command "`ftp    ftp.comlab.ox.ac.uk`" (or alternatively "`ftp 192.76.25.2`" if this does not work) and use "`anonymous`" as the login id and your e-mail address as the password when prompted. The FTP command "`cd Zforum`" will get you into the Z archive directory. The file `README` gives some general information and `00index` gives a list of the available files. The Z bibliography may be retrieved using the FTP command "`get    z.bib`", for example. If you have serious problems accessing the Z archive at the PRG and need human help, or if you wish to submit an item for the archive, please send e-mail to `<archive-management@comlab.ox.ac.uk>`.

[334] P. Zave and M. Jackson. Techniques for partial specification and specification of switching systems. In S. Prehn and W.J. Toetenel, editors, *VDM'91: Formal Software Development Methods*, volume 551 of *Lecture Notes in Computer Science*, pages 511–525. Springer-Verlag, 1991.

[335] P. Zave and M. Jackson. Techniques for partial specification and specification of switching systems. In J.E. Nicholls, editor, *Z User Workshop, York 1991*, Workshops in Computing, pages 205–219. Springer-Verlag, 1992.

[336] Z FORUM. Oxford University Computing Laboratory, 1986–1993. Electronic mailing list: vol. 1.1–9 (1986), vol. 2.1–4 (1987), vol. 3.1–7 (1988), vol. 4.1–4 (1989), vol. 5.1–3 (1990).

Z FORUM is an electronic mailing list. It was initiated as an edited newsletter by R. Macdonald of RSRE, Malvern, Worcestershire, UK, and is now maintained by J.P. Bowen at the PRG. Contributions should be sent to `<zforum@comlab.ox.ac.uk>`. Requests to join or leave the list should be sent to `<zforum-request@comlab.ox.ac.uk>`. Messages are now forwarded to the list directly to ensure timeliness. The list is also gatewayed to the USENET newsgroup `comp.specification.z` at Oxford and messages posted on either will automatically appear on both. A message answering some frequently asked questions is maintained and sent to the list once a month. A list of back issues of newsletters and other Z-related material is available via e-mail by sending a message of "`index z`" to the PRG archive server [333] on `<archive-server@comlab.ox.ac.uk>`. For a particular issue, send a message such as "`send z 5.3`"; for the latest messages, send the command "`send z zforum`".

[337] Y. Zhang and P. Hitchcock. EMS: Case study in methodology for designing knowledge-based systems and information systems. *Information Software Technology*, 33(7):518–526, September 1991.

Comp.specification.z and Z FORUM Frequently Asked Questions

Jonathan Bowen

Oxford University Computing Laboratory

11 Keble Road, Oxford OX1 3QD, UK

Email: <Jonathan.Bowen@comlab.ox.ac.uk>

Abstract

This appendix provides some details on how to access information on Z, particularly electronically. It is based on a message that is updated and sent out monthly on international computer networks.

1 What is it?

Comp.specification.z is an international computer-based USENET newsgroup that was established in June 1991 and is intended to handle messages concerned with the formal specification notation Z. It has an estimated readership of around 15,000 people worldwide. The Z notation, based on set theory and first order predicate logic, has been developed at the Programming Research Group (PRG) at the Oxford University Computing Laboratory and elsewhere for well over a decade. It is now used by industry as part of the software (and hardware) development process in both Europe and the US. It is currently undergoing BSI standardisation in the UK and has been proposed for ISO standardisation internationally. Comp.specification.z provides a convenient forum for messages concerned with recent developments and the use of Z. Pointers to and reviews of recent books, articles and research results are particularly encouraged. Suitable publications will be included in the Z bibliography (see later) if they appear in comp.specification.z.

2 What if I do not have access to USENET news?

Electronic mailing list: There is an associated Z FORUM mailing list that was initiated in January 1986 by Ruaridh Macdonald, RSRE, UK. Articles are now automatically cross-posted between comp.specification.z and the mailing list at the PRG for those whose do not have access to USENET news. This may apply especially to industrial Z users who are particularly encouraged to subscribe and post their experiences to the list. Please contact the list maintainer on <zforum-request@comlab.ox.ac.uk> with your name, address and e-mail address to join the mailing list (or if you change your e-mail address or wish to be removed from the list).

Readers are strongly urged to read comp.specification.z rather than the Z FORUM mailing list if possible to save on network resources. Messages for submission to the Z FORUM mailing list and the `comp.specification.z` newsgroup may be sent by e-mail to `<zforum@comlab.ox.ac.uk>`. This method of posting is particularly recommended for important messages like announcements of meetings since not all messages posted on `comp.specification.z` reach the PRG.

3 What if I do not have access to electronic mail?

Postal mailing list: If you wish to join the postal Z mailing list, please send your address to the Secretary of the Z User Group, Jonathan Bowen, Oxford University Computing Laboratory, 11 Keble Road, Oxford OX1 3QD, UK (tel +44-865-273838, fax +44-865-273839). This will ensure you receive details of Z meetings, etc., particularly for people without access to electronic mail. This service is currently free, although it may be necessary to introduce a charge to cover costs in the future.

4 How can I join in?

Subscribers: If you are currently using Z, you are welcome to introduce yourself to the newsgroup and Z FORUM list by describing your work with Z. You may also advertise publications concerning Z which you feel would be of general interest. These will then be added to a master Z bibliography maintained at the PRG and updated for the proceedings of the Z User Meetings. By subscribing to the newsgroup, Z FORUM or the mailing list you may consider yourself a member of the Z User Group.

5 Where can I obtain publicly available Z-related files?

Archive: There is an automatic mail-based electronic archive server at the PRG which contains back-issues and messages that have appeared on the Z FORUM mailing list and `comp.specification.z` newsgroup, as well as a selection of other Z-related files. Send an e-mail message containing the command "`help`" in the body of the message or in the "`Subject:`" line to `<archive-server@comlab.ox.ac.uk>` for further information on how to use the server. A command of "`index z`" will list the Z-related files.

FTP access: The archive is also available via anonymous FTP on the Internet. Type the command "`ftp ftp.comlab.ox.ac.uk`" (or alternatively try the command "`ftp 192.76.25.2`" if this does not work) and use "`anonymous`" as the login id and your e-mail address as the password when prompted. The FTP command "`cd Zforum`" will get you into the Z archive directory. The file README gives some general information and 00index gives a list of the files. (Retrieve these using the FTP command "`get README`", for example.)

6 What tools are available?

Tools: various tools for formatting, type-checking and aiding proofs in Z are available. A free LaTeX style file and documentation can be obtained from the PRG archive server. To receive this via e-mail, send send a message containing the command "`send z zed.sty zguide.tex`" to the PRG archive server (see above).

The *fuzz* package, a syntax and type checker with a LaTeX style option and fonts, is available from J.M. Spivey Computing Science Consultancy, 34, Westlands Grove, Stockton Lane, York YO2 0EF. It is compatible with the second edition of Spivey's Z Reference Manual (see later). Contact Mike Spivey on <`Mike.Spivey@comlab.oxford.ac.uk`> for further information, or send the command "`send z fuzz`" to the PRG archive server for an order form.

CADiZ, a suite of tools for checking and typesetting Z specifications is available from York Software Engineering, University of York, YORK YO1 5DD, UK (tel +44-904-433741, fax +44-904-433744). Support is available for UNIX *troff* and more recently for LaTeX. Contact David Jordan at York on <`yse@minster.york.ac.uk`> for further information.

ProofPower is a suite of tools supporting specification and proof in Higher-Order Logic (HOL) and in Z. Short courses on ProofPower-Z are available as demand arises. For further information, please contact R.B. Jones, International Computers Ltd, Eskdale Road, Winnersh, Wokingham, BERKS RG11 5TT, UK (tel +44-734-693131 ext 6536, fax +44-734-697636, email <`R.B.Jones@win0109.wins.icl.co.uk`>).

Zola is a tool that supports the production and typesetting of Z specifications, including a type-checker and and a proof checker. The tool is sold commercially and available to academic users at a special discount. For further information, contact K. Ashoo, Imperial Software Technology, 62–74 Burleigh Street, Cambridge CB1 1DJ, UK (tel +44-223-462400, fax +44-223-462500, email <`ka@ist.co.uk`>).

Th B-Tool, designed to assist software engineers in the construction of formal proofs using a Z-like notation, is licensed by Edinburgh Portable Compilers Ltd, 17 Alva Street, Edinburgh EH2 4PH, UK (tel +44-31-225-6262, fax +44-31-225-6644). Further information may be obtained by contacting the Distribution Manager on <`support@epc.ed.ac.uk`>.

7 How can I learn about Z?

Courses: There are a number of courses on Z run by industry and academia. Oxford University offers industrial short courses in the use Z. As well as introductory courses, advanced Z-based courses on proof and refinement are available. Courses are held in Oxford, or elsewhere (e.g., on a company's premises) if there is enough demand. For further information, contact Jim Woodcock (tel +44-865-272576, fax +44-865-273839) on <`Jim.Woodcock@comlab.ox.ac.uk`>.

Logica Cambridge offer a five day course on Z and a three day introductory course on formal methods (mainly Z). For dates and prices contact Debi Kearney on +44-223-66343 ext 4859.

Praxis Systems runs a range of Z (and other formal methods) courses. For details contact Anthony Hall on +44-225-444700 or <`jah@praxis.co.uk`>.

8 What has been published about Z?

Publications: A BⁱʙTₑX bibliography of Z-related publications is available electronical from the PRG archive server (see earlier). Information on Oxford University Computing Laboratory Technical Monographs and Reports, including many on Z, is available from the librarian on <library@comlab.ox.ac.uk>.

The following books specifically concerning Z have been published (in approximate chronological order):

- I. Hayes (ed.), Specification case studies, Prentice Hall International Series in Computer Science, 1987. 2nd ed. due 1993.

- J.M. Spivey, Understanding Z: a specification language and its formal semantics, Cambridge University Press, 1988.

- D. Ince, An introduction to discrete mathematics and formal system specification, Oxford University Press, 1988.

- J.C.P. Woodcock & M. Loomes, Software engineering mathematics, Pitman, 1988.

- J.M. Spivey, The Z notation: a reference manual, Prentice Hall International Series in Computer Science, 1989. 2nd ed., 1992. *

- A. Diller, Z: an introduction to formal methods, Wiley, 1990.

- J.E. Nicholls (ed.), Z user workshop, Oxford 1989, Springer-Verlag, Workshops in Computing, 1990.

- B. Potter, J. Sinclair & D. Till, An introduction to formal specification and Z, Prentice Hall International Series in Computer Science, 1991.

- D. Lightfoot, Formal specification using Z, MacMillan, 1991.

- A. Norcliffe & G. Slater, Mathematics for software construction, Ellis Horwood, 1991.

- J.E. Nicholls (ed.), Z user workshop, Oxford 1990, Springer-Verlag, Workshops in Computing, 1991.

- I. Craig, The formal specification of advanced AI architectures, Ellis Horwood, 1991.

- M. Imperato, An introduction to Z, Chartwell-Bratt, 1991.

- J.B. Wordsworth, Software development with Z, Addison-Wesley, 1992.

- S. Stepney, R. Barden & D. Cooper (eds.), Object orientation in Z, Springer-Verlag, Workshops in Computing, 1992.

- J.E. Nicholls (ed.), Z user workshop, York 1991, Springer-Verlag, Workshops in Computing, 1992.

---

*The first widely available reference manual for Z.

9   What is object-oriented Z?

Several object-oriented extensions to or versions of Z have been proposed. The book *Object orientation in Z*, listed above, is a collection of papers describing various OOZ approaches – Hall, ZERO, MooZ, Object-Z, OOZE, Schuman&Pitt, Z++, ZEST and Fresco (an OO VDM method) – in the main written by the methods' inventors, and all specifying the same two examples.

10   How can I execute Z?

Z is a (non-executable in general) specification language, so there is no such thing as a Z compiler/linker/etc. as you would expect for a programming language. Some people have looked at animating subsets of Z for rapid prototyping purposes, using logic and functional programming for example, but this work is preliminary and is not really the major point of Z, which is to increase human understandability of the specified system and allow the possibility of formal reasoning and development.

11   Where can I meet other "Z" people?

Other meetings: VDM'91 was held on 21–25 October 1991, at Noordwijkerhout, The Netherlands. The meeting included papers on Z, and the proceedings are available as two volumes in Springer-Verlag LNCS 551 (conference) and 552 (tutorials). The scope of the symposium has expanded during the last years to include other formal notations and techniques, including Z. Therefore the name of the symposium (and the associated organisation) has been changed to *Formal Methods Europe*. The first FME Symposium will be held at Odense Technical College in Denmark, during the week of 19–23 April, 1993. The programme chairman is Jim Woodcock, Oxford University Computing Laboratory, 11 Keble Road, Oxford OX1 3QD, UK (tel +44-865-272576, fax +44-865-273839, email <Jim.Woodcock@comlab.ox.ac.uk>).

The 5th Refinement Workshop was held on 8–10 January 1992, at Lloyd's Register of Shipping, Fenchurch Street, London, England. The proceedings for these workshops are currently published in the Springer-Verlag Workshops in Computing series. The next workshop is planned for January 1994. For further information, please contact Roger Shaw at Lloyd's Register of Shipping, Lloyd's Register House, 29 Wellesley Road, Croydon, Surrey CR0 2AJ, UK (tel +44-81-681-4747, fax +44-81-681-6814, email <ttercs@aie.lreg.co.uk>).

The 6th International Conference on Formal Description Techniques will be held at Boston, Massachusetts, USA on 26–29 October 1993. FORTE'93 will address formal techniques and testing methodologies applicable to Distributed Systems such as Estelle, Lotos, SDL, ASN.1, Z, etc. For further information, contact Richard L. Tenney (Chair), Math & Computer Science, University of Massachusetts, Boston, MA 02125-3393, USA (email <rlt@cs.umb.edu>).

The Z User Group is planning an 8th Z User Meeting to be held in Cambridge, UK. Details will be issued on comp.specification.z, Z FORUM and the Z mailing list.

Details of Z-related meetings may be advertised on comp.specification.z if desired. All the above meetings are part of regular series.

12 What if I have spotted a mistake or omission?

Updates: Please send corrections or new relevant information about meetings, books, tools, etc., to `<zforum-request@comlab.ox.ac.uk>`. New questions and model answers are also gratefully received!

Author Index

Published in 1990–92

AI and Cognitive Science '89, Dublin City University, Eire, 14–15 September 1989
A. F. Smeaton and G. McDermott (Eds.)

Specification and Verification of Concurrent Systems, University of Stirling, Scotland, 6–8 July 1988
C. Rattray (Ed.)

Semantics for Concurrency, Proceedings of the International BCS-FACS Workshop, Sponsored by Logic for IT (S.E.R.C.), University of Leicester, UK, 23–25 July 1990
M. Z. Kwiatkowska, M. W. Shields and R. M. Thomas (Eds.)

Functional Programming, Glasgow 1989
Proceedings of the 1989 Glasgow Workshop, Fraserburgh, Scotland, 21–23 August 1989
K. Davis and J. Hughes (Eds.)

Persistent Object Systems, Proceedings of the Third International Workshop, Newcastle, Australia, 10–13 January 1989
J. Rosenberg and D. Koch (Eds.)

Z User Workshop, Oxford 1989, Proceedings of the Fourth Annual Z User Meeting, Oxford, 15 December 1989
J. E. Nicholls (Ed.)

Formal Methods for Trustworthy Computer Systems (FM89), Halifax, Canada, 23–27 July 1989
Dan Craigen (Editor) and Karen Summerskill (Assistant Editor)

Security and Persistence, Proceedings of the International Workshop on Computer Architecture to Support Security and Persistence of Information, Bremen, West Germany, 8–11 May 1990
John Rosenberg and J. Leslie Keedy (Eds.)

Women into Computing: Selected Papers 1988–1990
Gillian Lovegrove and Barbara Segal (Eds.)

3rd Refinement Workshop (organised by BCS-FACS, and sponsored by IBM UK Laboratories, Hursley Park and the Programming Research Group, University of Oxford), Hursley Park, 9–11 January 1990
Carroll Morgan and J. C. P. Woodcock (Eds.)

Designing Correct Circuits, Workshop jointly organised by the Universities of Oxford and Glasgow, Oxford, 26–28 September 1990
Geraint Jones and Mary Sheeran (Eds.)

Functional Programming, Glasgow 1990
Proceedings of the 1990 Glasgow Workshop on Functional Programming, Ullapool, Scotland, 13–15 August 1990
Simon L. Peyton Jones, Graham Hutton and Carsten Kehler Holst (Eds.)

4th Refinement Workshop, Proceedings of the 4th Refinement Workshop, organised by BCS-FACS, Cambridge, 9–11 January 1991
Joseph M. Morris and Roger C. Shaw (Eds.)

AI and Cognitive Science '90, University of Ulster at Jordanstown, 20–21 September 1990
Michael F. McTear and Norman Creaney (Eds.)

Software Re-use, Utrecht 1989, Proceedings of the Software Re-use Workshop, Utrecht, The Netherlands, 23–24 November 1989
Liesbeth Dusink and Patrick Hall (Eds.)

Z User Workshop, 1990, Proceedings of the Fifth Annual Z User Meeting, Oxford, 17–18 December 1990
J.E. Nicholls (Ed.)

IV Higher Order Workshop, Banff 1990
Proceedings of the IV Higher Order Workshop, Banff, Alberta, Canada, 10–14 September 1990
Graham Birtwistle (Ed.)

ALPUK91, Proceedings of the 3rd UK Annual Conference on Logic Programming, Edinburgh, 10–12 April 1991
Geraint A.Wiggins, Chris Mellish and Tim Duncan (Eds.)

Specifications of Database Systems
International Workshop on Specifications of Database Systems, Glasgow, 3–5 July 1991
David J. Harper and Moira C. Norrie (Eds.)

7th UK Computer and Telecommunications Performance Engineering Workshop
Edinburgh, 22–23 July 1991
J. Hillston, P.J.B. King and R.J. Pooley (Eds.)

Logic Program Synthesis and Transformation
Proceedings of LOPSTR 91, International Workshop on Logic Program Synthesis and Transformation, University of Manchester, 4–5 July 1991
T.P. Clement and K.-K. Lau (Eds.)